Word and Music Studies

Selected Essays on Opera by Ulrich Weisstein

WORD AND MUSIC STUDIES
8

Series Editors

Walter Bernhart
Michael Halliwell
Lawrence Kramer
Suzanne M. Lodato
Steven Paul Scher†
Werner Wolf

The book series WORD AND MUSIC STUDIES (WMS) is the central organ of the International Association for Word and Music Studies (WMA), an association founded in 1997 to promote transdisciplinary scholarly inquiry devoted to the relations between literature/verbal texts/language and music. WMA aims to provide an international forum for musicologists and literary scholars with an interest in interart/intermedial studies and in crossing cultural as well as disciplinary boundaries.

WORD AND MUSIC STUDIES will publish, generally on an annual basis, theme-oriented volumes, documenting and critically assessing the scope, theory, methodology, and the disciplinary and institutional dimensions and prospects of the field on an international scale: conference proceedings, collections of scholarly essays, and, occasionally, monographs on pertinent individual topics as well as research reports and bibliographical and lexicographical work.

Word and Music Studies

Selected Essays on Opera by Ulrich Weisstein

Edited by
Walter Bernhart

Rodopi

Amsterdam - New York, NY 2006

The paper on which this book is printed meets the requirements of "ISO 9706: 1994, Information and documentation - Paper for documents - Requirements for permanence".

ISBN-10: 90-420-2111-X
ISBN-13: 978-90-420-2111-2
©Editions Rodopi B.V., Amsterdam - New York, NY 2006
Printed in The Netherlands

Contents

Preface vii

Selected Essays on Opera by Ulrich Weisstein

The Libretto as Literature (1961) 3

Cocteau, Stravinsky, Brecht, and the Birth of Epic Opera (1962) 17

Introduction to *The Essence of Opera* (1964) 33

Reflections on a Golden Style:
W. H. Auden's Theory of Opera (1970) 43

"Per porle in lista": Da Ponte/Leporello's Amorous Inventory
and its Literary and Operatic Antecedents from Tirso de Molina
to Giovanni Bertati (1981) 65

Educating Siegfried (1984) 91

(Pariser) Farce oder wienerische Maskerade?
Die französischen Quellen des *Rosenkavalier* (1987) 105

The Little Word *und*: *Tristan und Isolde*
as Verbal Construct (1987) 141

Benedetto Marcellos *Il Teatro alla moda*:
Scherz, Satire, Parodie oder tiefere Bedeutung? (1989) 171

Von Ballhorn ins Bockshorn gejagt:
Unwillkürliche Parodie und unfreiwillige Komik
in Ambroise Thomas' *Mignon* (1989) 201

"Die letzte Häutung". Two German *Künstleropern* of the
Twentieth Century: Hans Pfitzner's *Palestrina* and
Paul Hindemith's *Mathis der Maler* (1992) 229

Between Progress and Regression:
The Text of Stravinsky's Opera *The Rake's Progress*
in the Light of its Evolution (1992) 273

What is Romantic Opera?
Toward a Musico-Literary Definition (1994) 301

Böse Menschen singen keine Arien: Prolegomena zu einer
ungeschriebenen Geschichte der Opernzensur (1996) 337

Sources 369

Acknowledgments 371

Register of Persons and Operas
Mentioned in the Text 373

Preface

Ulrich Weisstein, well-known as an international authority in the fields of comparative literature and comparative arts, is one of those scholars of worldwide distinction who have paved the way for the now flourishing field of intermedia studies. His most extensive intermedial concerns have always been with the relations of literature to the visual arts and to music. Already his dissertation was devoted to opera, which is a form that has become his life-time obsession. It is in the operatic field that Professor Weisstein has most significantly contributed to the area of Word and Music Studies, which sufficiently explains why his work on opera is now naturally finding its way into the book series of that name.

What is here presented is a collection of essays which reflect fifty years of Ulrich Weisstein's involvement with opera and which represent thirty-five years of his publishing activity in the field. The necessarily restrictive selection of essays from his impressively large output on opera is primarily governed by the wish to present to an interested scholarly readership texts that are representative of their author's work and, at the same time, are unlikely to be readily available through other channels. Further selection considerations, concerning limits of space and the avoidance of occasional thematic duplications, have led to the sequence of fourteen essays collected in this volume, which are arranged in chronological order and – following the publisher's policy – are predominantly written in English. Only four – of a substantial number in that language – are in German, but the volume would have been sadly diminished without them as they address essential and particularly suggestive issues.

The title of the first essay here reprinted, "The Libretto as Literature", has the character of a motto for much of what follows, as it points to a central concern of Weisstein's work on opera. He introduced the serious study of libretti in their own right and, thus, can be seen as an early initiator of librettology as an independent branch of literary and intermedial studies. His keenest interest is in the genesis of dramaturgically successful operas, tracing adaptive processes from textual sources to final products and investigating the collaborative efforts of writers and composers in creating effective operas. A further innovative focus is on the social ambience of operas as, for example, reflected in Marcello's *Il Teatro alla moda* with its brilliant satire on operatic activities in early-eighteenth-century Italy, or in the surprisingly widespread practices of opera censorship, on which the most recent essay included in this selection throws a strong first light. Generally, the essays show a tendency to discuss works which are not necessarily the most popular and most frequently studied ones, which results in a welcome widening of perspective and offers opportunities for unexpected discoveries, such as a number of so-called artist operas, which reflect Ulrich Weisstein's most personal interests as an indefatigable art-lover. His wide range of experience allows for a bird's-eye overview of the various types of opera that have emerged over the centuries, an overview that he has given in his seminal earlier volume, *The Essence of Opera*, and which led to his attempts at defining the specific properties of such forms as the romantic opera or the epic opera, to be found in this selection. It is to be hoped that the essays here collected, written as they are in an accessible, essentially non-technical language, make not only a profitable reading, but a pleasurable one as well.

Thanks are due to Professor Weisstein himself for his untiring commitment and enthusiasm in collaborating on letting this book see the light of day, and to Ingrid Hable, who has once again been a most conscientious help in bringing a volume of Word and Music Studies into the printable shape as required by current publishing standards. All essays have been reset, but bibliographical documentation has not been unified and basically follows the principles of the original publications. Yet it has been carefully checked and, where necessary, made consistent and occasionally corrected. The sources of the essays and the acknowledgments of permissions for reprint are found at the end of the volume.

Graz, June 2006   Walter Bernhart

Selected Essays on Opera
by Ulrich Weisstein

The Libretto as Literature (1961)

Considering the wealth of operatic material hidden in the world's libraries, a disproportionately small amount of scholarship has, so far, gone into its critical evaluation. It seems especially desirable that the 'ancillary' genre of the libretto should receive fairer treatment both with regard to its dramatic and its poetic qualities, for the serious critical attempts to deal with this stepchild of literature are few and far between. All the greater is the challenge posed for the literary critic of the libretto.

By some sort of tacit agreement, the dramatic aspect of opera is generally considered to be the domain of musicologists, the more catholic of whom (Edgar Istel, Edward J. Dent, and a few others) have honestly striven to restore the dignity of the music drama. Most of their colleagues, however, incline to overemphasize the role of the composer, a sin exemplified by Kerman's statement, "For the composer, I should like to believe that the essential problem is to clarify the central dramatic idea, to refine the vision. This cannot be left to the librettist; *the dramatist is the composer.*"[1] (Italics mine). This opinion is shared by many composers who, without directly denouncing the libretto, claim sole authority for judging its 'operatic' qualities. Richard Strauss expresses the conviction that "except for the person who wants to set it to music, nobody is able to judge a serious and poetically accomplished libretto before having heard it performed together with its music".[2] And Giancarlo Menotti asserts that "to read and judge a libretto without its musical setting is unfair both to the librettist and the composer".[3]

---

[1] Joseph Kerman. *Opera as Drama* (New York. Knopf. 1956), p. 267.
[2] Letter to Hugo von Hofmannsthal of May 3, 1928. See their *Briefwechsel* (Zürich. Atlantis. 1952), p. 620. The translations are my own unless otherwise indicated.
[3] "Opera Isn't Dead". *Etüde*, Vol. LXVIII, No. 2, February, 1950.

There have indeed been literary critics with an interest in the non-musical aspects of opera (I think of Bulthaupt's *Dramaturgie der Oper* and the *Tristan* chapter in Francis Fergusson's *Idea of a Theater*); but their influence has hardly been such as to eflect an appreciable change in critical opinion. On the whole, then, we are still faced with the situation described by Dent: "The libretto, as a thing in itself, has never received the systematic analytical study which is its due."[4] This is all the more perplexing since, in a number of notable instances, the collaboration between composer and librettist has been exhaustively documented in their published correspondence (Verdi-Boito and Strauss-Hofmannsthal[5]).

When asked to furnish the names of the most prominent librettists in operatic history, even the most enthusiastic opera fan will find his knowledge restricted to Metastasio, Da Ponte, Scribe, Boito, Hofmannsthal and perhaps W. H. Auden. Rare is the operaphile who could cite Quinault, Calsabigi, Zeno, Helmine von Chezy, Ghislanzoni and Ramuz. Operatic audiences do not think of these individuals as authors in their own right, although Auden's poetry, Scribe's plays and Hofmannsthal's demanding *œuvre* enjoy a certain popularity among the intelligentsia of their native countries. Their librettos are offered for sale in the lobby of the Metropolitan, in Chicago, San Francisco, Dallas, and wherever there is an operatic *stagione*; but who bothers to read them from beginning to end? Most of the operas in the standard repertory have been heard so often that almost everybody knows their plots.

Even such plays as *Pelléas* and *Salome*, which have been composed integrally, seem to have lost their status as literature, the musical versions having, in a manner of speaking, superseded their literary antecedents. Such is the triumph of music in opera – a triumph which luckily has not as yet extended to Büchner's *Wozzeck*, Kafka's *Trial*

---

4 "Un Ballo in Maschere". *Music and Letters*, April, 1952.
5 The Verdi-Boito correspondence was published by Alessandro Luzio in *Carteggi Verdiani* (Rome. Reale Accademia d'Italia. 1935), Vol. II, p. 95ff.

(with music by Gottfried von Einem) and other works melodramatized by composers of the Expressionistic and post-Expressionistic generation. Viewing these facts, how can one expect the average listener to challenge the truth of Kerman's statement? Even in the mid-twentieth century it requires courage to come to the rescue of that much maligned and self-effacing individual, the librettist.

Kerman's point of view is certainly justified with regard to operas in which the music has overcome the obstacles presented by the underlying text. Beethoven's *Fidelio* and Mozart's *Magic Flute* offer examples of the transcendence of textual shortcomings, Verdi's *Il Trovatore* of the defeat of structural absurdities. The first two works reveal a loftiness not only of purpose (for such was certainly present in the plays of Bouilly and Schikaneder) but also of expression (masking the triteness of the poetry). In the quatrain assigned to the three *Knaben* in Act I of *The Magic Flute*, the banality of the verses is transcended by Mozart's sovereign treatment of the metrical pattern.[6] Similar instances abound in the songs of Schubert and Schumann.

Another abuse of the librettist's privilege consists in the practice, common in Handelian times, of inserting irrelevant arias borrowed from other works, adding *bravura* pieces (such as Constanze's "*Martern aller Arten*" in *The Abduction from the Seraglio*) at the request of prima donnas and *castrati*, and distributing arias in deference to the artist's reputation and salary. The following passage from a letter by Giuseppe Riva partly explains the dramatic failure of Handel's operas:

> For this year and for the following there must be two equal parts in the operas for Cuzzoni and Faustina. Senesino is the chief male character, and his part must be heroic; the other three male parts must proceed by degrees with three arias each, one in each act. The duet should be at the end of the second act, and between the

---

6 "Dies kund zu tun, steht uns nicht an;/ Sei standhaft, duldsam und verschwiegen./ Bedenke dies; kurz, sei ein Mann,/ Dann, Jüngling, wirst du männlich siegen."

two ladies. If the subject has in it three ladies, it can serve because there is a third singer here.[7]

It is this curious practice, as well as many others indulged in by the makers of late Baroque operas, which Benedetto Marcello scorns in *Il teatro alla moda*[8]. But even in our own age operatic arias are often detached from their context for the sake of recordings, recitals, and concerts.

It is well to remind the denunciators of the libretto that the spoken drama itself is based on a number of highly artificial conventions, few of which, to be sure, are as far removed from 'lived' reality as are their operatic counterparts. Every drama is a *Gesamtkunstwerk* whose printed text resembles a musical score in that it merely suggests the theatrical possibilities which are inherent in it. Soliloquy, aside, and chorus – which are a thorn in the flesh of the Naturalistic playwrights – still remain within the realm of language, the difference between them and ordinary discourse being quantitatively determined (at least by common consent, since it is wholly a matter of definition where to place the exact point at which the qualitative leap begins). The use of different meters to indicate different levels of consciousness is a more strictly musical device, however. It is illustrated by T. S. Eliot's *The Family Reunion,* where the progression from seven-stress to two-stress lines corresponds to the operatic sequence: dialogue-recitative-aria/ensemble.

But what are the specific conventions, at first strictly observed but later modified in the direction of greater realism, employed in the preclassical-classical-Romantic type of opera? The convention most likely to shock the naive observer derives from the principle of simultaneity which, negatively applied in the spoken drama, forbids the use of several individualized speakers at the same time – the chorus con-

---

[7] Letter to Muratori of September 7, 1725. See Alexander Streatfeild's article "Handel, Rolli and Italian Opera". *Musical Quarterly,* July, 1917.

[8] Published in an English version by Reinhard G. Pauly in *Musical Quarterly*, XXXIV (1948), p. 371ff.

sisting of persons expressing themselves collectively. In opera, contrasting moods may be rendered simultaneously with an entirely pleasurable effect upon the listener. Stendhal effectively counters the objections of the "poor frigid souls [who] say [that] it is silly for five or six persons to sing at the same time" by pointing out that "experience completely ruins their argument"[9]. This rationalistic approach is exemplified by Calvin S. Brown's interpretation of "the famous quartet from *Rigoletto,* with two persons inside a shack thinking they are alone, two outside spying on them, and all four singing full blast in sickly [sic] contrived harmony"[10]. For a very practical, but nonetheless superficial, reason this observation holds true with regard to the literary side of opera; for one cannot read several lines of poetry at once. Hence the awkwardness in the arrangement of the text in the printed versions of most librettos.

Opera also employs a different concept of time, the horizontally progressing dramatic time (which is conceived in analogy with actual time) being replaced by a 'timeless' moment of reflection and introspection. Beginning with Mozart, however, the great melodramaturgists have intuitively modified this procedure by combining action and reflection in their ensembles, something Gluck had not yet dared to do. This reemergence of dramatic time is especially noticeable in Verdi's maturest operas, where lyrical epiphanies (in the Joycean sense) go hand in hand with actions in which the scenic word (*la parola scenica*) rules.

Like the reiterated shifting of levels of consciousness, the musical momentum required for increasing and decreasing emotional tensions seriously affects the structure of the lyrical drama. It corresponds to the phenomenon of crystallization which Stendhal analyzes in *De l'amour.*

---

9   *Vie de Rossini* (Paris. Le Divan. [n. d.]), Vol. I, p. 249.
10 *Music and Literature* (Athens. University of Georgia Press. 1948), p. 89.

While affecting the listener much more directly than the spoken word (hence the empathic mode of reception presupposed in pre-Expressionistic operas), music is somewhat slower than language in reflecting the evolution of a feeling whose breadth is audibly manifested. Composed of arbitrary signs and primarily intended as a vehicle for thoughts and ideas, language denotes specific objects rather than picturing or reproducing them. It also has the advantage of knowing how to indicate rapid shifts of opinion and quick changes in attitude. But its very wealth points to its basic deficiency. Condemning music "because it cannot narrate"[11], however, is just as foolish as chastising language for its failure to convey the rhythm of the emotions. Music, according to Schopenhauer, does not express the phenomenon itself but only the inner nature of all phenomena (not joy, sorrow, horror and pain themselves but their rhythmic substratum)[12]. Language, however, names the emotions. The merger of music and words, the temporal and the spatial, the general and the particular, should theoretically result in a more satisfactory image of the mental universe than is furnished by either in isolation. But, alas, so great are the difficulties to be overcome in the process of unification that the desired effect is rarely achieved.

Returning to the musical momentum and its exigencies, we should take note of the fact that whereas in the spoken drama mood is usually the means to an end (the end being action), operatic action is commonly regarded as a point of departure, a hard core around which emotions may crystallize. The pyramidal scheme presented by Gustav Freytag in his *Technik des Dramas* has no place in pre-Expressionistic melodramaturgy. Instead of stressing the progression from scene to scene and from act to act (with the necessary retardations), the makers of opera concentrate on the act itself as their basic unit. Hence the need for intermissions at the conclusion of each act. Within this larger

---

11 Boileau in the preface to his fragmentary "Prologue d'opéra".
12 See *Die Welt als Wille und Vorstellung*, II, 3, p. 39.

unit a fluctuation of moods between lyric and dramatic is often discernible. Similar to the symphonic development, where a theme may be shifted from major to minor and otherwise played upon, the operatic action moves in a wavelike rhythm that is peculiar to the lyrical drama. This symphonic structure is outlined by Hofmannsthal in the following résumé of his method of composition:

> The most difficult and at the same time most challenging task consists in balancing the spiritual motives, and in determining the inner relation between the characters and among the parts of the whole; in short: in designing the exact scheme of inner motives which must be in the poet's – just as in the symphonist's – mind. [...] This spiritual web is the very essence [of opera].[13]

Since music lacks the speed and verbal dexterity of language, fewer words are needed in opera than would be required in a play of comparable length. Librettos are usually shorter than the texts of ordinary dramas, and often to the point of embarrassing the listener or reader[14]. Repetitions are frequently called for if the librettist has failed to leave sufficient space for the music. This drastic reduction in the quantity of text, in conjunction with the highly sensual nature of music, necessitates a simplification of both action and characters, the emotions expressed in the closed musical numbers occupying a large segment of the time normally reserved for the dramatic events. The poet in E. T. A. Hoffmann's dialogue "Poet and Composer" justly complains:

> It is the incredible brevity you demand of us. All our attempts to conceive or portray this or that passion, in weighty language are in vain; for everything has to be settled in a few lines which, in addition, have to lend themselves to the ruthless treatment which you inflict upon them.[15]

Opera seems often absurd because its characters are poorly motivated.[16] Character is defined succinctly and forthrightly and must be

---

13 Letter to Strauss of May 28, 1911.

14 "It is frightening to see how short is the libretto of *Tristan,* and how long the opera." Hofmannsthal to Strauss in a letter of June 3, 1913.

15 The dialogue forms part of the sequence of stories entitled *Die Serapionsbrüder.*

16 To make matters worse, it is often hard to understand the singers. Strauss's assertion that "in an opera, one third of the text is always wasted" is partly explained by the poor enunciation of the soloists and partly by the rich orchestral palette preferred by many modern composers.

accepted at face value. Passion being the operatic coin of the realm, everything is seen in relation to it, even to the point where it becomes impossible sensually to distinguish between good and evil characters. Kierkegaard asserts that music is ethically indifferent and W. H. Auden maintains that, in opera, "feelings of joy, tenderness and nobility are not confined to 'noble' characters but are experienced by everybody, by the most conventional, most stupid, most depraved"[17]. In the closed number, mood seems to lead an existence apart from character. But in spite of this transformation of individuals into mouthpieces of generalized emotions (types), every surge of passion appears to be fresh and personal. As far as their feelings are concerned, operatic figures are individuals because the listener identifies himself with the emotions they radiate. They revert into types in the very moment in which their action falls short of the expectations aroused by these emotions (Don Ottavio in *Don Giovanni*).

Taken by itself or in the melodramaturgical context, music is hard pressed when urged to represent falsehood, irony, or ambiguity. It was this deficiency which provided Hofmannsthal with a cogent explanation for the dramatic failure of *Così fan tutte*[18]. Nor is music capable of being humorous, at least not in the usual meaning of the word. Since humor results from the awareness of incongruity (it is a form of mental detachment), it cannot be rendered by music except indirectly. It is, after all, an intellectual rather than an emotional category. Perhaps the most ingenious way of expressing that incongruity in opera consists in the introduction of unmusical characters such as Beckmesser in *Die Meistersinger*.

The aesthetic principles so far discussed largely apply to the so-called *Nummernoper* which, in Wagner's time, began to give way to the *durchkomponierte Oper* (the opera composed integrally from beginning to end), whose structure shows a much greater conformity

---

17 "Some Reflections on Music and Opera". *Partisan Review*, January/February, 1952, p. 10ff.
18 See his letter to Strauss of August 13, 1916.

with the spoken drama. At its worst, the music of the *durchkomponierte Oper* will endeavor to illustrate even the minutest variations in speech and action. By thus trying to operate on too narrow a basis it will often defeat its own musical purpose. This threat to musical integrity induced Wagner to use the pseudo-literary device of the leitmotif, which must not be confused with Berlioz's *idée fixe*, a truly musical, because melodic and rhythmical, device. In the leitmotif, at least in its Wagnerian usage, the important musical category of repetition is turned into a literary cliché.

Used more discreetly, the music of the *durchkomponierte Oper* will seek to refine upon that which the spoken word expresses unsatisfactorily; but in contrast with the *Nummernoper* it will do so contemporaneously with language rather than biding its time until an occasion for crystallization arises. Adding a new dimension to speech, it brings to the surface what the characters cannot or will not utter. It is a mirror of the unconscious.[19] In *Tristan,* life is presented as a stratified temporal process, the drama showing the surface, and the music the depth, of existence.

If *Tristan,* intended for composition, is also a piece of literature, the same can be said with even greater veracity of the librettos fabricated by the Symbolists. Taking their clue from Verlaine's plea for "de la musique avant toute chose"[20], these writers were less concerned with the words themselves than with the mood evoked by them, i. e., with the latent music of their poetry[21]. If the music is thus regarded as being prefigured in the libretto, the question arises as to whether a musician is at all needed to spell it out, since 'to spell out', in the lan-

---

19 Busoni considers this to be the main function of music in opera. See his *Entwurf einer neuen Aesthetik der Tonkunst* of 1906.

20 In his poem "Art poétique".

21 Hofmannsthal begged Strauss to credit him not "with the words themselves as they appear in the libretto but with that which lies unspoken between them" (letter of January 20, 1913).

guage of the Symbolists, means to destroy the vagueness (*l'indécis*) essential to poetry.

What would happen if some composer were to apply his art to Chekhov's *Cherry Orchard* or *Sea Gull,* whose beauty is textural rather than structural? Shakespeare's *Othello,* too, comes so close to being a lyrical drama that Stanislavsky conceived of it altogether in musical terms[22].

Hofmannsthal's evaluation of his librettos recalls the favorite Romantic image for the relationship between poetry and music: the riverbed into which the composer pours the enlivening water of his melodies. Goethe, who idolized Mozart and Cherubini, enjoined his librettist "to follow the poetry just as a brook follows the interstices, juttings and declivities of the rocks"[23]. But whereas Hofmannsthal's theory of opera centers in the claim that poetry comes ever so close to being itself music, Goethe 'Romantically' believes in the subordination of the poetry. For him, as for Mozart, "the word is to be the obedient servant of the music"[24].

Another concept of melodramaturgy evolved with a view toward granting drama equal status within the *Gesamtkunstwerk* (a term sometimes inappropriately used in this connection) prevails among the Expressionists. In their epic operas, the constituent parts are meant to live a life of their own, each being asked to comment upon the other. In Stravinsky's *Histoire du soldat,* the orchestra is placed on the stage in full view of the audience – another example of Expressionistic alienation.[25] Neither Brecht's *Dreigroschenoper* nor *Histoire* is intended for empathic reception on the part of the audience. And although Brecht's drama can be enjoyed as literature, Weill's music

---

22 See especially p. 154 of *Stanislavsky Produces Othello,* Helen Novak, tr. (London. Geoffrey Bles. 1948).
23 From his letter to Philipp Christoph Kayser of June 20, 1785.
24 From a letter written by Mozart to his father.
25 See *Stravinsky: An Autobiography* (New York. Simon & Schuster. 1936), p. 110ff.

adds a new dimension, though hardly the one which Brecht envisaged. Indeed, now that the novelty of the work has faded, many of Weill's tunes are found to be ingratiating. Such is the fate of many experimental works that have since become classics.

A similar fallacy persisting in the short but varied history of opera underlies Gluck's melodramaturgy (his theory but fortunately not his practice). An ardent champion of the music drama, Gluck "sought to restrain music to its true function, namely that of serving poetry by means of the expression, without interrupting the action or spoiling its effect by useless and superfluous arguments"[26]. As Berlioz observed, the catch lies in the word "expression"; for any serious attempt by a great composer to fortify the language of a drama inevitably works in favor of the music[27]. It takes considerable effort and self-denial on the part of the composer to create the kind of musical arabesque which Verdi uses in his *Falstaff* and Strauss in his conversational operas[28].

An interesting sidelight on the classicistic approach to opera is shed by the eighteenth-century notion of counter-sense, which Rousseau defines as a "vice indulged in by the composer when he renders a thought other than that which he ought to render"[29]. Such misuse may refer to single words and phrases as well as to entire scenes or situations (depending on whether the composer is stimulated by language, character, or action). A Romantic perversion of this concept occurs in Stendhal's book on Rossini when he praises the composer for having overcome certain difficulties inherent in the libretto of one of his op-

---

26 Preface to *Alceste* in a dedicatory letter to Grand Duke Leopold of Tuscany (1769).

27 See his essay "L'*Alceste* d'Euripide, celles de Quinault, et de Calsabigi, les partitions de Gluck, de Schweizer, de Guglielmi et de Handel sur ce sujet". *A Travers Chants* (Paris. 1862), p. 130ff.

28 See Strauss's letter to Stefan Zweig of December 19, 1932, in their *Briefwechsel*, Willi Schuh, ed. (Frankfurt. S. Fischer. 1957).

29 Article "Contresens" in his *Dictionnaire de musique*. According to Rousseau, it was d'Alembert who claimed that "music being merely a translation of words into song, it is obvious that one can fall into countersense".

eras[30]. Here the counter-sense is understood to have originated in the literary substratum of opera, this being a parodistic view of the libretto as literature.

Two further observations may help to clarify the Romantic point of view with regard to the libretto. One would normally expect the libretto to form the basis of an opera, i. e., *prima le parole e poi la musica*[31]. But theatrically-minded composers have occasionally reverted to the unorthodox practice of demanding words for a piece of music already completed. Mozart, discussing *The Abduction from the Seraglio*, informs his father: "I have explained to Stephanie [the librettist] the words I require for this aria – indeed I had finished composing most of it before Stephanie knew anything whatever about it."[32]

Stendhal manifests his contempt for the librettos of the operas he heard at La Scala when informing his readers: "I take the situation envisaged by the librettist and ask for a single word, not more than one, to qualify the emotion which underlies it. Nobody should be so imprudent as to read the entire libretto."[33] And Auden says as much when stating:

> The verses which the librettist writes are not addressed to the public but are really a private letter to the composer. They have their moment of glory, the moment in which they suggest to him a certain melody; when that is over, they are as expendable as infantry is to a Chinese general; they must efface themselves and cease to care what happens to them[34].

Abandoning himself to his musical fancy, Berlioz epitomizes the Romantic attitude when defending his choice of Hungary as the setting for the initial scene of *Faust's Damnation*:

> Why did the composer cause his protagonist to go to Hungary? Because he wished to introduce a piece of instrumental music whose theme is Hungarian. [...]

---

30 *Vie de Rossini*, I, p. 297.

31 This is an inversion of the title of a one-act opera by Salieri (with a libretto by the Abbé de Casti) to which Strauss refers in the motto of his opera *Capriccio*.

32 Letter of September 26, 1781. See *The Letters of Mozart and His Family*, Emily Anderson, tr. (London. Macmillan. 1938).

33 *Vie de Rossini*, I, p. 102.

34 "Some Reflections on Music and Opera".

> He would have sent him anywhere if he had found the slightest *musical* [Italics mine] reason for doing so[35].

This much for the historical side of a critique of the libretto as literature. To those who object to this approach because it violates the spirit in which many librettos were conceived (i. e., their subordination to music) I can only answer that by the same token we would deprive ourselves of the pleasure of studying the sketches for a painting, the *bozzetto* of a sculpture, the plans for a building, or a film script. It may well be that in the case of the libretto the percentage of literary failures is exceptionally high and that much time would be required to separate the grain from the chaff. But why be discouraged by such a prospect? Chances are that the student of the libretto as literature will get a fair return for his investment in time and effort.

---

35 From his preface to the opera-oratorio.

Cocteau, Stravinsky, Brecht, and the Birth of Epic Opera (1962)

As its title indicates, this paper is not intended to be a comprehensive survey of anti-Romantic and anti-Wagnerian tendencies in modern opera, but merely an attempt to evaluate certain affinities among Jean Cocteau's *Le Coq et l'Arlequin*, a collection of brilliant *aperçus* about music and the theater, Stravinsky-Ramuz' *Histoire du Soldat*, Brecht-Weill's *Dreigroschenoper*, and the series of *Anmerkungen* which Brecht appended to the latter work. An historical outline of the epic trends on the musical stage of our day would necessarily entail consideration of such other key works as Erik Satie's *Parade*, Milhaud's *Le Boeuf sur le Toît*, Cocteau's *Les Mariés de la Tour Eiffel*, Milhaud's *La Création du Monde*, Sitwell-Walton's *Façade*, and Claudel-Milhaud's *Christophe Colomb*, whose authors, instead of wishing to place the audience at once in a "narcotic atmosphere", "wanted to show how the soul gradually reaches music"[1].

Taking the programmatic *Le Coq et l'Arlequin* as our point of departure, we note that Cocteau finished this manifesto toward the end of World War I, dedicating it to Georges Auric on March 19, 1918, exactly six days before Debussy's death. *Le Coq* furnishes a convenient summary of the artistic aims pursued by the group of French composers known as *Les Six* and consisting of Honegger, Milhaud (who joined the group after his return from South America), Poulenc, Auric, Georges Durey, and Germaine Tailleferre. *Les Six* had grown out of a nucleus of musicians whom Erik Satie, their patron saint, had dubbed *Les Nouveaux Jeunes* and who had made their first collective appearance in January, 1918. The name *Les Six* was attached to them by the music critic Henri Collet, whose article "Un livre de Rimsky et un

---

1 Paul Claudel, "Modern Drama and Music". *Yale Review*, XX (1930), p. 94ff.

livre de Cocteau – les cinq Russes et les six Français" had appeared in the January 16 and 23, 1920, issues of the magazine *Comoedia*. Collet defined the aims of the French artists in analogy to those spelled out by the Russian composers Balakirev, Moussorgsky, Borodin, Rimsky-Korsakov, and César Cui, popularly known as "The Five". Both schools were largely concerned with writing music conceived along national lines, freed, wherever possible, of foreign influence.

Cocteau, who is not a professionally trained musician but is known to possess an uncanny talent for grasping the aesthetic significance of musical phenomena, was ideally suited to become the spokesman of *Les Six*.[2] For him, to pretend that "one cannot talk music if one does not know its algebra" was tantamount to declaring "that one cannot enjoy good food without knowing how to cook, that one cannot cook without knowing chemistry, etc." (*Revue de Genève*, No. 21, March, 1922). As for the aesthetic of the group, it was a direct outgrowth of their anti-Romanticism, of their rebellion against Wagner (including his followers and the Impressionists), and of the Germanophobia which swept France at the outbreak of the global conflict. To Wagner and Debussy they opposed Erik Satie (much of whose laconic writing has entered into *Le Coq et l'Arlequin*), to Romantic murkiness a classical sense of form, proportion, and clarity, and to German music an art of decidedly Gallic persuasion. Viewing the group's classicist bent, it seems odd that Jean Cocteau should have acted as their self-appointed Musagete, for the author-to-be of *La Machine Infernale* and future champion of Surrealism would seem to have been ill-disposed for such a role. Indeed, as early as 1919, in *Carte Blanche*, he com-

---

2 "Jean Cocteau aura été un des très rares – je crois bien que, sans abus, on peut bien dire même le seul – qui ait toujours été en contact direct avec la musique; à l'avoir fréquentée pour elle-même, comme une chose en soi, en tant qu'élément essentiel; bien plus, à avoir su la regarder vivre et, partant d'une connaissance fort bien eclairée des époques ayant précédés la nôtre, partant d'une compréhension de l'enchâinement des faits musicaux, à avoir su l'aider à vivre, à accomplir son destin à une époque donnée." Claude Rostand in the special Cocteau issue of *La Table Ronde* (No. 94, October, 1955), p. 84.

pletely reversed his opinion when asserting that "the creative nations" – France prominently among them – "have always been the scene of salutary disorders" and accusing the Germans of indulging in "order, propriety and a clinical discipline"[3]. But in 1918 it was the Frenchman Cocteau who came to the rescue of Classicism, as in his own way the German-Italian composer Ferruccio Busoni had done ten years earlier in his *Entwurf einer neuen Aesthetik der Tonkunst*.

Seen with a view toward the evolution of musical taste in the last three centuries, Cocteau's Poetics marks the culmination of a rebellion against the *Gesamtkunstwerk,* the theatrical synthesis of the arts, with its empathic mode of being (according to Cocteau it "forces us to listen with our skin", [I, 36]) and its endless melody. Cocteau sided with Nietzsche who, cured of Wagnerism, had in *Der Fall Wagner* and *Nietzsche contra Wagner* used Georges Bizet as a whipping boy against the sorcerer of Bayreuth[4]. He rejected Romantic music and painting because they involved the emotions rather than the intellect, because he thought them to be eclectic, and because, in his opinion, they sacrificed form to content[5]. Romantic music is music created by dreamers; but the dreamer "est toujours mauvais poète"[6]. It is music as motley as the costume of the Harlequin which, as in Wagner's *Tristan*, does not like to be roused from its reveries. What Cocteau and *Les Six* prescribed as an antidote was a type of linear music based on melody

---

3 *Œuvres Complètes* (Paris, 1950), I, 99. Future reference to this work will be noted in the text by volume and page number.

4 In *Der Fall Wagner,* Nietzsche speaks of Wagner as a "Polyp in der Musik", a phrase which Cocteau borrowed when calling Wagner and Stravinsky "des pieuvres qu'il faut fuir ou qui vous mangent".

5 In *Le Coq,* Cocteau opposes Bach and – in an appendix – Mozart to Beethoven and Wagner. Beethoven is "fastidieux lorsqu'il développe [...] parce qu'il fait du développement du forme", whereas Bach "fait du développement de l'idée". Cocteau, of course, was never afraid of contradicting himself.

6 In 1929, Cocteau stated: "I do not have on my conscience many works written while awake, except the books which preceded *Le Potomak,* when I began to go to sleep; but I have some. How much would I give not to have them exist." *Opium,* tr. M. Crosland and S. Road (New York, 1958), p. 38. Was *Le Coq* one of the books he regretted having written?

but "sans la caresse des cordes", a music that, being simple, has also "l'air facile"[7], a music of "tous les jours" which ironically defeats the emotions, a music, above all, which is based on the principle of renunciation (I, 31).

The anti-Wagnerism of *Les Six* was most poignantly expressed in their feelings about the theater. Once again it was Nietzsche who set the tone for the group's violent reaction against traditional operatic modes of creation: "Aber Wagner macht mich krank. Was geht mich das Theater an? Was die Krämpfe seiner sittlichen Ekstasen, an denen das Volk – und wer ist nicht Volk? – seine Genugtuung hat? was der ganze Gebärden-Hokuspokus des Schauspielers?"[8] What Nietzsche especially disliked in the Wagnerian conception of the theater was its cultic, pseudo-religious nature manifested by every performance in the *Festspielhaus,* at whose opening in 1876 the Zarathustrian "said quietly farewell to Wagner".

In *Le Coq*, Cocteau voiced his antipathy by calling the theater corrupt and corrupting because it forced the audience to "listen with their faces buried in their hands" (I, 39). It was for similar reasons that subsequently Brecht encouraged the male members of his audience to take out their cigars and smoke them, so as to gain distance from the events portrayed on stage[9]. Stravinsky, too, whom Cocteau accused of having succumbed to theatrical mysticism in his *Sacre*, was soon to develop a dislike to music to which one must listen as if in a trance. It was this shutting out of the world, this act of concentration and forced identification which Cocteau signified by the phrase quoted at the beginning of this paragraph.

Exactly what did the proponents of the new aesthetic seek to substitute for the "Einopern" of opera in the theater? They resolutely turned to the music hall, to popular music, jazz, the café-concert –

---

7 Nietzsche, in *Der Fall Wagner,* asserts: "Das Gute ist leicht, alles Göttliche läuft auf zarten Füssen."
8 Nietzsche, *Werke* (Stuttgart, 1903), I. Abteilung, VIII, 187.
9 *Schriften zum Theater* (Frankfurt, 1957), p. 23.

where Satie himself had performed – and the circus.[10] These forms of light musical entertainment recommended themselves to the reformers because of the variety of tunes played in the course of a single evening and the necessary brevity of each piece. And just as Schönberg was to be disconcerted by the aphoristic quality of his first atonal compositions, Cocteau admitted that brevity was not in itself a virtue, but that it constituted an appropriate reaction against "l'interminable"[11].

Erik Satie, in whose name the war against the Wagnerian tribe was waged, has sometimes been called the Ingres of music. Such an analogy indeed suggests itself when one ponders the recently discovered *brouillon* for his *Socrate* to the effect that "the melody is the idea, the contour, just as much as it is the form and content of a work"[12]. One of the fiercest attacks launched by Satie was directed at the concept of program music, especially at Debussy's use of precious, descriptive titles in his short piano pieces. Instead of simply omitting such designations from his own compositions, Satie furnished many of his scores with titles totally unrelated to or, at best, ironically reflecting upon the music. It was in consequence of this abuse that some of his contemporaries regarded him as a practical joker or crank and as the typical product "of this exhausted civilization which jeers in order not to

---

10 "Le music-hall, le cirque, les orchestres americains de nègres, tout cela féconde un artiste au même titre que la vie. Se servir des émotions que de tels spectacles éveillent ne revient pas à faire de l'art après l'art. Ces spectacles ne sont pas de l'art. Ils excitent comme les machines, les animaux, les paysages, le danger." Cocteau, *Œuvres Complètes*, I, 28.

11 See Schönberg's lecture "Composition with Twelve Tones" in his book *Style and Idea* (New York, 1950), p. 103ff. In *Carte Blanche* (*Œuvres*, I, 120) Cocteau speaks approvingly of an essay by a certain Marnold "lorsqu'il reproche aux œuvres la brièveté [...] Mais la réaction centre l'interminable se faisait sentir, et toute réaction pèche par excès."

12 This *brouillon* is quoted in Roger Shattuck's *The Banquet Years* (New York, 1958), p. 131. Satie's life and art have been described and analyzed by Shattuck as well as by R. Templier and Rollo S. Myers (*Erik Satie*, London, 1948). Cocteau (*Œuvres*, 1, 25) affirms: "En musique la ligne c'est la mélodie. Le retour au dessin entraînera nécessairement un retour à la mélodie."

look death in the face"[13]. Satie's loyal followers, however, saw in the master's irony a decisive step in the direction of the coveted new classicism.

Cocteau had met Satie in 1915, when he was in the process of adapting Shakespeare's *A Midsummer Night's Dream* for the circus. The plan miscarried; but Satie and Cocteau became inseparable. During a brief furlough from the army in 1915, the poet conceived the idea for the Cubist ballet *Parade,* whose production in Rome in 1917 is a *cause celèbre* in the history of contemporary art, and which may be regarded as a live manifesto of the movement that had inscribed the words simplicity, brevity, and irony on its banners. *Parade,* whose music is "deliberately divested of subjective emotion, though a disturbing emotional experience results from the manner in which apparently banal fragments of melody and the simplest harmonies are deprived of their conventional associations and re-created in unexpected but logical patterns"[14], is far from being a prototype of epic opera. But the spirit of revolt which it breathes, and the reaction provoked by the adverse criticism which was levelled against it, strongly contributed to the rapid evolution of that genre in the hands of Igor Stravinsky.

A final glance at *Le Coq et l'Arlequin* may help to explain the paradoxical attitude which *Les Six* adopted toward Debussy and Stravinsky. The latter, though not actually Debussy's pupil (he had studied with Rimsky-Korsakov), was nevertheless strongly influenced by his music. *Les Six* found the composer of *Pelléas et Mélisande* laboring under the spell of Wagner and Moussorgsky. "Impressionism", their spokesman stated, "is a repercussion of Wagner, the last rumblings of the thunder" (I, 38). When gauging Debussy's accomplishments and comparing them with those of the neo-classicists, however, one does well to keep in mind that it was more in his practice than in his theory that the former differed from the latter. Musically speaking,

---

13 R. D. Chennevière in *Musical Quarterly*, V (1919), p. 474.

14 *Grove's Musical Dictionary*, fifth ed., VI, 417. See also Georges Auric's comments on *Parade* in the *Nouvelle Revue Française*, XVI (1921), p. 224ff.

Pelléas may well deserve to be called the Impressionistic *Tristan*. But when writing his opera, Debussy had long abandoned Wagner and turned toward a characteristically French manner of composing[15]. In this as well as in other respects he actually anticipated Satie's musical nationalism and the polemical use which Cocteau was to make of it. Yet it is an indisputable fact that he, to whom, according to Léon Vallas, the theater was "a false and inferior type of art"[16], wrote his *Pelléas* with the intention not of breaking up the Wagnerian synthesis of the arts, but of heightening its effect by giving it more psychological and musical continuity than Wagner had provided (see especially Debussy's letter concerning *Pelléas* to the Secretary General of the Paris Opéra Comique, as reproduced on p. 107f. of Vallas' book). Nevertheless, Cocteau, Satie, and *Les Six* manifestly wronged the composer who, belated Wagnerian though he was without fully realizing it, clearly foreshadowed some of the tendencies that were to crystallize almost immediately after his death. He, too, after all, was a master of the arabesque (his name for the linear element in music) who regretted that "the French forget too easily the qualities of clearness and elegance peculiar to them and allow themselves to be influenced by the tedious and ponderous Teuton".

Returning to Stravinsky, we observe that Cocteau, who, by the way, had only recently ceased to admire the Impressionists, in *Le Coq* denounced what he called that master's "musique française russe". Although in some ways he lumped the young Russian's music together with that of Wagner and the Impressionists, he left no doubt that he saw a marked difference in the way in which Wagner and Stra-

---

15 Debussy had been an ardent Wagnerian in his Prix-de-Rome days but had revolted as early as 1889 when he attended a performance of *Tristan* in Bayreuth. Edward Lockspeiser (*Debussy* [London, 1936], p. 72) quotes Tchaikovsky's patroness Nadeshda von Meck, in whose household the young Debussy served as an accompanist, as stating that already in 1880 the composer did not care for the Germans and maintained: "Ils ne sont pas de nôtre tempérament, ils sont si lourds, pas clairs."
16 Léon Vallas, *The Theories of Claude Debussy*, tr. M. O'Brien (London, 1929), p. 62.

vinsky sought to affect their audiences. What Wagner achieved by means of empathy, the author of *Le Sacre*, that "Georgics of Prehistory", accomplished through shock effect: "Wagner treats us to an extended meal. Stravinsky does not give us time to say 'ouf'. But both act on our nerves" (I, 39). However, when learning about *L'Histoire*, Cocteau quickly changed his mind and in a footnote appended to *Le Coq* apologized for having spoken ill of the composer as one who was not yet "de la race des architectes". In the appendix of 1924 he even went so far as to call Stravinsky a musical surgeon, "un homme dur auquel l'opinion amoureuse demande 'Brutalise-moi, frappe-moi encore,' et qui lui offre des dentelles"[17].

Judging by the evolution of Cocteau's views on music, one can see why, at a crucial point in his career, he denounced the Russian's sumptuous ballet scores of the ante-bellum period, notably that of the *Firebird*. Stravinsky, after all, had grown up with a decided penchant for rich orchestral palettes suffused with local color. However, his friendship with Debussy, beginning about 1910, was not to survive the premiere of *Le Sacre,* a work which the older man praised cautiously for having "enlarged the boundaries of the permissible in the empire of sound"[18]. Stravinsky later claimed that, all along, he suspected Debussy of duplicity and, at least in retrospect, showed annoyance at the latter's "incapacity to digest the music of the *Sacre* when the younger generation enthusiastically voted for it"[19].

That Stravinsky was generally considered to have turned anti-Debussyite by 1919 is shown by a letter in which Jacques Rivière, the

---

17 *Œuvres*, I, 58. By 1925, Stravinsky had become sufficiently inured to neoclassicism to think of writing his opera-oratorio *Oedipus Rex* on a Latin text. It was no other than Cocteau whom he commissioned to write the original French version of the libretto.

18 Quoted in *Conversations with Stravinsky*, ed. R. Craft (New York, 1959), p. 55.

19 *Conversations with Stravinsky*, p. 50. Cocteau, in his *Journals,* claims to have seen Debussy "sick at orchestra rehearsals of *Le Sacre du Printemps*. He was discovering the beauty of that music. The form he had given to his soul suffered from another form which did not match it."

newly appointed editor of the *Nouvelle Revue Française,* requested his services for the magazine, the attention of whose readers he wanted to direct to the "anti-impressionist, anti-symbolist, and anti-Debussy movements that are becoming more and more precise and threaten to take the form and force of a vast new current" (*Conversations,* p. 63).

But exactly when was it that Stravinsky began to shake off the tyranny of Romanticism-Impressionism? Around 1912 the Russian composer went to Bayreuth at the invitation of Diaghilev. He came away from a performance of *Parsifal* as a declared foe of Wagner. The overall impression he had received was one of sense-numbing boredom which made it impossible for him to concentrate on the music. He was equally appalled by the ritual and suprasensible element introjected into the operatic production. Trained primarily as a composer of music for the ballet, he subsequently embarked on a reform of the musical theater considered as a visual medium. As the composer and music critic Nikolas Nabokov put it in an essay entitled "Stravinsky and the Drama":

> Ballet had a meagre and sporadic tradition. This gave the modern composer a free, comparatively easy field for experiment and invention. It relieved him of the obligation to follow a poetic text and by its very nature worked against the principle of the mixture of the genres. Instead, it directed the composer toward the harmonious fitting together of the three arts, each one complete in itself[20].

It was in his second opera, *Reynard,* that Stravinsky began to destroy the much detested synthesis of the arts[21]; but only in the subsequent *Histoire* did his reformatory zeal lead to a systematic application of the epic principle. In his autobiography the composer stresses the advantage of having the instrumentalists in evidence during the entire performance of a stage work; for "the sight of the gestures and movements of the various parts of the body producing the music is funda-

---

20 *Stravinsky in the Theatre,* ed. M. Ledermann (New York, 1949), p. 106.
21 Stravinsky prescribed that *Reynard* be played "by clowns, dancers or acrobats, preferably on a trestle stage with the orchestra placed behind. If produced in a theatre, it should be played in front of the curtain. The players do not leave the stage." Quoted by E. W. White on p. 65 of his book *Stravinsky: A Critical Survey* (London, 1947).

mentally necessary if it is to be grasped in all its fulness. All music created or composed demands some exteriorization for the perception of the listener."[22]

In Switzerland, where he lived after 1914, Stravinsky became acquainted with the writer C. F. Ramuz, who collaborated with him in a number of ventures but made no original contribution until the spring of 1918 when, Stravinsky being in straitened financial circumstances, they "got hold of the idea of a sort of little traveling theater, easy to transport from place to place and to show in even small localities"[23]. The first epic opera thus did not result from purely aesthetic considerations but was partly conditioned by economic exigencies. Yet, whatever the role of the external circumstances involved in its creation, it can hardly be called coincidence that the genre which *L'Histoire* represents is so perfectly in keeping with the aesthetic developed by *Les Six*. For Cocteau and his friends were also to give battle in the name of simplicity, which was the *mot d'ordre* in the making of Stravinsky's chamber opera.

Histoire was to be a story presented in a threefold manner, namely read, played, and danced. Ramuz, who was not a man of the theater, had proposed to write a dramatic narrative to show "that the theater can be conceived in a much wider sense than is usually attributed to it"[24]. Making the most of Ramuz' deficiency, Stravinsky decided that in the work in progress "the three elements [music, narrative, and action] should sometimes take turns as soloists and sometimes combine as an ensemble" (*Autobiography*, p. 73). *L'Histoire*, in short, was to perpetuate alienation through constant shifts in emphasis and the deliberate avoidance of extended parallelisms.

---

22 *Igor Stravinsky: An Autobiography* (New York, 1962), p. 72.

23 For the whole question of the collaboration between Ramuz and Stravinsky see pp. 71ff. of the composer's autobiography as well as Ramuz' "Souvenirs sur Igor Stravinsky" (especially pp. 61-65 in Vol. XIV of his *Œuvres Complètes* [Lausanne, 1941]) and his *Lettres 1900-1918* (Lausanne, 1956) with Ernest Ansermet's account of "La Naissance de *l'Histoire du Soldat*".

24 Ramuz, *Œuvres Complètes*, XIV, 62.

Let us briefly explain the manner in which the principal ingredients of *L'Histoire* are treated both by themselves and in relation to each other. In an attempt to reduce the size of the orchestra, Stravinsky selected a group of seven instruments including "the most representative types, in treble and bass, of the instrumental families". He was beginning to realize the advantages to be gained by renunciation which, in many of his neo-classical works, became the cornerstone of his aesthetic[25]. As for the music of *L'Histoire*, its complexity is such that veritable virtuosi are needed to perform it – a serious obstacle in the way of the simplicity for which composer and librettist were striving. The instrumental parts, moreover, are not consistently integrated throughout the opera; but each solo instrument is encouraged to develop an independent linear existence. For Stravinsky it was also a foregone conclusion that his music should be so far detached from the underlying action that it could be performed as an orchestral suite.

A few words, finally, about the astounding variety of ways in which Ramuz designed each part of the action to operate both by itself and in conjunction with, or contrast to, the others. The *dramatis personae* of *L'Histoire*, for instance, lists four characters: the reader, the soldier, the devil, and the princess. But five performers are needed to fill their roles, since that of the devil is split up into a dancing and an acting part. The matter is further complicated by the fact that the reader is not restricted to narrating and interpreting the action, but frequently takes it upon himself to voice the soldier's innermost thoughts and feelings. In short, the unity of character is persistently denied to the major figures.

Scenically, effects of alienation in *L'Histoire* are achieved by the alternation of mute scenes with dialogic ones, of scenes played on center stage with others enacted in front of the curtain, and of dramatic action with 'epic' commentary. Another instance of neutralization is found in Stravinsky's use of non-Russian music to accompany this

---

[25] See the very interesting footnote on p. 97 of T. W. Adorno's *Philosophie der neuen Musik* (Tübingen, 1949).

Russian folktale[26]. The introduction of Jazz into the score offers perhaps the most striking instance of this deliberate rejection of local color. The plot upon which Ramuz and Stravinsky fastened was well suited to their non-Aristotelian dramaturgy since, in the course of its unfolding, the unity of the space-time continuum is disrupted and time treated in terms of spatial progression. Having been lured into extra-temporal territory, the soldier, upon his return to the real world, finds himself regarded as a revenant. He finally manages to outwit the devil and to win the princess whom, with the help of his recovered instrument, he has cured of melancholy. But the devil strikes promptly back when the soldier, crossing the border in order to enter his native country, finds himself deprived of the protection offered to him by the timeless realm. His punishment is deserved; for

> Il ne faut pas vouloir ajouter à ce qu'on a ce qu'on avait,
> on ne peut pas être à la fois qui on est et qui on était.
> On n'a pas le droit de tout avoir: c'est défendu.
> Un bonheur est tout le bonheur; deux c'est comme s'ils n'existaient plus.

Rather than pursue Stravinsky's operatic career beyond *L'Histoire*, we turn now to the artist who deserves credit for having brought the epic opera to its perfection both in practice and theory. Bertolt Brecht needs no special introduction as a writer. Yet it is relatively little known that he was also a practicing musician and that, in the early stages of his career, he composed the music for his own *Balladen*. Some of these songs made their appearance in his plays as well as in the *Hauspostille*, in which certain of the tunes are also reprinted. In his early plays, the young playwright, by his own confession, used music in the conventional manner by providing dramatic occasions for it[27]. It was only beginning with Kurt Weill's contributions to *Mann ist Mann*

---

26 "Restait à trouver le sujet: rien de plus facile. J'étais Russe: le sujet serait russe; Strawinsky était Vaudois (en ce temps-là): la musique serait vaudoise." Ramuz in *Œuvres Complètes*, XIV, 62.

27 "In den ersten paar Stücken wurde Musik in ziemlich landläufiger Form verwendet; es handelte sich um Lieder oder Märsche, und es fehlte kaum je eine naturalistische Motivierung dieser Musikstücke [...] Diese Musik schrieb ich noch selbst." (*Schriften zum Theater*, p. 239)

that the music achieved that *Kunstcharakter* or *Selbstwert* without which there can be no epic opera. Epic opera, however, as Ernst Schumacher points out in his book on Brecht, is the epitome of the epic theater, "since the musical elements serve as an epic, i. e. retarding factor"[28].

As with Cocteau and his friends, Brecht's break with musical Aristotelianism was largely due to his rejection of Wagner. In Wagner's music dramas Brecht saw an incarnation of the emotional and unconscious elements. But actually his critique was aimed less at Wagner himself and his own *Weltanschauung* than at the modern Wagnerians "who are satisfied with remembering that the original Wagnerians had ascribed a meaning to Wagner's opera"[29]. Brecht defied the so-called reforms of the musical theater under way in the twenties and aimed at modifying the outward form of opera without changing its apparatus. Desirous to change the apparatus itself, he pleaded for a *Literarisierung* of the theater, a process which he defined, in an untranslatable phrase, as "das Durchsetzen des 'Gestalteten' mit 'Formuliertem'".

Brecht's first venture into the musical theater, and his first collaboration with Weill, had taken place in 1927 when the original version of *Mahagonny* was written for performance at the Baden-Baden music festival. The plan for the most popular of Brecht's contributions to the genre materialized, in the following year, during a perusal of Gay's *Beggar's Opera*. In his analysis of the *Dreigroschenoper*, Schumacher underscores the similarity of the circumstances which led to the creation of Gay's satire and Brecht's parody. Artistically, the *Beggar's Opera* must be regarded as a protest against the totally unrealistic

---

28 *Die dramatischen Versuche Bertolt Brechts 1918-1933* (Berlin, 1955), p. 211. John Willett, *The Theatre of Bertolt Brecht* (London, 1959), p. 126ff., also deals with the problem of epic opera.

29 "Die heutigen Wagnerianer begnügen sich mit der Erinnerung, dass die ursprünglichen Wagnerianer einen Sinn festgestellt und also gewusst hatten. Bei den von Wagner abhängigen Produzierenden wird sogar die Haltung des Weltanschauenden noch stur beibehalten. Eine Weltanschauung, die, zu sonst nichts mehr nütze, nur noch als Genussmittel verschleudert wird." (*Schriften zum Theater*, p. 24)

style of Handel's late baroque operas. Analogously, the *Dreigroschenoper* mocks the Handelian Renaissance in post-war Germany, which the generation of *Neue Sachlichkeit* and the *Bauhaus* came to view as a sign that the bourgeoisie was beginning to reconstitute itself, for the rise of opera had long been associated with the emergence of that class.

Generically, the *Dreigroschenoper* stands halfway between the *Singspiel* and the Jazz Revue, traditional forms being consistently used with ironic overtones. The Wagnerian orchestra is replaced by a small jazzband, the set form of the aria by *Moritat* and Song[30]. Like Stravinsky, Brecht wants the musicians to be visible during the whole performance of the work[31]. On the whole, however, the German writer is more consistent in his use of alienating devices, which he deploys programmatically. Where Stravinsky totally eliminates the singers, Brecht retains them, but insists on neatly separating the various levels of verbal expression. In the *Dreigroschenoper,* there are to be no smooth transitions between spoken dialogue, recitative and singing; for "nothing is more detestable than for the actor to pretend that he does not notice the transition from speech to singing" (*Schriften zum Theater*, p. 32). Nor is the sequence of levels regarded as signifying an increase in emotional intensity. In order to forestall any such interpretation, Brecht uses titles and signs as "primitive attempts at making the theater literary" (p. 30), and as a means of training the audience in the art of "complex seeing".

---

30 For Brecht's defense of Jazz Revue and *Singspiel* see the essay "Über die Verwendung von Musik für ein episches Theater" (*Schriften zum Theater*, p. 239ff.), especially the paragraph culminating in the assertion: "Die sogenannte billige Musik ist besonders in Kabarett und Operette schon seit geraumer Zeit eine Art gestischer Musik; die ernste Musik hingegen hält immer noch am Lyrismus fest und pflegt den individuellen Ausdruck."

31 *Schriften zum Theater*, p. 240. With regard to the size of the orchestra to be used in the *Dreigroschenoper* Brecht states: "Die grosse Menge der Handwerker in den Opernorchestern ermöglicht nur assoziierende Musik" and demands a "Verkleinerung des Orchesterapparates auf allerhöchstens 30 Spezialisten" (see fn. 9).

Whereas in Stravinsky's opera the innovations came about for a variety of reasons not necessarily related to the final product, Brecht's revolution *in aestheticis* is the well-defined and carefully shaped by-product of a larger issue. In *L'Histoire*, for instance, the plot itself is treated quite seriously. Music and action, though not always running a parallel course, never clash or look at each other ironically. The fable of the *Dreigroschenoper*, on the other hand, is treated parodistically; and instead of leading up to a clearly defined moral, the action concludes with a literary cliché.

Throughout Brecht's work, music is used as a tool of alienation, especially in the sense that conventional tunes are applied to unconventional contexts: "By acting emotionally and rejecting none of the customary narcotic charms, it helped to unmask bourgeois ideology" (p. 241). From the musician's point of view, Kurt Weill arrived at a similar conclusion: "I found myself confronted with a realistic action, to which I had to oppose my music, since I consider music incapable of being realistic."[32] In the *Dreigroschenoper*, accordingly, traditional musical forms such as arias, duets, and chorales are used in contrast with the dramatic situations which give rise to them. This does not preclude the use of strictly musical parody in the form of dissonance, such as appears in the famous "Kanonensong". Further increasing the distance between words (or action) and music, Brecht advised the actors occasionally to speak against the music, an ironic perversion of the use which Schönberg and Alban Berg had made of *Sprechstimme*[33].

The limitation of scope and subject matter self-imposed upon the present paper renders impossible a discussion of the subsequent evolution of Brecht's ideas about the musical theater: his collaboration with

---

32 From an article in the *Monatsschrift für moderne Musik*, cited by Schumacher, *Die dramatischen Versuche Bertolt Brechts 1918-1933*, p. 249.

33 "Was die Melodie betrifft, so folge er [the actor] ihr nicht blindlings: es gibt ein Gegen-die-Musik-Sprechen, welches grosse Wirkungen haben kann, die von einer hartnäckigen, von Musik und Rhythmus unabhängigen und unbestechlichen Nüchternheit ausgehen." (*Schriften zum Theater*, p. 132; see fn. 9)

Weill on the expanded *Mahagonny,* his interest in the *Schuloper,* and his later theoretical writings. Suffice it to say that the *Anmerkungen* to *Mahagonny* offer a formal poetics of the epic opera with its total and permanent separation of ingredients, and that the *Little Organon* postulates a half-hearted return to art as 'culinary' entertainment, music having the task of "establishing itself in many ways and quite independently by expressing its attitude toward the subject" or merely that of "adding variety to the entertainment" (*Schriften zum Theater,* p. 170). This is a far cry from the relentless pursuit of alienation which characterized the author of the *Dreigroschenoper.*

Introduction to *The Essence of Opera* (1964)

The editor of a collection like the present one, which aims at acquainting the reader with as wide as possible a variety of views on opera broached by composers, librettists, and aestheticians during the last three hundred and fifty years, cannot possibly hope to unite all the important statements bearing on that subject in a single volume. It will rather be his task to proffer the most significant samples of each of the four basic approaches to opera which evolve in the course of the history of the form. The undertaking seems doubly justified by the fact that it has no precedent and that a considerable portion of the material appears for the first time in translations from the German, French, and Italian.

The omission of relevant utterances by such eminent librettists as Quinault[1], Apostolo Zeno[2], Marmontel[3], Goldoni[4], Eugène Scribe[5],

---

1 Concerning this principal librettist for Jean Baptiste Lully see Etienne Gros' *Philippe Quinault* (Paris: Champion, 1926).

2 Zeno, the predecessor of Metastasio and da Ponte, lived from 1668 to 1750. He wrote innumerable librettos for composers like Bononcini, Galuppi, Hasse, Porpora, and the Scarlattis. His letters in six volumes were published in 1785 (Venice: Sansoni).

3 Marmontel, the chief French author of librettos for comic operas in the second half of the eighteenth century (he wrote ten for Grétry and five for Piccinni), lived from 1723 to 1799. He is also known for his *Essai sur la révolution de la musique française* of 1777.

4 Goldoni's *Memoirs*, trans. by J. Black, edited by W. A. Drake (New York: Knopf, 1926), contains many interesting details and anecdotes about his experiences with managers and composers, especially with Baldassare Galuppi.

5 Scribe, the most prolific librettist of them all, not only wrote thirty-eight texts for Auber but provided the librettos for Verdi's *Vêpres siciliennes*, Boieldieu's *Dame blanche*, Meyerbeer's *Huguenots*, *Robert le diable*, and *Le Prophète*, and Halévy's *La Juive*. Verdi's *Un ballo in maschera*, Bellini's *Sonnambula*, and Cilea's *Adriana Lecouvreur* also derive from plays he wrote. Scribe's contribution is discussed by Neil C. Arvin in his book *Eugène Scribe and the French Theatre 1815-1860* (Cambridge: Harvard University Press, 1924).

and Gabriele d'Annunzio[6] is regrettable. But a line had to be drawn at some point and repetition would have been unavoidable. The number of first-rate and second-rate composers slighted in our anthology is naturally legion. Some of those whose works are still in the repertory (Donizetti, Bellini, Smetana, etc.) or formerly had a prominent place in it (from Cimarosa and Païsiello to Cherubini, Spontini, Meyerbeer, Gounod, and Auber) either found no occasion to verbalize their feelings about the art they practiced or merely echoed what their predecessors and contemporaries had to offer by way of comment, although some interesting material could have been drawn from the formal or informal writings of most of them. Evidence from the pen or mouth of older masters (Purcell, Hasse, Telemann, Alessandro Scarlatti) either does not exist or is extremely hard to come by. Nor did it seem desirable to burden the collection with views on comic opera. On the whole it is evident that unless they are conscious innovators or reformers, the makers of operatic music are not overly inclined to theorize about their art, except spontaneously during the creative process. Of the great masters in the field who are still acknowledged as such, Handel is the only one not directly quoted in the anthology, since his letters shed little light on his conception of opera as an art form. Haydn's annotations to his own works for the musical stage and Weber's communications with Helmina von Chézy are, unfortunately, unavailable.

One cannot help but notice that this anthology is largely composed of programmatic and quasi-programmatic statements, even though some of the selections appear to be of a strictly descriptive nature. In spite of the many disparities between intention and execution, no attempt has been made – except briefly as part of the introductory matter – to evaluate the material critically, i. e., to match an artist's theory with his practice. The reader who wishes to pursue that aspect should consult the books and articles listed in the succinct bibliographies

---

6 D'Annunzio wrote the *Mystère de Saint Sebastien*, for which Debussy supplied incidental music. Their correspondence, edited by G. Tosi, was published in 1948.

appended to each introduction. An excellent analysis of the relationship between music and drama and its effect on operatic history, theory, and criticism is made by Joseph Kerman in his stimulating though one-sided book *Opera as Drama.* In his judgment of works for the musical stage Kerman is guided by the belief that "in opera, the composer is the dramatist and [...] the clarification of the dramatic idea and the refinement of the vision cannot be left to the librettist," a view that flatly contradicts the neoclassical concept of opera. So far nobody has written a history of the libretto, a task we consider to be a prerequisite for that history of melo-dramaturgy for which our anthology might serve as a tentative basis and for that poetics of opera which Beaumarchais envisaged in his preface to *Tarare* and which a latter-day Algarotti should perhaps be encouraged to create.

The pieces assembled on the following pages are extremely diverse. Some constitute private, some semi-private documents, while others were intended for publication. Letters exchanged between individuals engaged in creating a symbiosis of music and drama are especially valuable insofar as their content directly reflects the creative process and acquaints us with the actual intentions of librettists and composers. Monteverdi's letters to Striggio, Goethe's to Christoph Philipp Kayser, Mozart's to his father, Verdi's to his numerous collaborators, and Puccini's to Giuseppe Adami belong to this category, which is nowhere better represented than in the extensive correspondence exchanged between Richard Strauss and Hugo von Hofmannsthal. Other epistles, such as St. Evremond's letter to the Duke of Buckingham, Gluck's to de la Harpe and the *Mercure de France*, and Debussy's to the Secretary General of the Opéra Comique in Paris, are much less spontaneous. The same applies to Rossini's conversations with his biographer Zanolini and to Lorenzo da Ponte's patently apologetic memoirs.

Prefaces to, and dedications of, specific works represent a rather formal type of communication between an artist and his patrons or his audience. Gluck used his dedication of *Alceste* to Grand Duke Leopold of Tuscany as an excuse for writing a manifesto. Corneille's *Examen* of *Andromède*; Dryden's preface to *Albion and Albanius*, Beaumarchais' to *Tarare*, Berlioz' to *La Damnation de Faust*, Hofmannsthal's to *Die ägyptische Helena*, Strauss' to *Intermezzo*; Berg's observations about *Wozzeck*; and Brecht's "Anmerkungen zur *Dreigroschenoper*" fall under this heading. Examples of treatises on the genre are found in Voltaire's *Dissertation sur la tragédie ancienne et moderne*, Diderot's *Le Neveu de Rameau*, Wieland's essay on the *Singspiel* (his term for *opera seria*), E. T. A. Hoffmann's dialogue between poet and composer, Wagner's *Oper und Drama*, Nietzsche's pro-Wagnerian and anti-Wagnerian polemics, Busoni's *Versuch einer neuen Ästhetik der Tonkunst*, Cocteau's aphoristic *Le Coq et l'Arlequin*, and Claudel's dissertation on "Modern Drama and Music". Stendhal's *Vie de Rossini* is a Romantic poetics of opera in disguise, Marcello's satire *Il Teatro alla moda* a melo-dramaturgy in reverse. Dictionary entries, like Rousseau's articles on opera and counter-sense from his *Dictionnaire de musique* and Voltaire's definition in his *Connaissance des beautés et des défauts de la poésie et de l'eloquence dans la langue française*, lay claim to greater objectivity but are by no means free of polemic overtones.

Several contributions consist of reviews of specific operas (Grillparzer on Weber's *Freischütz*, Weber on E. T. A. Hoffmann's *Undine*) and books (Shaw on Noufflard's *Richard Wagner d'après lui-même*) or, as in Addison's sarcastic *Spectator* essays, are journalistic attacks on contemporary operatic abuses. Aesthetics proper is represented in writings by Schopenhauer and Kierkegaard; and the volume concludes with a symposium on the present state of opera conducted by some of today's leading melodramatists.

Although it is quite impossible (and perhaps undesirable) to reduce the manifold views on opera to a set of clearly delimited, mutually exclusive categories, four basic approaches to melo-dramaturgy suggest themselves, with numerous intermediary positions completing the spectrum. A fifth approach – that which posits the absurdity of the genre "since music is unable to tell a story" (Boileau) – cannot be taken seriously by anyone concerned with enriching the repertory. The first approach, which is essentially that embraced by the classicists and neoclassicists of all nations and ages, rests on the assumption that in opera music must always remain a modest handmaiden. At its inception in the days of the Florentine *camerata*, opera was earmarked as the modern equivalent of ancient tragedy (of whose musical qualities we have only a faint idea based on, among other things, the notation of a few lines in Euripides' *Orestes*). Rinuccini, Caccini, Peri and their contemporaries agreed that the musical ingredient should underscore, perhaps enhance, but never overshadow the spoken word. From Corneille to Beaumarchais this was the position held, with a few notable exceptions, by one generation of French critics after another. Rousseau and the Encyclopedists never ceased to think of music – or, at any rate, of song – as a kind of language; and the venerable Pietro Metastasio, reminding us of the fact that Aristotle listed music as the fifth of the six constituent parts of drama, proudly reported that his dramas – the famous *Didone abbandonata* among them – were more frequently seen as plays than as operas.

By far the staunchest defender of the neoclassical view was Christoph Willibald Gluck, who thought it his mission to "reduce music to its true function", that of "serving the poetry by means of the expression". Luckily for us, the great reformer was much too inspired a musician to let his genius be quenched, although he too cherished the notion that music "even in the most terrible situations, must never offend the ear, but must please the hearer, or, in other words, must never cease to be *music*" (Mozart) – a view that was subsequently challenged by Diderot and Berlioz and refuted *in toto* by the Expressionists. Philosophically, the neoclassical theory of opera finds support in the writings of Kant, for whom reason is the supreme guide in human affairs and who, judging the arts according to the degree in which reason partakes in their execution and reception, finds fault with music on account of its sensuousness.

The Romantic theory of opera, radically opposed to its classical antecedents, celebrates the triumph of music over drama. Stepping out of the role assigned to it by the classically minded aestheticians, music now regards literature as its slave. Mozart, although a born melodramaturgist, nevertheless demands that "the poetry must be altogether the obedient daughter of the music", Stendhal wants the operatic audience to dispense (or nearly dispense) with the libretto, Berlioz shows sovereign contempt for dramatic values by dispatching his Faust to the plains of Hungary, and W. H. Auden offends his muse by asserting that "the verses which the librettist writes are not addressed to the public but are really a private letter to the composer". Romantically inclined composers – but, understandably, not only those – are at times so carried away by their inspiration that they compose the music for numbers whose text has not as yet been written. This paradox, bearing out the contention *Prima la musica e poi le parole* (the title of an opera by Salieri), is mentioned in the letters of Mozart, Verdi, Strauss, and Puccini. The philosophical blessing upon Romantic melodramaturgy was bestowed by none other than Schopenhauer who, revolting against the Kantian rationalism, glorified Rossini's music as one that speaks "its own language so distinctly and purely that it requires no words and produces its full effect when rendered by instruments alone".

The two radical positions just outlined are duly complemented by two others, which hinge on the conviction that the two principal ingredients of opera are equally valuable and that neither of them should be exalted at the expense of the other. Wagner proclaimed the union of music and drama in terms of a perfect marriage contracted and consummated between male and female, whose copulation renders the *Gesamtkunstwerk* possible, whereas, breaking away from the Wagnerian style, the founders of Epic Opera were determined to provide equal but separate facilities for music and drama. Both elements are thus assured their independence. Stravinsky, Brecht, and to a certain extent Claudel are fond of alienation, whereas Alban Berg, in his

Wozzeck, alienates music from drama *sub rosa* while emphasizing the expressive quality of his music.

Chronologically, the neoclassical view predominated in the seventeenth and eighteenth centuries (except when opera gave itself frankly as a baroque spectacle), whereas the Romantic concept prevailed in the first half, and the Wagnerian in the second half, of the following centennium. Twentieth-century melo-dramaturgy, when it avoids the charge of being conservative or reactionary, centers in the fourth approach. However, at times the rebellion against Wagner took so violent a turn that an exodus of opera from the theater to the concert hall (opera-oratorio) or music hall (Satie's *Parade*) was deemed advisable. Thus a period of operatic history is brought to a close under circumstances that bear a striking resemblance to those which led to the demise of Handelian opera under the impact of John Gay's *Beggar's Opera*.

Apart from the basic, and hence constantly repeated, question concerning the true nature of the relationship between music and drama (or poetry), a limited number of topics of a more specialized nature are intermittently discussed in our anthology. Those who affirm the role of opera as an important ingredient of the aesthetic universe are naturally eager to explain what makes it a form *sui generis*. What can opera do, they ask, that the exclusively literary or musical genres find themselves barred from achieving? Those who want to undermine the foundations of opera, on the other hand, seek to prove that it can never rid itself of its inherent flaws.

The champions of opera are only too quick to point out that what the spoken drama lacks most of all is the ability to handle several strands of action or emotion simultaneously. In the musical drama, however, simultaneity comes naturally and, as Stendhal explains, "experience completely ruins the arguments" of those "poor frigid souls [who] claim [that] it is silly for five or six persons to sing at the same time". Nor do the participants in an ensemble (Weber calls it a "Janus head") have to share identical feelings, a fact most beautifully illustrated in the quartet from *Otello* to which Boito refers in his letter to Verdi. What is more, considerable depth is gained in opera by the interplay between the singers and the orchestra, since the latter may be advantageously used to comment upon the action on stage, just as it can serve to reveal the subconscious motives and urges of the protagonists. Wagner even wants it to perform the role of historian and prophet.

Music being a mood-building art, its presence often adds a totally new dimension to the drama: the sensuousness which language, that arbitrary system of counters, lacks. In the spoken drama, mood can only be expressed negatively, for instance by means of significant pauses. In the lyrical plays of Hofmannsthal, Chekhov, and Maeterlinck, what is said often matters less than what remains unspoken, whereas Shakespeare's *Othello* – joined, perhaps, by the second part of Goethe's *Faust* – is the rare example of a play that is lyrical in the sense of aspiring to be music. Stanislavsky, I think, was right when treating it symphonically.

A further advantage enjoyed by opera, and repeatedly touched upon in our anthology, derives from the use of several levels of expression, and hence consciousness, which that art form renders feasible. The operatic composer commands a variety of means of expression – from the conversational to the symphonic, from ordinary speech via *Sprechstimme*, melodrama (of the type encountered in *Fidelio*), *recitativo secco* and *accompagnato* to full-fledged arias, ensembles, and purely instrumental music – that is unparalleled in regular drama. At best this wealth can be approximated in a poetic play like T. S. Eliot's *Cocktail Party*, where the number of stresses per line indicates the appropriate level of consciousness. This stratification, however, also has its disadvantages: for how is the composer to proceed from one level of discourse to another without breaking the continuity? Wagner fiercely attacked the fragmentation he noticed in operatic practice, a fragmentation defended by, among others, Alfred de Musset in his maiden speech at the Académie Française. Wagner insisted on writing through-composed operas, in which the levels imperceptibly merge in a continuous stream of musical progression. Today operatic abuses of the kind Wagner attacked are out of fashion and composers are no longer forced to bow to the wishes of prima donnas (as Mozart did in *Die Entführung aus dem Serail* and *Die Zauberflöte*) or the spoiled taste of a public set in its ways. To us even Puccini's striving for effect seems out of place.

What the critics of opera most violently object to in the genre is the artificiality of the conventions which gave rise to it and which make its existence possible. People don't sing in real life, these critics say; why should they do so in the theater? But, as Wieland points out astutely, the conventions of the spoken drama and of art in general, are hardly less constraining, and the difference is, at best, one of degree. Many champions of opera, anticipating this common objection, sought to assign to it a realm sufficiently remote from ordinary life to make these conventions tolerable. The musical theater, in their opinion, should never engage in realistic modes but should restrict itself to the presentation of mythological, pastoral, or otherwise 'marvelous' scenes and actions. Dryden, Wieland, Busoni, Hofmannsthal and, in part, Beaumarchais share this view; and Schiller, in a letter to Goethe of December 29, 1797, goes so far as to express the hope that a rejuvenation of drama might be effected by way of opera.

Other weighty objections consistently raised by the foes, and difficulties encompassed by the executants, of opera, include the undue brevity of the libretto (Hofmannsthal was frightened to see "how short is the libretto of *Tristan* and how long the opera"), the amount of repetition allowed and often required by music, music's inability to convey deception, contradiction, and even humor (*Hamlet* makes a very poor operatic subject; and perhaps the best way of being humorous in an opera consists in introducing unmusical characters such as Beckmesser in *Die Meistersinger* and the male protagonist of Strauss and Zweig's *Die schweigsame Frau*), and the often painfully noticeable unintelligibility of the singers (Richard Strauss claimed that one third of each operatic text is a total loss). These factors surely contribute to the failure of many a music drama and help to account for the excruciatingly small number of operatic masterpieces. All the more reason for us to ponder these questions anew and to sharpen our awareness of the hurdles any team of composer and librettist has to clear before it can proceed to the finish.

Reflections on a Golden Style:
W. H. Auden's Theory of Opera (1970)

For several decades now, W. H. Auden has been regarded as the most representative English writer (or, at least, the most representative British poet) of the generation following that of T. S. Eliot. In recent years, literary historians and critics have begun to scrutinize his works; and even his criticism – much of it conveniently gathered in the volume, *The Dyer's Hand and Other Essays*[1] – has attracted attention in the world of scholarship. Its growth and scope have been surveyed in essays by Edward Callan and Cleanth Brooks[2]. As a playwright, too, Auden has found himself in the critical limelight, notably regarding his contributions to the repertory of the British Group Theatre in the thirties (*The Dog Beneath the Skin* and *The Ascent of F 6,* both written in collaboration with Christopher Isherwood).

What literary scholars, with few exceptions, have thus far failed to realize is that, because of his close and intimate contact with music, Auden's theatrical interests have gradually shifted from the spoken verse drama to the music drama, which he now regards as one of the only two contemporary vehicles of the Golden and High Style required by a public art – the other being the ballet. As a sheer artifice, that is to say, opera is not ashamed of the rhetoric from which the modern playwright shies away. Whereas Joseph Warren Beach refuses to treat Auden's librettos "with critical solemnity" since they "have been one means of eking out a poet's slender income" and "represent

---

1 New York: Random House, 1962. Subsequently referred to as *DH*.
2 E. Callan, "The Development of W. H. Auden's Critical Theory". *Twentieth Century Literature*, IV (1958), 79-91; Cleanth Brooks, "W. H. Auden's Literary Criticism". *Kenyon Review*, XXVI (1966), 173-189.

[...] the hobbies of a highly gifted poet"[3], Monroe K. Spears is aware of the fact that "opera libretti [...] have been Auden's only long works [...] in recent years"[4], and John G. Blair admits that "in the opera [Auden] seems to have found a set of conventions that is most congenial to his poetic and dramatic talents"[5]. In our study of that author's poetics of opera, we shall proceed from this assumption.

Auden's collaboration with Benjamin Britten in a number of musical ventures – beginning with the "Symphonic Cycle for Soprano and Orchestra", *The Hunting Fathers* (1936), and ending in 1941 with the chamber opera (or operetta) *Paul Bunyan*[6] – need not detain us here, although it should be noted, if only for curiosity's sake, that the pair did not subsequently follow the example of Strauss and Hofmannsthal. Auden's profound and lasting interest in opera was apparently not aroused until after he had come of age, as he reports in an essay entitled "A Public Art":

> I was brought up to believe that opera was a bastard art-form. The great Mozart operas might just do because Mozart was Mozart, but Wagner in one way and Verdi in another were considered vulgar; as for Rossini, Bellini and Donizetti, they were simply beyond the pale. (Judging by some articles I have read, this prejudice still survives in certain English quarters.) In addition, we were put off, not entirely without justification, by the kind of public which *did* 'go to the op-

---

3   *The Making of the Auden Canon* (Minneapolis, 1957), 205. Beach nevertheless devotes a whole chapter (190-205) to Auden's librettos, focusing almost entirely on Britten's Op. 14, the *Ballad of Heroes*, which is partly based on the poem "Danse Macabre".

4   *The Poetry of W. H. Auden: The Disenchanted Island* (New York, 1963), 288. The opening section of the fourth chapter of Spears's book (262-289) deals exclusively with Auden's operatic contributions.

5   *The Poetic Art of W. H. Auden* (Princeton, 1965), 184. Blair analyzes the libretto of *The Rake's Progress* at some length (163-184), as does Joseph Kerman in his fine book, *Opera as Drama* (New York, 1956), 234-247.

6   The work remains unpublished, since the authors withdrew it after the premiere staged in May 1941 in Columbia University's Brander Matthews Theatre. Spears discusses it on the basis of information furnished by Daniel G. Hoffman. Auden's remarks concerning "Opera on an American Legend: Problems of Putting the Story of Paul Bunyan on the Stage" (*New York Times*, May 4, 1941, section 9, 7) constitute a first sketch of his theory of opera in-the-making.

era'; many of them seemed more interested in appearing at the appropriate social event for the London Season than in listening to music.[7]

The revelation must have occurred around 1940 for, as Auden puts it in his inaugural Oxford lecture, "I am eternally grateful [...] to the musical fashion of my youth which prevented me from listening to Italian opera until I was over thirty, by which age I was capable of really appreciating a world so beautiful and so challenging to my own cultural heritage" (*DH*, 40). Similarly, it was Nietzsche's polemic tract, *Der Fall Wagner*, "which first taught [him] to listen to Wagner, about whom [he] had previously held silly preconceived notions" (*DH*, 48).

Auden's poetic and musical views about opera began to crystallize in the late forties, largely in connection with his work on the libretto for *The Rake's Progress*, which Igor Stravinsky had commissioned from him at the suggestion of Aldous Huxley[8]. Since then, operatic problems have occupied him as intensely as they did Hugo von Hofmannsthal, "Austrian, European and Master Librettist", to whose memory the three makers of *Elegy for Young Lovers* were later to dedicate their work[9]. This incontrovertible fact explains why it is virtually impossible to do justice to Auden's mature art – both in theory and practice – without reference to music in general and melodrama in particular. Those literary critics who presume to do so act in ignorance and demonstrate, once again, the dire consequences which an arbitrary fragmentation of the arts entails.

In the following discussion, it will be our principal aim to furnish some guidelines for an understanding of Auden's poetic theory and to

---

[7] *Opera* (London), XII (1961), 12-15.

[8] Concerning the genesis of *The Rake's Progress* see the composer's report, Auden's letter, and the first scenario, as included in Stravinsky's book, *Memories and Commentaries* (Garden City, NY, 1960), 144-154.

[9] The hero of this opera – perhaps a caricature of the beloved model – is an "artist-genius [...] morally bound [...] to exploit others whenever such exploitation will benefit his work and to sacrifice them whenever their existence is a hindrance to his production". *Elegy for Young Lovers* (Mainz, 1961), 63.

state, as succinctly as possible, the reasons for his choice of opera and the dance as the preferred artistic media of our age. (We hardly need apologize for the omission of some particulars and details which – the standard fare of melo-dramaturgy – would only clutter up the pages.) As will shortly be seen, it was in Kierkegaard – more specifically in the section of *Either/Or* which deals with music in its sensuous and erotic aspects – that Auden encountered the most congenial treatment of this burning question. He candidly acknowledged his debt when, in a review of the first complete English translation of this treatise, he stated that "Kierkegaard's essay on music is the only illuminating suggestion for a musical esthetic that I have seen"[10].

In keeping with our announced purpose, we do not intend to analyze any of the original librettos Auden wrote jointly with Chester Kallman[11], except where the nature or evolution of such texts has a bearing on the subject of operatic theory, which constitutes the focus of our essay. Nor shall we explicitly concern ourselves with their translations of *Die Zauberflöte, Don Giovanni,* and Brecht's *Die sieben Todsünden der Kleinbürger*[12], especially since we have given an extended critique of the transmogrified *Magic Flute* in another context[13]. Auden himself has admitted his skepticism with regard to the translatability of librettos. In 1952, for instance, he put himself on record as believing:

---

10 "Preface to Kierkegaard". *The New Republic*, May 15, 1944, 683-685.

11 Disregarding the "corporate personality" (*DH*, 483) at work in these librettos – which also include *Delia or A Masque of Night* (*Botteghe Oscure*, XII, 1953, 164-210) – most critics annex them to the work of Auden. In the case of *The Rake's Progress*, the exact nature of the collaboration has been disclosed by Stravinsky (*Memories and Commentaries*, 150 footnote) and Auden's former secretary, Alan Ansen (*The Hudson Review*, IX, 1956, 319-320). Spears was informed by Auden that seventy-five per cent of the text of *Elegy for Young Lovers* must be credited to Kallman.

12 *The Magic Flute* (New York, 1956); *Don Giovanni* (New York, 1961); *Seven Deadly Sins* in *Tulane Drama Review*, VI (Sept. 1961), 123-129.

13 "Sarastro's Brave New World or *Die Zauberflöte* Transmogrified". *Your Musical Cue* (Bloomington), II (Dec., 1965/ Jan., 1966), 3-9.

> It is precisely because I believe that, in listening to song (as distinct from chant), we hear, not words, but syllables, that I am violently hostile to the performances of opera in translation. Wagner in Italian or Verdi in English sounds intolerable, and would still sound so if the poetic merits of the translation were greater than those of the original, because the new syllables have no apt relation to the pitch and tempo of the notes with which they are associated. The poetic value of the notes may provoke a composer's imagination, but it is their syllabic values which determine the kind of vocal line he writes. In song, poetry is expendable, syllables are not[14].

If within a few years following this pronouncement Auden had embarked on doing exactly what, in theory, he did not regard as being worth the trouble, this can be explained in a very pragmatic manner. For as the poet himself candidly admits: "The big broadcasting companies are willing to pay handsomely for translations and we saw no reason why, if a translation *was* going to be made, we shouldn't get the money."[15] Yet there is reason to assume that Auden and Kallman became intrigued by the problems involved in transposing an operatic text from one tongue into another. A note of hope and despair, triumph and defeat is sounded – by way of a *captatio benevolentiae* – in the preface to the Englished *Zauberflöte*:

> Translation is a dubious business at best and we are inclined to agree with those who believe that operas should always be given in their native tongue. However, if audiences demand them in their own, they must accept the consequences. Obviously, the texture and weight of the original words set by the composer are an element in his orchestration and any change of the words is therefore an alternation of the music itself. Yet the goal of the translator, however unattainable, must be to make audiences believe that the words they are hearing are the words the composer actually set, which means that a too-literal translation of the original text may sometimes prove a falsification[16].

---

14 "Some Reflections on Music and Opera," *Partisan Review*, XIX, (1952), 10-18. The passage was not contained in an earlier version of the "Reflections" published in the British periodical *Tempo*, No. 20 (Summer, 1951), 6-10. They form part of Auden's reply to a critique of his views on opera offered by Ronald Duncan in *Opera*, III (1952), 34-36, and were later incorporated in the revised notes. Readers are alerted to the excisions, additions, and emendations found in the various versions of the "Reflections".

15 "Translating Opera Libretti" (co-authored by Kallman), *DH*, 483-499.

16 *The Magic Flute*, XIV-XV. Under his own name, Auden presented similar views in a short essay entitled "Putting it in English: A Translator Discusses the Problems of Changing an Opera's Language". *New York Times*, January 8, 1956, section 2, 9. The

As we turn to the central topic of our discussion, we wish to emphasize that in order fully to savor the meaning of Auden's views on opera for the poet's esthetic orientation we must see them in relation to his attitudes toward the other art forms. Taken as a whole, these attitudes form a frame of reference in which all artistic media occupy their assigned stations and are judged according to a carefully drawn-up scheme of values. That Auden was relatively slow in arriving at this grand conception of a *harmonia artium* and that, nevertheless, this development was a natural one, is proved by the notions – however tentative – which the young author of the Group Theatre harbored. These notions (which must have found a sympathetic ear in T. S. Eliot, the author of the Agon, *Sweeney Agonistes*) in some ways clearly foreshadow the final epiphany.

In a paradigmatic utterance published in a program of the communal enterprise, Auden sought to establish the superiority of the poetic drama over any branch of dramatic realism. He wished to see all vestiges of "brute" reality transferred to the art of cinematography: "The development of the film has deprived drama of any excuse for being documentary. It is not in its nature to provide an ignorant and passive spectator with exciting news."[17] While the documentary elements of drama are thus relegated to the movies, character portrayal is handed over to the novel: "Similarly the drama is not suited to the analysis of character, which is the province of the novel. Dramatic speech, like dramatic movement, should possess a self-confessed, significant and undocumentary character." Only one step further, and the realization that opera was the perfect embodiment of this dream would have dawned upon the poet who, already at this early point, states unequivocally that "drama, in fact, deals with the general and

---

article "On *The Magic Flute*". *Center: A Review of the Performing Arts*, I (1954), was, unfortunately, unavailable.

17 From "What I Want the Theatre to Be", as quoted by Ashley Dukes in *Theatre Arts*, XIX (1935), 907-908.

universal [= the mythical], not with the particular and local." But Auden was not quite ready to take this step.

The expected development took place gradually in the course of the next decade, with the first crystallization – to use Stendhal's pet term – occurring in conjunction with the writing of *Paul Bunyan*, which deals precisely with a mythical subject; myths being, in Auden's view, "collective creations" which "cease to appear when a society has become sufficiently differentiated for its individual members to have individual conceptions of their own tasks"[18]. The opera, therefore, begins with a prologue "in which America is still a virgin forest and Paul Bunyan has not yet been born" and ends "with a Christmas party at which he bids farewell to his men because now he is no longer needed"; for "a collective mythical figure is no use, because the requirements of each relation are unique. Faith is essentially invisible."

Like Hofmannsthal who – for slightly different reasons – regarded mythological operas as the truest of all art forms[19], Auden, ever since he became involved in the creation of works for the lyrical stage, has persistently sought to embrace subjects expressing the universal and the general. Whereas in *The Rake's Progress* he fell somewhat short of the goal because this was a commissioned work and he was tied to the essentially didactic subject suggested by the composer, the *Elegy for Young Lovers* is concerned with the artist genius who, in the librettist's opinion, constitutes "not only a nineteenth and early twentieth century myth, but also a European myth"[20], while his latest libretto,

---

18 *New York Times*, May 4, 1941, section 9, 7. Spears discusses *Paul Bunyan* on pp. 264-269 of his study.

19 The operas that come to mind forge a link between the 'realistic' librettos for *Der Rosenkavalier* (1911) and *Arabella* (1933). They are *Ariadne auf Naxos* (1912), *Die Frau ohne Schatten* (1918), and *Die ägyptische Helena* (1928). It is in the preface to the latter work that Hofmannsthal enters his plea: "For if this age of ours is anything, it is mythical – I know of no other expression for an existence which unfolds in the face of such vast horizons."

20 *Elegy for Young Lovers*, 63.

Die Bassariden, is a revamping of Euripides' *Bacchae* and treats a myth which, though it may have been considered moribund in the nineteenth century, has taken on new meaning in the present one; for "today we know only too well that it is as possible for whole communities to become demonically possessed as it is for individuals to go off their heads"[21].

Here, then, is the core of Auden's poetics of opera as far as its subject matter is concerned, which must clearly belong to that "secondary world" which creates an ambience of its own while at the same time giving depth to the primary world inhabited by ordinary mortals:

> At the same time, no secondary world can fully hold our attention unless it has something significant to say [...] about our present life. The most successful heroes and heroines in opera are mythical figures. That is to say, whatever their historical or geographical setting, they embody some element of human nature or some aspect of the human condition which is a permanent concern of human beings irrespective of their time and place[22].

Since the theory of any art – whether it be literature, music, painting, sculpture, architecture, the film, or any mixture of these – must inevitably come to grips with form as well as *Stoff*, we must undertake to reconstruct Auden's esthetic universe *in toto* and, on the basis of this model, deduce the general and specific reasons responsible for the exalted place assigned to opera within that harmony of artistic spheres. First of all, we are surprised that a man who tends to emulate what we might call the Romantic view of opera should so brazenly insist on a neat separation of genres, or rather on assigning to each genre its uniquely proper function. Only a neoclassical purist could be expected to vouch that "each of the arts has its special field with which it can deal better than any rival medium can, and its special limitations which it transgresses at its peril"[23]. The practical applica-

---

21 "The Mythical World of Opera". *Times Literary Supplement*, November 2,1967, 1038. This is "a somewhat shortened version of the third of Mr. Auden's T. S. Eliot Memorial Lectures given at the University of Kent".

22 Ibid.

23 *Vogue*, July 1948, p. 65.

tion of this view was suggested in a document published three years later:

> Every artistic medium reflects some area of human experience. Those areas often overlap but never coincide, for if two media could do the same thing equally well one would be unnecessary.
>
> When someone, like myself, after years of working in one medium, essays another for the first time, he should always, I believe, try to discover its proper principles before starting work. Otherwise he is in danger of carrying over assumptions and habits of mind which have become second nature to him in a field where, as a matter of fact, they do not and cannot apply[24].

In light of this cautionary note, we justly expect Auden to strive for a systematic exploration of the arts in terms of their interrelationship. Although, for reasons which will soon become apparent, he pays relatively little attention to the plastic arts, he does not, on the whole, disappoint us in this respect. His discontent with the visual arts stems primarily from his awareness of their stationary and hence essentially passive character. Whereas "the possibility of making music [...] depends primarily, not upon man's possession of an auditory organ, the ear, but upon his possession of a sound-producing instrument, the vocal chords", in the case of painting, sculpture, etc. "it is a visual organ, the eye, which is primary, for without it, the experience which stimulates the hand into becoming an expressive instrument could not exist"[25].

Auden seems to regard the plastic arts as being mimetic and representational – a rather old-fashioned view regarding the predominance of abstract painting in the first half of the twentieth century. What really irks him, however, is the circumstance that, lacking the temporal dimension, painted characters are unable to choose or assert their wills in any recognizable way. They thus invariably appear to be products of their environment or victims of fate. This was the chief handicap with which Auden and Kallman found themselves saddled

---

[24] *Tempo*, No. 20 (1951), 6. This section is missing in subsequent versions of the "Reflections".

[25] *Partisan Review*, XXIX (1952), 13f.

when Stravinsky proposed an operatic subject based on Hogarth's series of engravings:

> A character in opera can never appear the victim of circumstances; however unfortunate, he or she is bound to seem the architect of fate. When we look at a picture of a couple embracing, we know for certain that they are interested in each other, but are told very little about what each is feeling; when we listen to a love duet on the opera stage, it is just the other way round; we are certain that each is in love, but the cause of that love will seem to lie in each as subject not as an object[26].

Kierkegaard certainly would have given his *placet*, for what mattered to him in his search for the most perfect expression of sensuous-erotic genius was the suitability of a given artistic medium for that purpose:

> The most abstract idea conceivable is sensuous genius. But in what medium is this idea expressible? Solely in music. It cannot be expressed in sculpture, for it is a sort of inner qualification of inwardness, nor in painting, for it cannot be apprehended in precise outlines; it is an energy, a storm, a passion, and so on, in all their lyrical quality, yet so that it does not exist in one moment but in a succession of moments, for if it existed in a single moment it could be modeled or painted[27].

As we move with Auden from painting to cinematography, we find some satisfaction in entering an ambit of temporal progression in a visual art. Yet in spite of the desired "immediacy" – a key term in Auden's and Kierkegaard's poetics – we are still on that side of the esthetic ledger which records the passive or negative assets. For the characters on the screen, while theoretically free to act and portrayed as acting, still remain subject to "the necessities of nature or the necessities of the social order"[28]. This view is broached in Auden's essay on Veristic opera, where he denounces Naturalism as an art which precludes choice on the part of the individual and which therefore fails to rise even to the level of ethics – not to mention the level of esthetics which constitutes the desired secondary world[29]. Auden would apply

---

26 *"The Rake's Progress,"* *Harper's Bazaar*, February 1953, 165.

27 *Either/Or*, tr. D. F. and L. M. Swenson, rev. by H. A. Johnson (Garden City, NY, 1959), I, 55.

28 "Cav and Pag". *DH*, 478. The essay originally appeared as an introduction to an RCA Victor recording of *Cavalleria rusticana* and *I Pagliacci*.

29 Auden interprets *verismo* very broadly as including Bizet's *Carmen* as well as Puccini's *Madama Butterfly*.

this stricture – although less stringently – to fiction and epic poetry as well.

The foregoing argument by no means exhausts the objections which Auden feels urged to raise against cinematography; for in addition to disqualifying the film artistically on the grounds of its 'documentary' nature, he also resents its didactic and magical properties. By the latter he means the "means for inducing desirable emotions and repelling undesirable emotions in oneself and others"[30]. More important still, the film – he argues – renders abortive any attempt on the artist's part to transcend nature by means of the spirit, whereas in opera the spirit decidedly triumphs over nature. Auden seeks to prove his contention by comparing Wagner's *Tristan* with Cocteau's *L'Eternel Retour* in the following manner:

> On the other hand, its pure artifice renders opera the ideal medium for a tragic myth. I once went in the same week to a performance of *Tristan und Isolde* and a showing of *L'Eternel Retour* [...] During the former two souls, weighing over two hundred pounds a piece, were transfigured by a transcendent power, in the latter a handsome boy met a beautiful girl and they had an affair. This loss of value was due not to any lack of skill on Cocteau's part but to the nature of the cinema as a medium. Had he used a fat middle-aged couple, the effect would have been ridiculous because the snatches of language which are all the movie permits have not sufficient power to transcend their physical appearance. Yet if the lovers are young and beautiful, the cause of their love looks 'natural', a consequence of their beauty, and the whole meaning of the Myth is gone[31].

Moving to the level of literature, we can confine ourselves, with Auden, to a brief consideration of the drama which, unlike epic poetry or fiction, retains little of the material dross – the documentary values and environmental factors – which weighs so heavily on the visual arts. (As for the nature of the relationship between lyrical poetry and music – chant and song – Auden discusses it at some length in his introduction to *An Elizabethan Song Book*[32].)

---

30 "Squares and Oblongs". *Poets at Work*, ed. C. D. Abbott (New York, 1948), 173.

31 *Partisan Review*, XIX (1952), 11. Elsewhere Auden calls Tristan and Isolde "two mountains of corseted flesh".

32 Garden City, NY, 1955.

Auden finds literature to be superior to painting because it is, first and foremost, a temporal art. However, in the more extended fictional forms it suffers – in his opinion – from leaving too much room for reflection, thereby allowing the other temporal dimensions to intervene: the past in the form of memories and regrets, and the future in the form of hopes, doubts, and anticipations. The gain – to use Kierkegaard's terminology – is to be credited to ethics, the loss, however, to esthetics. Moreover, the metaphorical nature of language encourages an implicit spatialization through imagery; and this in turn impairs and at times destroys that immediacy of feeling and directness of movement which is the hallmark of the esthetic constructs admired by Kierkegaard and Auden:

> A verbal statement and a musical phrase are both temporal successions of sounds that take time to say or play, but words, unlike notes, have denotative meanings. Consequently in most verbal statements there is little or no relation between the temporal expression of the words and the thought which they express. When we speak, that is to say, we are usually stopping to think, but music is always going on to 'become'[33].

Among the kinds of literature it is drama which comes closest to meeting the demands for an art of pure becoming in which every moment is felt in its immediacy while at the same time there is a contiguous sweeping movement, each choice leading to an action and each action compelling those involved in, or affected by, it to choose anew. In other words, drama is the only form of literature based on the premise that what really counts is the individual will and its assertion in thought (choice) or deed (action); the only disadvantage being that, as a verbal art, it is still ethically determined. The ethical, however, lacks immediacy; it is "sentimental" while the esthetic is "naïve".

Drama, in Auden's view, is based on the Mistake (i. e., the wrong choice unwittingly made) or on the deliberate choice of good or evil. Both choices entail some degree of responsibility on the part of their agents. That *hubris* (the tragic outgrowth of responsibility) is essential to drama is shown in Auden's essay "Cav and Pag" through an analy-

---

33 *Times Literary Supplement*, November 2, 1967, 1037.

sis of Naturalistic drama, in which suffering replaces choice, insofar as the blame is placed on the circumstances rather than the individual. While a playwright who believes "that the most interesting and significant characteristic of man is his power to choose between right and wrong, his responsibility for his actions" will select "situations in which the temptation to choose wrong is at the greatest and the actual consequences incurred by the choice are most serious", the writer "committed to a naturalist doctrine" is driven "to find a substitute for the tragic situation in the pathetic [...] and a substitute for the morally responsible hero in the pathological case"[34].

The final and irrevocable parting of ways occurs precisely at the point of transition from drama to opera – or, more generally but also more vaguely speaking, from literature to music; for the ethical is chained to the primary world by means of realism and psychology, whereas the esthetic belongs, ideally, to the domain of pure spirit which constitutes a world of artifice where ethical categories are no longer applicable. As a mimetic art, drama is more natural than opera (and the ballet) in many ways – and quite pragmatically so; for while "in any village twenty people could get together and give a performance of *Hamlet* which, however imperfect, would convey enough of the play's greatness to be worth attending", if the same people attempted "a similar performance of *Don Giovanni*, they would soon discover that there was no question of a good or a bad performance because they could not sing the notes at all"[35]. In other words, both opera and ballet are virtuoso arts since "without an exceptional physical endowment, vocal chords or a body, granted to very few human beings, no amount of intelligence, taste and training can make a great singer or dancer"[36].

---

34 *DH*, 476, 477. Auden objects to *La Bohème* precisely because Mimi is too passive a character.
35 *Partisan Review*, XIX (1952), 12.
36 "A Public Art". *Opera*, XII (1961), 14.

Expounding Kierkegaard – as early as 1944 – Auden surveyed the dialectic triangular relationship between Art, Morality, and Religion and concluded:

> In treating [...] theft as an individual act of will which cannot be judged in abstraction from the concrete temporal situation in which it occurs, the Religious sides with the Esthetic against the Ethical in upholding the unique importance of the individual will. But in asserting that the good act – not stealing – is always and only the product of good will, and the bad act – stealing – always the product of an evil will, it sides with the Ethical against the Esthetic belief that to will is valuable in itself. Lastly, it disagrees with both in blessing an act neither for its manifestly interesting appearance nor for its demonstrably good result, but for its hidden subjective intention.
>
> To the Esthetic, as the Ethical, any suffering involved in an act is accidental and without significance in itself, but to the Religious it is precisely in the suffering that the significance lies[37].

With Auden, as with Kierkegaard, the greatness and perfection of a work of art depends entirely on the extent to which it succeeds in attracting the spirit of sensuous genius and repelling the moral elements from its territory. In the case of Mozart, for example, *Don Giovanni* succeeds where *Die Zauberflöte* fails, mainly because of the "ethical" nature of its subject. While the esthetic, according to the body of opinions under discussion, insists on choice without tolerating any change in the character engaged in choosing, the ethical presupposes a change in consequence of the individual's choice. It is precisely this which makes an ethically determined story *interesting*:

> It is rare for the story of a successful opera to be interesting in itself. Even Don Juan, a character of profound extramusical significance, cannot be said to have a story since, by definition, he cannot or will not change himself; he can only be shown as triumphant and invulnerable (the Duke in *Rigoletto*), or in his fall (*Don Giovanni*) [...] The characters in *Die Zauberflöte,* on the other hand, have a real history in which what happens next always depends upon what they choose now[38].

This view is foreshadowed by the Danish philosopher who, while introducing Papageno as a prototype of the second stage of the musical-erotic, severely criticizes Mozart's German opera:

---

37 *The New Republic*, May 15, 1944, 684.
38 *The Magic Flute*, viii. Compare Auden's remarks on *Tristan*, *Don Giovanni*, and *Falstaff* in his essay, "The Prince's Dog". *DH*, 183f.

> It might not be without interest to run through the whole opera in order to show that its subject matter, considered as operatic material, profoundly fails of its purpose. Nor would we lack occasion to illuminate the erotic from a new side, as we noticed how the endeavor to invest it with a deeper ethical view [...] is an adventure which has ventured quite beyond the range of music, so that it was impossible for even a Mozart to lend it any deeper interest. This opera definitely tends toward the unmusical, and therefore it is, in spite of individually perfect concert numbers and deeply moving, pathetic utterances, by no means a classic opera[39].

Opera, then, must be ethically indifferent so that, in effect, every choice made by an operatic character is automatically a good – or, at any rate, the right – one. Moreover, since it is inevitably the wilful assertion of an emotion – supplying, as it does, an "illusion of absolute certainty out of the individual passions of [a character's] immediate moods"[40] – it is, by its very nature, pleasurable as well. Following Aristotle's precept to the effect that "objects which in themselves we view with pain, we delight to contemplate when reproduced with fidelity"[41], Auden validates the paradox by asserting "that emotions and situations which in real life would be sad or painful are on the stage a source of pleasure"[42]. In the operatic medium, he surmises, anomaly is heightened (an innocent bystander might say: to the point of absurdity), for

> the singer may be playing the role of a deserted bride who is about to kill herself, but we feel quite certain as we listen that not only we but also she is having a wonderful time. In a sense, there can be no tragic opera because whatever errors the characters make and whatever they suffer, they are doing exactly what they wish[43].

Conversely, "feelings of joy, tenderness and nobility are not confined to 'noble' characters but are experienced by everybody, by the most conventional, most stupid, most depraved"[44]. In Auden's opinion (which Mozart would certainly have shared), Alban Berg's *Wozzeck* is

---

39 *Either/Or*, I, 77f.
40 *The New Republic*, May 15, 1944, 683.
41 *Poetics*, chapter IV.
42 *Partisan Review*, XIX (1952), 13.
43 Ibid.
44 Ibid., 14.

a failure because "in any satisfactory opera the voices must make as beautiful noises as the orchestra"[45].

Choice, in the melo-dramatic world of Auden's making, is essentially "out of character", since the emotions projected are universal rather than being tied to any particular time, place, person, or situation. The proof of the pudding, he contends, lies in listening "to a recording of an opera sung in a language that one does not know"; for in spite of this barrier of communication "one can generally tell what is the particular emotional state – love, rage, grief, joy or so forth – which the singer is expressing at a given time, but one cannot tell whether the singer is a duchess, a chambermaid, a prince or a policeman", as "all social distinctions and all differences in age are abolished by song. In the case of some operas like *Rosenkavalier* and *Arabella* one cannot even tell the sex."[46] This observation calls to mind a passage in Stendhal's book on Rossini, where we are told that, at Vicenza, "on the first night, it was customary to skim through [the libretto] just sufficiently to gain some notion of the plot, glancing, as each new episode opened, at the first line, just so as to appreciate the emotion or the shade of emotion which the music was supposed to suggest"[47].

At least insofar as the text of arias, duets, and ensembles is concerned, Auden prefers to regard the libretto as a "private letter to the composer". In his eyes, "the verses which the librettist writes are not addressed to the public [...] They have their moment of glory, the moment in which they suggest to him a certain melody; once that is over, they are as expendable as infantry to a Chinese general; they must efface themselves and cease to care what happens to them."[48] This is a condition which, as Auden rather sadly remarks, Hofmanns-

---

45 "A Public Art". *Opera*, XII (1961), 14.
46 *Times Literary Supplement*, November 2, 1967, 1037.
47 Quoted in *The Essence of Opera*, ed. U. Weisstein (New York, 1964), 195.
48 *Partisan Review*, XIX (1952), 13.

thal's *Rosenkavalier* does not meet.[49] The translator of a libretto, accordingly, is free to alter the text of the vocal pieces as he sees fit, as long as the general mood is retained, no counter-sense produced, and the syllabic values are preserved. A literal translation is needed only in the recitatives – *secco* and *accompagnato* – and the prose dialogue, whose function it is to propel the action after it has been suspended in the closed numbers.

The process of musical 'depersonalization' just referred to also affects the personal interrelationships of the characters; one might go so far as to say, with Auden, that it renders communication as a social phenomenon impossible: "In verbal speech, I can say: 'I love you.' Music can, I believe, express the equivalent of 'I love' but it is incapable of saying who or what I love – you, God, or the decimal system. Music, one might say, is always intransitive, and in the first person."[50] Hence Auden's aversion to contemporary subjects like Menotti's *The Consul*, where the situation is "too actual, that is, too clearly a situation some people are in and others, including the audience, are not in, for the latter to forget this and see it as a symbol of, say, man's existential estrangement"[51].

The most pronounced assertion of wilful feelings (in opera as in real life) is the gratuitous act of the kind envisaged by Gide's Lafcadio. In the present context we are not so much concerned with the existential nature of this act – which Auden adumbrates in his essay "Squares and Oblongs" as well as in the introduction to his Kierkegaard anthology[52] – as with their role within the esthetic universe of opera. That the "free act" has always been what amounts to an obsession in Auden's work could be demonstrated in a number of ways. One need only think of the opening line of Prospero's address to Ariel

---

49 Ibid., 17. The passage is deleted in *DH*.
50 *Times Literary Supplement*, November 2, 1967, 1037.
51 *Partisan Review*, XIX (1952), 13.
52 *The Living Thoughts of Kierkegaard*, presented by W. H. Auden (New York, 1952), esp. 6-8.

in *The Sea and the Mirror*, the poet's "Commentary on Shakespeare's *The Tempest*". More relevant to our discussion is Auden's dramaturgical use of the concept in *The Rake's Progress*, where Nick Shadow, the Mephistophelian tempter, persuades the hero to marry Baba the Turk by arguing:

> Why? Because they are not free. Why? Because the giddy multitude are driven by the unpredictable Must of their pleasures and the sober few are bound by the inflexible Ought of their duty, between which slaveries there is nothing to choose. Would you be happy? Then learn to act freely. Would you act freely? Then learn to ignore those twin tyrants of appetite and conscience[53].

For Auden the gratuitous act, being unattached to ethics, religion, psychology, and the world of social taboos and biological urges, is the very epitome of esthetic behavior. Its archenemy is verisimilitude in its various guises: the sensible, the credible, the plausible, and the probable. The precise semantic implications of these terms have been the subject of an exchange of views between Auden and his fellow librettist Ronald Duncan[54]. However, even Auden's latest pronouncement on this topic reaffirms his conviction "that a good opera plot is one that provides as many and as varied situations in which it seems plausible that the characters should sing. This means that no opera plot can be sensible; for in sensible situations people do not sing. An opera plot must be, in both senses of the word, a melodrama."[55]

In terms of the context of operatic history, to which we now turn our attention in concluding, Auden's theory of opera finds its paragons exclusively in the Golden Age of opera which, in his opinion, extends from Gluck's *Orfeo ed Euridice* (1762) to Verdi's *Otello* (1887), with a center of gravity constituted by the works of Bellini and Donizetti. Puccini and Strauss foreshadow the decline of the High or Golden Style, which is complete in modern opera. On the whole, modern composers are suspect to Auden since they tend to write "a

---

53 *The Rake's Progress* (New York, 1951), 22.

54 "An Answer to Auden," *Opera*, II (1950), 630-632, and "Auden Replies," ibid., III (1952), 34-36.

55 *Times Literary Supplement*, November 2, 1967, 1038.

static kind of music in which there is no marked difference between its beginning, its middle and its end, a music which sounds remarkably like primitive proto-music"[56].

The views on opera we have traced here clash head-on with the neoclassical theory illustrated by Gluck's famous dictum: "[In *Alceste*] I sought to restrict music to its true function, namely to serve the poetry by means of the expression – and the situations which make up the plot – without interrupting the action or diminishing its interest by useless and superfluous ornament."[57] Auden comes much closer to agreeing with Mozart that "in an opera the poetry must be altogether the obedient daughter of the music"[58]. However, one suspects that he feels somewhat uneasy about Mozart's dramaturgical skill and finds greater satisfaction in the pure *bel canto* of *Norma* and *Lucia di Lammermoor*.[59] Chronological considerations apart, it is, therefore, fully appropriate that he teamed up with Stravinsky at a time when the latter wished to indulge in musical eclecticism, rather than during a phase of experimentation with Epic Opera (*Histoire du Soldat*) or ascetic neoclassicism (*Oedipus Rex*).

As for Wagner, Auden (much as he likes *Tristan* and *Die Walküre*) would hardly subscribe to the master's carefully elaborated theory of the total *Gesamtkunstwerk* in which the orchestra functions as an "agent which constantly completes the unity of expression and which, wherever the vocal expression of the dramatic characters lowers itself in order to define the dramatic situation more clearly [...] balances the

---

56 *DH*, 474. This passage is not found in the earlier versions of the "Reflections."

57 From Gluck's letter of dedication to Grand-Duke Leopold of Tuscany, as quoted in *The Essence of Opera*, 106.

58 Mozart, speaking about *Die Entführung aus dem Serail*, in a letter to his father dated October 13, 1781.

59 See Auden's list, "My Favorite Records", in *Saturday Review of Literature*, November 27, 1958, 48, where the only complete opera recordings referred to are *Lucia di Lammermoor, Don Pasquale, Così fan tutte*, and *Un Ballo in Maschera*. This is not necessarily a list of Auden's favorite operas, however.

abated expression of the dramatic characters"[60]. Both share a strong aversion to instrumental music, since – in Wagner's words – "the work of the composer of absolute music must be regarded as one altogether lacking in poetic intent; for although feelings may well be aroused by purely musical means, they cannot by such means be fixed as to their actual nature"[61]. Kierkegaard, too, questioned the alleged esthetic superiority of music over language by calling the common view that music is a more perfect medium "one of those sentimental misunderstandings which originate only in empty heads". He was out of sympathy "with that sublime music which believes that it can dispense with words"[62].

Auden would seem to be even less tolerant than Kierkegaard, who regarded the overture to *Don Giovanni* as a masterpiece rising high above the usual "labyrinthine hodgepodge of associated ideas"[63]. As he puts it in his "Reflections on Music and Opera",

> [i]n opera, the orchestra is addressed to the singers, not to the audience. An opera-lover will put up with and even enjoy an orchestral interlude on condition that he knows the singers cannot sing just now because they are tired or the scene-shifters are at work, but any use of the orchestra by itself which is not filling in time is, for him, wasting it. Leonora III is a fine piece to listen to in the concert hall, but in the opera house, where it is played between scenes one and two of the second act of *Fidelio* it becomes twelve minutes of acute boredom[64].

Exactly twenty years ago Auden publicly stated that, as a rule, the opera addict will be a conservative "who does not welcome new opera" because he has staged a "daydream repertoire of seldom performed operas by, say, Bellini or Rossini or Weber or Meyerbeer or Gounod or the young Verdi, which he longs to hear and fears he never will"[65]. Even for the author of *The Age of Anxiety*, opera (and art in general) was, and is, a "*fait accompli*" which "presents/ Already

---

60 From *Opera and Drama* (1851) as quoted in *The Essence of Opera*, 217.
61 Ibid., 216.
62 *Either/Or*, I, 68.
63 Ibid., 126.
64 *Partisan Review*, XIX (1952), 16.
65 *Vogue*, July 1948, 65.

lived experience/ Through a convention that creates/ Autonomous completed states", and an "abstract model of events/ Derived from dead experiments"[66]. For us who like the living experiments conducted on the lyrical stage in our day, such a view seems overly cautious if not downright reactionary.

---

[66] "New Year Letter" (1940), *The Collected Poetry of W. H. Auden* (New York, 1945), 267.

"Per porle in lista"
Da Ponte/Leporello's Amorous Inventory and its Literary and Operatic Antecedents from Tirso de Molina to Giovanni Bertati (1981)

In his *Memorie,* written when the author, then Professor of Italian at Columbia College in New York, was in his seventies, Lorenzo Da Ponte, one-time poet-in-residence of the Imperial Theatres in Vienna, relates an episode that must have taken place around 1792, i. e., approximately a lustrum after the world premiere of *Don Giovanni* in Prague (October 29, 1787) and roughly four years after that opera's first performance in the Austrian capital (May 7, 1788). His account, patently biased, must be read with several grains of salt and a pinch of pepper:

> Il nuovo poeta del teatro [Giovanni Bertati] era sovra tutti ansiosissimo di sapere s'io intendea partir da Vienna o rifermarmivi. Io conosceva le sue opere, ma non lui. Egli n'aveva scritto un numero infinite, e, a forza di scriverne, aveva imparato un poco l'arte di produr l'effetto teatrale. Ma, per sua disgrazia, non era nato poeta e non sapeva l'italiano. Per conseguenza l'opere sue si potevano piuttosto soffrir sulla scena che leggerle. Mi saltò il capriccio in testa di conoscerlo. Andai da lui baldanzosamente. [...] Mi domandò il mio nome, gli dissi ch'io aveva avuto l'onore d'essere stato il suo antecessore e che il mio nome era Da Ponte. Parve colpito da un fulmine. Mi domandò in un'aria molto imbarazzata e confusa in che cosa potea servirmi, ma sempre fermandosi sulla porta. Quando gli dissi ch'avea qualchecosa da comunicargli, trovossi obbligato di farmi entrar nella stanza, il che fece però con qualche renitenza. Mi offrì una sedia nel mezzo della camera: io m'assisi senza alcuna malizia, presso alla tavola, dove giudicai dall'apparenze ch'ei fosse solito a scrivere. Vedendo me assiso, s'assise anch'egli sul seggiolone e si mise destramente a chiudere una quantità di scartafacci e di libri, che ingombravano quella tavola. Ebbi tuttavia l'agio di vedere in gran parte che libri erano. Un tomo di commedie francesi, un dizionario, un rimario e la grammatica del Corticelli stavano tutti alla destra del signer poeta; quelli che aveva alla sinistra, non ho potuto vedere che cosa fossero. Credei allora d'intendere la ragione per cui gli dispiaceva di lasciarmi entrare[1].

---

1 Lorenzo Da Ponte, *Memorie, libretti mozartiani,* Milan (Garzanti) 1976, p. 163f.

Written three decades after the fact, this scathing indictment, culminating in the charge of verbal incompetence and poetic failure, mirrors, not unexpectedly, an attitude characterized by professional rivalry and envy. The report also strikes one as an act of bad faith, an implicit attempt to hide a bitter truth from posterity: for, sadly to say, the libretto of Mozart's next-to-the-last Italian opera is not original in conception and plot but has its very tangible model in a text authored by the object of Da Ponte's scorn in the passage cited above. More precisely, Bertati had recently collaborated with the composer Giuseppe Gazzaniga in the creation of a work for the musical stage entitled *Don Giovanni o sia Il Convitato di pietra.* That piece was successfully mounted during the Carnival season (on February 5, 1787, to be precise) at the Teatro Giustiniani di S. Moisé in Venice – only eight-and-one-half months, that is to say, before the *maestro di capella* Wolfgang Amadeus Mozart raised his baton to conduct the overture of his new work at the National- und Ständetheater of the Bohemian metropolis.

What a coincidence; or, surely, more than a coincidence! For Don Juan operas were the rage just then, at least in northern Italy, where more than half a dozen, some concurrently, ran in the decade from 1777 to 1787[2]. (Mozart's masterpiece, climaxing this trend so fashionable in the waning years of the Enlightenment, which produced a Cagliostro and Casanova as well as the *Encyclopédie*, demonstrated its melo-dramat(urg)ic superiority over its predecessors by putting a stop to all further attempts to exploit the theme operatically.) And while there is no reason to think that the collaborative effort of Bertati and Gazzaniga was then, or ever, staged in Vienna, the facts, speaking for themselves, demonstrate that Da Ponte was intimately acquainted with

---

2 For an account and an analysis of these works see Stefan Kunze, *Don Giovanni vor Mozart: Die Tradition der Don Giovanni-Opern im italienischen Buffa-Theater des 18. Jahrhunderts*, Munich (Fink) 1972.

the libretto, as Mozart seems to have been familiar with the music of their joint product[3].

As a seasoned *Dramaturg*, fresh from the triumph of *Le nozze di Figaro*, the Abbate, looking for a subject capable of providing a full evening's entertainment, must have been dissatisfied with what he saw: the text of a one-act *opera buffa* which, in performance, was usually preceded by a curtain raiser, the same team's *Capriccio drammatico*[4], in which, both literally and metaphorically, the stage was set for the principal fare of the night at the opera[5]. Da Ponte, shrewdly realizing the potential of the piece, ingeniously solved the problem. By splitting Bertati's action in half (Scenes 1 to 18 and 19 to 25 respectively), he had the beginning (Act I, Scenes 1 to 10) and end (Act II, Scenes 12 to 18) of his *dramma per musica* cut out for himself[6]. All he needed to do, borrowing freely from Molière's *Dom Juan ou Le Festin de Pierre* and other sources[7], and adding plot material of his own, was to furnish the middle section constituted by Act I, Scenes 11 to 21, and Act II, Scenes 1 to 11, of the opera *Don Giovanni* as we know it. This 'labor of love' he accomplished – if we are to trust the

---

[3] The text of the libretto of that one-act opera was first published by Friedrich Chrysander in the *Vierteljahrsschrift für Musikwissenschaft* 4 (1888), pp. 369-404. It is reprinted in Kunze, pp. 159-187.

[4] The full text of the capriccio is found in Kunze, pp. 140-158. Chrysander offers only an abridged version.

[5] In operatic history, the genre is represented by works like Mozart's *Der Schauspieldirektor*, Salieri's *Prima la musica e poi le parole* and, last but not least, Richard Strauss' *Capriccio*.

[6] Throughout the essay, Da Ponte's text is quoted from the *Memorie, libretti mozartiani*, where *Don Giovanni* appears on pp. 511-595.

[7] As the impresario Policastro puts it in Scene 11 of the *Capriccio drammatico* (Kunze, p. 155):

Ma la nostra Commedia
Ridotta com'ell è fra la Spagnuola
Di Tirso de Molina,
Tra quella di Molière,
E quella delli nostri Commedianti,
Qualunque sia, non fu veduta avanti.

memoirs, where his crib is at no point mentioned – in the space of sixty-three days, in which he also claims to have written the entire text for Padre Vincenzo Martini's *Arbore di Diana* and part of the libretto for Salieri's *Tarare*[8]. Outwardly adhering to the conventional structure of the *opera buffa* (two acts with one intermission) but aiming – one suspects, at Mozart's urging – at the more stately pattern of *opera seria*[9], he laid the foundation for *Il dissoluto punito ossia il Don Giovanni*, a *dramma giocoso* partaking of two conflicting traditions and forcing the unfortunate stage director to mount a four-act opera in two acts[10].

---

8   Da Ponte's account, as found in *Memorie...*, p. 125f., offers the following information (here condensed):

> Me ne presentarono l'occasione i tre prelodati maestri, Martini, Mozzart e Salieri, che vennero tutti tre in una volta a chiedermi un dramma. [...] Pensai se non fosse possibile di contentarli tutti tre e di far tre opere a un tratto. Salieri non mi domandava un dramma originale. Aveva scritto a Parigi la musica all'opera del *Tarar*, volea ridurla al carattere di dramma e musica italiana, e me ne domandava quindi una libera traduzione. Mozzart e Salieri lasciavano a me interamente la scelta. Scelsi per lui il *Don Giovanni*, soggetto che infinitamente gli piacque, e *L'arbore di Diana* pel Martini. [...] Io seguitai a studiar dodici ore ogni giorno, con brevi intermissioni, per due mesi continui. [...] La prima giornata [...] ho scritte le due prime scene del *Don Giovanni*, altre due dell'*Arbore di Diana* e più di metà del primo atto del *Tarar* [...] e in sessantatré giorni le due prime opere erano finite del tutto, e quasi due terzi dell'ultima.

9   In her biography of Da Ponte – *The Libertine Librettist*, New York (Abelard–Schuman) 1957, p. 142 –, April Fitzlyon quotes an American acquaintance of Da Ponte as having been told:

> Mozart determined to cast the opera exclusively as serious and had well advanced in his work. Daponte assured me that he remonstrated and urged the expediency on the great composer of the introduction of the *vis comica*, in order to accomplish a greater success, and I prepared the role with *Batti, batti: La ci darem ...* etc.

Although the account may well be apocryphal, it underlines a tendency corroborated by the fact that for the Viennese production of the opera Da Ponte supplied (on his own?) a number of additional scenes comical in nature and enhancing the scope of the Leporello/Zerlina/Masetto subplot. See Christoph Bitter's essay "*Don Giovanni* in Wien 1788" in the *Mozart-Jahrbuch 1959*, Salzburg, 1960, pp. 146-164. The scenes in question, which dropped out very quickly and are not included in the standard editions of the work, are found in the Reclam text (Universal-Bibliothek, # 2646) edited by Wilhelm Zentner.

10 For a treatment of this problem, see especially Emilio Carapezza's book *Figaro e Don Giovanni: Due folli giornate*, Palermo (Flaccovio) 1974, p. 82.

In the present essay, I am not so much interested in Da Ponte, the dramaturgist, as in Da Ponte, the poet and verbal artificer. In this, the linguistic, realm, too, Mozart's librettist owes a debt of gratitude to Bertati, whose text provides, in many instances, the basis on which his emulator's verbal structures rest. However, given the fact that Bertati's handling of language is often crude and lacks elegance, Da Ponte's assessment ("He was not a born poet and did not know Italian") seems fully justified. Indeed, Da Ponte's stylistic superiority is such that a major publishing house – Garzanti in Milan – felt the need for including his *Memorie e libretti mozartiani* (but only those!) in a series of *grandi libri* not only of Italian vintage (Ariosto, Goldoni, Leopardi) but of world literature (Shakespeare, Goethe, Balzac) as well. Thus, like Metastasio, the unchallenged *librettista laureatus* of Italy, Da Ponte may be regarded as a minor classic in T. S. Eliot's sense – a label hardly applicable to, say, Apostolo Zeno or Verdi's Antonio Ghislanzoni.

It would be both illuminating and instructive to show – as I have tried to do in another paper[11] – how deftly Da Ponte handled his mother tongue, not only in the way of phrasing or word choice, but also in the manner in which he wove verbal patterns that are almost entirely lost in most translations. But the task which I have set myself for the present occasion is, at once, more limited and more encompassing; for I intend to show, with reference to a small but significant and characteristic sample, that both Bertati and Da Ponte are links in a chain that originates, like so many features of Don Juan lore, with Tirso de Molina. The snippet I have chosen to focus on is the catalogue exemplified, at its very best, by Leporello's two-part aria (#4 in the score of Mozart's opera) beginning with the lines

Madamina!/ Il catalogo è questo
Delle belle che amò il padron mio.

---

11 "So machen's eben nicht alle: Da Ponte/Mozarts *Don Giovanni* und die vergleichende Erotik", in: *Festschrift für Elisabeth Frenzel zum 65. Geburtstag*, Stuttgart (Kröner) 1980, I, pp. 81-94.

While the piece itself, a staple of Don Juan plays and operas, has been scrutinized before, mostly from a musicological standpoint[12], the tradition of which it forms part has not, to my knowledge, been traced in any detail. It clearly warrants an investigation from the comparative angle.

Before embarking on that enterprise – a Cook's tour, as it were, of catalogue speeches and arias in various literatures –, I would like to reflect a) on the plot function of such a list, b) the place assigned to it in the sequence of events/adventures which make up the story of the seducer, c) the person asked to redact, and charged with delivering, it, and d) the audience to be addressed. The reasons for offering a statistical chart in a work dealing with Don Juan are simple and persuasive: the noble seducer, incarnation of male prowess and endowed with an almost Herculean sexual *Potenz*, is, after all, a quasi-mythical or legendary figure whose exploits exceed the narrow bounds of verisimilitude. A quality rather than a person (to use Kierkegaardian terminology), he can do the impossible. But insofar as the drama, for which type of literature the theme has a decided *Gattungsaffinität*, operates in the realm of the actual rather than in that of the possible, the need for limiting the scope of the action by presenting a concrete, though still approximate, number of victims arises. From the human – all too human – perspective, such a figure will still seem hyperbolic, if not fabulous, whereas from the mythical perspective it will seem unnecessarily restrictive and, hence, disenchanting. Whatever the case, it is a compromise – a strictly narrative, or epic, device mediating between the levels of myth and plot.

On the level of plot, a further reduction in the number of characters is, obviously, required to achieve manageable proportions and pre-

---

12 By far the most elaborate treatment was given by Rolf Dammann in his article "Die Register-Arie in Mozarts *Don Giovanni*", *Archiv fur Musikforschung* 23 (1976), pp. 278-308, and 24 (1977), pp. 56-77. Pp. 278-294 are devoted to the text, the rest to its musical setting. Dammann does not proceed historically, nor does he specifically compare Bertati's catalogue aria with Da Ponte's.

serve the clarity of structure. This presents a serious problem, insofar as the fewer women the playwright-librettist introduces, the more representative they must be. Nor must one overlook a weighty pragmatic factor, namely the limited size of the operatic companies, stationary or ambulatory, that were active in the latter part of the eighteenth century. Thus the troupe which performed Bertati/Gazzaniga's piece consisted of eight singers charged, in this particular case, with embodying a total of ten roles. This necessitated the doubling up of one male (Biagio/Commendatore) and one female (Donna Ximena/ Maturina) member and mandated a juggling of the plot, as these pairs of characters could not jointly appear in any given scene.

The whole question enters meaningfully, and amusingly, into the dialogue of the *Capriccio drammatico*, where the realization of the Impresario's plan to stage a Don Juan opera in the cultural hinterland of Germany is pinned to his own willingness to take on the role of the servant Pasquariello assigned to a *buffo caricato* not otherwise present in the company[13]. In Prague, the Bondini troupe which premiered *Don Giovanni* in the fall of 1787 was even smaller than the one operating out of the Teatro Giustiniani di S. Moisé, consisting, as it did, of no more than seven singers. Having cut the number of *dramatis personae* from ten to eight by eliminating the part of the second servant (Lanterna) and distributing that of Donna Ximena among Donna Elvira (primarily) and Zerlina (secondarily), Da Ponte thus still saw

---

13 The matter is taken up in Scene 2 of the *Capriccio* (Kunze, p. 144):

Valerio: *Quel che dite sarà; ma il Convitato,*
 O Signor Impresario,
 Certo non sì può far.
Polic.: *Per qual ragione?*
Valerio: *Perchè adesso ci manca*
 Un Buffo Caricato. E qual ripiego
 C'è a questo Signor mio?
Polic.: *Da Buffo Caricato farò io.*

The impresario promptly demonstrates his talents as a *buffo caricato* by singing an aria beginning with the lines
 In Teatro siamo adesso,
 Pronta sta la compagnia.

himself faced with the need for assigning two basso roles (Masetto and the Commendatore) to one artist, Giuseppe Lolli.

On the whole, the reduction of Bertati's quartet of women (Anna, Elvira, Ximena, Maturina) to a tercet (Anna, Elvira, Zerlina) was a clever stroke since Elvira and Ximena were poorly differentiated, to begin with. Concurrently, Da Ponte (at Mozart's request?) enhanced the significance of Donna Anna. In the model, that luckless lady had vanished for good at the end of the third scene, in order to hide in a cloister until her father's assassin was identified and the assassination revenged:

> *Finchè il reo non si scopre, e finchè il padre*
> *Vendicato non resta, in un Ritiro*
> *Voglio passar i giorni;*
> *Nè alcun mai vi sarà, che me n'distorni.*
> (Kunze, p. 163)

In Mozart's opera, she is with us to the end, a dramatically static but musically dynamic figure bent on keeping the milksop Ottavio – another dramatic non-entity – on the *qui vive*[14].

The tripartite scheme which Da Ponte has adopted *ad usum Delphini* is most ingenious and, in the terms which I have just laid down, eminently appropriate: for both the social standing of the three women who cross the seducer's path and their current status in relation to Giovanni are taken into account and ably correlated. To begin with Donna Anna who, being of noble birth, is a perfect match for the impetuous wooer: having the strength of character lacking in Elvira, she resists his rather brutal advances – one is tempted to say: manfully – and subsequently becomes the backbone of the counter-movement fighting for the restoration of order and morality. Judging by her treatment of Ottavio, whom she loves rather primly and, it would seem, impassionately, she appears to lack sensuality, not to speak of erotic fervor. Yet, could not her seeming detachment be a mask, the *persona*

---

14 In their analyses of the opera, Hermann Abert and several other critics have underscored this fact and, by implication, suggested that it was Mozart who gave them their present melo-dramatic stature.

on public display that hides the true, seething Self underneath? Such, certainly, was the view taken by E. T. A. Hoffmann, who maintained that she was hopelessly enthralled with Don Juan and succumbed to him, much against her conscious will, at the critical moment of their nocturnal encounter:

> Wie, wenn Donna Anna vom Himmel dazu bestimmt gewesen wäre, den Don Juan in der Liebe [...] die ihm innewohnende göttliche Natur erkennen zu lassen und ihn der Verzweiflung seines nichtigen Strebens zu entreissen? – Zu spät, zur Zeit des höchsten Frevels, sah er sie, und da konnte ihn nur die teuflische Lust erfüllen, sie zu verderben. – Nicht gerettet wurde sie. Als er hinausfloh, war die Tat geschehen. Das Feuer einer übermenschlichen Sinnlichkeit, Glut aus der Hölle, durchströmte ihr Inneres und machte jeden Widerstand vergeblich.[15]

This depth-psychological approach which, forming the basis of a different character portrait, could pose a real challenge for the *Regisseur*, finds verbal justification in the ambiguity of the language she uses in her account of the traumatic event:

> *Alfino il duol, l'orrore*
> *dell'infame attentato*
> *accrebbe sì la lena mia, che, a forza*
> *di svincolarmi, torcermi, e piegarmi*
> *da lui mi sciolsi.* (P. 537)

The last of the three verbs aligned in the infinitive is double-edged: used transitively, *piegar* means to bend, twist or, militarily, retreat: but used reflexively it means to yield or give way.

By comparison, Elvira's position is more clearly defined and her character less ambiguous. A representative of what might be called the upper middle class, she has fallen in love with, and yielded to, Don Giovanni, who has played his usual trick by vowing to marry her. (In doing so, he has committed blasphemy by mocking what Molière's Sganarelle calls a "mystère sacré"[16].) Although she has been jilted – Don Giovanni having left her behind in Burgos after spending three days in her company –, she is more than willing to forgive and forget:

---

15 "Don Juan" in *Fantasie- und Nachtstücke*, ed. Walter Müller-Seidel, Munich (Winkler) 1960, p. 77.

16 *Dom Juan* I, 2, in *Œuvres complètes*, ed. Maurice Rat, Paris (NRF Bibliothèque de la Pléïade), I (1959), p. 780.

and, being jilted once again, the *abbandonata* does her level best to make him repent, wrestling to the very end with his immortal soul while cursing his mortal flesh. In doing so, she attests, more poignantly than words can do, to his lasting appeal and to the undiminished fascination which he exerts. At the center of the feminine trio, she is the hero's true antagonist, locked in a fierce struggle that reflects their mutual attraction in love and hatred.

Zerlina, who complements the two ladies, represents still another social class, the peasantry – corresponding to the shepherdesses and fisher girls in Tirso's *Burlador de Sevilla* and their numerous descendents. She is the only true 'exhibit' in Da Ponte's libretto: for Don Giovanni is shown in the very act of seducing her. Cocksure of his success, he flaunts not only his manhood but also his social superiority, in order to bowl her over. And she, in her coquettish naiveté, escapes by the skin of her teeth, awakened to her own sensuality and thus emotionally transcending the level of her clodhopper fiancé.

In Da Ponte/Mozart's *dramma giocoso*, Anna, Elvira and Zerlina are flanked by three shadowy figures whose names do not appear among the *dramatis personae*: the *bella dama* of Act I, Scene 4 (p. 518), a relic of Bertati's Ximena, whom Don Giovanni literally smells out (*mi pare sentir odor di femmina*) and of whose imminent surrender he is, as usual, convinced: Elvira's maid, of whom in Act II, Scene 1 (p. 558) he says ecstatically:

Non (ho) veduto
Qualche cosa di bello

and whom, dressed in Leporello's cloak, he serenades; and the *fanciulla/Bella, giovin, galante* (Act II, Scene 12; p. 577) whom he meets at night on the way to the cemetery and who mistakes him, still disguised, for Leporello, her sweetheart or, who knows, her husband. While doubling the 'score', these women – all potential victims – do not significantly broaden the spectrum of representative female characters in the opera. The *bella dama* adds little variety since she seems to conform, more or less, to Elvira as a prototype, whereas the *cameri-*

era and the *fanciulla*, city cousins of Zerlina, reflect the comic rivalry which, on account of Don Giovanni's fishing in his servant's pond, exists between him and Leporello. The full documentation and corroboration of the hero's omni-potence, then, is left to the *index nominum* and/or *rerum* which forms the principal object of this study.

As for the placing of the list within the dramaturgical framework, it should be strategic – more so with regard to the audience in the pit and the gallery than in view of the characters on stage to which the catalogue is addressed. Psychologically, its effect will be enhanced, and the *Erwartungshorizont* more clearly defined, if it is introduced at an early point since, in this manner, it will inform the spectator/listener, from the outset, *welch Geistes Kind* the hero is. (For cogent reasons, the catalogue records no failures such as the Don, whose luck is about to run out, is suffering before our very eyes.) Its most suitable author is Leporello, the servant who doubles as bard and bookkeeper since his master, like all those active in the seduction trade, has no time or inclination to keep score[17]. The factotum greatly enjoys the counting, though not the reporting, which invariably exposes him to the wrath of the irate women from whom he is supposed to shield his master.

Regarding the person at whom the recital should be aimed, tradition – which carries its own weight – will have it that it should be a woman 'after the fall'. Read at the master's behest, or for the servant's pleasure, it offers proof that Don Giovanni will have his way with women and that, having had it, he cannot be counted on to assume responsibilities of any kind. Repetition – the lethal enemy of *élan vital* – is not his style. Thus the shorthand account offers some sort of consolation and 'reassures' the betrayed woman that she is in good, though hardly exclusive, company. It cannot well be used as an

---

17 "Fast möchte man Leporello bedauern, der nicht nur, wie er selber sagt, vor der Tür Wache halten muß, sondern außerdem noch eine so weitläufige Buchführung zu erledigen hat, daß es einem routinierten Expeditionssekretär genug zu schaffen machen würde." Søren Kierkegaard, *Entweder/Oder*, tr. H. Diem and W. Rest, Cologne/Olten (Hegner) 1960, p. 113.

incentive; for, true to his nature, Don Giovanni tells every woman with aplomb that she is, and will remain, the only one, and proves his point by offering to marry her on the spot, without any further pomp and circumstance. In this, but only in this sense, he is indeed what Pasquariello cynically calls him: *il marito universale*.

Now to the catalogue itself and its history as a symptomatic feature of dramatic versions of the Don Juan story from Tirso de Molina down to Da Ponte/Mozart. The brief overview I shall attempt will not be exhaustive, nor even comprehensive, but will seek to pinpoint the chief varieties of its use in different contexts, and to outline its theatrical (gesture) and literary potential. I begin, *ab ovo*, with *El Burlador de Sevilla*, the matrix of all plays and operas on the subject. On reading both the early, shorter play (*Tan largo me lo fiáis*) and its ampler sequel, one notes that neither offers what could be regarded as a direct ancestor of the item in question. Rather, the place into which the catalogue would fit dramaturgically – following Tisbea's discovery of Don Juan's desertion and preceding her "aria" of despair (11. 985ff. of *El Burlador...*)[18] – is empty, in contrast to Da Ponte/Mozart's *Don Giovanni*, where it appears exactly at this point, namely at the end of Act I, Scene 5 (p. 522f.) and before Elvira's *recitativo secco* "In questa forma dunque/ Mi tradì il scellerato" (p. 523). Actually, in the tradition the piece is closely linked with the figure of Elvira, an affinity psycho-sociologically explained by the fact that a compilation of this kind is hardly needed to impress (or: depress) a mere peasant girl, and that it would be inappropriate in the case of the highly placed Donna Anna, whom it would only 'drag into the mud'.

However, the search for the roots of the compilation yields some results within the body of Tirso's *comedia*, where the "playboy" –

---

18 The edition I have used, and from which I am quoting, is *El Burlador de Sevilla y convidado de piedra*, ed. Gerald E. Wade, New York (Scribner's) 1969.

Oscar Mandel's rendition of *burlador*[19] – upon returning to Seville engages in a curious dialogue with his friend, the Marquis de la Mota. Their exchange, showing Don Juan in the role of Tom Rakewell, concerns the city's most notorious prostitutes and runs, in part, as follows:

> Juan: *¿Que hay de Sevilla?*
> Mota: *Está ya*
> *Toda esta corte mudada.*
> Juan: *¿Mujeres?*
> Mota: *Cosa juzgada.*
> Juan: *¿Ines?*
> Mota: *A Vejel se va.*
> Juan: *Buen lugar para vivir,*
> *La que tan dama nació*
> Mota: *El tiempo la desterró*
> *A Vejel.*
> Juan: *Irá a morir.*
> *¿Costanza?*
> Mota: *Es lástima vella*
> *Lampiña de frente y ceja.*
> *Llámala el portugués vieja*
> *Y ella imagina qne bella.* (ll. 1210-1221)[20]

---

19 Oscar Mandel's translation of the shorter version appears under the title *The Playboy of Seville in The Theatre of Don Juan: A Collection of Plays and Views, 1630-1963*, ed. Oscar Mandel, Lincoln (University of Nebraska Press) 1963, pp. 47-99.

20 In the racy but inaccurate rendition by Harry Kemp (*The Love Rogue*, New York: [Lieber & Lewis] 1923, p. 89ff.) the passage reads:

> Juan: *How goes it in Seville these days?*
> Mota: *Great changes, friend, have taken place*
> *In a short time.*
> Juan: *The women?*
> Mota: *They*
> *Are ... well, what can a fellow say?*
> Juan: *Inez?*
> Mota: *She's gone to Vejel.*
> Juan: *A rare*
> *Abiding place if she be there.*
> Mota: *Time has retired her to that town.*
> Juan: *Time that must bring all beauty down.*
> *Constanza?*
> Mota: *Ay, but it is sad*
> *To see the eyebrows she once had*
> *Grown bald now on her thinning hair.*

And so on through Teodora, who cures her French disease by profuse sweating

> (*se escapó del mal francés*
> *Por un rió de sudores*)

and the application of quicksilver that makes her teeth fall out. In short, the catalogue portion of the conversation is a specimen of low, coarse humor serving entirely satirical ends.

The catalogue proper would seem to be an Italian invention linked to the *lazzi* executed, and largely improvised, by *commedia dell'arte* figures – in this case, Pulcinella. It makes its debut – or so we surmise – in an early adaptation of Tirso's play that was staged in Naples and has been preserved in the form of a scenario entitled *Il Convitato di pietra*[21]. Set in the countryside by the sea near Naples, Act I, as epitomized, ends as follows:

> Tisbea vorrebbe andar con lui; ma Don Giovanni non vuole, dicendo che a lei deve bastare la gloria di essere stato goduta da un cavaliere della sua qualità; e dice a Policinella [= Leporello] che la ponga capolista. Tisbea fa suo lamento e, buttandosi in mare, si annega.

Appropriately, the *lista per Policinella* finds its place among the props (*robbe*) enumerated in an appendix to the scenario. In a slightly later version of the play, published under the same title by the prolific Andrea Cicognini, we have a corresponding dialogue between Don Giovanni, his servant Passarino and the seduced girl Rosalba. Responding to the latter's complaint that she has been jilted, Passarino coolly observes: *Si l'attendesse la parola a tutte le donne, al bisognaria ch'al n'havesse sposade quattro milla*[22]. And when Don Giovanni has left, claiming priority for some other 'business', the Zanni (as Passarino,

---

> They call her the "old Portuguese trull";
> But still she thinks she's beautiful.

21 "Lo Scenario italiano 'Il Convitato di pietra'", published by Giannina Spellanzon in the *Rendiconti della Reale Accademia dei Lincei*, vol. 5 (1901), pp. 376-384.

22 The text is reproduced in G. Gendarme de Bevotte's edition of *Le Festin de Pierre avant Molière: Dorimon, De Villiers, Scénario des Italiens, Cicognini*, Paris (Cornely et Cie.) 1907, undertaken on behalf of the Société des Textes Français Modernes. The quotation appears on pp. 391f.

showing his true colors, is now called in the stage directions), addressing himself to the audience in broad dialect, throws the catalogue into the pit, exclaiming: "See for yourselves, my friends, if there aren't several hundred on the list."

Two new features of the catalogue scene make their appearance in this passage, one of them relatively short-lived and basically limited to the *commedia dell'arte,* the other destined to become a permanent fixture. Taking the latter first: Passarino's obsession with figures will be shared by his descendants in the next century-and-a-half, with the perplexing result that the total number of victims, while always considerable, varies from a few dozen to a few thousand, with Leporello's *mille ottocento* occupying the middle ground. Mimetic rather than verbal, the other feature invites audience participation and provokes audience reaction. Still a mere insinuation in Cicognini, it blossoms into an outright challenge in the *Convitato di pietra* which in 1658 an Italian troupe of comedians displayed in Paris. In the scenario drawn up by one of its members, Biancolelli, the action at this point is described as follows:

> La pêcheuse [...] dit a Don Juan qu'elle compte qu'il lui tiendra la parole qu'il lui a donnée de l'épouser. Il lui répond qu'il ne le peut et que je lui en dirai la raison. Il s'en va et cette fille se désespère. Alors je lui remontre qu'elle n'est pas la centième qu'il a promis d'épouser. 'Lisez, lui dis-je, voilà la liste de toutes celles qui sont dans le même cas que vous, et je vais y ajouter votre nom'. Je jette alors cette liste roulée au parterre, et j'en retiens un bout, en disant: 'Voyez, Messieurs, si vous n'y trouverez pas quelqu'une de vos parentes.'[23]

The Paris *stagione* of the Locatelli troupe, in whose production Biancolelli took the role of Don Giovanni's servant, was apparently sensational and had a threefold literary aftermath. Already in the following year (1659) there appeared, in print and on the stage, two *tragicomédies* entitled *Festin de Pierre ou Le Fils criminel,* the one authored by M. Dorimon, the other by a certain De Villiers; and six years later (in 1665) Molière's *Dom Juan ou Le Festin de pierre* made its debut. Poquelin's handling of the situation substantially differs

---

23 Ibid., p. 343.

from the solution – prevalent in the long run – embraced by his less talented predecessors. In his *comédie,* the issue, rather than coming to a head, is diffused and only morsels of the set piece are retained. Thus, in the opening dialogue Sganarelle, the loquacious groom portrayed by the playwright himself, tells his colleague Gusman, *inter multa alia*:

> Un mariage ne lui [Dom Juan] coûte rien à contracter; il ne se sert point d'autres pièges pour attraper les belles, et c'est un épouseur à toutes mains. Dame, demoiselle, bourgeoise, paysanne, il ne trouve rien de trop chaud ni de trop froid pour lui; et si je te disais le nom de toutes celles qu'il a épousées en divers lieux, ce serait un chapître à durer jusques au soir. (Pleïade ed., p. 777)

On the other hand, the scene into which this snatch of information most suitably fits – Act I, Scene 3 of *Dom Juan* corresponding to Act I, Scene 5 of *Don Giovanni* – merely proceeds to Sganarelle's empty chatter (*Madame, les conquérants, Alexandre et les autres mondes sont causes de notre départ,* p. 784), to be followed directly by Elvira's accusations – here levelled at Dom Juan in person[24]. What is new and pacemaking about this *abrégé* is the division of the unnamed and unnumbered women into four estates (nobility, upper middle class, lower middle class, peasantry), to be refined and elaborated by subsequent authors.

In contrast to Molière, whose psychological finesse and overriding concern with motivation caused him to eliminate as many *lazzi* as possible, Dorimon and De Villiers expanded the catalogue, with the latter even retaining the stunt of shooting "un papier roulé ou il y a beaucoup de noms de femmes écrites"[25] into the audience. The lists which their servant figures – Briguelle and Philipin – recite are unsophisticated and largely undifferentiated. Thus Briguelle, speaking to

---

24 The passage is faithfully copied in Karl von Marinelli's *Dom Juan oder Der steinerne Gast,* Lustspiel in vier Aufzügen nach Molière und dem Spanischen des Tirso de Molina *el Combidado de piedra*..., as reprinted in *Die romantisch-komischen Volksmärchen,* ed. Otto Rommel, series 13d, vol. 2 of the collection *Deutsche Literatur ... in Entwicklungsreihen,* Leipzig (Reclam) 1936. The catalogue is missing in the majority of German popular and puppet plays on Don Juan.

25 Gendarme de Bevotte (footnote 22 above), p. 95f.

Amarante, manages, before being interrupted by the arrival of his master, to reel off the names of more than thirty women whom, in his *pays natal*, Don Juan has either seduced or raped (note the coarsening of the tone!), throwing in an occasional epithet for good measure. Neither he nor the author seems to have noticed – or bothers to mention – the fact that theirs are French, rather than Spanish, names, suggesting various social stations and extending from the stately Dorinde, Angélique and Amarillis to the menial Margot, Janneton and Gillette. Comprising twenty-four lines and offering thirty-four names in all, some of them borrowed from Dorimon, De Villiers' compilation is more extensive and colorful

> *(la belle Joconde,*
> *Dont l'œil sçait embrazer les cœurs de tout le monde* [ll. 1263f.])

but equally fragmentary, as its perpetrator freely admits in closing his 'sermon':

> *Et si je pouvois bien du tout me souvenir,*
> *De quinze jours d'icy je ne pourrois finir* (ll. 1276f.)[26]

With a substantial and richly varied tradition, extending over roughly half a century, behind it, the Don Juan-*Stoff* entered the world of opera on February 17, 1669, when Filippo Acciajoli's "dramma per musica" *L'Empio punito*, with music by Alessandro Melani, premiered at the Palazzo Colonna in Borgo near Rome. It is a highly stylized version of the plot set not in a tangible and identifiable place or country, but in an Arcadian land by the name of Pella; and its *dramatis personae* are called Acrimante, Atamira and Bibi rather than Don Giovanni, Donna Anna and Leporello/Passarino/Pasquariello or the like. In such a work, aimed at literary connoisseurs rather than the *hoi polloi*, there is little room for popular entertainment and *commedia*-style *lazzi*. Yet, nodding in that direction, the librettist has Bibi most un-Leporello-like tell his master, upon arriving at an idyllic place where shepherdesses are seen fishing (!), to start keeping score:

---

26 Ibid., p. 239.

Allegrezza, padrone,
Tien pur lesta la penna;
Se non erra la vista,
Ecco robba da scriver nella lista –

but that is where the matter rests[27].

Generally (and as far as the available texts allow one to judge), the early phase of Don Giovanni's operatic career is marked by relative indifference, on the part of librettists and composers, toward the by now familiar *Register*. Thus, as Stefan Kunze reports in his invaluable monograph, the servant Malorco in *La pravità castigata*, a piece with music by Eustachio Bambini performed in Brno (now Czechoslovakia) in 1734, apes Cicognini's Passarino by showing the catalogue to Rosalba; but he does not break into song. Nor does, fifty years later, the Pulcinella of Giacomo Tritti's *Il Convitato di pietra* (1783), with text by Giambattista Lorenzi. By and large, however, the aria, well ensconced by 1780, had begun to lose some of its improvisational character, as method began to take the place of humorous madness. Still, the 'progress' was by no means unencumbered, and an occasional 'relapse' can be noted. Thus, a one-act adaptation of Francesco Gardi's "dramma tragicomico" *Il nuovo convitato di pietra* of 1787 – a rashly concocted piece that sought to make hay of Bertati/Gazzaniga's success – made as late as 1802 by one Giuseppe Foppa lapses into sheer buffoonery, as the women on the list, numbered with actuarial pedantry, are graced not with their baptismal names but with grotesquely characteristic designations such as Cecca (the blind one), Storta (the deformed one), Tortigliona (the spiral one), Burchiella (canal barge) and Lasagna[28].

None of these precedents could have sufficiently interested or impressed Da Ponte for him to wish to emulate or plagiarize it. He was,

---

27 Quoted from the text as found in Giovanni Macchia, *Vita, avventure e morte di Don Giovanni*, Bari (Laterza) 1966, p. 240.

28 The full text is given by Kunze (op. cit., p. 86), who also reproduces the words of the aria as sung in the original performance of the opera – a rather innocuous piece which culminates in an *Aufforderung zum Tanz*.

after all, a poet of fairly high literary aspirations, well versed in the Latin and Italian classics, and with a sure sense of how to draw the line between the various levels of style, whether in speech, gesture or action. Thus, even though Marinelli's recent success made the Don Juan theme a logical choice for the libretto which Mozart asked him to write, he, pressed as he was for time, might never have chosen this particular subject had it not been for a crutch on which he could lean with confidence. It so happened that Bertati's text for *Don Giovanni o sia Il convitato di pietra* offered a mould into which he could pour the treasures of his own wit and ingenuity. A comparison of the two matching pieces, entrusted to Pasquariello and Leporello respectively, may help us to qualify the nature of Da Ponte's inspired plagiarism.

Pasquariello's relatively short piece – a dozen lines of recitative and an aria based on nineteen lines of text – opens with a reference to Don Giovanni as *Il Grande Alessandro delle femmine* (a parallel inspired by Molière) who, in order to carry out his amorous plans, deflowers country after country. In contrast to Da Ponte's imitation-cum-variation, Bertati's original ends in a *duettino* between Elvira and her seducer's Certified Public Accountant – an unsatisfactory conclusion insofar as, at least by implication, it lowers Elvira in our esteem by bringing her down to Pasquariello's level.

Thematically, the organization of the aria is quite simple. Its first three lines tackle the geographic question by designating Italy, Germany and France as well as, naturally, Spain as the countries that have suffered the greatest damage during Giovanni's erotic siege. The next three lines deal with social status and convey the notion that the protagonist distributes his favors about equally between upstairs and downstairs: next to countesses (*contadine*), ladies (*madame*), middle-class women (*cittadine*) and craftsmen's wives (*artigiane*), he 'flirts' with chamber maids (*cameriere*), cooks (*cuoche*) and scullery maids (*guattere*) thereby descending – and condescending – below the level of what Da Ponte would subsequently find to be appropriate, his hero being cut of somewhat finer cloth.

On the whole, Bertati's Don is not particular, giving no hoot whether a wench is ugly or beautiful

(Vi dirò che egli ama tutte,
Che sian belle o che sian brutte);

but he draws a line where age is concerned, shunning intimate rapport with those tired of the amorous sport

(Delle vecchie solamente
Non si sente ad infiammar).

Having made this stricture, Pasquariello concludes his 'sermon' with the, by now stereotypical, apology that the list actually presented is no more than a symbolic gesture, a *pars pro toto* necessitated by the size of the catalogue, a full rendition of which would amount to a rhetorical marathon

(Vi dirò che si potria
Fin domani seguitar)[29].

As for Da Ponte's catalogue aria, it is verbally – as Mozart's is musically – the culmination of the series. Justifiably, the author took pride in his accomplishment and, hardly a person to excel in modesty, inserted it, with a partly rewritten recitative, in the adaptation of Bertati's libretto which, in 1794, he undertook for a London production of

---

29 Kunze (op. cit., p. 43f.) reproduces the words of two catalogue arias substituted for the standard text at regional performances of Gazzaniga's opera in 1788 and 1789, i. e., after the premiere of *Don Giovanni*. One of them does not offer a list but deals with the tribulations of love, while the other consists of two parts, the first of which

(Sei fra Indiane e del Perù
Tre di Gubbio, a forse più
Per adesso questo sono
Nove belle per mia fe.
Niente dico delle Gobbe,
Guercie, zoppe, e lacrimose;
Belle, brutte, e ancor meschine
Serve, Dame e Contadine
A diluvio qui ce n'e.
Tutta a queste, gioja mia
Tutta siete si per me)

is a grotesque and scaled-down version of the model, while the second evokes a ballroom scene dominated by Don Giovanni and his girl of the hour dancing to the tune of various instruments.

Gazzaniga's opera. In that recitative, Don Giovanni, still compared to the King of Macedon, is described as a person whose principal aim it is to transform the world of women into a harem:

> *Il mio padrone invece,*
> *Che conquistar non vuol paesi, e ville*
> *A dieci, a cento, a mille*
> *Cerca di conquistar tutte le belle,*
> *Onde andiamo girando a quadro, e a tondo*
> *Per convertir in un serraglio il mondo.*[30]

In the *dramma giocoso* fashioned for Prague's opera fans, Leporello is given more time to go through his files than is his twin in Bertati/Gazzaniga's one-acter. While the recitative portion of the piece is slightly shorter than its model – from which it borrows the punchline

> *Ogni villa, ogni borgo, ogni paese*
> *e testimon di sue donnesche*
> [in substitution for Bertati's clichéd *amorose*] *imprese* –,

the text of the aria proper is appreciably longer (thirty instead of nineteen lines of text). Between the two parts there is a grey zone, however; for the first four lines of the fully orchestrated number

> *(Madamina, il catalogo è questo*
> *Delle belle che amò il padron mio:*
> *Un catalogo egli è che ho fatto io:*
> *Osservete, leggete con me)*

exactly correspond to Bertati's transitional verses

> *(Se voi volete averle in vista*
> *Ecco Signora mia, quest'è la lista)*

and would seem to be better placed at the end of the recitative than at the beginning of the aria. Could it be that Mozart who, in *Le nozze di Figaro*, was so eager to supply music that he mistakenly composed a stage direction[31], have blundered in this instance as well? Hardly so; for as the rhyme scheme of the first eight lines (abbc deec), to which the music closely adheres, implies, Da Ponte wished the actual aria to begin at this particular point.

---

30 Kunze, op. cit., p. 192.

31 I am referring to the opening phrase of the "Canzonetta sull'aria" (# 20) duet in Act III of the opera.

The second quartet of lines closely parallels its equivalent in Bertati's piece, except that here the land of the seraglios, Turkey, broadens the geographic scope of Don Giovanni's campaigns and adds a measly ninety-one captives to the specific but clearly non-verisimilar number[32]. The last six lines of this segment are, once again, patterned after the model. The *contadine, cameriere* and *cittadine* are retained; but the *artigiane, cuoche* and *guattere* are replaced by women of more exalted rank (*contesse, baronesse, marchesane* and even *principesse*), a sign that this Don Giovanni who, like all his *alter egos*, is required to love *donne d'ogni grado* and *d'ogni forma*, has more aristocratic tastes than they and does disdain to mingle with the *plebs*.

At this point in the score, Mozart breaks the musical continuity by substituting an *andante con moto* for the opening *allegro*, while retaining the dominant key of D Major. This change of 'tone' not only serves to stave off monotony – the bane of statisticians, even if their name be Alfred Kinsey – but effects a transition from the level of scientific generalization to one of greater intimacy and specificity. Leporello now turns into a painter of mores and depicts physiological/physiognomic types that can be visualized by the mind's eye and, hence, empathized with to some degree. Being verbal, his portraits easily combine physical traits (hair color, teint, figure and size) with behavioral characteristics (*gentilezza, costanza, dolcezza*) and seasonal appeal

*(vuol d'inverno la grassotta,
vuol d'estate la magrotta)*,

---

32 Not surprisingly, given W. H. Auden's peculiar sense of translational adequacy, the Auden/Kallman version of the libretto, as reprinted in *The Great Operas of Mozart*, New York (Norton) 1962, destroys the geographical balance by substituting England for Germany and San Marino for France and Turkey in the original lines, and by adding, in a stanza capriciously invented for the purpose, Arabia, Dalmatia and Helvetia (p. 177).

Only after my essay went to press I was alerted to Franz Walter Müller's study "Zur Genealogie von Leporellos Liste", *Beiträge zur romanischen Philologie* 7 (1970), pp. 199-226; I apologize for the partial overlap.

thereby greatly enriching the somewhat barren structure erected by Bertati. Mozart's music – needless to say – further enlivens the proceedings by indulging in a bit of jolly tone painting on words like *grande*, *maestosa* and *piccina*, to mention only the most ear- and eye-catching examples.

This task completed, Leporello once again changes mood. Now his sarcasm comes to the fore. Going Pasquariello, who saved the elderly from Giovanni's clutches, one better, he reaffirms the collector's zeal by showing him to be indiscriminate in his choice, if only for the sake of being able *di porle in lista*, while still insisting on his preference for spring chickens

> (*sua passion predominante
> e la giovin principiante*)

– thus allowing his master to have his cake and eat it too. With coarse cynicism, underscored by the titillating music which Mozart provided, he winds up his aria with a highly suggestive punchline

> (*Purché porti la gonella
> voi sapete quel che fa*)

which, stripping off all aristocratic pretenses, ends the piece with a bang, rather than with Bertati's more conventional and rather poorly placed whimper

> (*Perche basta che sian femmine
> Per doverle amoreggiar*).

At this point, having had his fun and having vicariously enjoyed his master's triumphs in retrospect, he quickly exits, avoiding the box on the ears which he so richly deserves for his impudence, and the psychologically false situation into which Bertati manœuvers his predecessor by having Elvira chime in with her

> *Il mio cor da gelosia
> Tutto sento a lacerar.*

We have reached the end of what I promised would be a Cook's tour of catalogue speeches and arias in various literatures. Our critical survey, itself an annotated, historically sequential catalogue, has demonstrated – I hope successfully – that, both dramatically and melo-dramatically, a tradition, evolving out of a mere convention, invariably leads to a climactic fulfillment of its promise, and that once the promise has been fulfilled there is little room for further experimentation.

Giovanni Bertati/Giuseppe Gazzaniga

DON GIOVANNI o sia IL CONVITATO DI PIETRA
(1787)

Scene VII
Pasquariello, Elvira

E:	*E mi lascia così! Parla tu: dimmi*
	La cagione qual fù del suo abbandono;
	E pensa ben che disperata io sono.
P:	*Per me ... Sentite ... Vi dirò ... Siccome ...*
E:	*Non confonderti.*
P:	*Oibò: non v'è pericolo.*
	Siccome io dico, che Alessandro il Grande ...
E:	*E che c'entra Alessandro!*
P:	*C'entra: e statevi cheta.*
	Siccome, io dico, che Alessandro il Grande
	Non era giammai sazio
	Di far nuove conquiste, il mio padrone
	Se avesse ancora cento spose, e cento,
	Sazio non ne saria, nè mai contento:
	Egli è il Grande Alessandro delle femmine;
	Onde per far le sue amorose imprese
	Spesso, spesso cangiar suol di paese.
E:	*Dunque ha dell'altre femmine?*
P:	*Ih! ih! Se voi volete averle in vista*
	Ecco Signora mia, quest'è la lista.
	(Getta una lista di alcuna braccia di carta)
	Aria *Dell'Italia, ed Alemagna*
	Ve ne ho scritte cento, e tante.
	Della Francia, e della Spagna
	Ve ne sono non so quante:

	Fra Madame, Cittadine,
	Artigiane, Contadine,
	Cameriere, Cuoche, e Guattere:
	Perchè basta che sian femmine
	Per doverle amoreggiar.
	Vi dirò ch'e un'Uomo tale,
	Se attendesse alle promesse,
	Che il marito universale
	Un dì avrebbe a diventar.
	Vi dirò che egli ama tutte,
	Che sian belle, o che sian brutte:
	Delle vecchie solamente
	Non si sente ad infiammar.
	Vi dirò ...
E:	*Tu m'hai seccata.*
P:	*Vi dirò ...*
E:	*Non più: và via.*
P:	*Vi dirò che sì potrìa*
	Fin domani seguitar.
E:	*(Il mio cor da gelosia*
	Tutto sento a lacerar.)

Lorenzo Da Ponte/Wolfgang Amadeus Mozart

IL DISSOLUTO PUNITO ossia IL DON GIOVANNI
(1787)

Act One, Scene Five

Elvira:	*Stelle! L'iniquo*
	Fuggi, misera me! ... Dove? in qual parte ...
Leporello:	*Eh! lasciate che vada. Egli non merta*
	Che di lui ci pensiate ...
E:	*Il scellerato*
	M'ingannò, mi tradì ...
L:	*Eh! consolatevi:*
	Non siete voi, non foste, e non sarete
	Né la prima né l'ultima. Guardate
	Questo non picciol libro: è tutto pieno

Dei nomi di sue belle.
Ogni villa, ogni borgo, ogni paese
È testimon di sue donnesche imprese.
[# 4 Aria]
Allegro   *Madamina, il catalogo è questo*
Delle belle che amò il padron mio:
Un catalogo egli è che ho fatt'io:
Osservate, leggete con me.

In Italia seicento e quaranta,
In Lamagna duecento e trentuna,
Cento in Francia, in Turchia novantuna,
Ma in Ispagna son già mille e tre.

V'han fra queste contadine,
Cameriere, cittadine,
V'han contesse, baronesse,
Marchesane, principesse,
E v'han donne d'ogni grado,
D'ogni forma, d'ogni età.
Andante con moto *Nella bionda egli ha l'usanza*
Di lodar la gentilezza:
Nella bruna, la costanza;
Nella bianca, la dolcezza.
Vuol d'inverno la grassotta,
Vuol d'estate la magrotta:
È la grande maestosa.
La piccina è ognor vezzosa.
Delle vecchie fa conquista
Pel piacer di porle in lista:
Ma passion predominante
È la giovin principiante.

Non si picca se sia ricca,
Se sia brutta, se sia bella:
Purché porti la gonnella,
Voi sapete quel che fa.
      (parte)

Educating Siegfried (1984)

"A born anarchist, the ideal of Bakoonin."
 G. B. Shaw, *The Perfect Wagnerite*[1]

"A regular L'il Abner type."
 Anna Russell, "*The Ring of the Nibelung*, An Analysis"[2]

Contrary to Wagner's sure hopes and certain expectations[3], *Siegfried*, the third instalment of *The Ring,* is the least popular and least frequently performed part of the tetralogy, even though it is chock-full of ingratiating musical numbers, such as Mime's lullaby, the forging song, *Forest Murmurs,* horn calls, real and imitated bird song, and the glorious duet at its conclusion. And the comedienne, Anna Russell, speaking for those who regard Wotan's scenes with Mime and Erda as tedious stretches of conversation which repeat information already familiar from *The Rhinegold* and *The Valkyrie,* in her plot summary, undertaken from the perspective of the 'average opera-goer', dismisses this 'heroic *opéra-comique*'[4] by observing: "There is not much you need to know about [it] except that Wotan comes down and plays 'Twenty Questions'." The work is, however, pivotal to the action of the cycle and offers vital insights into Wagner's overall conception. For Siegfried is, like Wolfram von Eschenbach's Parsifal, the *tumbe*

---

1 The quotation is drawn from *The Works of Bernard Shaw* (London, 1930), XIX, 212.

2 *The Anna Russell Album* published in 1972 by Columbia Masterworks.

3 "I am now convinced that as my most popular work *The Young Siegfried* will have a quick and happy dissemination and will pull along the other pieces, one by one, so that it will probably be the founder of a whole Nibelung dynasty." Wagner in a letter to Julie Ritter dated May 6, 1857. This letter, as well as all other relevant statements by the composer, is culled from Richard Wagner, *Sämtliche Werke*, vol. 29/1: *Dokumente zur Entstehungsgeschichte des Bühnenfestspiels* Der Ring des Nibelungen, ed. W. Breig and H. Fladt (Mainz: Schott, 1976).

4 Wagner uses that term in a letter to Hans Richter written in 1868, where it applies both to *The Mastersingers* and *Siegfried*. In *Mein Leben* he calls it a 'heroic comedy'.

Tor (the ignorant fool), and it is he who, with Brünnhilde, is destined to lay the foundation for a new world unencumbered by brute force (the giants), cunning (the dwarfs) and legal power upheld by contracts (Wotan). This part of the cycle thus sets the stage for *Twilight of the Gods (Götterdämmerung),* an anarchist's dream of total destruction which paves the way for a new order of things.

Unlike the scores of *The Ring* (originally *Der Reif des Nibelungen,* i. e. *The Circlet of the Nibelung*), which were written in the order of the dramatic action between 1853 and 1874, with a seven-year break for *Tristan and Isolde* and *The Mastersingers of Nuremberg*[5], the texts were produced in reverse order, from *Twilight of the Gods* (originally *Siegfried's Death,* 1848) by way of *Siegfried* (originally *Young Siegfried,* 1851) backwards to *The Valkyrie* (June, 1852) and *The Rhinegold* (originally *The Theft of the Rhinegold,* mid-September to early November, 1852), because Wagner felt the need to work out the action in a fully realised visual concept[6]. After major revisions of *Siegfried's Death* and relatively minor surgery on *Young Siegfried,* the first integral version of the poem was printed in February, 1853, in a private edition of fifty copies. Following further cosmetic changes, primarily affecting Parts Three and Four, the final draft of the cycle appeared, at long last, in 1863, thirteen years before the quadruple premiere in Bayreuth. Thus the text of each unit of *The Ring* evolved, by way of extrapolation, from narrative passages in the one chronologically preceding it: the action of *Siegfried* was derived from the hero's retrospective account in Act Three, Scene Two, of *Siegfried's*

---

5   The exact point of interruption is marked by a letter to Liszt dated June 28, 1857, where Wagner states: "I have led my young Siegfried into the lonely beauty of the forest. There I have left him lying under the linden tree and have said farewell to him with heartfelt tears. There he is better off than elsewhere."

6   As Wagner points out in his autobiography, *Mein Leben*, it was the actor/director Eduard Devrient who, as early as 1848, demonstrated the need for a scenic, i. e. visual, realization of the entire story of the *Ring*. The first comprehensive outline of the tetralogy is sketched in letters to Uhlig (Nov. 12, 1851) and Liszt (Nov. 20, 1851).

Death[7], just as that of *The Valkyrie* originated in Brünnhilde's report in Act Three of *Young Siegfried*[8]. Wagner discarded that report when he gave *Siegfried* its final form; but Siegfried's narrative, though modified and slightly abridged, is retained in *Twilight of the Gods*. Although the scenes in which previous events are recapitulated may at first seem redundant to audiences attending the whole cycle, Wagner considered them intrinsic to his overall plan. Each of Wotan's question-and-answer sessions in *Siegfried*, for example, offers a new interpretation of the crucial incidents of the myth and consequently builds up for us a terrifying picture of the complex forces in Wotan's world. It is this world into which Siegfried, the Wälsung hero, ignorantly blunders.

Structurally, *Siegfried*, a veritable tragi-comedy[9], is peculiar in so far as it consists of two interlarded sets of scenes, those concerned with Siegfried and those dominated by the Wanderer (i. e. Wotan in disguise). Originally, this drama exclusively focussed on the overgrown boy-scout (Ernest Newman's label for Siegfried), and the action, accordingly, was more or less straightforward comedy, first farcical and then sublime. There is no reference to the Father of the Gods in the relevant section of the original outline, *The Nibelung Myth as Sketch for a Drama* (1848); nor does he figure in *Siegfried's Death*. Wotan makes his grand entrance only in the prose sketch for *Young Siegfried* (early May, 1851), where we are told of an encounter with the dwarf: "The [Wanderer] comes. Conversation while Mime works at his forge. The origin of the Nibelungs, etc." In the prose version, finished in late May of the same year, his role is considerably ex-

---

7 The full text of *Siegfrieds Tod* is found in vol. 6 of Wagner's *Gesammelte Schriften*, ed. J. Kapp (Leipzig, n. d. [1914]), 150-193.

8 This text, like all other *Skizzen und Entwurfe zur Ring-Dichtung*, was edited by Otto Strobel (Munich, 1930). Relevant portions of *Der junge Siegfried* are reproduced in III, 315-333, of the Jubiläumsausgabe of the *Dichtungen und Schriften*, ed. D. Borchmeyer (Frankfurt, 1983).

9 The generic question is raised in Patrick McCreless's *Wagner's 'Siegfried': Its Drama, History and Music* (Ann Arbor, 1982), to which I am greatly indebted.

panded and the dialogue with Mime augmented by conversations with Erda and Siegfried (Act Three), to which the verbal exchange with Alberich (and, briefly, Fafner) was subsequently added in lieu of a scene featuring the Nibelung hordes.

Wagner's reasons for enlarging Wotan's role are obvious: he needed to integrate Siegfried's *comédie humaine* with the remainder of *The Ring* and to juxtapose his hero's antics with the metaphysical drama of the rest of the cycle. This was done at the expense of stylistic unity and theatrical effectiveness, except in the truly Sophoclean confrontation between father and son in Act Three, where the two strands of the action overlap as Wotan vainly seeks to bar Siegfried's way. (In the draft, Wagner permitted the Wanderer to let the youth pass without a struggle; but in the final version the scene ends with the shattering of Wotan's spear by Siegmund's reconstituted sword – a parallel in reverse of the conclusion of Act Two of *The Valkyrie*, where it was the sword that was shattered by the spear.) For Wotan's scenes, in which the power structure of the universe is described (scenes according to Anna Russell of "crashing boredom" especially when Erda the "green-faced torso" is involved), Wagner adopts rhetorical devices very different from the sprightly character of the scenes which highlight Siegfried's boisterous apprenticeship – his *Lehrjahre* – under the tutelage of a misshapen pedagogue[10]. It is on these that we shall concentrate. To appreciate the results of Siegfried's upbringing in the backwoods, it is useful to know something about his teacher, and before scrutinizing Mime's unorthodox educational methods, we shall do well to draw a portrait of this guardian who justifiably presents himself to his ward as midwife, nurse, father and mother rolled into one. Our understanding of the standard text will be greatly enhanced by tracing the evolution of certain significant traits, especially the change of tone from serious to mock-heroic. In *The Nibelung Myth as Sketch for a Drama*,

---

10 The Wanderer scene in Act One of *Siegfried* has been thoroughly analyzed by Reinhold Brinkmann in an essay published in 1972 in the *Jahrbuch des Staatlichen Instituts für Musikforschung Preussischer Kulturbesitz*.

Mime is still conceived as a person worthy of his calling, a veritable Chiron to his Siegfried/Achilles. The following epitome of what would have been Act One of *Siegfried* shows him to be well-meaning and supportive:

> After a long pregnancy, the cast-out Sieglinde gives birth to Siegfried in the Wilderness [...] Reigin [Mime], Alberich's brother, emerged from clefts in the rock when she cried out in her birth-pangs and lent her a helping hand. Shortly after having given birth to Siegfried, Sieglinde dies, after telling Reigin her story and entrusting the boy to him. Reigin brings Siegfried up, informs him of his father's death, teaches him how to forge metal and procures the two pieces of his father's splintered sword, out of which, under his direction, Siegfried fashions Balmung [= Notung].

Up to this point, Mime's portrait is altogether positive. The catch, which in the final poem is manifest from the beginning, is revealed only in a subsequent passage:

> Now Mime incites the youth to kill the worm, in order to show his gratitude. Siegfried first wishes to avenge his father's death. He leaves the cave [...] and kills Hunding. Only after having done so, he fights and kills the dragon. When he puts his fingers, which are hot from the worm's blood, to his mouth in order to cool them, he involuntarily tastes the blood and in this way suddenly understands the language of the forest birds [here still in the plural] [...] They praise his deed [...] and warn him of Mime, who, they say, has used him only to get to the treasure and now craves his life in order to win the treasure for himself[11].

The complimentary image of Mime as skilled artisan and devoted teacher is not only retained but strengthened in *Siegfried's Death*, where the hero, no longer the Innocent Abroad but still essentially without gall or guile, recalls his childhood from the perspective of the trusting ward. In the prose version of the proto-*Twilight of the Gods*, for example, his hunchback foster-father is called a strong dwarf, splendid smith, and wise counsellor; and in the metrical version he appears, with alliterative force, as a manly creature, excellent smith and prudent counsellor to the orphaned boy[12].

---

11 Siegfried's revenge on Hunding, which formed part of the action in the early versions, was finally eliminated by Wagner.

12 "Mime hiess ein mannlicher Zwerg./ Zierlich und scharf wusst' er zu schmieden./ Sieglind, meiner lieben Mutter,/ half er im wilden Walde./ Den sie sterbend gebar,/ mich Starken zog er auf/ mit klugem Zwergenrat."

By the time Wagner set out to write *Young Siegfried*, Mime's character had changed for the worse, and the well-intentioned craftsman/philosopher/pedagogue had turned into a bundle of ill-assorted and unsavoury features. In both versions of *Siegfried* he shows himself to be a windbag, hypocrite, liar, weakling and coward. The fact that Mime, the clownish mimic, does not honour the truth is repeatedly demonstrated, although some of the apparent contradictions between the truth and his deceptive representation of it can be resolved by a comparison between the texts of *Siegfried* and *Young Siegfried*, which shows that Wagner was not uniformly successful in eliminating discrepancies[13].

Thus, in an aside during his verbal sparring with Wotan in the first act of *Siegfried*, Mime admits having stolen the pieces of Siegmund's sword which, in Act Three of *The Valkyrie*, Brünnhilde had handed over to Sieglinde: "Cursed steel,/ that I stole you!", thereby contradicting the evidence he himself had recently provided to Siegfried: "This your mother gave me./ For labour, food and service/ it was my wretched wage./ Look here, a broken sword!/ She said your father bore it/ when he died in his last fight."[14] There are two ways of interpreting this passage: either Mime is deliberately misrepresenting the facts in order not to arouse Siegfried's suspicion or, as Newman considers to be more likely, Wagner simply overlooked the discrepancy[15].

That Mime is insidious and hides his dubious purposes under a torrent of deceitful phrases is made explicit when Siegfried, coached by the little Woodbird, learns to distinguish between essence and appearance. The comic dialogue in Act Two where, much against his will ("I didn't say that./ You get me all wrong"), Mime is forced to speak the

---

13 Daniel Coren compares the texts of the two versions in an unpublished dissertation "A Study of Wagner's *Siegfried*" (Univ. of California, Berkeley, 1971).

14 All quotations are based on Andrew Porter's English version (New York, 1977) but have been amended to make the text more literal for literary analysis.

15 In general, the reader is alerted to Ernest Newman's subtle analysis in Chapter 17 ("Difficulties in the Rounding of the *Ring*") of vol. II of his *Life of Richard Wagner*.

truth – a device purportedly borrowed from a nineteenth-century Faust play – offers irrefutable proof of his duplicity[16].

As a weakling, the Mime of *Siegfried* is no longer fit to assist the protagonist in remaking his father's weapon but is reduced to playing the role of an onlooker. Admitting his own inferiority as a craftsman, he decides to change his profession and with mordant black humour exchanges the smith's apron for the cook's: "When the master finds his skill has gone,/ he serves as cook to the child./ If he makes a paste from the steel,/ I shall brew him/ a broth out of eggs." A picture of cowardice, he spends much of his time quaking in his boots, crouching behind the anvil or hiding in a corner, whether in response to Siegfried's roughhousing (in the episode with the bear), Wotan's threatening gesture with the spear, or the waking nightmare of Father's arrival. How ironic, and yet how appropriate, that it is he who should offer to give lessons in fear!

Turning to Siegfried, we note that in his physical and psychological makeup he combines traits derived from heroic legend (*Sage*) and fairy tale (*Märchen*). As a slayer of patently allegorical dragons ("Here I rest and possess", says Fafner, the perfect capitalist) he is quite at home in the heroic legend, and as the Youth Who Knew No Fear of fairy tale, he would seem to have no place in the weighty mythological context of *The Ring* – not so, however, according to Wagner. For in a conversation with the sculptor Gustav Kietz, in 1849, the composer programmatically stated: "I shall write no more Grand Operas. I shall write fairy tales, like the one about the Youth Who Went Forth to Learn What Fear Was."[17] Wagner had fallen in love with this idea. Having completed the prose sketch for *Young Siegfried*, he told his friend Theodor Uhlig of the discovery which,

---

16 After an oral report recorded in Gustav Adolph Kietz's *Erinnerungen*.

17 Here, too, the versions are at odds; for whereas in *Young Siegfried*, alerting the audience to things yet to pass, Wotan admonishes Mime to watch his tongue ("Hab' acht, wenn die Zunge dir schwankt,/ Schwatze kein albernes Zeug!"), in *Siegfried* no such warning is sounded.

striking him with the force of inspiration, had enabled him to graft one genre upon the other:

> All winter long I have been haunted by an idea which, quite recently, has so completely captivated me that I shall now bring it to fruition. Didn't I tell you, some time ago, about a humorous subject, i. e., the story of the fellow who sets out to learn what fear is but cannot bring himself to do so? Consider my surprise when suddenly I realized that that fellow is none other than – the young Siegfried who acquires the treasure and awakens Brünnhilde[18].

Almost concurrently it dawned on him that placing the folktale before the legend/myth – *The Ring* being then conceived as a mere diptych – would permit him, in line with the Horatian formula *utile dulci* (i. e. both instructive and entertaining), to ease his audience into the high tragic mode: "*Young Siegfried* offers the enormous advantage of acquainting the audience with the weighty myth in a playful manner, just as the fairy tale does with children. Everything is engraved upon the mind by distinct, sensuous impressions; everything is understood – and when the serious *Siegfried's Death* arrives the audience knows everything that is presupposed there or could only be hinted at, and I've won the game."

Let us now trace the development of the text of the scenes which deal with Siegfried's acquisition of knowledge and experience. Wagner had considerable difficulty making 'ends meet' in this particular instance. If, once again, we search for evidence in the original plot outline of *The Ring*, *The Nibelung Myth as Sketch for a Drama*, we find that, at that point, Wagner had not yet linked fairy story and heroic legend, although even then he must have known that in the Teutonic legends Siegfried is commonly referred to as one who knows no fear, which, naturally, is a far cry from saying that, for whatever reasons, he must learn it.

The question of fear (*Furcht*) – whose existential analogue is anguish (*Angst*), a notion which is introduced at a much later stage in Act Three with reference to Sieglinde and Brünnhilde – is first raised in the prose sketch for *Young Siegfried*. The motivation furnished in

---

18 The letter was written on May 10, 1851.

this context is extremely poor, however, for it is Siegfried himself who broaches the subject 'out of the blue'. Asked by his tutor what he would do once Mime had mended the sword, the pupil emphatically states: "That I have told you long ago. Into the world will I fare and learn fearing since I will never learn it from you." Surely, this explanation is unsatisfactory since we cannot be certain when and under what circumstances the notion popped into Siegfried's head or whether Mime planted it there to begin with. Wagner must have noticed that this was a grave lacuna and, resolving the issue in his mind, added a note which supplies the much needed rhyme and reason:

> Siegfried now feels himself quite free of Mime. He will leave him in order to go into the world: for this reason he once more demands the sword. Mime tries to instil into him fear of the world so as to keep him in the wood. He paints for him one terror after another in the world beyond the wood. [...] Argument over fearing. Mime must explain it. He describes fear. Siegfried cannot learn it and now will go forth just to learn it. (Mime resolves quickly to teach it to him *himself*. Fafner? ...)

In the corresponding passage of *Young Siegfried*, Wagner realizes this idea but unduly complicates matters by coupling the notion of fear with that of cunning (*List*). Here Mime acquaints his ward with what he claims to be the educational policy framed by his mother on her deathbed: "Mime ...,/ you clever man!/ When my child grows up one day/ keep the courageous one in the wood!/ The world is malicious and false;/ it sets traps for the simpleton./ Only he who has learned fear/ may keep himself tolerably safe."[19] Whereupon the impetuous Siegfried expresses his wish to acquire fear. Mime will teach it to him (or so he thinks) together with its antidote *List*: "It is cunning/ which fear teaches us./ It is the fruit of fear." On second thought, while working on the final version of the text, Wagner must have observed that, from the dwarf's point of view, such instruction would be counterproductive; for if Mime succeeded in teaching Siegfried cunning he would quickly be up to his teacher's tricks.

---

19 In *Siegfried*, the corresponding passage reads: "Your mother's counsel/ speaks through me./ What I vowed/ I must now fulfill:/ not to dismiss you/ into the cunning world/ until you have learned how to fear."

Accordingly, in the text that finally emerged and served as a basis for the composition of the music, Mime does not teach Siegfried anything (except speech, and even that reluctantly[20]). As for cunning, it is the Woodbird, which introduces him, with Father's posthumous help, to the art of double hearing, which enables him to cope with Mime's double talk in what may be the most amusing scene in all of *The Ring*:

MIME:	Siegfried, my son,
	you see it yourself:
	you will have to yield your life to me.
SIEGFRIED:	That you hate me
	I am pleased to hear,
	but must I yield my life as well?
MIME:	That's not what I said.
	You get me all wrong.

Although the intrinsic motif of fear was retained, it was altered from phase to phase of the creative process. Thus both in *Young Siegfried* and in *Siegfried* it is neither the protagonist nor Mime but the Wanderer who brings up the subject, and each time in a different manner. In the *Ur*-libretto Wotan insinuates to Mime that it is his own disciple who will slay him ("Only Siegfried himself/ can forge his sword./ Your clever head/ keep for yourself;/ I do not need useless things./ But take good care of it/ from now on!"); but the dwarf, blind for all his shrewdness, fails to put two and two together. In *Siegfried*, on the other hand, Wotan, linking the forging of the sword with the acquisition of fear and embedding both motifs in a riddle, prophesies: "Now, Fafner's dauntless destroyer,/ hear, you doomed dwarf:/ 'Only he who has never/ learned to fear/ will fashion Notung anew.'/ Your wise head/ guard in future;/ I leave it forfeit to him/ who has not learned to fear."

Much against his better knowledge, which he seeks desperately to suppress, Mime himself tries to piece Notung together but quickly

---

20 This is evidenced in Act One, Scene One, where Siegfried, seizing Mime by the throat, violently complains: "Then I must choke you/ to learn anything;/ of your own will/ you tell me nothing./ Thus everything/ I had to wrest from you./ I would hardly have learned/ how to use speech/ if I had not forced the scoundrel/ to teach me."

realizes that the task is beyond him and that, accordingly, his life is doomed ("My wise head/ I have lost in the wager./ Doomed, I lost it to him/ who has not learned to fear."); but at this point he still fails to identify his slayer as Siegfried. That is the next step, for once Siegfried has done the seemingly impossible by forging Notung, there can be no doubt as to who will kill him. It is then that he decides on a new course of action, namely that of instilling fear in the youth, since, according to Wotan's prophecy, one who has learned to fear cannot be Mime's murderer. Yet, on second thought he realizes that he is now caught on the horns of a dilemma: if things are to work out as he wants, Siegfried must forge the sword and dispatch the dragon but, having been struck with fear in the process, must then meet his own fate:

> How do I hide
> my anxious head?
> It is forfeited to the bold youth
> unless Fafner teaches him fear.
> But woe, poor me!
> How could he wring the worm's neck
> if it taught him to fear?
> How would I attain the ring?
> Darned fix!
> I would be stuck
> if I didn't find a way
> to subdue the fearless one[21].

Since the scenario that would suit Mime best – Siegfried killing Fafner and, in turn, being killed by him – is unlikely to be enacted, the resourceful dwarf literally concocts an alternate plan: he will cook a poisonous broth (*Sudel*) which he will dish up to the thirsty boy after the fight. The plan backfires, and Siegfried emerges unscathed but without having learnt to fear. Still uncertain of his calling but acting on another hint from the Woodbird, he embarks on a new adventure

---

21 Wagner deliberately couched the farcical passages of *Siegfried* in the colloquial language of low comedy. Thus "darned fix" renders "verfluchte Klemme" more closely than the "accursed problem" of Andrew Porter's performing translation.

beyond the *selva oscura*, the dark wood of ignorance and sexual innocence in which Mime has raised him.

Having, still fearless, pierced the wall of flames, he meets his Beatrice, Brünnhilde, whom at first he mistakes for his mother. In her realm he is to acquire his sentimental education. What he is to learn now is a kind of fear that is in no way physical. Rather he, the loner, who has until now met only animals, dwarfs, giants and gods, is to become a thinking and feeling member of the human race. Face to face with the woman (of divine origin) who is to initiate him into love, he is consumed by the very fear which he is 'burning' to possess. Approaching the sleeping Valkyrie, he reflects:

> How do I, coward, feel?
> Is this what fear is?
> O mother! mother!
> Your brave child!
> There's a woman asleep
> who taught him fear.
> How conquer fear?
> How muster courage?
> To awake myself
> I must awaken the maiden.

Fear it is, but of an entirely different order. In the words of Patrick McCreless, "Siegfried is involved with two very different kinds of fear: physical fear, or fear of death, and the perfectly valid emotional fear which is the basis of sensitivity to other human beings and underlies human relationships. Although the two seem to be equated in the drama – they are in no way differentiated in the text – the story simply does not make sense if there is no distinction drawn between them." This is exactly the point and, accordingly, the progression from physical fear to emotional fear signals genuine progress. This different type of fear is the first step in his experience of human love, which in turn gives him back the confidence to forget self-doubt. Indeed, as soon as he has discovered what it feels like to be afraid in an emotional sense he also learns that another new experience, that of human love, enables him to overcome it.

> As the fire in the blood is kindled,
> as we pierce each other with our glances,
> as we burn in ardent embraces,
> my keen courage
> returns to me,
> and the fear, ah!
> which I never learned,
> the fear which you
> taught me just now:
> that fear, it seems,
> fool that I am,
> I forgot altogether.

Unlike the boy in the Grimm Brothers' fairy tale who, having passed through his ordeals with flying colours, finally gets his wish when a waiting-maid dumps a bucket of gudgeons over his head, Siegfried, having been gripped by fear on the threshold of his humanity, quickly unlearns it. Love, united with knowledge and free of anguish, is about to conquer the world and, in the process, topple the mythological edifice erected in the earlier portions of *The Ring*. Like Pamina and Papageno in Mozart's *The Magic Flute*, Siegfried and Brünnhilde can dispense with heaven because love is heavenly: "Mann und Weib und Weib und Mann/ reichen an den Himmel an" ("Man and woman, and woman and man/ reach up to heaven"). In gaining this insight, they have learned their lesson, and no further schooling is needed.

(Pariser) Farce oder wienerische Maskerade?
Die französischen Quellen des *Rosenkavalier* (1987)

> Man wird sagen, dass dies ganz und gar nicht
> die komische Oper ist, welche das deutsche
> Volk Jahrzehnte mit Sehnsucht erwartet.
> Richard Strauss[1]
>
> Sein wir in Frankreich? Sein wir unter die
> Kurutzen? Oder in Kaiserlicher Hauptstadt?
> Ochs von Lerchenau[2]

I.

Dem Hofmannsthal-Spezialisten wird der Gegenstand dieser Studie vertraut vorkommen, und er wird sich fragen, ob eine neuerliche Behandlung der Materie über Gemeinplätze hinausführen und mehr als ein paar dürftige Varianten zu einem geläufigen Thema hinzufügen kann. Doch mag er sich täuschen; denn einige kleine Überraschungen sind ihm gewiß. Zunächst freilich sei ohne weitere Umschweife festgestellt, daß die dem Meisterwerk und seinem Ambiente gewidmete Sekundärliteratur aus unerfindlichen Gründen bis heute unzureichend ist[3]. Gewiß gibt es zahlreiche Aufsätze und Kurzmonographien über Hofmannsthal und Frankreich; doch ist eine umfassende Darstellung

---

1 Von Hofmannsthal zitiert in „Zum Geleit" (1927). Siehe *Gesammelte Werke: Dramen V Operndichtungen* (Frankfurt: S. Fischer, 1979), S. 149. Von hier an durchgehend als *Dramen V* zitiert.

2 *Der Rosenkavalier*, Dritter Akt. Ebd., S. 83.

3 Horst Weber, *Hugo von Hofmannsthal: Bibliographie des Schrifttums 1892-1963* (Berlin: De Gruyter, 1966), die Standard-Bibliographie, wird ergänzt durch Hans-Albrecht Koch, *Hugo von Hofmannsthal: Bibliographie 1964-1976* (Freiburg i.Br.: Deutsches Seminar der Universität, 1977) und die periodischen Nachträge in: *Blätter der Hofmannsthal-Gesellschaft*.

dieses Komplexes weiterhin Desideratum[4]. Welch' einmalige Gelegenheit für Doktoranden und Habilitanden der Germanistik, sich wissenschaftlich einen Namen zu machen! Was den *Rosenkavalier* selbst anbetrifft, so liegen zwar zahllose Arbeiten, Rezensionen usw. vor – auch über die literarische Komponente; auch hier fehlt aber ein panoramischer Überblick[5].

Unter den französischen Autoren, die im Hinblick auf den Dramatiker Hofmannsthal behandelt worden sind, nimmt Molière unzweifelhaft die erste Stelle ein, und dies sowohl allgemein als spezifisch in bezug auf den *Rosenkavalier*[6]. Aber selbst diese für das Verständnis des Werks unabdingbar wichtige Beziehung ist m. W. noch nie erschöpfend behandelt worden, wenngleich kein Zweifel über die Hauptlinien der Filiation besteht. Die Aufmerksamkeit wurde vor allem auf *Monsieur de Pourceaugnac,* eine *comédie-ballet* aus dem Jahre 1669[7], gelenkt, daneben aber auch auf den *Bourgeois gentil-*

---

[4] Weber führt sechs Arbeiten unter dieser Rubrik auf und drei weitere unter der Rubrik „Romania". Darunter befinden sich ein kleines Buch von Francis Claudon (*Hofmannsthal et la France* [Bern: Peter Lang, 1979]) und Aufsätze von Geneviève Bianquis (*Revue de Littérature Comparée* 27 [1953], S. 301-318) und Claude David (*arcadia* 5 [1970], S. 163-175).

[5] Weber führt etwa fünfundziebzig Arbeiten auf. Es bleibt abzuwarten, was in dieser Hinsicht der inzwischen erschienene, von Dirk O. Hoffmann und Willi Schuh betreute *Rosenkavalier*-Band der Kritischen Hofmannsthal-Ausgabe (Bd. XXIII) leistet. Hoffmann erläutert editorische Probleme in einem Beitrag in: *Zeitschrift für Deutsche Philologie* 101 (1983), Beiheft, S. 80-95.

[6] Weber katalogisiert sechs Nummern, darunter Essays von Hilde Burger, Victor Oswald und Helmut Wocke sowie eine Akademie-Rede von Wolfram Mauser. Was Molière und den *Rosenkavalier* angeht, so gibt Leonhard M. Fiedler einen nuancierten Überblick zu Beginn seines Buches: *Hugo von Hofmannsthals Molière-Bearbeitungen: Die Erneuerung der comédie-ballet auf Max Reinhardts Bühnen* (Darmstadt: Agora Verlag, 1974), S. 17-27. Man vergleiche hierzu die sich auf eine geplante, aber nur teilweise ausgeführte Übersetzung des ganzen Molière durch Sternheim und Hofmannsthal beziehenden Briefe, von Fiedler gesammelt und kommentiert in: *Hofmannsthal-Blätter* 4 (1970).

[7] Siehe Hilde Burgers Essay „Hofmannsthal's Debt to Molière: Monsieur de Pourceaugnac and Baron Ochs von Lerchenau". In: *Modern Languages* 39(1958), S. 56-61.

homme[8] und die beiden Stücke, in denen eine Geronte genannte Figur vorkommt[9]. Louvet de Couvrays vierbändiger Roman *Les Amours du Chevalier de Faublas* (1791-1795), die zweite literarische Hauptquelle des *Rosenkavalier*, ist von den Einflußforschern wiederholt aufs Korn genommen worden. Als Vorbild wurde er schon 1911 von einem Kritiker namens Felix Poppenberg gewürdigt[10]. Jedoch nahm die Forschung bisher fast einhellig an, es sei der Roman selbst gewesen, den Hofmannsthal damals zumindest schon ein Jahrzehnt lang kannte[11], der diese frappante Wirkung ausgeübt habe. Zwar liegt eine solche Wirkung auf der Hand und läßt sich relativ leicht dokumentieren;

---

8   Der Text der Tenor-Arie im ersten Akt des *Rosenkavalier* stammt aus dem *Bourgeois gentilhomme*, dem Werk Molières, das bei der Planung und Gestaltung der *Ariadne auf Naxos* eine entscheidende Rolle spielen sollte.

9   Es handelt sich um *Le Medécin malgré lui* und *Les Fourberies de Scapin*. Wie der Name dieser Figur andeutet, handelt es sich bei ihr um einen ausgesprochenen Typencharakter.

10 In einer „Die Ahnen des *Rosenkavalier*" betitelten Rezension in: *Literarisches Echo* 14 (1911), Sp. 1254-1259. Poppenberg weist auch auf den Unterschied zwischen den *Amours du Chevalier de Faublas* und dem weitaus bekannteren Roman von Choderlos de Laclos, den *Liaisons dangereuses*, hin, den Heinrich Mann gerade ins Deutsche übertragen hatte: „Wenn Choderlos de Laclos in seinen *Liaisons dangereuses* der ‚galanten Zeit' einen unerbittlichen Spiegel vorhielt, mittels raffinierter Gefühlschemie Beispiele kaltherziger Freude am Bösen darstellte und virtuos zeigte, wie in dieser Gesellschaft, die sich selbst verbrauchte, nur noch eine mephistophelische Gehirnfreude am Verderben und Zur-Strecke-Bringen unschuldiger Opfer als letzte Sensation übrigblieb, so sehen wir in Louvet de Couvrays *Abenteuern des Chevalier Faublas* das interessante Gegenstück, nämlich die ‚schöne Lüge'" (Sp. 1254). Hilde Burgers Aufsatz „Trois Visages d'un ingenu libertin ou Les Chevaliers sans et avec rose (Louvet de Couvray, Louis Artus et Hofmannsthal)" war mir nur in einer gedruckten Zusammenfassung zugänglich. In: *Australasian Universities Language and Literature Association Proceedings* 14 (1972), S. 140-141. Es handelt sich um einen Kongreß-Beitrag, dessen voller Wortlaut anscheinend nie veröffentlicht wurde.

11 Es gibt mehrere deutsche Fassungen des Romans, deren früheste aus dem Jahre 1837 stammt. Hofmannsthal hatte möglicherweise Zugang zu Franz Bleis Übersetzung in vier Bänden mit Illustrationen von Karl Walser (München: Georg Müller, 1910) und zu Bleis kritischer Einführung in das Werk. Wie ein Brief an Hermann Bahr (*Briefe 1890-1901* (Berlin: S. Fischer, 1935), S. 32f.) beweist, kannte er das französische Original spätestens seit 1891. Im Jahre 1901 erwähnt er Victor Hugos Kenntnis des Romans in seiner *Studie über die Entwicklung des Dichters Victor Hugo*.

doch beschränkt sie sich, wie ein näheres Hinsehen zeigt, vor allem auf einzelne Details[12]. Den eigentlichen Anstoß gab aber eine Bühnenbearbeitung, eine von Louis Artus textierte und von Victor Terrasse komponierte Operette, die am 11. Dezember 1907 in Offenbachs Theater, den Bouffes Parisiennes, Premiere hatte. Dort sah sie Hofmannsthals Freund und Mitarbeiter Harry Graf Kessler[13].

Bei einem Zusammentreffen in Weimar im Februar 1909 muß Kessler dem Dichter den Inhalt von *L'Ingenu libertin ou La Marquise et le marmiton* – so hieß dieses Produkt der leichten Muse – ausführlich erzählt haben. Hierauf bezieht sich Hofmannsthal in einem Brief vom Juli des gleichen Jahres, in dem von einer „Faublas-Operette, die in den ersten Weimarer Stunden uns den Anstoß gegeben hat"[14], die Rede ist. Im gleichen Schreiben teilt er Kessler mit, er habe sich „auch das Textbuch [...] verschafft"[15]. Wie ich im Folgenden zeigen werde, ist die szenische Anordnung des dritten Aktes des *Rosenkavalier*, vor allem die Schluß-Szene, ohne dieses Vorbild nicht zu denken.

Zu jenem Zeitpunkt scheint der Dichter das in Arbeit befindliche Werk als ein – zugegebenermaßen auf höherem Niveau angesiedeltes

---

12 Eine Zusammenstellung der zahlreichen Einzelheiten, die Hofmannsthal den *Amours du Chevalier de Faublas* entnommen haben könnte, wäre in diesem Zusammenhang kaum zweckdienlich. Ich erwähne ein charakteristisches Beispiel. Wenn die Marschallin im *Rosenkavalier* zu Oktavian sagt: „Jedes Ding hat seine Zeit" und dieser erwidert: „Soll das heißen, daß ich Sie nie mehr werde küssen dürfen, bis Ihr der Atem ausgeht", so klingt das wie ein Echo auf folgende Stelle aus Louvet de Couvray (I, 130 in Bleis Übersetzung): „‚Komm jetzt' sagte die Marquise, mich umarmend, ‚ich muß meine Tochter ankleiden.' Ich versuchte, den Augenblick des Rückzugs mit einem letzten Sieg zu bezeichnen. ‚Nein, mein Freund' wehrte sie ab, ‚man darf nichts mißbrauchen'."

13 Kessler, der sich als wahrer Mitarbeiter verstand, war von Hofmannsthals Angebot, ihn als Helfer zu bezeichnen, nicht gerade angetan. Die Briefe, in denen diese Frage behandelt wird, finden sich in dem von Hilde Burger herausgegebenen *Briefwechsel 1898-1929* (Frankfurt: Insel-Verlag, 1968) der beiden. Siehe vor allem S. 296-303.

14 Ebd., S. 253. Die ‚Gattungsbezeichnung' im Untertitel der Operette von Artus und Terrasse lautet *Conte galant en trois actes*. Das Textbuch erschien 1909 in der Pariser Librairie Théâtrale.

15 Brief vom 28. Juli 1909. Ebd., S. 255.

– Pendant zur Pariser Operette verstanden zu haben. Jedenfalls fand er den Text des *Ingenu libertin* „reizend" und bemerkte: „Wenn das meinige im *Ganzen* ebenso gut wird, und dann noch ein kleines darüber hinaus, will ich sehr zufrieden sein." Kessler, der sich vorstellen konnte, daß unter Hofmannsthals Händen das Sujet eine der trivialen und klischeehaften Ausführung durch die französischen Boulevard-Autoren weit überlegene Gestaltung erfahren würde, schmeichelte ihm, indem er schrieb: „Natürlich wird *Quin-Quin* viel besser als der Artus'sche *Faublas*, weil der dichterische ‚Charme', das Individuelle und Seltene deiner Vision hinzukommt", versuchte ihn aber gleichzeitig zu überreden, auch den farcenhaften Zügen von „Molières kleinen Spielen" Beachtung zu schenken[16].

Soweit die französischen Hauptquellen des *Rosenkavalier*. (Eine Nebenquelle wird uns weiter unten kurz beschäftigen.) Wie bekannt sind dies die stärksten literarischen Quader, deren sich Hofmannsthal bei der Errichtung seines Operngebäudes bediente. Die Summe der zu diesem Zweck herbeigeschafften Blöcke ist freilich größer und deren Ursprung keinesfalls rein französisch[17]. Und zusätzlich zur Literatur lieferten auch die Oper (Mozarts *Le nozze di Figaro*[18], Wagners *Tristan und Isolde*[19] und *Die Meistersinger von Nürnberg*[20] sowie Verdis

---

16 Brief vom 3. August 1909. Ebd., S. 258.

17 Auf mögliche Vorbilder in der deutschsprachigen Literatur, vor allem bei Lenau und Fontane, hat Katharina Mommsen in ihrem Buch *Hofmannsthal und Fontane* (Bern: Peter Lang, 1978) hingewiesen, und zwar in den Abschnitten „Lenau in *Graf Petöfy, Arabella* und *Rosenkavalier*" und „*Die Poggenpuhls* im *Rosenkavalier*". Ich komme später auf ihre These zurück.

18 In einem Schreiben an seinen Verleger Otto Fürstner vom 4. Mai 1910 demonstriert Strauss die Übereinstimmung der Tessituren der Marschallin, Oktavians und Sophies mit denen der Gräfin, Cherubinos und Susannas. Siehe: Der Rosenkavalier: Fassungen, Filmszenarium, Briefe, hsg. von Willi Schuh (Frankfurt: S. Fischer, ²1972), S. 265. Und in „Zum Geleit" (*Dramen V*, S. 149) bezeichnet der Dichter einen der Typencharaktere (später Oktavian) als den „Cherubin", während Kessler in einem Brief an den Freund vom 18. Mai 1909 die gleiche Figur als „Cherubin mouillé" charakterisiert.

19 Willi Schuh weist in seinem Aufsatz „Die Entstehung des *Rosenkavalier*" (*Trivium* 9, Nr. 2 [1951], S. 65-91) darauf hin, daß Text und Musik des Anfangs der Oper

Falstaff[21]), die Bildende Kunst und die Geschichtsschreibung – vor allem Graf Khevenhüller-Metschs Memoiren *Aus der Zeit Maria Theresias*[22] – Materialien zur Konstruktion des Operntextes.

Unter den Werken der Bildenden Kunst, deren Hofmannsthal sich freigebig bediente, nimmt Hogarths *Marriage-à-la-Mode*, ein graphischer Zyklus von sechs Darstellungen aus dem Jahre 1744, bekanntlich eine besondere Stellung ein. Bei der Gestaltung des Lever der Marschallin im ersten Akt stand, szenisch gesehen, die vierte Nummer dieser Folge Pate. Das volle Ausmaß der Verschuldung, die indirekt auch Lichtenbergs *Ausführliche Erklärungen der Hogarthschen Kupferstiche* (1798)[23] mit einschließen mag, wurde erst vor relativ kurzer Zeit von Mary E. Gilbert erkannt, die freilich in ihrer Argumentation zu weit geht[24]. Weniger bekannt ist der von Hans Swarowsky erwähnte, auf Hofmannsthals eigener Aussage beruhende Umstand, daß drei Bilder im

> Palais Harrach in Wien, die heute im Stiegenhaus hängen und feierliche Auffahrten des Aloys Thomas Raimund Graf Harrach, Vizekönig von Neapel, von Nicolo Maria Rossi, einem Schüler Solimenas, [darstellen], indirekt am Geschehen des

---

(„Du, du – was heißt das ‚du'? Was ‚du und ich'?") sich direkt auf Wagners Oper beziehen.

20 Hinweise auf die *Meistersinger* finden sich an zahlreichen Stellen im Hofmannsthal/Strauss Briefwechsel. Willi Schuh zufolge erstellt Roland Tenschert sogar ein „Schema der Figuren-Analogien" in seinem Buch *Dreimal sieben Variationen über das Thema Richard Strauss*.

21 Hofmannsthal und Strauss nennen Ochs eine Falstaff-Figur. Eine spezifische Parallele wird uns im zweiten Teil dieser Arbeit beschäftigen.

22 *Aus der Zeit Maria Theresias: Tagebuch des Fürsten Johann Josef Khevenhüller-Metsch,* hsg. Rudolf Graf Khevenhüller-Metsch und Hanns Schütter (Wien: Holzbauer), S. 1907f.

23 Georg Christoph Lichtenberg, *Schriften und Briefe,* hsg. Wolfgang Promies (München: Hanser), III (1972), S. 921-989.

24 „Painter and Poet: Hogarth's *Marriage-à-la-mode* and Hofmannsthal's *Der Rosenkavalier*". In: *Modern Language Review* 64 (1969), S. 818-827. Professor Gilberts Darstellung ist insofern einseitig, als sie sich nur auf Hogarth bezieht und andere Bildquellen außer acht läßt.

zweiten Aktes beteiligt sind, weil sie die von Marianne [Leitmetzerin] aus der Fensternische vermeldete Auffahrt Rofranos in direkter Wiedergabe zeigen[25]. Zusätzlich wies Willi Schuh, *Rosenkavalier*-Spezialist *par excellence*[26], als einer der ersten auf die Rolle hin, die Pierre-Antoine Baudoins berühmt-berüchtigtes Gemälde *Le Coucher de la Mariée*, das heute verschollen und nur auf dem Umweg über zeitgenössische Kupferstiche zugänglich ist[27], in Alfred Rollers Konzeption und Ausführung des Bühnenbildes des ersten Aktes der Oper spielte. Aber selbst dieser feinsinnige Beobachter übersah die ungleich wichtigere Beziehung zwischen diesem Paradebeispiel des erotischen Kitsches aus dem achtzehnten Jahrhundert, das Diderot in seinem *Salon* des Jahres 1767 als „propre au boudoir d'une petite-maîtresse, à la petite maison d'un petit-maître, faites pour de petits abbés, de petits robins, de gros financiers ou autres personnages sans moeurs et d'un petit goût"[28] abkanzelte, und der Oper von Strauss und Hofmannsthal, und zwar auf dem Umweg über den Gebrauch, den Louis Artus im dritten Akt des *Ingenu libertin* von diesem einst als spektakulär geltenden Tableau machte[29].

---

25 Hans Swarowsky in: *Österreichische Musikzeitschrift* 24 (1969), S. 586.

26 *Der Rosenkavalier: Fassungen, Filmszenarium, Briefe*, S. 302f.

27 Zwei Fassungen sind in Emile Daciers Buch *La Gravure en France au XVIIIe siècle: La gravure de genre et de moeurs* (Paris/Brüssel: Van Oest, 1925), Ill. LII und LIII, abgebildet.

28 *Salon de 1767* in: Denis Diderot, *Oeuvres Complètes...*, hsg. Roger Lewinter (Paris: Le Club Français du Livre, 1970), V, S. 225.

29 So wird das Bühnenbild des dritten Aktes des *Ingenu libertin* als „celui du tableau fameux de Baudoin, ‚Le Coucher de la Mariée'" beschrieben; und in der sechsten Szene dieses Aktes (*L'Ingenu libertin*, S. 140) singt Faublas, als die Marquise aus dem Bett steigt: „Cela ressemble, d'un peu loin,/ A la pose refugiée/ Du joli tableau de Baudoin/ Le Coucher de la Mariée". Die Regiebemerkungen hierzu lauten: „*Et, en effet, c'est le tableau célèbre qu'évoquent, en outre du décor, le nègligè de la marquise et l'attitude des personnages, Faublas, un genou à terre, figurant lui-même l'heureux mari.*" Es handelt sich also um eine Art lebendes Bild.

Genau wie Brecht, mit dem er trotz seiner ironisch gefärbten Faszination von dessen dramatischem Erstling *Baal*[30] weder im ästhetischen noch im ideologischen Bereich viel gemein hatte, war Hofmannsthal ein großer Eklektiker, will sagen: ein Autor, dessen wahres Genie und dessen eigentliche Originalität sich vielfach in der Verknüpfung heterogener Teile unterschiedlichster Herkunft zu einem neuen Ganzen manifestierte. Er selbst gestand in einer schwachen Stunde, daß er kein Erfinder von Themen oder Handlungen sei; und Kessler, der auf Anerkennung seiner Verdienste am *Rosenkavalier*, wenn auch höflich und zurückhaltend, pochte, traf ins Schwarze mit dem in einem Brief an den gemeinsamen Freund Eberhard von Bodenhausen enthaltenen Hinweis:

> Du wunderst Dich, daß ich überhaupt auf diese Form der Mitarbeit mit Hofmannsthal eingegangen sei und nicht lieber allein Stücke oder Ballets verfaßt habe. Die Erklärung liegt in einer durchaus klaren Erkenntnis der Grenzen sowohl von Hofmannsthal wie von meiner dichterischen Begabung. Hofmannsthal fehlt ganz genau das zu einem dramatischen Dichter, was ich besitze, und umgekehrt, Hofmannsthal hat gar kein konstruktives Talent sogar zur Auswicklung und dramatisch-wirksamen Ordnung eines schon gegebenen Stoffes; deshalb hat er sich immer, außer in bloß lyrischen Dramen, an vorhandene Szenarien angelehnt[31].

So geartete Dichter sind ein ideales Objekt für komparatistische Forschung, die sich zunächst einmal darum kümmert, daß das Fremde in einem Werk als solches erkannt wird, darüber hinaus aber bemüht sein muß aufzuzeigen, ob und inwieweit es verarbeitet, also zum Eigenen geworden ist; denn eine *creatio ex nihilo* ist unvorstellbar. Hofmannsthal war ein Zauberkünstler, der Ingredienzien unterschiedlichster Herkunft so subtil vermischen und mit eigenen Zutaten durchsetzen konnte, daß das Endprodukt seiner Bemühungen den arglosen, weil

---

30 „Das Theater des Neuen", ursprünglich erschienen in: *Neue Freie Presse*, wiederabgedruckt in: *Lustspiele IV*, hsg. Herbert Steiner (Frankfurt: S. Fischer, 1956), S. 407-425.

31 Im gleichen Brief behauptet Kessler: „Von einem bloßen Umarbeiten, Korrigieren oder Beraten kann gar keine Rede sein, da schon das Thema des Stückes zur Hälfte von mir stammt, nämlich die Idee der Verkleidung und die Figur des Quinquin, des Rosenkavaliers selber." Eberhard von Bodenhausen/Harry Graf Kessler: *Ein Briefwechsel 1894-1918*, hsg. Hans-Ulrich Simon (Marbach: Deutsches Literaturarchiv, 1978), S. 92.

uneingeweihten Rezipienten wie ein auf heimischem Boden gewachsener Organismus anmutet. Und da er sich bei seinen Anleihen keineswegs auf die Literatur beschränkte, sondern die anderen Künste immer mit in Betracht zog, schuf er Gesamtkunstwerke, denen nur Gesamtinterpreten gewachsen sind.

Was den Text des *Rosenkavalier* anbetrifft, so wird es vor allem meine Aufgabe sein zu zeigen, mit welchen Mitteln, in welchem Umfang, mit welcher Absicht und mit welcher Wirkung Elemente der französischen Literatur und Kunst in ihn eingebettet wurden. Der Ordnung halber und im Hinblick auf die mit der Materie nicht vertrauten Leser sei zunächst kurz auf die Entstehungsgeschichte des Librettos eingegangen bzw. auf diejenigen Aspekte der Genese, die für unsere spezifische Fragestellung von Belang sind.

Die genaue Abfolge der Ereignisse im Anfangsstadium der gemeinsamen Arbeit Kesslers und Hofmannsthals läßt sich nur in groben Zügen ausmachen, da wir uns gänzlich auf die sich zum Teil widersprechenden Aussagen der Hauptbeteiligten stützen müssen. Dabei werden wir den schriftlichen Dokumenten, die den Schaffensprozeß unmittelbar widerspiegeln, natürlich größeres Gewicht beimessen als späteren, unter Umständen mehr oder minder leicht frisierten Aussagen. Denn im Nachhinein war Hofmannsthal zusehends darauf bedacht, Kesslers Anteil, wie er meinte, ins rechte Licht zu rücken, d. h. im Grunde zu verkleinern, wobei zuzugeben ist, daß, sobald das Wort zum Zuge kam, der Dichter unverwechselbar in seinem eigenen Element war. Wie Dirk O. Hoffmann es treffend ausdrückt,

> verkannte Kessler leider, daß das Wesen des *Rosenkavalier* sich während der Niederschrift grundlegend geändert hatte – und damit auch sein Anteil. Während der Weimarer Tage [...] war es sicherlich mehr als eine Höflichkeitsfloskel, wenn Hofmannsthal ihm sagte, daß er ‚eigentlich als Verfasser des Stückes auf dem Titelblatt stehen' müsse. Doch anderthalb Jahre später [...] traf dies nicht mehr zu. Jetzt beruhte die ‚Substanz' des *Rosenkavalier* nicht mehr, oder nicht in erster Linie, auf der von Kessler in den Vordergrund gerückten gemeinsamen Ausarbeitung des Pantomimischen[32].

---

[32] „Zu Harry Graf Kesslers Mitarbeit am *Rosenkavalier*". In: *Hofmannsthal-Blätter* Nos. 21-22 (1979), S. 158.

Wenn man außerdem bedenkt, daß, sobald Richard Strauss in Erscheinung trat und seine eigenen, Dramaturgie und Text mit einbeziehenden Ansprüche anmeldete, der Anteil Kesslers proportional weiter sank, so wird man zugeben müssen, daß Hofmannsthal im Grunde recht hatte, seinem Freund das Attribut „Mitverfasser" vorzuenthalten. Aber trotzdem darf nicht vergessen werden, daß Kessler auch im späteren Stadium der Textzubereitung sich keineswegs mit der passiven Rolle eines bloßen Beobachters zufrieden gab, sondern als akribischer Kommentator fungierte, dem es von Fall zu Fall gelang, den Dichter von der Treffsicherheit seiner Kritik an der Gestaltung einzelner Charaktere zu überzeugen und Modifikationen zu erzwingen[33].

Wie die von Willi Schuh in dem vor über zwei Jahrzehnten im Fischer-Verlag publizierten *Rosenkavalier-Buch* gesammelten Dokumente bezeugen, erarbeiteten Hofmannsthal und Kessler gemeinsam das Szenarium eines ursprünglich als *comèdie-ballet* konzipierten Stückes[34]. Hofmannsthal hatte Strauss, der von todernsten Stoffen, wie sie *Salome* und *Elektra* behandeln, die Nase voll hatte und nichts so sehr ersehnte wie eine Art Fortsetzung der *Meistersinger*, einen auf einer für Max Reinhardt in Arbeit befindlichen Komödie beruhenden Operntext versprochen. Der Plan zerschlug sich aber, als der Dichter erkannte, daß das Werk – es handelt sich um *Christinas Heimreise*, zu der ein weiteres erotisches Werk des achtzehnten Jahrhunderts, Ca-

---

33 Siehe vor allem den Briefwechsel Kessler/Hofmannsthal, S. 222-254.

34 „Auf- und abgehend arbeiteten wir vormittags drei bis vier Stunden an dem Szenario; abwechselnd trug jeder von uns eine Idee dazu bei, so daß es heute ausgeschlossen wäre herauszufinden, bei welchem von uns beiden jede Idee ihren Ursprung nahm" schrieb Kessler am 10. Februar 1909 an seine Schwester. Und Hofmannsthal teilte Strauss am 11. Februar mit: „Ich [sic] habe hier in drei ruhigen Nachmittagen ein komplettes, ganz frisches Szenar einer Spieloper gemacht, mit drastischer Komik in den Gestalten und Situationen, bunter und fast pantomimisch durchsichtiger Handlung, Gelegenheit für Lyrik, Scherz und Humor und sogar für ein kleines Ballett. Ich finde das Szenarium reizend, und Graf Kessler, mit dem ich es durchsprach, ist entzückt davon." *Briefwechsel*, hsg. Franz und Alice Strauss (Zürich: Atlantis, 1952), S. 47.

sanovas Memoiren, den Stoff geliefert hatte – auf die Sprechbühne gehörte und nicht auf die Opernbühne transponiert werden konnte.

So war alles in der Schwebe, als Kessler, der oft in Frankreich war und dort viel mit Künstlern verkehrte, den Freund auf ein frivoles Singspiel aufmerksam machte, das er in Paris gesehen hatte. Ihre Phantasie entzündete sich sofort, und in drei Tagen intensiver Arbeit erstellten die Freunde das pantomimische Gerüst einer *satura* aus zwei Hauptbestandteilen, dem von Kessler eingebrachten *Ingenu libertin* und dem von Hofmannsthal ergänzend beigebrachten *Monsieur de Pourceaugnac*. Nach ihrer vermischenden Aufbereitung wurden diese Ingredienzien vom Dichter mit einer dicken österreichisch-ungarischen Soße übergossen, die dem kulinarischen Leckerbissen sein Aroma und damit sein eigentliches Gepräge gibt.

Die Skizze, die Kessler und Hofmannsthal zwischen dem 8. und 10. Februar 1909 entwarfen, muß mit dem sogenannten Zweiten Entwurf, der erst 1976 ans Tageslicht kam, identisch sein[35]. Es ist daher unwahrscheinlich, daß der Dichter, als er am 13. Februar nach Berlin fuhr, um das Projekt mit Strauss zu besprechen, dieses Dokument zurückließ und, wie er in dem 1927 verfaßten Aufsatz „Zum Geleit" behauptet, „ohne eine Notiz als das Personenverzeichnis auf die Rückseite einer Tischkarte gekritzelt, aber mit einer erzählbaren Handlung im Kopf"[36] in der Reichshauptstadt anlangte. Hofmannsthal korrigierte also höchstwahrscheinlich die Geschichte.

Ob Hofmannsthal mit „Personenverzeichnis" ein individualisiertes Instrumentarium von *dramatis personae* oder eine Liste von Typen-Charakteren meinte, läßt sich nicht mit Sicherheit ausmachen; denn obgleich sowohl der Erste[37] als auch der Zweite Entwurf den einzelnen Handlungsträgern konkrete Namen zuerkennt, scheint es eine Vorstufe gegeben zu haben, auf der dies noch nicht der Fall war. Hofmannsthal berichtet nämlich in „Zum Geleit":

---

35 Abgedruckt in *Dramen V*, S. 111-116.
36 Ebd., S. 149.
37 1951 veröffentlicht. Abgedruckt *in Dramen V*, S. 110.

> Die Gestalten waren da und agierten vor uns, noch ehe wir Namen für sie hatten: der Buffo (= Ochs), der Alte (= Faninal), die Junge (= Sophie), die Dame (= Marschallin), der Cherubin (= Oktavian). Es waren Typen, die zu individualisieren der ausführenden Feder vorbehalten blieb. Aus dem ewig typischen Verhältnis der Figuren zueinander entsprang die Handlung, fast ohne daß man wußte wie[38].

Wie die Phrase „ohne daß man wußte wie" beweist, bestand bei Hofmannsthal, wenigstens in diesem Fall, die Tendenz, dem Schaffensvorgang einen mystischen Anstrich zu geben[39].

Der erste greifbare Text zum *Rosenkavalier*, dessen Thema Kessler (auf Englisch) mit den Worten „two antithetic characters playing around a woman"[40] und sein Partner mit dem Satz „Ein dicker, älterer, anmaßender Freier, vom Vater begünstigt, wird von einem hübschen jungen ausgestochen"[41] umschrieb, ist jedenfalls ein durch stenographische Kürze gekennzeichneter Abriß, der in drei Abschnitten, die jeweils einem Akt entsprechen, die Handlung des geplanten Stücks zusammenfaßt. Aber hier erscheinen die Akte noch nicht in der gewohnten Reihenfolge, sondern der erste Akt schließt sich dem zweiten an. In ihrer Urform beginnt also die Oper nicht mit dem doppelten Lever der Marschallin, sondern mit der Szene im Haus Gerontes, in der die Rosen-Zeremonie, das Mittelstück in der endgültigen Fassung, ausgespart bleibt[42]. In diesem Kontext ist das Lever gleichsam die Endphase des „Stelldicheins für die Nacht", das die Marquise dem Faublas anbietet und zu dem dieser sich einstellt, obwohl er, der sich

---

38 Ebd., S. 149.

39 Es scheint symptomatisch für Hofmannsthal, daß er in seinen Briefen an Strauss keine anderen literarischen Vorbildern als Molière erwähnt. Und Kesslers Bemerkung in einem Brief vom 18. Mai 1909 nach zu urteilen („Eine famose Erfindung sind die drei adeligen Waisen und der Friseur; ferner die Szene mit dem Sänger; auch der kleine Mohr, der die Schokolade bringt"), scheint der Dichter seinem engsten Mitarbeiter auch das Modell, das Hogarths Kupferstiche lieferten, vorenthalten zu haben.

40 Kessler an seine Schwester am 21. Februar 1909.

41 Hofmannsthal an Strauss am 12. Mai 1909.

42 Dieses Mittelstück fehlt auch im Szenarium. Im Ersten Entwurf wird die Lücke durch die Ankunft Pourceaugnacs mit „2 ältlichen Tanten, Tieren und sonderbarem Gepäck" gefüllt, während die Szene im Szenarium („Entree F[aublas] mit Läufern und Negern [...] 3 Stühle gerückt. Sie freut sich auf die Ehe [...]") völlig fehlt.

gerade erst in Sophie verliebt hat, „nicht so rückhaltlos erfreut" über diese Entwicklung ist[43].

Wie läßt sich Hofmannsthals (und Kesslers?) Sinnesänderung in Hinsicht auf die Verteilung der Akte erklären? Und hängen die möglichen Erklärungen irgendwie mit der Notwendigkeit, die verschiedenen Quellen miteinander in Einklang zu bringen, zusammen? Mary E. Gilbert zum Beispiel vertritt die Ansicht, die ursprüngliche Reihenfolge der Haupteinheiten des *Rosenkavalier* gehe auf Hogarth und seine *Marriage-à-la-Mode* zurück und entspreche den auf dem ersten (Unterzeichnung des Heiratskontrakts), vierten (Lever) und fünften (Bagno-Szene) dargestellten Ereignissen[44]. Ohne zu leugnen, daß dies im Bereich des Möglichen liegt, möchte ich anführen, daß die ursprüngliche Lösung des dramaturgischen Problems dem Roman Louvet de Couvrays und damit auch der Operette von Artus und Terrasse näher stand, weil dort bei der Begegnung mit der Marschallin die Bekanntschaft Faublas' mit Sophie vorausgesetzt wird und handlungsbildend ist. (Wäre Hofmannsthal dem Modell des Romans treugeblieben, so hätte er die Oper mit einer Szene im Kloster, in dem Sophie erzogen wird und wo sie Faublas durch seine Schwester kennenlernt, beginnen lassen müssen – eine Lösung, die ihm selbst wohl kaum behagte und die, auch wenn er sie angestrebt hätte, gewiß auf heftigen Widerstand von Seiten des Komponisten gestoßen wäre. So verlegte er die Begegnung kurzerhand in den Salon[45].)

Die Vertauschung der beiden ersten Akte, für die sich Hofmannsthal letztendlich entschied, hatte zur Folge, daß die Frivolität, die sowohl den Roman Louvet de Couvrays als auch dessen theatralischen Ableger kennzeichnet, auf ein Mindestmaß reduziert und somit das

---

43 *Dramen V*, S. 110.
44 Mary E. Gilbert (Anmerkung 24), S. 820ff.
45 Im *Rosenkavalier*, wo bekanntlich die Begegnung des Liebhabers mit der älteren Frau der mit dem jüngeren Mädchen vorausgeht, spiegelt sich die klösterliche Erziehung Sophies in ihrer klischierten Sprache. Hofmannsthal legte großen Wert auf diesen Charakterzug und nannte Faninals Tochter in einem Brief an Strauss von 12. Juli 1910 „ein hübsches gutes Dutzendmädchen".

Niveau der Opernhandlung stark angehoben wird. Im *Rosenkavalier*, wie wir ihn kennen und lieben, ist das Verhältnis des Jünglings mit der reiferen Frau nicht mehr ein Aufbegehren frustrierter körperlicher Liebe wie in den *Amours du Chevalier de Faublas* oder ein durch die Aufstachelung eines Dritten zustandegekommener Racheakt wie im *Ingenu libertin*, sondern das eher spontane Zusammenfinden zweier Liebesbedürftiger. Die ‚Verführung' wird nicht als Prozeß vor Augen gestellt, sondern ist eine Tatsache, mit der wir uns abfinden müssen. Auch wirkt, stärker noch als bei den Vorbildern, Oktavians Hinwendung zu Sophie natürlich; und die Marschallin ist keine Circe mehr, die Männer, figürlich gesprochen, in Schweine verwandelt[46], sondern eine eher mütterliche Geliebte, die das Herz auf dem rechten Fleck hat. Was den ältlichen Freier angeht, so ist aus dem passiven und pathetischen[47] Möchtegern ein zwar komischer, aber doch irgendwie respektabler Gegenspieler in der Intrige geworden.

Soweit die Charaktere. Deren Namen, die zunächst durchweg denen ihrer französischen Vorgänger entsprachen, änderten sich von Stufe zu Stufe. Im Ersten Entwurf heißen die Figuren Faublas, Sophie, Marquise (aus Louvet de Couvray), Pourceaugnac und Geronte (aus Molière). Auch der Zweite Entwurf verwendet diese Bezeichnungen; doch in den Zusätzen treten sie bereits als Baron – noch nicht Ochs –, Oktavian und Marschallin auf, während Geronte sich namensmäßig treu bleibt. Den Namen Sophies zu ändern war nicht notwendig, weil er kosmopolitisch und sozusagen aller Welt geläufig ist[48]. Die von ihren Vorbildern gelösten Namen der ‚Fassung letzter Hand' des *Rosenkavalier* hingegen verraten auf den ersten Blick kaum das Geheimnis ihres Ursprungs. So wurden der der Marschallin (Maria-Theresia

---

46 In deutschen Fassungen des Stücks erscheint Pourceaugnac als Schweinfeld oder Schweinichen.
47 *Pathos* bedeutet Leiden, also ein passives Verhalten. Pourceaugnac ist pathetisch im komischen Sinn, weil er eine Zielscheibe des Spottes ist.
48 Der Name ist insofern ironisch, weil er Weisheit bedeutet, die von einem „Dutzendmädchen" kaum zu erwarten ist.

Fürstin Werdenberg) und der Oktavians (Maria Ehrenreich Bonaventura Fernand Hyazinth Rofrano) aus Khevenhüller-Metsch entlehnt[49], und der des Barons erweist sich als zweckdienliche Transposition aus dem Schweinischen Molières in das Rindische der prätendierten Zeus-Figur[50].

Wie viele Bearbeiter liebte es Hofmannsthal, die Spuren seiner Arbeit zu verwischen und überließ es den Spürhunden unter den Kennern seines Werkes, sie aufzudecken. Im *Rosenkavalier* dehnte er dieses Versteckspiel auch auf manche Nebenfiguren aus. Wer unter den unbeleckten Lesern oder Zuschauern würde z. B. vermuten, daß die zwei Intriganten Valzacchi und Annina gleichfalls dem *Monsieur de Pourceaugnac* entstammen, wo sie thematisch und linguistisch das verdächtige italienische Element repräsentieren. Ihre direkten Vorfahren sind der neapolitanische ‚homme d'intrigue' Sbrigani[51] und Nerine, eine ‚femme d'intrigue' französischer Herkunft. Und der allerdings nicht ausdrücklich als Italiener bezeichnete Sänger, dessen Muttersprache nicht auszumachen ist, da er kein Wort *spricht* – Lichtenberg identifiziert die Hogarthsche Figur, die hier Modell stand, als den Kastraten Carestini –, verwendet in seiner Arie den Text eines *air* aus

---

49 Sophie zitiert Oktavians Namen *(Dramen V, S. 49)* mit dem naiven Ausruf: „Ich weiß, wie alt Euer Liebden sind:/ Siebzehn Jahr' und zwei Monat'. Ich weiß alle Ihre Taufnamen..."

50 In seiner „Katalog-Arie" *(Dramen V, S. 26f.)* enthüllt Ochs seinen Wunsch, wie Zeus zu sein („Wollt' ich könnt' sein wie Jupiter selig/ in tausend Gestalten,/ wär' Verwendung für jede"), wozu die Marschallin ironisch bemerkt: „Wie, auch für den Stier? So grob will Er sein?"). Die Mythologie will es bekanntlich, daß Zeus als Stier sich der Io nahte und Europa auf seinem Rücken forttrug. Mary E. Gilbert (Anmerkung 24, S. 823) weist ferner darauf hin, daß Correggios „Io" eines der im vierten Stich der Hogarthschen Folge sichtbaren Bilder ist und daß Hofmannsthal in einer handschriftlichen Skizze ausdrücklich auf dieses Vorbild hinwies. (Die Skizze ist im Faksimile reproduziert im Katalog der von Fritz Hadamovsky arrangierten Hofmannsthal-Ausstellung des Österreichischen Kultur-Instituts in London [1961]).

51 Wie der Herausgeber von Molières *OEuvres Complètes* (Paris: Bibliothèque de la Pléiade, 1959), II, S. 272, anmerkt, ist Sbrigani „un nom forgé par Molière sur l'italien sbricco (= fripon)".

dem Ballet des Nations, mit dem der *Bourgeois gentilhomme* schließt[52].

In einem ziemlich locker gefügten Essay über den *Rosenkavalier* hat der als Thematologe bekannte österreichische Germanist Robert Mühlher überdies auf einige Parallelen zwischen den beiden Liebespaaren – Eraste/Julie, Oktavian/Sophie – aufmerksam gemacht[53], die sich gleichfalls in die Debatte einbringen ließen, wobei die Unterschiede allerdings überwiegen. Eraste, das Haupt der Verschwörung gegen den unliebsamen Eindringling Pourceaugnac, hält nämlich von Anfang an alle Fäden in der Hand, während der lebensunerfahrene Oktavian nur, wenn auch sehr gut, eine Rolle spielt, die ihm aufgedrungen wird. Und während Julie, sobald sie Lunte riecht, den ihr zugedachten Part mit großem Geschick zu spielen weiß[54], ist Sophies Aufbegehren ihrem Vater gegenüber ein spontaner Akt der Selbstfindung und -bestätigung[55], bei dem Molière freilich Pate stand.

In der Regel üben Einflüsse zu Beginn eines Umsetzungs-Prozesses die größte Wirkung aus und schwächen sich in dessen Verlauf zusehends ab, sofern kein neuer Impuls aus der gleichen – oder einer anderen – Richtung erfolgt. *Der Rosenkavalier* bietet ein klassisches Beispiel des Verfahrens, bei dem eine allmähliche Absorption erfolgt und die zunächst getreulich abgespiegelten Personen des Modells zusehends mit den für den beeinflußten Dichter charakteristischen Zügen begabt werden, die sie, in diesem Fall, ästhetisch gesehen weit über ihre Vorbilder erheben. Bei Hofmannsthal, dessen lyrische Ader und psychologische Finesse von jeher Bewunderung erregten, erwer-

---

52 Ebd. II, S. 589f. Im *Rosenkavalier* ersetzt natürlich Straussens Musik diejenige Lullys. Straussens Suite *Der Bürger als Edelmann*, in der Lullys Musik Verwendung findet, gehört zu seinen häufig gespielten Kompositionen.

53 „Hugo von Hofmannsthal: Die ‚Komödie für Musik' *Der Rosenkavalier*" in: *Österreichische Dichter seit Grillparzer: Gesammelte Aufsätze* (Wien: Braumüller, 1973), S. 321-338.

54 Zweiter Akt, sechste Szene. *OEuvres Complètes* II, S. 443f.

55 Der Zusammenhang ist jedoch auch insofern ein anderer, als hier die Geliebte ihrem Liebhaber, und nicht ihrem Vater, damit droht, ins Kloster zu gehen.

ben sie, wenn auch in unterschiedlichem Maße, geistige und gefühlshafte Eigenschaften, die ihnen bei Molière und Louvet de Couvray abgehen. Ochs wird leicht veredelt, indem einige Charakteristika Don Juans auf ihn übertragen werden; Oktavian ist mehr als ein abenteuernder Galant; und Sophie, die man sich kaum im *travesti* vorstellen kann, ist trotz ihrer von Hofmannsthal ausdrücklich bestätigten Naivität weitaus liebenswerter als ihre Namens-Base.

Keine der Figuren des *Rosenkavalier* hat soviel Noblesse wie die Marschallin, die, obwohl sie nur sieben Jahre älter ist als die Marquise in den *Amours du Chevalier de Faublas*[56], sie an Reife weit überragt. Hofmannsthals Briefe spiegeln getreu des Dichters steigendes Bedürfnis zu solcher Aufwertung. Im endgültigen Text erhellt die neue Dimension der Figur, die sogar zu einer psychoanalytischen Untersuchung Anlaß bot[57], aus ihren philosophischen Betrachtungen. Strukturell gesehen wurde die anfangs schwache Position der Marschallin während der Arbeit am Libretto zusehends verstärkt und ihre Abwesenheit im zweiten Akt durch die *acte de présence* im dritten reichlich wettgemacht. Während im ersten Entwurf ihre Rolle im Schlußakt sich darauf beschränkt zu bestätigen, daß der verkleidete Faublas kein Mädchen ist („Faublas' Stiefel unterm Kleid. Geronte kompromittiert vor der Hofgesellschaft. Faublas im Travesti meldet sich. Marquise bestätigt, daß er ein Mann."[58]), nähert sich das Szenarium der Schlußfassung, indem sich die Marquise, wenngleich mit einem Anflug von Sarkasmus, dem Unvermeidlichen beugt („*Geronte verzweifelt, will Sophie in ein Kloster geben. Faublas erbleicht. Marquise spöttisch:*

---

56 Strauss charakterisierte die Marschallin im nachhinein (*Erinnerungen an die ersten Aufführungen meiner Opern* [1942]) als eine „schöne junge Frau von höchstens 32 Jahren". Seinen Ochs stellte er sich ähnlich vor, nämlich als eine „ländliche Don-Juan-Schönheit von etwa 35 Jahren" (ebd.), d. h. als erheblich jünger als Boito-Verdis *vecchio John*.

57 Peter A. Martin, „A Psychoanalytic Study of the Marschallin from *Der Rosenkavalier*". In: *Journal of the American Psychoanalytic Association* 14 (1966), S. 760-784. Ich persönlich finde es absurd, eine fiktive Figur auf die Couch zu legen, ohne daß man ihrem Erfinder die gleiche Behandlung zukommen läßt.

58 *Dramen V*, S. 110.

,Wollen Sie sie vielleicht heiraten?' *Faublas:* ,Darf ich?' *Marquise:* ,Es kommt ja doch so.' *Gibt Geronte die Hand. Die Liebenden allein.*"[59]) In den Zusätzen zum Zweiten Entwurf erfolgt die Hinwendung zu Nostalgie und Resignation in einer letzten Begegnung mit Oktavian, nachdem Sophie abgegangen ist:

> *Marschallin durchschaut die Situation. Sophie ab zum Vater.*
> Marschallin: Schon gestern, wie du bei mir warst,
>   hab' ich gewußt, wieviel's geschlagen hat.
> Octavian: Deswegen hast du mich nicht geküßt.
> Marschallin: Heirat' sie doch, bist ihr's schuldig.
>   Euch Männern wird sowas leicht.[60]

Im komponierten Text ist es, wie wir wissen, die Marschallin, welche abgeht und die jungen Liebenden allein zurückläßt.

II.

Der zweite Teil meiner Ausführungen, in dessen Mittelpunkt Hofmannsthals Verschuldung an die Artus'sche Bühnen-Bearbeitung des Romans von Louvet de Couvray stehen wird, ist als Nachvollzug der Handlung des *Rosenkavalier* unter Betonung der in diesem Werk enthaltenen und in dasselbe eingearbeiteten Fremdkörper konzipiert. *To begin with the beginning*: Die erste Szene des ersten Aktes erinnert stark an den Anfang des dritten Aufzugs von *L'Ingenu libertin* und ist sicher von diesem abgeleitet, ohne daß ein Rückgriff auf den Roman erfolgt wäre. Schon vom Bühnenbild her drängt sich ein anderes Vorbild auf, nämlich das schon erwähnte Bild von Baudoin[61]. Die Ähn-

---

59 Ebd., S. 116.

60 Ebd., als „spätere Ergänzung" bezeichnet.

61 Mary E. Gilbert (Anmerkung 24, S. 821) weist darauf hin, daß „in the first draft of *Der Rosenkavalier* Hofmannsthal describes as part of the scenery of the act the bed which the lovers have only just left as ,großes zeltförmiges Himmelbett oben zusammengehalten von einer Krone und Straußenfedern'". Sie erkennt, daß die Krone „is plainly visible in Hogarth's picture". Aber wie Willi Schuh im *Rosenkavalier*-Buch (Anmerkung 26, S. 303) mitteilt, stammen die Straußenfedern aus dem Bilde Baudoins. (Ich verweise erneut auf den in Anmerkung 27 erwähnten Katalog der Londoner Ausstellung und die darin faksimilierte Skizze.) Im Roman (*Les Amours du Chevalier de Faublas*, hsg. Michel Crouzet [Paris: Bibliothèque 10/19, 1966, S. 71]) lautet die entsprechende Stelle:

lichkeit der Regiebemerkungen ist so frappant, daß eine kausale Beziehung anzunehmen ist. In der Druckfassung des *Ingenu libertin* heißt es:

> Le décor est celui du tableau fameux de Baudoin „Le Coucher de la Mariée". Au fond un grand lit, de riche décoration Louis XV. A gauche et au fond une porte derrière un paravent. A droite, premier plan, une autre porte. Siège et table à coiffure de style exact.
> Quand le rideau se lève, la marquise dort encore, derrière les courtines closes. Faublas, qui vient de sortir du lit, est dans sa petite culotte et chemisette de cavalier. Sa robe de nuit est sur un meuble. Avec des airs las, devant la glace de la table à coiffer, il s'arrange un peu. Ensuite il s'approche du lit et ouvre les rideaux. La marquise sommeille encore, sa jolie tête abandonnée sur l'oreiller, une main hors du lit. Faublas, un genou à terre, s'empare de cette main qu'il couvre de baisers. (S. 125)

Und bei Hofmannsthal liest man:

> Das Schlafzimmer der Feldmarschallin. Links im Alkoven das große zeltförmige Himmelbett. Neben dem Bett ein dreiteiliger chinesischer Wandschirm, hinter dem Kleider liegen. Ferner ein kleines Tischchen und ein paar Sitzmöbel. Auf einem kleinen Sofa links liegt ein Degen in der Scheide. Rechts große Flügeltüren in das Vorzimmer. In der Mitte kaum sichtbare kleine Tür in die Wand eingelassen. Sonst keine Türen. Zwischen dem Alkoven und der kleinen Türe stehen ein Frisiertisch und ein paar Armsessel an der Wand. Die Vorhänge des Bettes sind zurückgeschlagen. Oktavian kniet auf einem Schemel vor dem Bett und hält die Feldmarschallin, die im Bett liegt, halb umschlungen. Man sieht ihr Gesicht nicht, sondern nur ihre sehr schöne Hand und den Arm, von dem das Spitzenhemd abfällt.

Um wenigstens den Schein des Anstands zu wahren – wie sich sehr bald herausstellen sollte, bei weitem nicht genug, um die moralischen

---

> Je ne tardai pas à m'endormir profondément. Quand je me réveillai le jour pénétrait dans l'appartement, malgré les rideaux. Je songeai à mon père. [...] hélas! Je me souviens de ma Sophie. Une larme s'échappa de mes yeux; la marquise s'en aperçut. Déjà capable de quelque dissimulation, j'attribuai au chagrin de la quitter la pénible agitation que j'éprouvais; elle m'embrassa tendrement. Je la vis si belle! L'occasion était si pressante! Quelques heures de sommeil m'avaient ranimé mes forces [...] L'ivresse du plaisir dissipa les remords de l'amour.
> Il faut enfin songer à nous séparer. La marquise me servit de femme de chambre; elle était si adroite que ma toilette eu bientôt fait, si nous avions pu sauver les distractions. Quand nous crûmes qu'il ne manquait plus rien à mon ajustement, la marquise sonna ses femmes. Le Marquis attendait depuis plus d'une heure qu'il fit jour chez madame.

Bedenken von Sängerinnen und Intendanten zu zerstreuen[62] –, brachte Hofmannsthal einige Veränderungen an, und zwar in der Weise, daß die Marschallin in den Aufführungen, denen wir beiwohnen, beim Aufgehen des Vorhangs nicht länger schläft und Oktavian bereits völlig angezogen ist. (Analog zu einer Regiebemerkung bei Artus [„Dans la coulisse, on entend comme un grand murmure voluptueux, encourageant les amours de Faublas et de la marquise"[63]], die ihm ganz sicher unbekannt war, bediente sich Strauss in der Ouvertüre zum *Rosenkavalier* übrigens der Musik als Klangkulisse für das „verliebte Geschäft".) In beiden Fällen kniet der Liebhaber vor dem Bett, und der Blick richtet sich auf die schöne Hand seiner Maîtresse.

Die teilweise Deckungsgleichheit der beiden Texte endet bezeichnenderweise nicht an diesem Punkt, sondern erstreckt sich darüber hinaus bis über den Beginn des Dialogs, welcher aufgrund des gattungsspezifischen Unterschieds im *Ingenu libertin* in der Form eines Duetts erfolgt. Bei Artus singt Faublas vor dem Erwachen der Marquise zwei Strophen und diese selbst die restlichen zwei, während die entsprechende Stelle im *Rosenkavalier* rezitativisch gehalten ist, also handlungsmäßig gewichtiger anmutet. Beiden Paaren ist nicht nur das Bedauern über die Kürze der Nacht eigen – dem „Il est vrai que cette nuit fut trop courte. Mais voici, maintenant, qu'il fait grand jour" der Marquise (S. 127) entspricht Oktavians „Warum ist Tag? Ich will nicht den Tag! Für was ist der Tag! Da haben Dich alle!" –, sondern

---

62 Hofmannsthal und Strauss mußten sich viel mit der ‚Zensur' herumplagen – in diesem Falle mit der des Intendanten der Sächsischen Staatsoper, Graf Seebach. Wie der folgende Passus aus einem Brief des Dichters an den Komponisten vom 12. Juli 1910 beweist, beugte sich Hofmannsthal der Stimme des Volkes: „Die Einwendungen Graf Seebachs scheinen mir beachtenswert. Denn was ihn so choquiert, wird auch andere choquieren (nicht bloß in Hoftheatern), und wozu sich vor ein Teil des Publikums überflüssigerweise entfremden? Also [...] daß die Marschallin schon außer Bett ist ja mit Roller (bezüglich Regiebuch und Dekoration) schon längst fixiert."

63 *L'Ingenu libertin*, S. 124. Dies ist also das eigentliche coucher, während das, was sich in der Pause zwischen dem zweiten und dritten Akt abspielt, die Liebesnacht ist, welche Strauss in der Ouvertüre darstellt. Und der dritte Akt repräsentiert, wie Faublas selbst erklärt, „le lever de la Marquise" (S. 141).

Die französischen Quellen des Rosenkavalier 125

auch die Furcht vor dem Ertapptwerden. „Qu'avez-vous, charmant enfant, et pourquoi n'est-ce pas, seulement, de la joie que je lis sur votre visage?" fragt die Marquise, und Faublas erwidert: „C'est que je tremble, madame, que tout ne soit bientôt découvert, et que le marquis [...]" (S. 126). Und seine Befürchtungen finden ein Echo in Hofmannsthals Text, wo der Feldmarschall, der sich gegenwärtig „im Raitzenland,/ noch hinterwärts von Esseg" auf der Jagd befindet, in den Alpträumen seiner Frau unvermutet seine Aufwartung macht.

Auf die schon erwähnte Abhängigkeit des öffentlichen Levers im Zenith des ersten Aktes vom vierten Stich aus Hogarths *Marriage-à-la-Mode* soll hier nicht eingegangen werden, da es sich um sattsam bekannte, auf der Hand liegende und oft detaillierte Übereinstimmungen handelt. Beachtung verdient andererseits das Vorliegen eines französischen Modells innerhalb des Schlußteils dieses Aktes, der mit der brüsken Verabschiedung der „bagagi"[64] einsetzt. Die Marschallin bleibt allein zurück und sinnt nostalgisch über „die Schwäche von allem Zeitlichen" (S. 40) nach. Ihr, den theatralischen Gepflogenheiten Rechnung tragend, nach außen projizierter und in Worte umgesetzter innerer Monolog, der später von Oktavian-Mariandl parodiert wird[65], lautet an der Kernstelle:

> Die Zeit, die ist ein sonderbar Ding.
> Wenn man so hinlebt, ist sie rein gar nichts.
> Aber dann auf einmal.
> Da spürt man nichts als sie:
> Sie ist um uns herum, sie ist auch in uns drinnen.
> In den Gesichtern rieselt sie, im Spiegel da rieselt sie.
> In meinen Schläfen fließt sie.
> Und zwischen dir und mir da fließt sie wieder,
> Lautlos wie eine Sanduhr. [...]
> Manchmal hör' ich sie fließen unaufhaltsam,

---

64 In ihrem in Anmerkung 17 erwähnten Buch weist Katharina Mommsen auf einige frappante Ähnlichkeiten zwischen dem *Rosenkavalier* und *Die Poggenpuhls* hin, darunter Fontanes Hinweis auf die „Adelspackage" (S. 102).

65 „Wie die Stund' hingeht, wie der Wind verweht,/ so sind wir bald alle zwei dahin./ Menschen sein ma halt, richt's nicht mit Gewalt,/ weint uns niemand nach, net dir und net mir". *Dramen V*, S. 80.

> Manchmal steh' ich auf mitten in der Nacht
> Und laß' die Uhren alle stehen[66].

Diese echt Hofmannsthalisch anmutenden Reflexionen über Zeit und Vergänglichkeit sind ein Widerhall der Gedanken einer viel jüngeren Frau, der Heldin von Alfred de Mussets Novelle *Emmeline* aus dem Jahre 1837, die wie folgt auf eine Bemerkung ihres schachspielenden Gatten reagiert:

> „Vous aimez donc beaucoup ce jeu?" demanda Emmeline en souriant. „Comme la musique, pour passer le temps," répondit le comte. Et il continua sans regarder sa femme.
> „Passer le temps!" se répeta tout bas Mme de Marsan, dans sa chambre au moment de se mettre au lit. Ce mot l'empêchait de dormir. „Il [ihr zukünftiger Geliebter, M. de Sorgue] est beau, il est brave [...] il m'aime." Cependant son coeur battait avec violence; elle écoutait le bruit de la pendule; et la vibration monotone du balancier lui était insupportable. Elle se leva pour l'arrêter. „Que fais-je," se demanda-t-elle. „Arrêterai-je l'heure et le temps en forçant cette petite horloge à se taire?" Les yeux fixés sur la pendule, elle se livra à des pensées qui ne lui étaient pas encore venues. Elle songea au passé, à l'avenir, à la rapidité de la vie; elle se demanda pourqoi nous sommes sur terre, ce que nous y faisons, ce que nous attend après [...][67]

In beiden Fällen ist die zerstörerische Rolle der Zeit im Leben einer liebenden Frau der Gegenstand von halb gedachten und halb gefühlten Überlegungen existentieller Art – mit dem handlungsmäßig gewichtigen Unterschied freilich, daß wir es bei Musset mit einer ganz jungen Frau zu tun haben, die ihren Mann verlassen wird, bei Hofmannsthal aber mit einer reiferen, deren Liebhaber Abschied nehmen wird[68].

Im Gegensatz zum ersten Akt des *Rosenkavalier* weist der zweite relativ wenige Züge auf, die sich auf fremde Vorbilder beziehen lassen; er stellt eine im wesentlichen eigenständige Leistung dar, an der freilich neben dem Dichter auch der Komponist dramaturgisch beteiligt ist. Bekanntlich ist nur der erste Teil dieses Aufzugs, einschließ-

---

66 Katharina Mommsen (Anmerkung 17, S. 87ff.) vermutet einen indirekten Einfluß von Lenaus Gedicht *Nach Süden* auf dem Umweg über Fontanes *Graf Petöfy*. Hier sehen sich Germanistik und Komparatistik vor eine gemeinsame Aufgabe gestellt.

67 Alfred de Musset, *Nouvelles* (Paris: La Renaissance du Livre, [o.D.]), S. 23.

68 Auch verkleidet sich Oktavian, um von der Marschallin wegzukommen, während Artus' Sophie ihr *travesti* dazu benutzt, um zu Faublas zu gelangen.

lich des frei erfundenen Zeremoniells der Rosen-Übergabe[69], zur Gänze dem Dichter zuzuschreiben – wenigstens in der Fassung letzter Hand[70]. Die Linienführung des zweiten Teils hingegen geht letztendlich auf Strauss zurück, der sich sehr genaue Vorstellungen über die musikdramatische Architektonik der fallenden Handlung machte und Hofmannsthal von der Richtigkeit seiner Auffassung zu überzeugen vermochte[71]. Strukturell standen weder *Monsieur de Pourceaugnac* noch *L'Ingenu libertin* Modell für das Mittelstück der Oper, was allerdings die Entlehnung gewisser für Molière charakteristischer farcenhafter Kleinbauformen nicht ausschließt. Diese wären noch stärker zum Tragen gekommen, wenn Harry Graf Kessler dem Dichter gegenüber seinen Willen durchgesetzt hätte. Er schrieb nämlich dem Freund am 5. Juni 1909:

> Ich finde, dieser [Aktschluß] sollte laut buffonesk sein, als Kontrast zu den leisen und gefühlvollen Schlüssen von Akt I und III. Auch gleichzeitig mimischer, ballettmäßiger. Am liebsten möchte ich nicht bloß Annina sondern auch Valzacchi auftreten lassen, einen buffonesken ballettmäßigen Streit (cf. *Pourceaugnac*) zwischen Ochs und den beiden sehen, wobei Ochs sich truthahnmäßig bläht, womöglich seine Livree hereinruft, die dann in einem „pas de coups de pieds au cul" mit Annina und Valzacchi abgeht, die Rache schwören.

Hofmannsthal folgte zunächst diesem Rat, wie folgende Stelle aus dem Ersten Entwurf beweist:

> Baron (*munter*): Man dreh' mir das Gesindel da fix dort zur Tür hinaus. (*Es geschieht, wobei sich die Balgerei zu einem grotesken kleinen Ballett „un pas de coups de pieds au cul" entwickelt*)
> Valzacchi (*sich wehrend, drohend*): Ihre Gnade wird bereuen.
> Annina (*ebenso*): Euer Gnaden werden sich schaden [...][72].

---

69 Wie es im *Ungeschriebenen Nachwort* (*Dramen V*, S. 147) heißt: „Von den Sitten und Gebräuchen sind diejenigen meist echt und überliefert, die man für erfunden halten würde, und diejenigen erfunden, die echt erscheinen."

70 Die zuerst in *Neue Rundschau* 64 (1953) veröffentlichte Erstfassung des zweiten Aktes ist in *Dramen V*, S. 117-145 abgedruckt.

71 Man sehe vor allem die Briefe, die Strauss am 9. und 10. Juli 1909 an den Dichter schrieb.

72 *Dramen V*, S. 144.

Aber der Dichter erhob Einspruch gegen die viel drastischeren und weitaus einschneidenderen Modifikationen, die Kessler nach Kenntnisnahme der von Strauss vorgeschlagenen Änderungen vorschlug:

> Nur eine Klippe scheint mir zu vermeiden, das Herausfallen aus dem tanzmäßig Ornamentalen beim Duett, bei der Verbandszene usw. Diese Motive müssen m. E. im Gegenteil ganz aufs Rhythmische zugespitzt werden, durch Wiederholungen, Parallelfiguren etc., so wie in Molières kleinen Spielen (in *Fourberies de Scapin* z. B. die Sackschlagenszene usw.). Nichts reizt mehr zum Lachen als komische Situationen in stylisierter Vorführung[73].

In seiner Erwiderung erläuterte Hofmannsthal seine Gründe für die Weigerung, den *Rosenkavalier* in die Form einer *comèdie-ballet* zu gießen:

> Nicht wahr, du erwartest von mir vom 2ten Act der Operette ebenso wenig eine complete Durchsetzung mit diesen Figuren der Molièreschen Comödie (Parallelismen, Wiederholungen etc.) als der 1ste sie hat. Ich habe nicht diesen Ton angeschlagen, sondern einen gemischteren, mit mehr Realität[74].

Nichtsdestoweniger finden sich im zweiten Akt einzelne rhythmisch-gestisch bewegte Stellen, die eindeutig auf Molière verweisen, so der mit „Wiederholungen" und „Parallelismen" gespickte Wortabschlag zwischen Faninal und seiner Tochter:

> Faninal (*zu Sophie*): Hör' Sie mich. Sie heirat' ihn. Und wenn er verbluten tät', so heirat' Sie ihn als Toter. [...] *Faninal macht Oktavian eine Verbeugung, übertrieben höflich, aber unzweideutig. Oktavian* [...] *erwidert* [...] *Faninals Verbeugung durch ein gleiches tiefes Kompliment.*
> Sophie ([...] *mit einer Reverenz*): Heirat' den Herrn dort nicht lebendig und nicht tot. Sperr' mich zuvor in meine Kammer ein.
> Faninal (*in Wut und nachdem er abermals eine wütende Verbeugung gegen Oktavian gemacht hat, die Oktavian prompt erwidert*): Ah. Sperrst dich ein. Sind Leut' genug im Haus, die dich in Wagen tragen werden.
> Sophie (*mit einem neuen Knix*): Spring' aus dem Wagen noch, der mich zur Kirche fährt.
> Faninal (*mit gleichem Spiel zwischen ihr und Oktavian, der immer einen Schritt gegen den Ausgang tut, aber von Sophie in diesem Augenblick nicht loskann*): Ah, springst noch aus dem Wagen. Na, ich sitz' neben dir, werd' dich schon halten.
> Sophie (*mit einem neuen Knix*): Geb' halt dem Pfarrer am Altar Nein statt Ja zur Antwort.

---

73 Briefwechsel Hofmannsthal/Kessler, S. 155.
74 Brief vom 15. August 1909.

> Faninal (*mit gleichem Spiel*): Ah, gibst Nein statt Ja zur Antwort. Ich steck' dich in ein Kloster, stante pede. Marsch, mir aus den Augen, lieber heut' als morgen. Auf Lebenszeit. (S. 69)

Ein ziemlich gewichtiger Fehler in der Konstruktion des zweiten Aktes resultierte aus den Schwierigkeiten, die sich bei Hofmannsthals Versuch ergaben, zwei literarische Quellen miteinander im *tertium comparationis,* das heißt dem neuen, als *Rosenkavalier* bekannten Gebilde, in Einklang zu bringen und das Verhalten der aus verschiedenen Kontexten stammenden Figuren richtig zu motivieren. Während nämlich im *Monsieur de Pourceaugnac* die zwei Intriganten von Anfang an Erastes Geschöpfe sind und von ihm bezahlt werden, sind sie in der Komödie für Musik zunächst unabhängig und bieten ihre Dienste der Reihe nach der Marschallin („die swarze Zeitung"), dem Baron („Ihre Gnade sukt etwas. Ik seh'") und Oktavian an. Als drahtziehender Autor war aber Hofmannsthal verpflichtet zu erklären, aus welchen Gründen und unter welchen Umständen sie in das Lager des Letzteren überwechseln. Wie sich bald herausstellte, war das gar nicht so einfach.

Im Ersten Entwurf sind die diesbezüglichen Angaben noch recht vage.

Allerdings deuten zwei Phrasen im Handlungsabriß für den ersten Akt („Sophie bittet um Befreiung. Die Intriganten") darauf hin, daß das Paar wie in Molières *comèdie-ballet* bei der Vertreibung des unerwünschten Freiers eine Rolle spielen wird. Das wird im letzten Satz des zweiten Abschnitts („P. geht. Intrigant kommt und sagt, wie es zu machen"), der auf einen Plan der Marquise, den Eindringling zu kompromittieren, hinzuweisen scheint, bestätigt.

Im Szenar tritt Faublas'/Oktavians Komplizität deutlich zutage. Der von den Intriganten beim spontanen tête-à-tête mit Sophie überraschte Liebhaber fängt sich schnell und wirft dem Paar eine gespickte Geldbörse zu (S. 114). Das Gleiche gilt für die ausgearbeitete Erstfassung des Aktes, in der Oktavian Valzacchi und Annina ausdrücklich herbeiruft:

> *Oktavian tut einen Pfiff, die Italiener kommen hinter den Stühlen hervor. Oktavian hat sich gesetzt, sie stehen vor ihm.*
> Valzacchi und Annina: Zu Euer Exzellenz Befehl. Mit Leib und Leben.
> Oktavian: Ah, solche seid's ihr. Na, ihr seid's die rechten. Ich trau' euch nicht. (*V. und A. beteuernde Gebärde?*) Aber ich zahl' euch halt, solang's mir passen wird. (S. 135)

Aber in der endgültigen Fassung muß ihr Gesinnungswechsel aus folgender Geste im dritten Akt erschlossen werden: „*Oktavian greift in die Tasche* [...] *und wirft Valzacchi eine Börse zu.*" (S. 74) Im Gegensatz zu Hofmannsthal, dem die Lösung viel Sorge bereitete, schien Strauss die Sache kaum der Rede wert, und er riet dem Dichter, sie einfach auf sich beruhen zu lassen: „Seien Sie mit der Motivierung des Stimmungsumschwunges bei den Italienern nicht ängstlich. [...] Das Publikum braucht sie nicht. Errat' ja auch was"[75].

Ein weiteres Einsprengsel im zweiten Akt verdient abschließend unsere Aufmerksamkeit, obwohl es sich nicht um ein französisches, sondern sozusagen um ein anglo-italienisches Vorbild handelt, das hier seine Umsetzung erfuhr. Im Zuge des dramaturgischen Eingriffs, den Strauss seinem Mitarbeiter schmackhaft zu machen suchte, bezeichnete er einen Passus aus Verdis *Falstaff* als mögliches Vorbild für die von ihm gewünschte Coda:

> In Verdis *Falstaff* ist so ein hübscher Monolog zu Anfang des letzten Aktes. Er beginnt mit dem Wort „Schandvolk". Ich denke mir die Szene des Barons nach dem Abgang des Oktavian ähnlich: der Baron auf dem Sofa, Arzt bei ihm, die Diener stumm am Bettende aufgestellt, und der Baron in Pausen sprechend, halb für sich, halb zu den andern: halb Siegesstimmung, halb Katerstimmung, immer von Orchesterzwischenspielen unterbrochen: Schmerzen leidend, auf Quinquin fluchend, die Braut glossierend[76].

Hofmannsthal, dem die Affinität Ochsens mit Sir John aufging, scheint die entsprechende Stelle des Texts von Boito konsultiert zu haben, die mit den Worten „Mondo ladro. Mondo rubaldo. Reo mondo" einsetzt, dann in eine Art Katerstimmung („Mondo reo. Non c'e più virtù. Tutto declina") übergeht und in ein Lob des Weines als wahrem Trostspender („Buono. Ber del vin dolce e sbottonarsi al sole,/

---

75 Strauss an Hofmannsthal, 9. Juli 1909.
76 Strauss an Hofmannsthal, 13. August 1909.

dolce cosa. Il buon vino sperde le tetre folle/ dello sconforto, accende l'occhio e i pensier"[77]) mündet, denn schon am 18. September konnte er Strauss mitteilen: „Umstehend serviere ich Ihnen als Monolog mit Pausen für Orchesterzwischenspiel: a) Katerstimmung, b) Zorn auf Oktavian, c) erwachendes Behagen, d) völliges Behagen (mit Übergang zum Refrain-Liedchen)"[78]. Dem Brief lag der Text eines Selbstgesprächs bei, das uns von „Da lieg' ich. Was ei'm Kavalier nicht alles passieren kann in dieser Wienerstadt" (a) über „Der Satan. Sakramentsverfluchter Bub" (b) und „Und doch lachen muß ich, wie sich so ein Bub mit seine siebzehn Jahr' die Welt imaginiert", (c) zum Ausdruck der selbstzufriedenen Gemütlichkeit in den Sätzen „Bin willens jetzt, mich in mein Kabinettl zu verfügen und eins zu ruh'n. Herr Medicus, begeb' Er sich indes voraus. Mach' Er das Bett aus lauter Federbetten. Ich komm'. Erst aber trink' ich noch" (71) transportiert.

Wie die ersten zwei Akte des *Rosenkavalier*, so erweist sich auch der echt wienerisch anmutende dritte beim näheren Hinschauen als ein mixtum compositum aus Molière, Louvet de Couvray/Artus und Hogarth. Was die *Marriage-à-la-Mode* des letzteren anbetrifft, so hat Mary E. Gilbert mit Recht darauf hingewiesen, daß das fünfte Bild dieser Folge die Anregung für das Bühnenbild der Beisl-Handlung gab. Freilich sind sowohl die Situation/Aktion als auch der Ausgang – bei Hogarth melodramatisch und tödlich, bei Hofmannsthal komisch und versöhnlich – grundverschieden. Auf jeden Fall besteht zwischen den Bühnenanweisungen „Ein Extrazimmer in einem Gasthaus. Im Hintergrund links ein Alkoven, darin ein Bett. Der Alkoven durch einen Vorhang verschließbar, der sich auf- und zuziehen läßt" (S. 74) und dem Dekor des Hogarthschen Stichs eine Ähnlichkeit, die sich nur zum Teil durch Stereotypie erklären läßt.

---

77 Ich zitiere den auf S. 107 des English National Opera Guide zu *Falstaff*, hsg. Nicholas John (London: Calder, 1982) wiedergegebenen Text der Oper.
78 Hofmannsthal an Strauss, 18. September 1909.

Adepten der Vergleichenden Literaturwissenschaft lernen früh, daß Deckungsgleichheit in der Kunst sehr rar ist und meist nur in der Form des Zitates auftritt. Neben Ähnlichkeiten gibt es Unterschiede, die vom Forscher erklärt und bewertet werden müssen. Bei einem Vergleich zwischen Hogarth und Hofmannsthal müssen wir zum Beispiel berücksichtigen, daß der englische Künstler im fünften Tableau nicht den Maskenball selbst, an dem Silvertongue und seine Maîtresse teilgenommen haben, zur Darstellung bringt, sondern, wie die auf dem Fußboden des unordentlich aussehenden Zimmers herumliegenden Masken beweisen, dessen trauriges Nachspiel. Im Schlußakt des *Rosenkavalier* hingegen sind wir Augenzeugen der Maskerade.

Wenn die Marschallin, die keiner Verkleidung bedarf, von den turbulenten Begebenheiten, in die sie nur zum geringen Teil selbst verwickelt war, als einer Farce und kurz darauf als einer „Wienerischen Maskerad" spricht[79], so meint sie das wörtlich *und* symbolisch, d. h. sie bezieht diese Gattungsbegriffe sowohl auf das unmittelbare Geschehen als auch auf die ganze Kette der Ereignisse. (Im Roman *Les Amours du Chevalier de Faublas*, den man zum Vergleich heranziehen mag, dient der Ball, bei dem auch der Held im *travesti* erscheint, nur als Auslöser, während er sich im *Ingenu libertin* auf die gesamte Handlung erstreckt; denn dort herrscht der Geist des Karnevals und in Verkleidung erscheint nicht nur Faublas [als *La Belle Jardinière*], sondern auch Sophie, die ihm als *marmiton* in das Haus der Marquise nachfolgt.)

Im dritten Akt des *Rosenkavalier*, den Hofmannsthal trotz Straussens Versicherung[80] des Gegenteils als viel zu lang empfand und einem ungleich empfindlicheren Publikum zuliebe erheblich kürzen wollte, finden sich einzelne Molièreske Elemente. So stammt die Szene, in der Annina im Geiste der Mozartschen Donna Elvira die verlas-

---

79 *Dramen V*, S. 96.
80 Siehe Hofmannsthals Brief vom 30. August 1909 und Straussens Antwort vom 12. September.

sene Gattin spielt und ihre verwaisten Kinder plärren läßt[81], direkt aus dem *Monsieur de Pourceaugnac* (7. und 8. Szene des zweiten Aktes), wo die Wirkung verdoppelt wird, weil gleich zwei verschmähte Frauen – Nerine, eine „feinte Picarde", und Lucette,eine „feinte Gasconne"[82] – ihren ehelichen Anspruch geltend machen. Ähnliches gilt für die dem Pourceaugnac drastisch vor Augen gestellten rechtlichen Folgen der Bigamie bzw. Polygamie[83] sowie für den Gestus des zweckentfremdeten Gebrauchs, den die beiden Figuren von ihren Hüten machen[84].

Aber dies sind nur kleine Details, dazu angetan, den Unterhaltungswert des *Rosenkavalier* zu erhöhen durch augenfällige Gags, die das Publikum erheitern. Sobald Ochs endgültig aus dem Bereich des adeligen Anstands und der bürgerlichen Wohlanständigkeit vertrieben und von der Bildfläche verschwunden ist, beginnt erneut der ‚Ernst des Lebens'. Mit Hilfe des Komponisten, der ein ausgezeichnetes Gespür für musikalische Proportionen hatte, erstellte Hofmannsthal ein Finale als letztes Glied der Kette, die das Duett Marschallin/Oktavian im ersten, das Duett Oktavian/Sophie im zweiten und das auf ein Ter-

---

81 Strukturell entsprechen sie den „drei armen adeligen Waisen" im Lever des ersten Aktes, die es ihrem Vater, der, wie sie berichten, „jung auf dem Felde der Ehre gefallen" ist (*Dramen V*, S. 31), nachtun wollen – etwa, indem sie auch „fallen"? Situationsmäßig besteht, wie Katharina Mommsen (Anmerkung 17, S. 102) aufzeigt, auch hier eine Parallele zwischen dem *Rosenkavalier* und den *Poggenpuhls*.

82 Molière, *Oeuvres Complètes* II, S. 445-448. Im Gegenzug zu Nerine und Lucette, die Lokaldialekte verwenden, bedient sich Annina als Italienerin, die nur gebrochen Deutsch spricht, hier „eines böhmisch-deutschen Akzents, aber gebildeter Sprechweise" (*Dramen V*, S. 81).

83 Wirt: „Halten zu Gnaden, gehen nicht zu weit,/ Könnten recht bitterböse Folgen von der Sach' gespüren. [...] Die Bigamie ist halt kein Gspaß" (ebd., S. 83). – Sbrigani: „Voilà une méchante affaire, et la justice en ce pays-ci est rigoureuse en diable contre cette sorte de crime" (*Oeuvres Complètes* II, S. 449); und der Anwalt, „*trainant ses paroles*" singt am Ende des zweiten Aktes: „La polygamie est un cas,/ Est un cas pendable".

84 Im *Rosenkavalier* „schlägt Ochs mit dem Hut unter die Kinder" (*Dramen V*, S. 98), nachdem er vorher die Serviette zum gleichen Zweck verwendet hat (ebd., S. 82). Im *Monsieur de Pourceaugnac* benutzt der Titelheld seinen Hut „pour se garantir des seringues", die der Apotheker und zwei als „médecins grotesques" verkleidete Musikanten in seinen Hintern schieben wollen.

zett folgende Duett im dritten Akt bilden. Zwar sind die Worte, die in der Schluß-Szene der Oper gesprochen bzw. gesungen werden, Hofmannsthals geistiges Eigentum, doch ist die Konstruktion, die das Gerüst für die Gesangsnummern und die dazwischenliegenden Rezitative bildet, der *communis opinio* zum Trotz durchaus keine eigenständige Leistung, sondern trägt deutlich die Züge eines bestimmten Modells. Was nämlich die Hofmannsthal-Forschung bisher übersehen oder zumindest unbeachtet gelassen hat, ist die Tatsache, daß hier zwei Szenen des *Ingenu libertin* (III, 9 und 10, S. 151-160) Pate gestanden haben. Das gilt es zu beweisen.

Gewiß, in der Pariser Operette, die Hofmannsthal hier zu Rate zog, ist die Lösung des Handlungsknotens, die bei Louvet de Couvray schon im zweiten Band – also lange vor dem Ende des Romans – erfolgt, zwar bühnenwirksam, aber nicht eben elegant. Verzichtet in *Les Amours du Chevalier de Faublas* die Marquise, wie übrigens auch die Marschallin des *Rosenkavalier*, aus freien Stücken und uneigennützig auf den jungen Liebhaber, so ließen sich Artus und Terrasse eine spielerisch anmutende Szene einfallen, in der sie mit Sophies halb erzwungener Zustimmung den Faublas auffordert, mit sich selbst Blindekuh zu spielen. Vor die Notwendigkeit gestellt, sich für die himmlische – seine Seelenbraut Sophie – oder die irdische Liebe[85] – die erotisch reizvolle Marquise – zu entscheiden, optiert der *ingenu libertin* für die höhere Sphäre, aber mit offensichtlichem Bedauern: „Je le sais bien, vous êtes la plus belle,/ Chère mamam. Pourquoi m'aveugle-t-on?/ J'aime Sophie. Ah marquise si bonne,/ Daignez-vous m'accorder mon pardon?" (S. 160). Die gewünschte Absolution wird prompt erteilt, und die Verschmähte, sich erst an Faublas und dann an Sophie wendend, ruft großmütig aus: „Je vous pardonne [...] C'est vous qui le méritez mieux. Gardez-donc cette enfant que j'adore."

Freilich endet *L'Ingenu libertin* nicht, wie man erwarten würde, an diesem Punkt; denn sobald die Binde von den Augen des Faublas ent-

---

[85] So Robert Mühlher (Anmerkung 50, S. 315).

fernt worden ist, tritt der Gatte der Marquise, der *cocu* wie er im Buche steht, ein, gefolgt von den übrigen *dramatis personae*, die in ein an Carmens *L'Amour est un oiseau rebelle* gemahnendes, aber ungleich trivialeres Chanson folgenden Wortlauts einstimmen:

> Amour va venir et sans qu'on veuille.
> Vous tous, prenez votre part
> Du bonheur qu'il sème.
> Il veut que l'on s'aime.
> Il peut naître d'un hasard,
> D'une mèche folie,
> D'un baiser qu'on vole,
> Ou bien d'un regard. (S. 165)

Man kann sich vorstellen, wie Hofmannsthals verfeinerter Geschmack auf diesen Edelkitsch reagierte. Auch in diesem Fall war sein Interesse an dem Produkt der Pariser leichten Muse weder sprachlicher noch thematischer Art, sondern erstreckte sich einzig und allein auf die Art, wie der französische Dutzendschreiber seine Figuren auf den Brettern, die die Welt bedeuten, bewegte und sich je nach der seelischen Konfiguration verteilen ließ. Die aus diesen Beobachtungen gezogene Nutzanwendung auf die Schluß-Szene des *Rosenkavalier* ließe sich am besten graphisch darstellen. Doch muß der Leser in Ermangelung einer Wandtafel mit einer verbalen Umschreibung der wechselnden Stellungen vorliebnehmen.

Beginnen wir mit dem *Ingenu libertin*. Am Ende der achten Szene des dritten Aktes dieser Operette sehen wir Faublas vor Sophie, die er vergebens um Verzeihung gebeten hat, knien und ihre Hand küssen (F/S)[86]. In diesem Augenblick tritt die Marquise, von den beiden unbemerkt, ein (M S/F). Als er sie sieht, erhebt sich Faublas, wohl mit schuldiger Miene, und entfernt sich ein wenig von Sophie. Während des nun folgenden Dialogs nähert er sich ihr aber wieder und vergißt beinahe die Gegenwart seiner Maîtresse[87]. Als er in süßer Erinnerung mit der Geliebten die Schluß-Strophen der Romanze singt, mit der er

---

[86] *L'Ingenu libertin*, S. 150: „Il tombe à ses pieds et lui baise les mains."
[87] Ebd., S. 153: „Et voici que Faublas oublie, presque, la présence de la marquise."

an der Klostermauer um sie warb, kommt er ihr erneut ganz nah (M F/S)[88]. Doch sobald ihn die Marquise ruft, trennen sich die beiden, und einen Augenblick lang steht Faublas genau in der Mitte zwischen ihnen (M F S)[89]. Dann macht sich die Marquise entschlossen zur Herrin der Lage und schlägt ihm das schon erwähnte Blindekuh-Spiel vor, das sein und Sophies Geschick entscheiden soll. Als sie ihm die Augen verbindet, kniet er vor ihr genau so wie er vor Sophie gekniet hatte (M/F S)[90]. Am Ende der Szene, als die Entscheidung gefallen ist, löst Sophie die Binde des Faublas, der vor ihr kniet. So hat sich der Kreis geschlossen: (M F/S)[91].

Hier wird Hofmannsthal – gewiß zum Vergnügen Kesslers, dem diese sentimentale Variante Molièrescher Technik gefallen haben dürfte – Nahrung für die ungleich subtilere Behandlung dieses ‚Themas' im Finale seines *Rosenkavalier* gesogen haben, allerdings erst bei der endgültigen Festlegung des Textes, also nachdem er die Druckfassung des *Ingenu libertin* gelesen hatte. Die Entwürfe bieten jedenfalls keinerlei Hinweis auf derartige ‚Stellungnahmen'[92]. Im Libretto wird in der Szene, die in der überstürzten Flucht des Ochs von Lerchenau endet, bereits auf das nachfolgende Konfigurationsspiel hingewiesen. Der verblüffte Baron, jetzt im Wortsinn ein Mann zwischen drei Frauen, steht nämlich genau in der Mitte zwischen der Marschallin und Sophie, die verwunderte und bedeutsame Blicke wechseln[93]. (Hofmannsthal weigerte sich übrigens, auf den Vorschlag Straussens einzugehen, Ochs an dieser geometrischen Variante des

---

88 Ebd., S. 154: „Il est tout près d'elle, des larmes dans les yeux et dans la voix."
89 Ebd.: „Il est entr'elles deux."
90 Ebd., S. 156: „Il se met à genoux sur un coussin devant la marquise assis dans une bergère."
91 Ebd., S. 160.
92 Im Gegensatz zu den Szenarien für den ersten und zweiten Akt bietet das zum dritten Akt kein Standorts- bzw. Bewegungs-Schema.
93 *„Die Blicke der beiden Frauen begegnen sich. Sophie macht der Marschallin einen verlegenen Knix. Der Baron, zwischen Sophie und der Marschallin stehend:* ‚Bin gar nicht willens [...]'" *Dramen V*, S. 96.

Kämmerchen-Vermietens teilnehmen und ihn wild gestikulierend umhertaumeln zu lassen[94].) Im nächsten Moment, als er endlich erkannt hat, daß die angebliche Kammerzofe ein „Manndl" ist, läßt er seine Blicke zwischen ihm und der Marschallin hin- und herschweifen.[95] Aber dieser flüchtige Augenblick völliger Paralyse bezeichnet nur die Stille vor dem Sturm, der ihn hinwegfegt.

Nach Ochsens Abgang beruhigt sich die Szene, und das lyrische Moment, das sich bis zur Schluß-Apotheose der Liebenden hin steigert, kommt zu seinem Recht. Hofmannsthal, der wieder einmal mit Strauss, der stets für das Burleske plädierte, uneins war, erläuterte in einem Schreiben an den Komponisten seine Strategie wie folgt:

> Daß die Sophie links, die Marschallin rechts auf einen Stuhl fällt, ist rein im konventionellen, burlesken Sinn ganz richtig, verwischt mir aber zu sehr den für die Schluß-Situation nötigen Ranges- und Standesunterschied der zwei Frauen. Sophie muß trotzig links stehen, die Marschallin traurig rechts sitzen. Oktavian zwischen beiden hin- und herpendeln[96].

Die Parallelen mit dem Szenen-Komplex des *Ingenu libertin* werden deutlicher, wenn man die Anwendung dieses Programms auf das Bühnengeschehen näher ins Auge faßt. Da sehen wir Sophie „rechts stehend, blaß" und Oktavian „hinter dem Stuhl der Marschallin, verlegen" (O/M S), bis dieser auf Geheiß der Marschallin („Geh' er doch schnell und tu er, was sein Herz ihm sagt") zu seiner künftigen Braut tritt (M O/S). Aber die letzte Entscheidung ist noch nicht gefallen. Oktavians Unsicherheit bleibt bestehen und veranlaßt ihn, fast ohne sein Zutun, sich wieder der Marschallin zu nähern: „Oktavian ist ein paar Schritte gegen die Marschallin hingegangen, steht jetzt zwischen

---

94 Strauss an Hofmannsthal (20. Mai 1909): „Der Brennpunkt ist die enorme Verlegenheit des Barons, als er sich plötzlich den drei starr ihm gegenüberstehenden Gesichtern gegenübersieht. [...] Wie er zwischen den drei hin- und hertaumelt, muß äußerst drastisch sein."

95 „Der Baron *(allmählich der Situation beikommend)*: ‚Kreuzelement! Komm' aus dem Staunen nicht heraus'. *(Mit einem ausgiebigen Blick, der von der Marschallin zu Oktavian, von Oktavian wieder zurück zur Marschallin wandert)*: ‚Weiß bereits nicht, was ich von diesem ganzen qui pro quo mir denken soll'." *Dramen V*, S. 97.

96 Hofmannsthal an Strauss, 23. Mai 1910.

beiden verlegen [...] in der Mitte [und] dreht den Kopf von einer zur andern" (S O M)[97].

Als Oktavian endlich zurücktritt, um der nunmehr verabschiedeten Geliebten Platz zu machen, nähert sich diese noch einmal Sophie, als wolle sie sich vergewissern, daß sie richtig gehandelt habe, und tritt nach einem kurzen Wortwechsel ab. Als sie die Tür erreicht, begibt sich Oktavian erneut in ihre Nähe. Erst als sie den Raum verlassen hat, steht das junge Paar in intimer Pose beisammen: „Oktavian ist dicht an Sophie herangetreten; einen Augenblick später liegt sie in seinen Armen." Aber der Augenblick des höchsten Glücks verschiebt sich, als die Marschallin, von Faninal begleitet, eintritt, um das Paar gerührt, doch mit leicht ironischer Überlegenheit zu betrachten. Für wenige Sekunden steht das ältere Paar dem jüngeren von Angesicht zu Angesicht gegenüber (M/F O/S). Dann gehen sie und versetzen Oktavian und Sophie in den siebenten Himmel: „Sie sinkt an ihn hin, er küßt sie schnell. [...] Dann laufen sie Hand in Hand hinaus."

Obgleich es der Hauptzweck dieser Arbeit war, die französischen Quellen des *Rosenkavalier* aufzudecken und ihre Umfunktionierung zu dokumentieren, erwies es sich letzten Endes als unmöglich, die anderen Vorbilder völlig auszuschalten. So geriet das ganze Libretto in unser Blickfeld. Insgesamt bewies unsere Untersuchung erneut, daß die Oper für Hofmannsthal das „erreichte" Gesamtkunstwerk[98] war und daß insbesondere das Werk, dem diese Studie gewidmet ist, eine äußerst gelungene Mischung aus eigenen und fremden Bestandteilen verschiedener Künste ist. Die Sprache ist des Dichters eigener und eigentlichster Beitrag; die Handlung und die ‚Bewegungsregie' verbindet – nicht immer ganz unauffällig – den *Monsieur de Pourceaugnac* mit dem *Ingenu libertin* (nicht mit den *Amours du Chevalier de Faublas*, wie man bisher angenommen hat), die Bühnenbilder grei-

---

[97] *Dramen V*, S. 101.
[98] Für Hofmannsthals Auffassung des (lyrischen) Dramas als Oper ohne Oper siehe den Schlußteil des Vorworts zur *Ägyptischen Helena* (1928) in Gestalt eines imaginären (?) Gesprächs zwischen ihm und Strauss. *Dramen V*, S. 510-521.

fen zum Teil auf Hogarth und Baudoin zurück, die gestisch-pantomimische Gestaltung beruht im manchen Zügen auf Molière, und einige der Namen verdanken den Memoiren von Khevenhüller-Metsch ihr Dasein. Und doch schwebt bei aller Eklektik über alledem ein Geist, der unverkennbar derjenige Hofmannsthals ist und dem Werk Anmut in der Fülle verleiht[99].

---

99 Die langwierigen Überlegungen, die von allen Beteiligten über die Titelgebung des Werkes angestellt wurden, reflektieren nicht nur die Ungewißheit darüber, wer denn eigentlich die Hauptperson sei, sondern verraten auch seine literarischen Ursprünge. So schrieb Kessler am 12. Oktober 1909 an Hofmannsthal:

> Warum nicht *Die galanten Abenteuer des Barons von Lerchenau*? (oder *Baron von Ochs*). Was sich sehr hübsch auf *Die galanten Abenteuer* im laufenden Sprachgebrauch abkürzt. Ouvertüre zu den *Galanten Abenteuern*, Duett aus den *Galanten Abenteuern*, Menuett aus den *G. A.* klingt alles ganz hübsch. Übersetzt gibt es: *Les Aventures galantes du Seigneur de Lerchenau* und *The Amorous Adventures of Mylord Ochs* or *Herr von Ochs*, was noch komischer klingt. Ich hatte auch an *Die Liebeslist* gedacht oder an *Die Schule der Unverschämten* oder *Ochsens Schulung*; aber das alles ist weit weniger amüsant und treffend.

Hofmannsthal erwiderte am 18. Dezember:

> Ich bin ziemlich fest für den Titel *Ochs von Lerchenau* entschlossen, der den Buffo in die Mitte stellt, das derbe Element andeutet und ganz gut klingt und aussieht. Für solche preciöse archaische Titel wie Du vorschlägst, hab ich selbst große Neigung. Doch sind sie ganz unmöglich auf dem Zettel, unmöglich auf dem Wochenplan, unmöglich im Mund des hastigen, alles abbreviierenden Publicums. Die Verkürzung zu *Die galanten Abenteuer* scheint mir *dieses* Lustspiel nicht gut zu charakterisieren; es kommt wohl auch ein galantes Abenteuer (der Marschallin) und ein sentimentales Abenteuer (der Sophie und des Quinquin) vor, aber was die Sache zusammenhält, ist der Pourceaugnac, der buffo, der Ochs von Lerchenau, also bleiben wir dabei.

Man blieb natürlich nicht dabei.

The Little Word *und*
Tristan und Isolde as Verbal Construct (1987)

> Der Literat legt den "Operntext" beiseite,
> weil er nur den Musiker angehe, der
> Musiker, weil er nicht begreift, wie
> dieser Operntext komponiert werden solle.
> Das eigentliche Publikum verlangt [...]
> die "Tat".
> (Richard Wagner[1])
>
> Wagner vor allem als Musiker zu beachten;
> seine Texte sind "Musikdunst".
> (Friedrich Nietzsche[2])

I.

There are surely more than thirteen ways of looking at opera, and any scholar or critic worth his salt is well advised to make up his mind early on as to the kind of approach he wishes to take in a given case. Up to this point in the history of interdisciplinary studies involving the musical drama, theoretical and methodological reflections have been few and far between, and no latter-day Aristotle has come to the rescue to unfold a cogent systematic Poetics of Opera[3]. Especially the

---

1   From Wagner's "Vorwort zur Herausgabe der Dichtung des Bühnenfestspiels *Der Ring des Nibelungen*" (1863) as reprinted in *Richard Wagner: Dokumentarbiographie*, ed. Egon Voss, 2nd enlarged edition (Munich: Goldmann/Schott, 1983), p. 389.

2   From writings and aphorisms related to *Die Geburt der Tragödie aus dem Geiste der Musik* (1870/1871) as reproduced in Friedrich Nietzsche, *Der Fall Wagner: Schriften, Aufzeichnungen, Briefe*, ed. Dieter Borchmeyer (Frankfurt: Insel-Verlag, 1983), p. 278.

3   I have assembled historical documents for such a Poetics in my anthology *The Essence of Opera* (New York: The Free Press, 1964). In a recent essay, "Librettology: The Fine Art of Coping with a Chinese Twin" (*Komparatistische Hefte*, Nos. 5/6 [1982], 7-22), I have tried to systematize the study of operatic texts with reference to the six elements of drama that Aristotle discusses in his *Poetics*.

literary scientists who have sporadically dabbled in such matters have tended to let the chips fall where they may and steered a more or less erratic course[4]. It will therefore behoove me to preface my paper with a few observations on the various choices open to the practitioner of *Opernforschung* in general and its subdivision, librettology, in particular. This will serve to introduce and justify my enterprise, which is based on an assumption, shared by Leo Spitzer, that it is precisely with a poet like Wagner, "whose texts we ordinarily hear mixed with, or drowned out by, an intoxicating music, that a sober philological interpretation of the words [and concepts] might be considered most necessary"[5].

Disregarding, with some regret, the theatrical or 'spectacular' side of opera, Aristotle's *opsis*, which looms so large in Wagner's mimetic conception of his art, we may conveniently, though somewhat schematically, divide the study of the *Gesamtkunstwerk* into three main divisions: the musicological, the literary, and the musico-literary, which combines both. (Needless to say, both *Musik-* and *Literaturwissenschaft* err when assuming that either the libretto or the score of an opera can be meaningfully viewed in isolation. An interaction between the two disciplines is absolutely necessary, and an emphasis on one or the other collaborative art at the expense, or to the exclusion, of the other is merely a matter of convenience or professional competence.) Let us illustrate this tripartite and, in the original sense of the word, trivial scheme with a few examples drawn from the literature on *Tristan und Isolde*.

---

[4] A good example of such aimless weaving in and out is Gary Schmidgall's *Literature as Opera* (New York: Oxford University Press, 1977), which lacks both a method and a sense of direction.

[5] Leo Spitzer, *A Method of Interpreting Literature* (Northampton, Mass.: Smith College, 1949). The quotation is culled from the first of three lectures, which bears the title "Three Poems of Ecstasy".

The strictly musicological approach was first taken by Hans von Bülow in a letter to the editor of the *Neue Zeitschrift fur Musik*[6]. It is represented by Alfred Lorenz's monumental study, *Das Geheimnis der Form bei Richard Wagner*[7], which almost totally disregards the text, a particularly striking example of myopia, although among compositional techniques, chromaticism would seem to fall wholly into the lap of the musical theorist. But insofar as chromaticism also subserves a dramatic purpose, even here the literary dimension is not lacking. As Joseph Kerman so aptly puts it, "Wagner's regular and exasperating cliché, the evasion of solid harmonic setting, finds its true symbolic place in [this] drama of the agony of yearning and its transformation"[8]. Furthermore, what Wagner calls "die Kunst des Überganges," that is, "die Vermittlung und innige Verbindung aller Momente des Überganges der äussersten Stimmungen ineinander"[9], must also be considered under this heading since in explicating the technique, the composer relies solely on musical elements – rhythm, harmony and melody. In short, Wagner, too, seems to treat *Tristan und Isolde* more or less as a symphonic poem[10].

Given the fact that Wagner was an artistic *Doppelbegabung* of the first order who believed that language and music – the male and female principles – were destined to join hands in marriage, it is hardly surprising that most of the devices he uses, and often introduces, pertain somehow to both spheres of artistic activity and should ideally be judged by those endowed with scholarly *Doppelbegabung*. In the

---

6 The letter was addressed to Franz Brendel and published on 9 September, 1859; it is reproduced in the *Dokumentarbiographie*, pp. 362-364.

7 The work, in four volumes, appeared between 1924 and 1933.

8 Joseph Kerman, *Opera as Drama* (New York: Knopf, 1956), p. 212.

9 Letter to Mathilde Wesendonck dated 29 October, 1859 in: *Richard Wagner an Mathilde Wesendonck: Tagebuchblätter und Briefe 1853-1871*, 27th ed. (Berlin: Duncker, 1906), p. 189. Carl Dahlhaus discusses the concept in his essay, "Wagner's 'Kunst des Übergangs': Der Zwiegesang in *Tristan und Isolde*" in: *Zur musikalischen Analyse*, ed. Gerhard Schuhmacher (Darmstadt: Wissenschaftliche Buchgesellschaft, 1974), pp. 475-486. Wagner's spelling is modernized throughout this essay.

10 Kerman actually calls his *Tristan* chapter "Opera as Symphonic Poem".

past, nearly all attempts to come to grips with Wagnerian opera have failed either because the literary scholars interested in the subject lacked the requisite technical know-how or because musicologists – including such eminent ones as Dahlhaus and Kerman (whose claim that "in opera the true dramatist is the composer" is a tautology when applied to Wagner) – treated their colleagues in the other camp as unwanted children toying with their own selected hobby-horses.

Among the features that enjoy what might be called dual citizenship in the land of opera, the most obvious, and obsessively treated, is the leitmotif. Indeed, in some of its applications it must be regarded as a quasi-literary device transferable to literature (Thomas Mann). Less well understood but equally important, at least from Wagner's point of view, is the "dichterisch-musikalische Periode"[11], and with direct application to *Tristan und Isolde*, that "unendliche Melodie" or "Kunst des tönenden Schweigens" which the composer defines in the following terms: "In Wahrheit ist die Grösse des Dichters am meisten danach zu ermessen, was er verschweigt, um uns das Unaussprechliche selbst schweigend sagen zu lassen; der Musiker ist es nun, der dieses Verschwiegene zum hellen Ertönen bringt, und die untrügliche Form seines laut erklingenden Schweigens ist die unendliche Melodie."[12]

As a more practical example of how music and language complement and, by pitting subjectivity against objectivity, comment upon each other, I should like to mention the beginning of Act Two, where Isolde's wishful thinking, blatantly contradicted by the musical evi-

---

11 Regarding this concept, see Carl Dahlhaus, "Wagners Begriff der 'dichterisch-musikalischen Periode'" in: *Beiträge zur Geschichte der Musikanschauung im 19. Jahrhundert*, ed. W. Salmen (Regensburg: Bosse, 1965), pp. 179-194.

12 The expression "die tiefe Kunst des tönenden Schweigens" occurs in a letter to Mathilde Wesendonck dated 12 October, 1858 (*Richard Wagner an Mathilde Wesendonck*, p. 68). The term "unendliche Melodie" is used in "Zukunftsmusik" as reprinted in Richard Wagner, *Dichtungen und Schriften: Jubiläumsausgabe in zehn Bänden*, ed. Dieter Borchmeyer (Frankfurt: Insel-Verlag, 1983), VIII, pp. 45-101, here specifically p. 93. – "Tristans Schweigen" is the title of an essay by Hans Mayer, originally published in the latter's *Anmerkungen zu Wagner* (Frankfurt: Suhrkamp, 1966).

dence, actually causes the sound of the horns that betray the presence of King Marke's hunting party to be replaced by the rustling leaves and the murmuring spring: "Nicht Hörnerschall/ tönt so hold,/ des Quelles sanft/ rieselnde Welle/ rauscht so wonnig daher./ Wie hört' ich sie,/ tosen noch Hörner?/ Im Schweigen der Nacht/ nur lacht mir der Quell."[13]

As for strictly literary analysis, there are many ways in which to approach the work as a drama or *sprachliches Kunstwerk*. Since it was intended for performance in the theater, *Tristan und Isolde* shares certain basic structural features with all plays; hence the option of treating it within a dramaturgical framework, following the examples set by Francis Fergusson[14] and Kerman, whose analysis of the paroxysmal cycle experienced by Tristan in Act III is primarily, though not exclusively, structural[15]. Unlike the structuralists among *Tristan* scholars, the thematologists act in the capacity of literary historians, tracing the evolution of the plot as developed in various genres (epic, drama and perhaps even the cinema) subsequent to Gottfried von Strassburg's poem and its medieval analogues. In fact, thematology as practiced by a long string of critics from Wolfgang Golther to Michael S. Batts and Egon Voss has long been a staple of *Tristan und Isolde* criticism[16].

---

13 The problem is discussed in Ernst Bloch's essay, "Paradoxa in Wagner's *Tristan und Isolde*" as reprinted in vol. 9 (*Literarische Aufsätze*) of the Gesamtausgabe of his works (Frankfurt: Suhrkamp, 1965).

14 Francis Fergusson, *The Idea of a Theater* (Princeton: Princeton University Press, 1949). Chapter III is entitled "*Tristan und Isolde*: The Action and Theater of Passion".

15 See section 2 of the *Tristan* chapter in Kerman's book, pp. 197-204.

16 Wolfgang Golther's '*Tristan und Isolde' in den Dichtungen des Mittelalters und der Neuzeit* was published in 1907 (Leipzig: Hirzel), his *Tristan und Isolde in der französischen und deutschen Dichtung des Mittelalters und der Neuzeit* (an updated version) in 1929. The fifth chapter of Michael S. Batts' monograph *Richard Wagner* (New York: Twayne, 1971) is entitled "Modern Literary Versions and Scholarly Interpretations of *Tristan*" (pp. 109-150). Egon Voss' "Wagner's *Tristan*: Die Liebe als furchtbare Qual", which discusses 19th-century versions that must have been

A third road toward the comprehension of *Tristan und Isolde* as a literary phenomenon – the one, curiously enough, least travelled in the 120-year reception of that masterpiece – is the verbal or linguistic one. The neglect of this obviously important aspect is demonstrated by the glaring absence of relevant material in a recently published rororo/Ricordi monograph, which does not even include the elaborate prose sketch Wagner redacted in preparation for writing the libretto[17]. The few efforts that have been made to assess the work from this point of view have been largely polemical. Thus, Richard Weltrich's book on *Tristan* as poetry devotes a chapter to the "sprachliche Beschaffenheit des Wagner'schen Textes" and arrives at the disheartening conclusion:

> Ich verkenne nicht, dass im Text [...] auf ein paar Strecken hin wahre Empfindung durchbricht, dass namentlich in der ersten Szene des dritten Aktes stellenweise die Sprache sich hebt; aber dieses Bessere gleicht Oasen in der Wüste, ohne Misshandlung des Sprachsinns geht es auf den wenigsten Seiten ab, und als eine Mischung von steifer Prosa und schwulstigem Wortgekünstel, unerträglich, unausstehlich für jeden, der Geschmack, der ein Ohr für Dichtersprache und ein lebendiges Verhältnis zu deutscher Poesie hat, liest sich das Ganze. Das Sprachgefühl des Dichters Wagner ist stumpf, über alle Massen stumpf[18].

The other extreme, that of lavish praise for Wagner's linguistic daring, especially with regard to his ingenious use of Middle High German vocabulary and syntax, is represented by Johann Cerny's essay, "Die Sprache in Richard Wagners *Tristan und Isolde*" which appeared, half a century ago, in the *Bayreuther Blätter*[19]. It is a paean to Wagner's linguistic genius, even though on occasion the author chides the Master for his capriciousness in matters grammatical. The piece

---

known to Wagner, appeared in the *Programmheft* of the Bayerische Staatsoper issued in conjunction with a 1980 production of the opera.

17 Richard Wagner, *'Tristan und Isolde': Texte, Materialien, Kommentare*, ed. Dietmar Holland (Hamburg: Rowohlt, 1983) includes several of the essays previously mentioned. The *Prosaentwurf* for the opera is reprinted in the *Jubiläumsausgabe*, IV, pp. 84-103.

18 Richard Weltrich, *Richard Wagners 'Tristan und Isolde' als Dichtung nebst einigen allgemeinen Bemerkungen über Wagners Kunst* (Berlin: Georg Reimer, 1904), p. 61.

19 *Bayreuther Blätter* 57 (1934), pp. 14-30.

concludes with an attack on Weltrich: "Als Schwulst erscheint die Dichtung des *Tristan* nur denjenigen, die nicht fähig sind, Wort und Ton im Musikdrama als untrennbare Einheit zu betrachten."

There is no denying that as a literary text *Tristan und Isolde* can fend for itself and must be judged on its own merits, notwithstanding the fact that Wagner himself subsequently regretted having published it 'before its time' and stressed the need for reading it, as it were, in musical terms.

> Bei der Gelegenheit fiel mir aber auch ein, dass es unüberlegt von mir war, den *Tristan* jetzt schon zu veröffentlichen. Zwischen einem Gedicht, das ganz für die Musik bestimmt ist, und einem rein dichterischen Theaterstück muss der Unterschied in Anlage und Ausführung so grundverschieden sein, dass das erstere, mit demselben Auge wie das letztere betrachtet, seiner eigentlichen Bedeutung nach fast ganz unverständlich bleiben muss – ehe es eben nicht durch die Musik vollendet ist[20].

That Wagner was clearly of two minds on this matter, the demands of the poet clashing, or at least conflicting, with those of the composer, is amply documented in *Zukunftsmusik*, his open letter "an einen französischen Freund als Vorwort zu einer Prosaübersetzung meiner Operndichtungen". "[...] wenn ich zu gleicher Zeit hoffen durfte, dass Sie meiner dichterischen Ausführung des *Tristan* an sich mehr Wert beilegen können als der bei meinen früheren Arbeiten mir möglichen, so müssten Sie schon aus diesem Umstande schliessen, dass die im Gedichte vollständig bereits vorgebildete musikalische Form zunächst mindestens eben der dichterischen Arbeit vorteilhaft gewesen wäre."[21]

There is plenty of evidence that Wagner harbored distinctly literary ambitions throughout his life and expressed them intermittently in his public and private utterances. In an unpublished title page for his treatise *Die Kunst und die Revolution* (1849), for example, he stated: "geschichte der musik: =christlicher ausdruck: 'wo das wort nicht mehr weiter kann, da fängt die musik an': Beethoven, 9. Symfonie: beweist dagegen: 'wo die musik nicht mehr weiter kann, da kommt das wort'.

---

20 *Jubiläumsausgabe* VIII, p. 86.
21 Ibid.

(das wort steht höher als der ton)."[22] More surprising perhaps is his reiterated wish to abandon music for literature. Thus, speaking of *Tristan* and *Die Sieger*, he unburdens himself to Liszt: "Eigentlich möchte ich jetzt lieber dichten als componiren; es gehört eine ungeheuere Hartnäckigkeit dazu, so bei der Stange zu bleiben."[23] Outlining his *Parsifal* to Mathilde four years later, he sighs: "Wenn Alles einmal ganz reif in mir ist, muss die Ausführung dieser Dichtung ein unerhörter Genuss für mich werden. Aber da können noch gute Jahre darüber hin gehen! Auch möchte ich's einmal bei der Dichtung allein bewenden lassen."[24]

As a verbal entity, *Tristan und Isolde* lends itself to a wide spectrum of specialized investigations. On the lexical level, Wagner, who prided himself on being a perceptive etymologist, excels (or, in the eyes of his severest critics, sins) in proliferating neologisms, some of which form part of a carefully designed pattern. Syntax is another subject warranting closer scrutiny than has so far been accorded it, for simply to affirm that the text is muddled throughout and an early example of willed unintelligibility is an act of critical cowardice. It merely proves that those who hold this view are unwilling to cope with ambiguity or unable to fathom the musical reasons for Wagner's linguistic deformations.

Perhaps the most promising area of linguistic-literary research on the text of *Tristan und Isolde* is Wagner's skilful handling of rhetorical devices and his dexterous use of certain figures of style[25]. A whole

---

22 Reprinted from *Nachgelassene Schriften und Dichtungen* (1895) in the *Dokumentarbiographie*, p. 342.
23 Letter dated 12 July, 1856, in *Briefwechsel zwischen Wagner und Liszt* (Leipzig: Breitkopf und Hartel, 1887), II, p. 131.
24 Letter dated 22 July, 1860, in *Richard Wagner an Mathilde Wesendonck*, p. 243.
25 This is partly prefigured in Gottfried's *Tristan*. Apart from the word play Tristan/Tantris, to which Wagner also refers, these include numerous paradoxical references to Tristan and Isolde's two-in-oneness, such as "ein man ein wip, ein wip ein man,/ Tristan Isolt, Isolt Tristan" (ll. 129/130 of the standard text in the edition by Gottfried Weber [Darmstadt, 1967]); "sie wurden ein und einvalt, die zwei und zwivalt waren

monograph could be devoted to his use of explicit or implicit oxymora (*Freundesfeindin, Wonne-Grausen, kühn und feig*) which, by their very abundance and often strategic placement in the poem, forcefully remind us of the duality which is here at work and presupposes a double perspective on the beholder's part. A similar role is assigned to puns and word plays – from the intriguing *double entendre* in the sailor's song ("Wehe, wehe, du Wind!/ Weh, ach wehe, mein Kind!") in Act I to the pervasive presence of *Schein*, quintessentially used, as in Mörike's "An eine Lampe", to refer to both illumination and illusion[26].

In the second section of this paper, I shall combine the linguistic with the conceptual approach and the two together, related as the thing contained is to the container, will constitute the final rubric in my *catalogue raisonné* of ways to approach *Tristan und Isolde*. In fact, in dealing with rhetorical figures, I have already arrived at the level of *Gehalt*, which must now occupy us for a moment.

Seeking to discover an integral meaning in *Tristan* and to determine its underlying *Weltanschauung* has been the occupation of many Wagnerites, often indulged in with a passion rarely encountered in scholarly pursuits. Since I shall face the philosophical issue head-on in the course of analyzing a central passage from Act II, the only kind of approach I need to deal with at this juncture focuses on the sexual issue.

With respect to the role of sex in *Tristan und Isolde*, two scholarly factions are at loggerheads with each other, the one upgrading, the other downplaying its importance. The most outspoken representative

---

ê; sie zwei enwaren do nieme" (ll. 11716-18), there are several other, related passages, eg. ll. 11725-30, 14327-39.

26 See especially the passage in Act II, Scene 1 (Isolde speaking to Brangäne): "Lösche des Lichtes/ letzten Schein/ [...] O lösche das Licht nun aus,/ lösche den scheuchenden Schein." P. 38 of *Tristan und Isolde*, vollständiges Buch, herausgegeben und eingeleitet von Wilhelm Zentner [Stuttgart: Reclam, 1966]). All textual references will be to this edition. Except in one potentially significant case, the discrepancies between this version and the one found in vol. 4 of the *Jubiläumsausgabe* will not be noted.

of the first is Eric Bentley, who staunchly maintains that "in its symbolism" the work – he does not specifically say: Act II – is "one long representation of the sexual act"[27]. Bentley protects himself with the qualifying phrase "in its symbolism", which raises the problem to a metaphorical level. Yet it is abundantly clear from the stage directions accompanying the climactic moment that the lovers, whether or not theirs is a "hot encounter" as Fergusson maintains, will not be caught *in flagranti delicto* since they are not wildly clutching each other at that point, but merely striking a pose ("Sie bleiben in verzückter Stellung"). Bentley would have scored a point if he had looked at Wagner's prose sketch, which gives the following instruction: "Gesteigerte Ekstase. Neue, höchste Berauschung – brünstigste Umarmung"[28]. Stage directors, take care! or you will make the audience complain, as did the composer's estranged wife Minna: "Es ist und bleibt ein gar zu verliebtes und ekliges Paar!"[29] In the *Tristan* section of his book *L'Amour et l'Occident*, Denis de Rougemont has rightly condemned the kind of interpretation offered by Bentley: "A force de l'entendre répéter par les bons juges, on a fini par croire que le *Tristan* de Wagner est un drame du désir sensuel. Qu'un tel jugement ait pu s'accréditer en dépit de flagrantes evidences, voilà qui est significatif au plus haut point de la *nécessité sociale* des mythes. (Mensonges d'auto-défense d'une société qui veut sauver sa forme, tandis que les individus qui la composent se prêtent obscurément, sous le couvert d'un refus, aux passions qui tendent à sa perte)."[30]

---

27 Eric Bentley, *The Playwright as Thinker* (New York: Reynal, 1946), p. 88.

28 *Jubiläumsausgabe* IV, p. 96.

29 Minna Wagner in a letter dated 15 December, 1861 addressed to an unidentified friend (reproduced in *Dokumentarbiographie*, p. 383). Similarly, a reviewer writing for the *Allgemeine Musikalische Zeitung* spoke of the scene as a "Verherrlichung der sinnlichen Lust mit allem aufregenden Apparat" and objected to its "trostloseste Materialismus" (quoted ibid., p. 409).

30 Denis de Rougemont, *L'Amour et l'Occident*, 2nd improved and enlarged edition (Paris: Plon, 1956), p. 212.

The reverse of Bentley's coin – but still the same coin – is presented to us by Morse Peckham who, flying in the face of all textual and musical evidence, especially as offered by Isolde's *Verklärung* (not her *Liebestod,* as is often suggested[31]), argues that in so far as "transcendental-erotic love [...] is an unrealizable ideal because it pursues a symbol and not a reality", *Tristan und Isolde* is not an "apotheosis of love" but was meant, from the very start, "to strip the mask from one of mankind's most cherished orientative gratifications"[32]. In his monograph on Wagner the writer, Peckham's disciple Robert Raphael echoes the same sentiment[33].

Rather than seeing the work as steeped in irony, de Rougemont places it in the context of medieval mysticism – more specifically, the ideal of *askesis* or voluntary renunciation of the carnal desire "that stands between the lovers"[34]. Whatever the merits of this assessment, the analysis fails to take into account that the text is not strictly Christian and that *Tristan und Isolde* aims not at renunciation but at fulfillment. Put differently: caught between Bentley's Scylla and de Rougemont's Charybdis, Wagner, far from being the ironist Peckham suspects him of being, simply wavered between various possible solutions. Depending on the mood of the moment and, one guesses, his readings of the day, he planned at different times to end his drama in different ways. With reference to the two flags introduced by Thomas in the final chapter of his *Tristran*[35], he wanted first to cover himself

---

31 The word "Liebestod" occurs at the end of the dialogue between the lovers in Act II, Scene Three (p. 52): "Nun banne das Bangen,/ holder Tod,/ sehnend verlangter/ Liebestod!"

32 Morse Peckham, *Beyond the Tragic Vision* (New York: Braziller, 1962), p. 256.

33 Robert Raphael, *Richard Wagner* (New York: Twayne, 1969), chapter 4 ("The Redemption from Love").

34 "Toutes les obstacles surmontés, quant les amants sont seuls enveloppés de ténèbres, c'est le désir charnel qui les sépare encore. Ils sont ensemble et pourtant ils sont deux." *L'Amour et l'Occident*, p. 213.

35 The references to the signal agreed upon between Tristan and Isolde are deliberately misread by Isolde of the White Hand in the final section of Thomas' *Tristran*. See pp. 349-353 in Gottfried von Strassburg, *Tristan [...] with the Surviving*

with the black one "which flutters at the end"[36], then hoped to introduce "the black and white flags"[37], but finally decided to use only the white one ("Der Freude Flagge/ am Wimpel lustig und hell"[38]).

With two mutually exclusive endings, contradictions abound, but may be resolved with reference to *Die Sieger,* the Buddhist drama about renunciation of carnal love as a precondition for the release from earthly fetters and for rejoining the God in his Nirvana. This work was to have formed a diptych with *Tristan und Isolde.* Wagner never proceeded beyond a brief prose sketch[39]; but the work, pondered for many years, entered the mainstream of his art by way of *Parsifal.* Two letters to Liszt written within the space of three months indicate how Wagner hoped to extricate himself from the dilemma caused by the conflicting views. The relevant passage in the first letter, which includes the allusion to the black and white flags, reads:

> Wenn Ihr mir recht gute Laune macht, krame ich Euch vielleicht auch meine *Sieger* aus; wiewohl es damit seine große Schwierigkeit haben wird, da ich die Idee dazu zwar schon lange mit mir herumtrage, der Stoff zu ihrer Verkörperung mir aber eben erst nur wie im Blitzesleuchten angekommen ist, zwar *für mich* in höchster Deutlichkeit und Bestimmtheit, aber nicht so für die Mitteilung. Erst müsstet ihr auch meinen *Tristan* verdaut haben, namentlich seinen dritten Akt mit der schwarzen und der weissen Flagge. Dann würden erst *Die Sieger* deutlicher werden[40].

Fragments of the 'Tristran' of Thomas, tr. A. T. Hatto (Harmondsworth: Penguin Books, 1960).

36 Letter to Liszt dated fall, 1854: "Ich habe im Kopfe einen *Tristan und Isolde* entworfen, die einfachste, aber vollblutigste musikalische Konzeption. Mit der 'schwarzen Flagge', die am Ende weht, will ich mich dann zudecken, um zu sterben." *Briefwechsel zwischen Wagner und Liszt,* p. 46.

37 Letter to Liszt dated 20 July, 1856. Ibid., p. 137.

38 P. 72 of the Reclam edition.

39 The text of this sketch is reproduced in IV, 380f. of the *Jubiläumsausgabe.* It is dated 16 May, 1856. References to *Die Sieger,* some of them rather extended, abound in Wagner's correspondence (see his letter to Mathilde dated 5 October, 1858) and in his autobiographical writings (see p. 542 of *Mein Leben,* vollständige, kommentierte Ausgabe, ed. Martin Gregor-Dellin [Munich: List, 1976]).

40 From the letter to Liszt mentioned in note 37. Here: pp. 136f.

And on a Sunday morning in the fall of 1856 (date unspecified) he expostulates, dwelling on the *concordia discors* of the pair:

> Alles was ich tat ist, dass ich die 'Madonna' und die 'Franceska' gut plaziert habe, was mir viel zu schaffen machte, ich habe gehämmert wie Mime. Nun ist aber alles fest; die Madonna über'm Arbeitstisch und Franceska über dem Sopha unter'm Spiegel , wo sie sich vortrefflich ausnimmt. Wenn es aber einmal an den *Tristan* geht, wird wohl die Franceska über den Arbeitstisch müssen; dann kommt die Madonna erst wieder dran, wenn ich an *Die Sieger* gehe. Für jetzt will ich mich immer etwas an der Siegerin [=Madonna] berauschen und mir einbilden ich könnt's auch[41].

What could be more enlightening about the two souls that dwelt in Wagner's breast than the juxtaposition of two paintings, one presumably of Dante's heroine from Canto V of the *Inferno* forever buffeted by the fierce winds of desire (presiding, as it were, over the making of *Tristan und Isolde*) and the Virgin Mary (hovering over the creation of *Die Sieger*)!

We must now take two more preliminary steps in order to reassure ourselves that it is, indeed, 'legitimate' to treat Wagner's opera as a verbal construct, shorn of its musical context. We must look, first of all, at the sequence of events relating to the genesis of *Tristan und Isolde*, in order to ascertain whether the words came before the music (*prima le parole e dopo la musica*)[42]. As it turns out, the matter is more complicated, and the answer less decisive, than one would wish it to be.

The documents at our disposal indicate that Wagner began to think about writing *Tristan und Isolde* in late 1854. As he puts it in a letter to Liszt of 16 December of that year: "Da ich nun aber doch im Leben nie das eigentliche Glück der Liebe genossen habe, so will ich diesem schönsten aller Träume noch ein Denkmal setzen, in dem vom Anfang bis zum Ende diese Liebe sich einmal so recht sättigen soll"[43]. The direct impulse for that enterprise was his response to another dramatic

---

41 *Briefwechsel zwischen Wagner und Liszt*, p. 142.

42 This in contrast to the situation prevailing in the title of Antonio Salieri's opera *Prima la musica e poi le parole*.

43 *Briefwechsel zwischen Wagner und Liszt*, p. 46.

version of the theme prepared by Karl Ritter, a disciple of Robert Schumann[44]. Wagner objected to Ritter's focus on the frivolous elements (*die übermütigen Situationen*) of Gottfried's epic and decided to sketch a *Gegen-Entwurf*: "Von einem Spaziergang heimkehrend, zeichnete ich eines Tages mir den Inhalt der drei Akte auf, in welche zusammengedrängt ich mir den Stoff für künftige Verarbeitung vorbehielt"[45]. Unfortunately, this sketch has not survived.

After a two-year period of gestation, Wagner decided in mid-1857 to carry out the project. On 28 June he notified Liszt of his decision not to complete *Der Ring des Nibelungen* at this time: "Ich habe meinen jungen Siegfried noch in die schöne Waldeinsamkeit geleitet; dort hab' ich ihn unter der Linde gelassen und mit herzlichen Tränen von ihm Abschied genommen."[46] On 20 August he began to write the long prose sketch and, following it, the full text, which was completed by 18 September and published roughly one year later in December 1858.

The first musical sketches for *Tristan*, most likely based on the early outline, were made in December, 1856[47]. However, the systematic, sequential *Vertonung* did not begin until after the libretto was finished. Wagner completed the full score of Act I on 3 April, 1858, in

---

44 Schumann himself was planning a *Tristan und Isolde*, for which Robert Reinick prepared a scenario, first published in 1925.

45 *Mein Leben*, p. 524.

46 Letter to Liszt 28 June, 1857, in *Briefwechsel zwischen Wagner und Liszt*, p. 173. As early as June 18 Wagner had written into the orchestral sketch for Act II of *Siegfried*: "*Tristan* bereits beschlossen." The parallels and interconnections between *Der Ring des Nibelungen* and *Tristan und Isolde* were repeatedly stressed by Wagner, for example in his "Epilogischer Bericht über die Umstände und Schicksale, welche die Ausführung des Bühnenfestspieles *Der Ring des Nibelungen* bis zur Veröffentlichung der Dichtung begleiteten" (1871) in *Jubiläumsausgabe* III, pp. 335-351.

47 According to Dahlhaus (*'Tristan und Isolde': Texte, Kommentare*, p. 235f.), Wagner wrote to Marie Wittgenstein in November 1856 that while working on *Siegfried* he suddenly found himself involved with *Tristan* and added: "Vorläufig Musik ohne Worte. Zu manchem werde ich wohl auch eher die Musik als die Verse machen." And in early 1857 he sent Mathilde a piece of *Tristan* music without text.

Tribschen[48], that of Act II in March 1859, in Venice, and that of Act III on 6 August, 1859, in Lucerne[49]. In January 1860, the score in its entirety was published, but five years elapsed before the premiere of the opera on 10 June, 1865, at the Munich Hof- und Nationaltheater[50].
These are the ascertainable facts and the raw chronological data. They do not offer a satisfactory answer to our question as to what came first, the text or the music. Take the following excerpt from "Zukunftsmusik":

> Ein Blick auf das Volumen dieses Gedichtes zeigt Ihnen sofort, dass ich dieselbe ausführliche Bestimmtheit, die vom Dichter eines historischen Stoffes auf die Erklärung der äusseren Zusammenhänge der Handlung, zum Nachteil der deutlichen Kundmachung der inneren Motive angewendet werden musste, nun auf die letzteren einzig anzuwenden mich getraute. Leben und Tod, die ganze Bedeutung und Existenz der äusseren Welt, hängt hier allein von der inneren Seelenbewegung ab. [...] Wenn [im *Fliegenden Holländer*] die Verse darauf berechnet waren, durch zahlreiche Wiederholung der Phrasen und der Worte, als Unterlage unter die Opernmelodie, zu der dieser Melodie nötigen Breite ausgedehnt zu werden, so findet in der musikalischen Ausführung des *Tristan* gar keine Wortwiederholung mehr statt, sondern im Gewebe der Worte und Verse ist bereits die ganze Ausdehnung der Melodie vorgezeichnet, nämlich die Melodie dichterisch bereits konstruiert[51].

This passage appears to teach us two things in respect to Wagner's musico-dramatic intentions: first, that the construction of the plot is subject to the laws of *internal* rather than *external* form ("innere Motive" instead of "äussere Zusammenhänge") according to Wagner's terminology; passion rather than action in Fergusson's; secondly, that the music is somehow implied in and anticipated by the text. What

---

48 The so-called *Wesendonck-Lieder*, which Wagner considered to be studies for *Tristan und Isolde*, were composed between late November, 1857 and early May, 1858.

49 Inspiration for the *Hirtenweisen* in the final act was drawn from popular songs in Venice and Lucerne.

50 This is hardly the place to recapitulate the story of the many frustrations and aborted attempts at staging the opera between 1861 and 1865.

51 *Jubiläumsausgabe* VIII, pp. 85f. Wagner's original intention to produce "ein seiner szenischen Anforderungen und seines kleineren Umfanges wegen leichter und eher aufführbares Werk" (ibid., p. 80), and the hilarious circumstances surrounding the Emperor of Brazil's commission for an opera in the Italian style, warrant full-blown treatment.

complicates the reading of Wagner's statement is that he seems to use the term *Melodie* both in a conventional and a highly idiosyncratic way. As "enge Form"[52] characteristic of the *Nummernoper* (of which traces are still to be found in *Tristan und Isolde*) it is linked to our conception of singable tunes and rounded phrases, but as "unendliche Melodie" it is all-pervasive and continual.

In the section "Zur Entstehungsgeschichte des *Ring* und des *Tristan*" of his book, *Wagners Konzeption des musikalischen Dramas*, Dahlhaus touches on this issue, pointing out that extreme views which give primacy either to the words or to the music are somewhat naive and stand in dire need of correction. Carefully weighing the slender and fairly ambiguous evidence, he arrives at the following preliminary conclusion:

> So unleugbar es ist, dass Wagner von einer dichterisch-musikalisch-szenischen Gesamtkonzeption ausging, so ungewiß ist das Ausmaß, in dem der Entwurf und die Ausarbeitung des Textes durch musikalische Vorstellungen mitbestimmt wurden. Und vor allem steht nicht fest, wie die musikalischen Ideen, die in die dichterisch-szenische Konzeption eingriffen, beschaffen waren. Die Voraussetzung, es müsse sich um melodische Gedanken gehandelt haben, ist ein bloßes Vorurteil aus Befangenheit in einer verschlissen romantischen Einfallsästhetik[53].

Dahlhaus suggests that what Wagner actually means by "unendliche Melodie" is a structural principle linked to the composer's notion of *Periode*. In his view, which applies to both *Der Ring des Nibelungen* and *Tristan und Isolde*, Wagner "trug [...] unbewußt eine mit den Versen verbundene musikalische Allgemeinvorstellung, eine Formidee ohne festen melodischen Umriss in sich" (p. 95). According to Dahlhaus, these *Formideen* were vague and yet firmly embedded in the text. This raises the question as to the exact point at which, in the genesis of the work, the embedding took place. A partial answer could, in my opinion, be arrived at on the basis of a detailed comparison between the prose sketch, which already contains a number of

---

52 This term actually surfaces in "Zukunftsmusik" (*Jubiläumsausgabe* VIII, p. 92).
53 *Wagners Konzeption des musikalischen Dramas* (Regensburg: Bosse, 1971), p. 94.

direct 'quotations' from the final text, and the libretto text itself. Among other things, such a study would surely reveal a tendency on the author's part to enrich the musical and impoverish the rhetorical substance of the work-in-the-making. In other words, *Tristan und Isolde* progressively ceased to be a literary product.

I do not wish to prolong the argument unduly, which was broached mainly in order to show that there is no easy solution to the problem and that, with all due respect to Wagner the musician, we do have a right to treat *Tristan und Isolde* as a verbal construct – a better right, at any rate, than can be claimed by those who choose to treat it as a symphonic poem. If in the literary analysis of the work that follows I ignore the 'rational' aspect of the text, that is, the day-action revolving around King Marke and the whole plethora of courtly terms such as honor, fame, custom and loyalty, I do so because it merely serves dramaturgically as background and because, musically, it yields little more than recitative. If as a literary scholar I venture occasionally onto territory that is more essentially musical, I do so in full awareness of the pitfalls and quicksands that are in store for me.

II.

In a letter to Mathilde Wesendonck of early August 1860, Wagner offered an exegesis of the true existential meaning he attached to his recently completed opera and, in so doing, revealed the secret of its *raison d'être*. "So wäre alle furchtbare Tragik des Lebens nur in dem Auseinanderliegen in Zeit und Raum zu finden; da aber Zeit und Raum nur unsere Anschauungsweisen sind, außerdem aber keine Realität haben, so müßte dem vollkommen Hellsehenden auch der höchste tragische Schmerz nur aus dem Irrtum des Individuums erklärt werden können."[54] This programmatic statement may be complemented, on the psychological plane, with an equally pertinent passage from "Zukunftsmusik". "Dürfen wir die ganze Natur im großen Über-

---

54 *Richard Wagner an Mathilde Wesendonck*, p. 242.

blick als einen Entwicklungsgang vom Unbewußtsein zum Bewußtsein bezeichnen und stellt sich namentlich im menschlichen Individuum dieser Prozeß am auffallendsten dar [...]."[55] Taking these statements together I shall seek to show that, conceptually as well as structurally, *Tristan und Isolde* is a carefully planned and neatly executed presentation of the process of *Ent-Individualisierung* on several levels.

The evidence I am prepared to offer is so forthright and cumulative that it is strange, even shocking, that it has never been marshalled before. Once again Peckham, shrewd but purblind observer that he is, will serve as our whipping boy. Realizing full well that *Tristan und Isolde* is all about the *principium individuationis*, he once again completely misses the mark. While it is rational enough to maintain that "when you are dead you can scarcely enjoy the loss of identity"[56], paradox insists that in the metaphysical and esthetic cosmos of *Tristan und Isolde* it is precisely the annihilation of Self, with its concomitant *Vergessen*[57], that brings ultimate joy, at least to Isolde, whose transfiguration Wagner celebrates at the conclusion of the opera.

There are many ways of looking at *Tristan und Isolde* conceived as a poem, a symphony or a mixture of both, but also as possible models of or analogues to its underlying world view, that is, the realization that Non-Being is preferable to Being[58]. Various religious and philosophical systems advocating the dissolution of self (preceded by abdication of the will) and its re-absorption into a larger, depersonalized or disembodied, stream may have gone into the making of this music drama, whether directly or indirectly. Among them are medieval

---

55 *Jubiläumsausgabe* VIII, p. 46.
56 *Beyond the Tragic Vision*, p. 256.
57 On the cognitive or gnoseological level, *Vergessen* corresponds to *Unbewußtsein* on the psychological one. It is a noun frequently used in *Tristan und Isolde*.
58 See especially Paul Valéry's greatest poem, "Le Cimétière marin", where the sky-as-diamond symbolizes the purity of Non-Being in which the thinking Self is but a flaw that mars it: "Mes repentirs, mes doutes, mes contraintes/ Sont le défaut de ton grand diamant".

mysticism, Novalis[59], Schopenhauer's philosophy, Buddhist theology and, *post festum*, the views on Dionysus developed in Nietzsche's *Die Geburt der Tragödie aus dem Geiste der Musik*.

My specific aim in the pages that follow, however, is not to mull over Wagner's philosophical eclecticism but to show the verbal strategies by which he manages to reproduce before our very eyes and ears the full cycle of developments from Non-Being by way of Being back to Non-Being. The model that the creator of *Tristan und Isolde* selected was provided by Indian, specifically Buddhist thought, in which he had steeped himself since 1854. It is described at length in a letter to Liszt of 7 June, 1855, whose central (for our purposes) passage reads:

> Die Bramanen-Lehre stellt [...] den Mythos von einer Entstehung der Welt durch Gott auf; allein sie preist diesen Akt nicht als eine Wohltat, sondern stellt ihn als eine Sünde Bramas dar, die dieser, der *sich selbst in diese Welt verwandelte*, durch die ungeheueren Leiden eben dieser Welt abbüßt, und sich in denjenigen Heiligen erlöst, die durch vollständige Verneinung des Willens zum Leben in der einzig nur noch sie erfüllenden Sympathie für alles Leidende in das Nirwana, d. h. Land des Nicht-mehr-seins, übergehen[60].

This sounds like a slightly foreshortened plot outline for *Die Sieger*, of which *Tristan und Isolde* is a secular mirror image, *Heilige* having here been replaced by *Liebende*.

In so far as music, before its elements have been formally assembled, pertains to a more 'primitive' condition, it stands, unadulter-

---

59 See especially Arthur Prüfer's essay "Novalis' *Hymnen an die Nacht* in ihren Beziehungen zu Wagners *Tristan und Isolde*" in *Richard-Wagner-Jahrbuch* 1 (1906), pp. 290-304.

60 *Briefwechsel zwischen Wagner und Liszt*, p. 83. The close relationship, in terms of the metaphysical underpinning, between *Tristan und Isolde* and Strindberg's *Dream Play* has surely been noted before. Both men were profoundly interested in Buddhism at the time of writing their masterpieces. Let us bear in mind the resemblance between the overall structure of Wagner's opera and the Daughter's account of the creation of the world in the last scene of Strindberg's drama: "In the dawn of time [...] Brahma [...] let himself be seduced by Maya, the World Mother, that he might propagate. This mingling of the divine element with the earthly was the Fall from heaven. This world, its life and its inhabitants are therefore only a mirage, a reflection, a dream image" (Elizabeth Sprigge's translation). The symbolic action of the *Dream Play* is a dramatization of Brahma's "Fall".

ated by the human voice, at the beginning of the opera, antedating but concurrently prefiguring individuation. Logically, then, the act of creation occurs in the Prelude, that is, before the curtain rises, the *dramatis personae* appear and the action gets under way. As Wagner puts it in a letter to Mathilde:

> Alles ist mir fremd, und sehnsüchtig blicke ich oft nach dem Land Nirwana. Doch Nirwana wird mir schnell wieder *Tristan*. Sie kennen die buddhistische Weltentstehungstheorie. Eine Hand trübt die Himmelsklarheit: das schwillt an, verdichtet sich, und in undurchdringlicher Massenhaftigkeit steht endlich die ganze Welt wieder vor mir. Das ist das alte Los, solange ich noch solche unerlöste Geister um mich habe[61].

The final stage of this ineluctable development, the fragmentation of the phenomenal world and its ultimate submersion in Nirvana, is attained not so much in Buddhist as in Schopenhauerian terms, that is to say, the unfettering of the will as symbolized by "des Welt-Athems wehendem All". In Act I the wind – objective correlative of the *Welt-Atem* – is still seen as a hostile and destructive force with entirely negative connotations. Thus Isolde, vowing revenge and lamenting the loss of her, and her mother's, magic power, calls upon the "wehenden Atem" to atomize the ship and its human cargo, including Tristan:

> Hört meinen Willen,
> zagende Winde!
> Heran zu Kampf
> und Wettergetös'!
> Zu tobender Stürme
> wütendem Wirbel!
> Treibt aus dem Schlaf
> dies träumende Meer,
> weckt aus dem Grund
> seine grollende Gier!
> Zeigt ihm die Beute,
> die ich ihm biete!
> Zerschlag es, dies trotzige Schiff,
> des zerschellten Trümmer verschling's!
> Und was auf ihm lebt,
> den wehenden Atem,
> den lass' ich euch Winden zum Lohn!

---

61 The letter, dated 3 March, 1860, is reproduced on pp. 208ff. of *Richard Wagner an Mathilde Wesendonck*. The quotation comes from p. 217.

And toward the end of the act, just before drinking the 'fatal' potion, Tristan seems to express a similar view. "Wild auffahrend", he cries, "Los den Anker!/ Das Steuer dem Strom! Den Winden Segel und Mast!" Needless to say, the two cannot have their wish but must, both separately and jointly, undergo the agonies and ecstasies of love before being inhaled by the universal breath.

In analyzing the process by which the world constructed in the Prelude is slowly but surely deconstructed, I shall focus on that portion of the dialogue between hero and heroine in Act II, Scene Two, in which the *Ent-Ichung* is thematic.

>Tristan: Lass' mich sterben!
>Isolde: Neid'sche Wache!
>Tristan: Nie erwachen!
>Isolde: Doch der Tag
>muß Tristan wecken?
>Tristan: Lass' den Tag
>dem Tode weichen!
>Isolde: Tag und Tod
>mit gleichen Streichen,
>sollten uns're
>Lieb' erreichen?
>Tristan: Uns're Liebe?
>Tristans Liebe?
>Dein' und mein',
>Isoldes Liebe?
>Welches Todes Streichen
>könnte je sie weichen?
>Stünd' er vor mir,
>der mächt'ge Tod,
>wie er mir Leib
>und Leben bedroht,
>die ich so willig
>der Liebe lasse,
>wie wäre seinen Streichen
>die Liebe selbst zu erreichen?
>Stürb' ich nun ihr,
>der so gern ich sterbe,
>wie könnte die Liebe
>mit mir sterben,
>die ewig lebende
>mit mir enden?
>Doch stürbe nie seine Liebe,

>   wie stürbe dann Tristan
>   seiner Liebe?
> Isolde: Doch uns're Liebe,
>   heißt sie nicht Tristan
>   und – Isolde?
>   Dies süße Wörtlein: und,
>   was es bindet,
>   der Liebe Bund,
>   wenn Tristan stürb',
>   zerstört es nicht der Tod?
> Tristan: Was stürbe dem Tod,
>   als was uns stört,
>   was Tristan wehrt,
>   Isolde immer zu lieben,
>   ewig ihr nur zu leben?
> Isolde: Doch dieses Wörtlein: und –
>   wär' es zerstört,
>   wie anders als
>   mit Isoldes eig'nem Leben
>   wär' Tristan der Tod gegeben?
> Beide: So stürben wir,
>   um ungetrennt,
>   ewig einig,
>   ohne End',
>   ohn' Erwachen,
>   ohn' Erbangen,
>   namenlos
>   in Lieb' umfangen,
>   ganz uns selbst gegeben,
>   der Liebe nur zu leben![62]

A close reading of the passage reveals that Wagner has carefully chosen each word or phrase and subtly distinguished between Tristan's and Isolde's share in the dialogue. (It is hardly coincidental, for instance, that it is Isolde, rather than Tristan, who stresses the *und*,

---

[62] I have omitted the stage directions. As Thomas Mann points out in his essay "Leiden und Grösse Richard Wagners" (1933), part of the section so closely resembles a passage from Friedrich Schlegel's *Lucinde* that a direct influence must be posited. The passage in question: "Warum sollten wir nicht die herbste Laune des Zufalls für schönen Witz und ausgelassene Willkür halten, da wir unsterblich sind wie die Liebe? Ich kann nicht mehr sagen, meine Liebe oder deine Liebe; beide sind sich gleich und vollkommen Eins, so viel Liebe als Gegenliebe. Es ist Ehe, ewige Einheit und Verbindung unsrer Geister, nicht bloß für das, was wir diese oder jene Welt nennen, sondern für die eine, wahre, unteilbare, namenlose, unendliche Welt, für unser ganzes ewiges Sein und Leben."

occurring three times within the space of a dozen lines, for it is she who, at this point, hangs on to life and does not wish to be summarily dislodged from her Self.) I must emphatically disagree with Dahlhaus's blanket judgment: "Das Zwiegespräch Tristans und Isoldes ist der Antithetik des traditionellen Dramas so weit entrückt, daß es beinahe gleichgültig erscheint, ob es Isolde oder Tristan ist, der redet: die Sätze und Satzfragmente sind austauschbar und werden auch manchmal ausgetauscht."[63] As the evidence shows, this is true only for the duet-like unison part at the conclusion of the segment.

The strategical blueprint to be used for our subsequent analysis specifies that each stage in the unfolding process of disintegration in *Tristan und Isolde* be marked and justified. However, since Wagner was an artist rather than a logician, he had to take musico-esthetic factors into account and was not, or was not primarily, concerned with fashioning solid causal links within the chain I shall construct here, rearranging the order in which the steps are presented in the opera so as to lay bare the ideal sequence, or rather sequences, for there are actually two series which run parallel to each other: a short one revolving around the notion of consciousness, and a long one gauged to that of identity. I shall start with the former, in which the adverb *bewußt* and its lexical offshoots play the pivotal role, usually at the climactic conclusion of a scene or segment of dialogue.

The brief but impassioned exchange between the two lovers in Act I, Scene Five, which opens with the drinking of the *Liebestrank* and ends abruptly as the curtains are torn open to reveal "das ganze Schiff mit Rittern und Schiffsvolk", concludes with the lines: "Welten entronnen,/ du mir gewonnen!/ Du mir einzig bewußt,/ höchste Liebeslust!" This ecstatic moment, which foreshadows the long tryst in the second act, thus culminates in the narrowing of focus and shutting out of reality, *Bewußtsein* here to be understood as awareness not of the

---

63 Carl Dahlhaus, *Richard Wagners Musikdramen* (Velber: Friedrich, 1971). The chapter from which the quote is taken is reproduced in *'Tristan und Isolde': Texte, Materialien, Kommentare*, pp. 231-243, here p. 231.

world at large but of the partner and/or (since the syntax is slippery) of *Liebeslust*. After this false start, a new beginning is made in Act II, Scene Two, where, after three hundred lines of rhetorical 'warming-up' exercises, the matching level of ecstasy is attained in the analogous lines, "Nie-wieder-Erwachens/ wahnlos/ hold bewußter Wunsch", which already suggest a sliding over into the realm of the unconscious.

Following the interruption by Brangäne, and a second, briefer intervention by the loyal guard, the unduly extended scene moves rather quickly toward its climax, which it reaches in perfect parallel to the corresponding scene of Act I just before the arrival of King Marke, with the joint exclamation "ewig, endlos,/ ein-bewußt;/ heiß erglühter Brust/ höchste Liebeslust!" Thus we have progressed from *einzig bewußt* and *hold bewußt* to *ein-bewußt*, a neologism expressly coined for the occasion and perfectly suitable for a more advanced but still intermediary stage in the de-individualization process, a condition of oneness in which consciousness continues to function but is no longer tied to the individual.

The final step, a qualitative leap, is taken in the concluding scene of Act III when the transfigured Isolde, following her suicidal Tristan into death, uses the telling phrase "In dem wogenden Schwall,/ in dem tönenden Schall,/ in des Welt-Atems/ wehendem All, –/ ertrinken,/ versinken, –/ unbewußt – höchste Lust!" Leo Spitzer has made a syntactic analysis fully in keeping with the spirit of the passage and Wagner's overall intentions[64]. Pinpointing the stage at which consciousness vanishes, these words terminate the series, whose parts, scattered over the three acts of the opera, make up a pattern that correlates with the inner action.

The second, longer, and much more intricate series focuses in its first, phenomenal phase on the way in which the names of the two

---

64 Leo Spitzer, *A Method of Interpreting Literature*, pp. 49f., where the notion of "syntactical disintegration" is used with regard to the "semi-independent" infinitives *ertrinken* and *versinken*.

protagonists are juxtaposed in the text. (Let us note, in passing, that this is the only one of Wagner's works for the musical stage in whose title two names are linked – a fact worth considering in light of the circumstance that such importance is attached to the coordinating conjunction.) In the first stage, marked by that portion of Act I which precedes the drinking of the love potion, Tristan and Isolde are kept apart inasmuch as their names are not permitted to occur in one and the same line or without intervening text. But right after the ceremonial act, having reached a new plateau, they are, for the first time, directly confronted ("Tristan!/ Isolde!"), until at long last the point is reached where, though still parted by the exclamation point, they appear side by side on the same line ("Isolde! Tristan!")[65].

With the sudden intrusion of external reality, no further progress toward the perfect union of the lovers is made in Act I. In fact, the movement is retrogressive in so far as at the very end of the act Wagner reverts to the initial formula "Tristan!/ Isolde!". At this point, then, no *und* is in sight, at least not in the finished libretto. Curiously enough, in the prose sketch Wagner introduces it just before the curtains are torn open: "Tristan! Isolde! O Wonne! o höchste Seligkeit! Ich nur dein! Nur dein! – Die Welt vergessen, alles besiegt – nur Tristan und Isolde!"[66] In finalizing his text, however, he wisely postponed the appearance of the crucial word.

Stages two to eight in our schematic presentation are all encompassed within the passage from Act II, Scene Two. We might call the second stage of the irreversible sequence possessive, that is, a condition in which the lovers, still very much themselves, seek to appropriate each other in preparation for the actual exchange of identities that is to follow. The requisite verbal formula is "mein und dein" which, at

---

[65] I must reiterate that mine is a verbal analysis, which must link up with a musicological one if full complementarity is to be achieved. In this case, for instance, anticipatory overlappings occur on the musical plane.

[66] *Jubiläumsausgabe*, IV, p. 92.

its very first occurrence is already seen as a precondition for "ewig, ewig einig!".

The third stage, foreshadowed in the title of the opera and fully thematized in our excerpt, is that in which a perfect balance is struck, but not yet at the cost of lost identities. The *und* which plays so weighty a role in the central portion of the interchange is used like an anchor to show that, while it is still in place, all is well with the phenomenal world. For Isolde it is a true conjunction vouchsaving "der Liebe Bund", whereas from Tristan's already transcendent perspective it is decidedly a disjunction ("Was stürbe dem Tod,/ als was uns stört,/ was Tristan wehrt,/ Isolde immer zu lieben,/ ewig ihr nur zu leben?").

Stage four in the 'loss of identity' sequence brings about a veritable exchange of selves. This manoeuver is neatly executed, near the end of our key passage in the following verbal exchange:

    Tristan: Tristan du,
              ich Isolde,
              nicht mehr Tristan!
    Isolde: Du Isolde,
              Tristan ich,
              nicht mehr Isolde![67]

Here identity is still within reach, but only barely as the lovers, moving toward *Ein-bewußtsein,* attain a quasi-androgynous condition by transforming themselves, as it were, into Istan und Tristolde. This metamorphic act has taken us to the very brink of the world of phenomena which, if Tristan is to have his way, must be thrown over for that of *noumena*. On the fringes, linking the physical with the metaphysical realm, lies the domain of myth, for which Wagner, throughout his career, displayed a very special affinity. As he explains in a passage from "Zukunftsmusik":

> Als den idealen Stoff des Dichters glaubte ich daher den 'Mythos' bezeichnen zu müssen [...], denn bei ihm verschwindet die konventionelle, mit der abstrakten Vernunft erklärliche Form der menschlichen Verhältnisse fast vollständig, um

---

67 The exchange of personalities is prefigured in Act II, Scene Two in the lines "Bin ich's?/ Bist du's?" spoken alternately by Tristan and Isolde.

dafür nur das ewig Verständliche, rein Menschliche, aber eben in der unnachahmlichen, echten Form zu zeigen, welche jedem Mythos seine so schnell erkenntliche individuelle konkrete Gestalt verleiht[68].

Whereas mythical figures are embodiments of concrete natural or, as the case may be, abstract supernatural forces, the figures of legend, as Tristan and Isolde, are fictional counterparts of historical or pseudo-historical personages that may ultimately rise to the level of myth. In both cases, it is the names which, firmly affixed to their bearers, offer stability and give permanence. For that reason, the loss of names, resulting in anonymity, entails the destruction of the very fabric of which myths and legends are made, a return to a chaotic sphere in which the *principium individuationis* has ceased to function and where individuals are, at best, reduced to qualities[69]. Tristan and Isolde reach and – given the inverse perspective which here prevails – celebrate this condition, which constitutes the sixth rung of the ladder: "So stürben wir,/ um ungetrennt, –/ ewig einig/ ohne End', –/ ohn' Erwachen, –/ ohn' Erbangen, –/ *namenlos*/ in Lieb' umfangen,/ ganz uns selbst gegeben,/ der Liebe nur zu leben!"[70]

Stage seven, already outside of the fence that encloses the world as *Vorstellung*, is marked by the point at which Tristan, abstracting from and, in fact, conceptualizing his own existence, postulates the coincidence of self and love: "Stünd' er vor mir,/ der mächt'ge Tod,/ wie er mir Leib/ und Leben bedroht,/ die ich so willig/ der Liebe lasse,/ wie wäre seinen Streichen/ *die Liebe selbst* zu erreichen?" Beyond the pale of love with a lower case "l", Tristan now regards himself as Love incarnate, a mutant of the Kantian *Ding an sich* which is, quite naturally, indestructible. This is quite another matter from Isolde's pat

---

68 *Jubiläumsausgabe*, VIII, p. 64.

69 According to Fergusson (*The Idea of a Theater*, p. 81), "even the characters are not to be thought of as real, but only as shifting moral qualities which express passion".

70 My emphasis. The *Jubiläumsausgabe* (IV, p. 51) is the only edition among those consulted which replaces Tristan's, but not Isolde's, *stürben* by *starben*. It would lead too far to ponder the implications of this substitution here.

allegorical solution of the problem, according to which it is *Frau Minne*, an outside force ("des kühnsten Mutes/ Königin,/ des Weltenwerdens/ Walterin") that is to blame (and be praised) for their predicament[71].

The process of conceptualization, in which allegory constitutes no more than a crude and preliminary form of philosophical abstraction, continues in stage eight, the next-to-the-last-one, which is adumbrated at the end of the duet "O sink hernieder,/ Nacht der Liebe".

Tristan:	Von deinem Zauber sanft umsponnen, vor deinen Augen süß zerronnen;
Isolde:	Herz an Herz dir, Mund an Mund;
Tristan:	eines Atems ein'ger Bund;
Beide:	bricht mein Blick sich wonn'-erblindet, erbleicht die Welt mit ihrem Blenden:
Isolde:	die uns der Tag trügend erhellt,
Tristan:	zu täuschendem Wahn entgegenstellt,
Beide:	*selbst dann bin ich die Welt*[72].

Like so much else in the opera, this may seem preposterous at first glance; yet it fits perfectly into the pattern that I am here attempting to trace. Sung in unison in the last line, the phrase lifts us to a level of abstraction which transcends the world as *Vorstellung* or *Erscheinung*, except for the *Ich* which stubbornly resists the force of the universal will.

---

71 With a probable allusion to Euripides' *Hippolytus*, Wagner states in the "Programmbuch zu drei Pariser Konzerten" (*Gesammelte Schriften*, ed. Julius Kapp [Leipzig: Hesse & Becker, n. d.] IX, p. 61): "Die auf ihre Rechte eifersüchtige Liebesgöttin rächt sich."

72 My emphasis. This is the exact reversal of the process outlined in the letter to Liszt, where it is said that Buddha "sich selbst in diese Welt verwandelte".

As the world was created by mistake or as a consequence of sin, so, according to Wagner, must it be destroyed. This is precisely what happens in Act III of *Tristan und Isolde*. Tristan having destroyed himself by a voluntary act (on the level of plot, he commits suicide by tearing off his bandages and bleeding to death[73]), it remains for Isolde to bring down the world through her negation of the will which finds its ultimate expression "in der vollständigen Aufhebung des persönlichen Bewußtseins"[74]. Symptomatically, Isolde remains attached to the world even as she is about to leave it. More specifically, in her case the desired erasure of consciousness is effected in a setting that is truly sensuous, namely through the medium of synesthesia. As a psycho-physical phenomenon, synesthesia, which denotes the fusion or confusion of the senses, entails the breakdown of the highly differentiated human sensorium and a return, quite appropriate in this context, to a more primitive form of multiple perception. Isolde experiences this deprivation (which for her is an enrichment) in a state of complete euphoria. Anticipated by the dying Tristan's exclamation "Wie, hör' ich das Licht?" and several other quasi-synesthetic formulations interspersed throughout, it sets the tone for her *Verklärung*. In an orgy involving the lower as well as the higher senses – almost a premonition of Des Esseintes' experiments in Huysmans' *A Rebours* –, she is lifted to a climax before breathing her last:

> Heller schallend,
> mich umwallend,
> sind es Wellen
> sanfter Lüfte?
> Sind es Wogen
> wonniger Düfte?

---

[73] This theatrically effective assertion of the will is not prefigured in the prose sketch, where the corresponding passage reads: "In der furchtbarsten Aufregung springt er auf, der Ankommenden entgegentaumelnd. Auf der Mitte der Bühne begegnen sie sich. Lauter Schrei des Entzückens. Er sinkt in Isoldens Armen langsam leblos zu Boden." *Jubiläumsausgabe* IV, p. 102.

[74] From the letter to Liszt referred to in note 72. Wagner adds: "Es gibt aber kein anderes Bewußtsein als das persönliche, individuelle."

> Wie sie schwellen,
> mich umrauschen,
> soll ich atmen,
> soll ich lauschen?
> Soll ich schlürfen,
> untertauchen?
> Süß in Düften
> mich verhauchen?

With the final lines of this strange monologue the world as we know it comes to an end along with Isolde's awareness of it. There will be no reconstitution of identity, no subsequent recourse to consciousness, no restoration of the sensory apparatus. Language will fail; and how long can music, of which Nietzsche maintains that it antedates the *principium individuationis*, survive? For the audience in the Festspielhaus or wherever *Tristan und Isolde* may be performed, it would be futile to think of the future either of the 'dissipated' protagonists or of the survivors, Marke and Brangäne. If empathy has carried the day, listeners and viewers will feel deprived of the chance to follow the pair into the Schopenhauerian Nirvana. Wagner agonized over the risk he thought he was taking. Thus in the course of writing the music for Act III he told Mathilde: "Kind! Dieser Tristan wird was furchtbares! Dieser letzte Akt! Ich fürchte die Oper wird verboten – falls durch schlechte Aufführung nicht das Ganze parodiert wird –; nur mittelmäßige Aufführungen können mich retten! Vollständig gute müssen die Leute verrückt machen."[75] And during the agonizing and ultimately abortive rehearsals in Vienna, he wrote: "Die Leute sind mir hier gut; keines kennt aber eigentlich die Gefahr, in die ich sie mit meinem *Tristan* bringe, und vielleicht wird noch alles unmöglich, wenn sie dahinter kommen. [...] Was werden sie alle erschrecken, wenn ich ihnen eines Tages offen sage, dass sie alle mit mir zu Grunde gehen müssen!"[76]

---

75 Letter to Mathilde dated April 1859, in *Richard Wagner an Mathilde Wesendonck*, p. 123.

76 Letter dated 19 August, 1861. Ibid., p. 279.

Benedetto Marcellos *Il Teatro alla moda*
Scherz, Satire, Parodie oder tiefere Bedeutung? (1989)

> Si vous voulez savoir ce que c'est qu'un Opéra, je vous dirai que c'est un travail bizarre de Poésie et de Musique où le Poète et le Musicien, également genés l'un par l'autre, se donnent bien de la peine à faire un méchant ouvrage.
> (Saint-Evremond)[1]

> Un abito intiero da Poeta moderno di scorza d'albero color di febbre, guarnito di metafore, traslati. iperbole, etc., con bottoniera di soggetti vecchi rifatti d'opera, foderato di versi di varie misure con sua spada compagna con manico di pelle d'orso.
> (Benedetto Marcello)[2]

Satire und Parodie, zwei Formen kritischer Auseinandersetzung mit der zeitgenössischen Wirklichkeit bzw. Kunst, in deren Rahmen die anvisierten Phänomene in der ausgesprochenen oder unausgesprochenen Absicht, den status quo zu ändern, verzerrend beschrieben werden, kommen besonders dann zum Tragen, wenn die jeweilige Entwicklung ihren Höhepunkt überschritten und in eine Phase des Exzesses und des Verfalls (Dekadenz) eingetreten ist. Sie sind also an einen bestimmten historischen Kontext gebunden und nur im Hinblick auf das *hic et nunc*, dessen Kenntnis beim Rezipienten und Interpreten vorausgesetzt werden muß, verständlich. In beiden Gattungen gibt es, bei unterschiedlicher Intensität und Dichte, sowohl allgemeine als auch besondere Modi und Verfahrensweisen. So tritt neben die Partikular-Satire, die sich mit Aktualität begnügt, die Universal-Satire, in der ‚zeitlose' menschliche Schwächen bloßgestellt werden. (Oft

---

1 *Oeuvres melées*, hrsg. von Charles Giraud (Paris: Techener, 1965). S. 359f.
2 *Il Teatro alla moda*, hrsg. von G. A. Caula (Turin: Caula. [o. J.]). S. 52. Von hier an zitiert als *Teatro*.

kommt es bei diesen Untergattungen zur Personal-Union – so bei den berühmtesten Exemplaren des Genres, Swifts *Gulliver's Travels* und Voltaires *Candide*.)

Parodien hingegen sind meist Partikular-Parodien, die ein konkret greifbares Modell anpeilen und karikieren – so Nestroys Meyerbeer-Parodie *Robert der Teuxel* und der *Tannhäuser* des gleichen Verfassers. Universal-Parodien sind verhältnismäßig selten und beziehen sich, wenn sie auftreten, eher auf scharf umrissene und relativ kurzlebige Unterarten als auf Grundtypen wie Tragödie und Komödie (siehe August von Platens Schicksalsdrama-Parodie *Die verhängnisvolle Gabel*).

Insofern als es Satirikern (seltener Parodisten) vor allem darum geht, Auswüchse zu geißeln und womöglich den status quo wiederherzustellen, sind ihre Werke gewöhnlich Ausdruck einer konservativen Gesinnung (progressive, d. h. futurologische Satiren nennt man Dystopien). Ästhetisch tendieren ihre Verfasser zum Klassizismus und schlagen sich in den jeweiligen *querelles des anciens et des modernes* mit Vorliebe auf die Seite der Alten. *Moderno*, *alla moda* und *al suo modo* sind in ihrem Lexikon Schimpfworte, in denen sich die Wut über alles Modische und somit Kurzlebige entlädt[3]. Bei Opernsatiren fällt zum Beispiel auf, daß sie sich mit Vorliebe auf die Poetik des Aristoteles berufen und demzufolge das Drama höher stellen als das *dramma per musica*. (Im Frankreich des achtzehnten Jahrhunderts galt bekanntlich die Oper als eine Unterart des Dramas, d. h. als eine literarische Gattung.) Im geistigen und weltanschaulichen Bereich sind Satiriker im Schnitt Vertreter der Aufklärung und somit mehr oder minder stark ausgeprägte Rationalisten, die den Intellekt höher bewer-

---

3 *Alla moda* erscheint im Titel, wie bei Hogarths Bilderfolge *Marriage-à-la-mode* aus dem Jahre 1745; auf S. 13 ist von der *confusione moderna* die Rede; und der Ausdruck *al suo modo* wird fast stereotyp auf den Dichter, den Komponisten und die Sänger angewendet. Zur Begriffsgeschichte von ‚modernus' siehe den entsprechenden Abschnitt in Ernst Robert Curtius' Buch *Europäische Literatur und lateinisches Mittelalter* (Bern: Francke, 1948).

ten als die Sinne. In der Opernsatire des aufgeklärten Jahrhunderts gehen folglich *classicismo* und *illuminismo* Hand in Hand[4].

In diesem Zusammenhang erhebt sich die Frage, welche Beweggründe ein schriftstellerndes Individuum jeweils dazu veranlassen mögen, Satiren zu schreiben. Man darf annehmen, daß hierbei zwei Faktoren im Spiele sind, nämlich ein äußerer (historischer) und ein innerer (psychologischer). Geschichtlich gesehen setzt, wie schon angedeutet, diese schöpferische Form der Kritik eine unmittelbare, detaillierte Kenntnis der herrschenden Zustände voraus, wobei anzunehmen ist, daß die Kritik an diesen Zuständen um so wirksamer sein wird je tiefer die Kenntnis davon in das Bewußtsein der Öffentlichkeit gedrungen ist. Was das Opernwesen bzw. -unwesen anbetrifft, so war das Venedig des frühen 18. Jahrhunderts in der Tat ein ideales Sujet für den Satiriker, machten doch hier, wo seit 1637 öffentliche Opernhäuser existierten, zur Zeit Marcellos ein halbes Dutzend einander Konkurrenz[5]. Kein Wunder also, daß sich diese Institutionen durch Anwendung spektakulärer szenischer Effekte gegenseitig das Wasser abzugraben suchten und keine Mühe scheuten, das in dieser Hinsicht zwar nicht anspruchsvolle aber wählerische Publikum für sich zu gewinnen. Wohl niemals zuvor oder danach waren also die Voraussetzungen für Satire besser und die Angriffsflächen offensichtlicher, und es war wirklich schwer *saturam non scribere*.

Was den venezianischen Adeligen, Staatsbeamten, Komponisten und Schriftsteller Marcello dazu bewog, das im Mittelpunkt unserer Betrachtungen stehende Pamphlet zu schreiben, läßt sich heute natürlich nicht mehr mit Sicherheit ausmachen, da wir über die Umstände, denen *Il Teatro alla moda* seine Entstehung verdankt, nicht im Einzel-

---

4 Die Standard-Terminologie des Klassizismus beherrscht durchwegs die Debatte auf Seiten der *anciens*; und Begriffe wie *verismiglianza, proprietà, probabilità* sowie deren Gegenteil finden sich z. B. besonders häufig bei Muratori.

5 Siehe hierzu vor allem Simon Towneley Worsthornes *Venetian Opera in the Seventeenth Century* (Oxford: Clarendon Press, 1954), Taddeo Wiels *I Teatri musicali veneziani del settecento* (Venedig: Forni, 1897) und den Ausstellungskatalog *I Teatri pubblici di Venezia (secoli XVII-XVIII)* (Venedig: Biennale, 1971).

nen unterrichtet sind[6]. Mehrere Gesichtspunkte wären beim hypothetischen Nachvollzug der Genese zu berücksichtigen. So besaß Marcello, wie ähnliche Ergüsse, die aus seiner Feder flossen, zur Genüge beweisen, von Natur aus eine satirische Ader[7]. Hinzu kam gewiß die Tatsache, daß zwar seine Psalmen-Vertonungen schon zu Lebzeiten höchste Anerkennung fanden und als vorbildlich galten[8], seine Opern aber erfolglos blieben und sehr schnell dem Vergessen anheimfielen. Jedenfalls erwähnt der Chronist Taddeo Wiel in seinem umfassenden Katalog der im 18. Jahrhundert in der Lagunenstadt aufgeführten Opern kein einziges ihm als musikalischem Urheber zugeschriebenes Werk[9], und noch heute streiten sich die gelehrten Geister darüber, welche Opern er wirklich komponiert hat[10].

Das *Teatro alla moda* mag also unter anderem auch ein Produkt enttäuschter Liebe und mangelnden Erfolgs gewesen sein, denn wie ein moderner Satiriker, Heinrich Mann, unter Hinweis auf seinen Roman *Der Untertan* treffend bemerkt: „Eine gute Satire schrieb noch keiner, er hätte denn irgendeine Zugehörigkeit gehabt zu dem, was er

---

6 Am 2. April 1721 schreibt Apostolo Zeno an Antonio Francesco Marmi: „Quel *Teatro alla moda* del Sig. Marcello è una satira gentilissima". *Lettere* (Venedig: Valvasense, 1752), II, S. 202.

7 Diese Frage behandelt Alfred Einstein in seiner exemplarischen Ausgabe: Benedetto Marcello. *Das Theater nach der Mode*, zum erstenmal ins Deutsche übertragen (München: Georg Müller. 1917. S. 114ff.). Von hier an zitiert als *Einstein*.

8 In seinem *Saggio sopra l'opera in musica* (1762) spricht Francesco Algarotti vom Komponisten Marcello als einem „uomo forse a niun altro secondo tra gli antichi e primo certamente tra' moderni". In: *Illuministi italiani. tomo II: Opere di Francesco Algarotti e di Saverio Bettinelli*, hrsg. von Ettore Bonora (Mailand: Ricciardi. 1969). S. 543. Von hier an zitiert als *Saggio*. – Auch E. T. A. Hoffmann war ein großer Marcello-Verehrer und nennt dessen Psalmen-Vertonungen ein „tiefsinniges Werk", das „wohl an der Spitze jener geistlichen Hymnen steh[e]. die später so vielfältig komponiert wurden". Zitiert aus dem Aufsatz „Alte und neue Kirchenmusik" (1814) in *Schriften zur Musik*, hrsg. von Friedrich Schnapp (München: Winkler. [o. J.]). S. 225.

9 In Wiels (vgl. Anm. 5) Namensregister erscheint der Name Marcello nur einmal unter den „poeti", ist aber auf der angegebenen Seite nicht zu finden.

10 Man vergleiche hierzu die Artikel von Franz Giegling in *Die Musik in Geschichte und Gegenwart* (Band 8, Sp. 1615-1619) und Michael Talbot in *The New Grove Dictionary of Music and Musicians* (Band II, S. 648-650).

dem Gelächter preisgab: ein Apostat oder ein Nichteingelassener. In Satire ist Neid oder Ekel, aber immer ein gehässiges Gemeinschaftsgefühl. Einem Fremden gelingt keine"[11].

Zu den vermutlich persönlichen Gründen gesellte sich im Falle Marcellos ein beruflicher: die nachweisliche Rivalität mit Antonio Vivaldi, seinem Spiegelbild. Denn analog zu ihm flocht die Mitwelt (und flicht die Nachwelt) dem *prete rosso* schöne Kränze für seine Instrumental- und Vokalmusik, kümmert sich aber keinen Deut um die zu seinen Lebzeiten im Teatro S. Moisé aufgeführten und schon damals wenig populären Bühnenwerke[12]. Daß Marcello seine satirischen Pfeile auf ihn richtete, erhellt eindeutig daraus, daß er, wie Francesco Malipiero eruieren konnte[13], unter karikaturistischen Vorzeichen in Schrift und Bild auf dem Titelblatt der Erstausgabe des *Teatro alla moda* erscheint, und zwar in Gesellschaft anderer mehr oder minder prominenter Figuren aus dem damaligen Opernbetrieb[14]. Die wirklich erfolgreichen Opernkomponisten Venedigs in diesem Zeitabschnitt waren Giuseppe Maria Buina, Michelangelo Gasparini, Giuseppe Maria Orlandini und die Brüder Antonio und Carlo Francesco Pollarolo,

---

11 Zitiert aus Heinrich Manns Essay über Gustave Flaubert und George Sand in *Essays* (Düsseldorf: Claassen. 1960). S. 113.

12 Tartini soll in einem Gespräch mit dem ‚President' De Brosses gesagt haben: „I have been asked to write operas for Venice but I never consented, knowing full well that a throat and a violin fingerboard are two different things. Vivaldi, who tried his hand at writing for both, was always hissed in one of the fields though he was very successful in the other". Zitiert bei Reinhard G. Pauly, „Benedetto Marcello's Satire on Early Eighteenth-Century Opera", *Musical Quarterly* 34 (1948). S. 230 (Anm. 22).

13 Die Entschlüsselung erfolgte durch Francesco Malipiero („Un frontespizio enigmatico" in der *Bolletino Bibliografico Musicale* 5 (1930). S. 16) und, unter Heranziehung eines anonymen Stückes (*Li Diavoli in maschera*, 1726), durch Ulderico Rolandi („A. Vivaldi nell'enigmatico frontespizio del *Teatro alla moda*" in *Musica d'Oggi* 22 [1940]. S. 5).

14 Die möglichen Kriterien für Marcellos Wahl seiner ‚Opfer' erwägt Andrea d'Angeli im Kapitel „Venezia musicale ai tempi di Marcello" seiner Studie *Benedetto Marcello: Vita e Opere* (Mailand: Bocca, 1940).

deren Namen längst Schall und Rauch und deren Werke auf Nimmerwiedersehen aus dem Spielplan der Opernhäuser verschwunden sind[15].

Zum Objekt von Satire und Parodie eignet sich das musikalische Bühnenwerk aus mehreren Gründen weitaus besser als andere Gattungen, ganz gleich in welchem Medium. Zum ‚idealen' Angriffsziel wird es, wie das Schauspiel und das Ballett, schon deshalb, weil es als öffentliche Kunst ein Publikum voraussetzt und erfordert und somit eine ausgesprochen gesellschaftliche Funktion ausübt – in Venedig, wo Oper und Karneval ohnehin in wilder Ehe lebten, noch mehr als in anderen Städten Italiens, geschweige des Auslands. Hierzu kommt zusätzlich, daß die Oper, viel mehr noch als andere theatralische Vergnügungen, einen wahren Rattenschwanz von Mitwirkenden und Hilfskräften erfordert, der den beim Sprech- und Tanztheater üblichen an Länge und Gewichtigkeit übertrifft.

Zu den wahren Urhebern des *dramma per musica* – dem Dichter und dem Komponisten, die E. T. A. Hoffmann in seinem Dialog aus dem Jahre 1813 auftreten und über das Wesen des romantischen Gesamtkunstwerks diskutieren läßt[16] – gesellen sich nämlich nachschöpferische Kräfte wie Regisseur, Bühnenbildner bzw. -architekt und Ausstatter, musikalische Gestalter wie Dirigent, Sänger und Orchester-Musiker und untergeordnete Chargen wie Statisten, Souffleure, Garderobiers, Bühnenarbeiter und Logenschließer. Über allem thront – allerdings nicht in unserer Satire – der Intendant, dem die unlösbare Aufgabe zufällt, das ganze *corps* zusammenzuhalten, damit die *stagione* zustandekommt und der Vorhang jeden Abend aufgehen kann. Aber auch damit ist es nicht getan; denn wie ließe sich die Welt der Oper, ob in der Metropole oder der fast schon sprichwörtlichen ‚Kleinen Stadt', denken ohne die Gönner, Mütter und Rechtsanwälte, die auf das Wohlergehen ihrer Schützlinge achten und auch im künstleri-

---

15 Zum Spielplan der venezianischen Opernhäuser in dem hier in Frage kommenden Jahrzehnt siehe Wiel (Anm. 5). S. 26-59.
16 „Der Dichter und der Komponist" in *Die Serapionsbrüder*, hrsg. von Wulf Segebrecht (München: Winkler. [o. J.]), S. 76-99.

Scherz, Satire, Parodie oder tiefere Bedeutung? 177

schen Ressort fleißig mitmischen wollen? So wird verständlich, warum der gute Ali in Goldonis *Impresario delle Smirne* die Flucht ergreift, als man ihm die zum Aufbruch in den Nahen Osten bereite, nach gewerkschaftlichen Prinzipien straff eingeteilte Truppe vorstellt:

> (*Fabrizio e detti* [Ali, der Agent Nibio und der Dichter Maccaro], *poi tutte quelle persone che da Nibio vengono nominate.*)
>
> Fabrizio: Mio signore (*ad Ali*)
>
> Ali: E quest'altro, chi star?
>
> Nibio: Quest'è un bravo pittore da teatro, il quale farà le scene, e condurrà con lui tutti i suoi scolari e tutti i suoi operai. Venite innanzi, signori (*verso la scena*).
>
> Ali: Quanta gente venir?
>
> Nibio: Ecco i pittori ed i lavoranti. Questo e il capo dell'illuminazione. Eco qui il capo delle comparse con trentadue compagni, bella gente e pratica del teatro. Questi sono i tre portinari. Questi sono i due paggi da sostener la colla alle donne. Ecco un bravo suggeritore, capace di suggerire le parole e la musica. Ecco due uomini per dispensare i biglietti. Ecco quei che devono assistere ai palchetti, per dare e ricuperare le chiavi. Questo sa far da orso. Quest'altro sa far da leone. E quest'altro, forte e robusto come vedete, è destinato per batter le mani.
>
> Ali: Condur Smirne tutta questa canaglia?
>
> Nibio: Tutte persone necessarie.
>
> Ali: Mangiar impresa e impresario. Sensal maledetto. Tu voler Ali precipitar. Ma se mal riuscir, omo d'onor, tu far impalar. (*parte*)[17]

Auch wenn man von der sozialen Komponente und der komplexen und bis ins Kleinste ausgeklügelten und durchgefeilten Arbeitsteilung absieht und sich gänzlich auf das Gesamtkunstwerk (*componimento*) selbst konzentriert, wird man einsehen, daß es sich hierbei um ein prekäres und äußerst anfälliges Gebilde handelt, ein Wesen bzw. Unwesen, das auf tönernen – wie selbstverständlich auch auf tönenden – Füßen steht. Den Angriffen der Kritik ist die Oper schon deshalb fast wehrlos ausgesetzt, weil ihre Bestandteile oder Glieder – im Grunde dieselben, die Aristoteles in der *Poetik* aufzählt und in ein hierarchi-

---

17 *Tutte le Opere*, hrsg. von Giuseppe Ortolani (Mailand: Mondadori, 1946), Band VII. S. 529f.

sches Verhältnis zueinander bringt[18] – selten miteinander in Frieden leben und sich allzu oft um den Vorrang streiten.

Die völlig gelungene und in sich stimmige Oper besitzt Seltenheitswert; denn meist breitet sich ein künstlerisches Ingrediens auf Kosten der anderen aus. So ist denn die Frage, welchem von ihnen die Palme gebührt, die Gretchenfrage der Opernkritik vom 17. Jahrhundert bis heute. Meist wurde sie auf die zwei allgemein als Hauptbestandteile gekennzeichneten Elemente ‚Text' und ‚Musik' reduziert, kategorisch so oder so beantwortet; und es hieß entweder *prima le parole e dopo la musica* – so der klassizistische Slogan – oder *prima la musica e poi le parole*[19]. Anlaß zur Parodie bzw. bei Ausweitung der Kontroverse vom Kunstwerk an sich auf dessen Schöpfer, Interpreten und Publikum zur Satire war stets der Umstand, daß der künstlich errichtete Bau zusammenbrach und man statt des geistigen Bandes, das ihn umschlingen sollte, nur die *disjecta membra* in der Hand hielt, was nachmals den Verfechtern des Prinzips der Epischen Oper zugute kam[20].

Die Geschichte der Kritik an der Oper (nicht der Opernkritik), welche diejenige der Opernsatire mit einschließt, kann hier nur im typologischen Sinn umrissen werden, und zwar vor allem unter Berücksichtigung des Stellenwertes von Marcellos nachhaltig wirkender Schrift[21]. Sie ist, so hat es den Anschein, fast so alt wie die Oper

---

18 Zur Methodologie der Libretto-Forschung unter Berücksichtigung der Aristotelischen Kategorien siehe meinen Aufsatz „Librettology: The Fine Art of Coping With a Chinese Twin" in *Komparatistische Hefte*, Nos. 5/6 (1982). S. 23-42.

19 Letztere Position, im Extrem vertreten, könnte man als die romantische bezeichnen. In gemäßigter Form wird sie relativ oft sowohl in der Musikgeschichte (Mozart) als auch in der Musikwissenschaft (Joseph Kerman) eingenommen. Siehe hierzu die entsprechenden Hinweise in meinem in Anm. 18 erwähnten Aufsatz sowie in der Einleitung zu meiner Anthologie *The Essence of Opera* (New York: Norton, 1964) [wiederabgedruckt in diesem Band].

20 Ich behandle die vier Grundtypen des Verhältnisses von Musik und Text in der Oper und ihre jeweilige Dominanz in der Operngeschichte in der Einleitung zu *The Essence of Opera* (Anm. 19).

21 Zur Nachwirkung des *Teatro alla moda* siehe unter anderem Pauly (Anm. 12). S. 231.

selbst, die bekanntlich nach einigen Anläufen und einem kurzen Vorspiel im Jahre 1600, in welchem die Äußerungen dreier Mitglieder der *camerata* – des Dichters Ottavio Rinuccini und der beiden Vertoner seines *Euridice*-Textes, Jacopo Peri und Giulio Caccini – publiziert wurden, einsetzt[22]. Ich sage ‚fast so als‘, denn wenn der Schock, den entscheidende Neuerungen (nicht nur auf künstlerischem Gebiet) auszulösen pflegen, überwunden und der anfängliche Widerstand gebrochen ist, vergeht gewöhnlich einige Zeit, bis sich die Gegenkräfte sammeln und einsetzende Verfallserscheinungen – man denke an die Exzesse von Cestis *Pomo d'Oro* aus dem Jahre 1663, dem Kulminationspunkt der barocken Prunkoper – zum Widerstand reizen.

Alfred Einstein, dem sachkundigen Übersetzer des *Teatro alla moda*, zufolge beginnt die ernsthafte kritische Auseinandersetzung mit der Oper mit dem zweiten, *Trattato della musica scenica* betitelten Band der *Descrizione delle opere sulla musica* des Florentiners Giovanni Battista Doni aus dem Jahre 1643, dem Todesjahr Monteverdis, des ersten Großmeisters des *stile rappresentativo*[23]. Sie beschränkt sich in ihren Anfängen auf Italien, verbreitet sich aber schnell nach Frankreich (Saint-Evremonds oft zitierter, im Londoner Exil geschriebener Brief „Sur les Opéra"[24]) und England (John Drydens Vorwort zu *Albion und Albanius*) sowie mit einiger Verspätung nach Deutsch-

---

22 Diese Dokumente sind gesammelt in dem von Angelo Solerti herausgegebenen Band *Le Origini del Melodramma: Testimonianza dei contemporanei* (Turin: Bocca, 1903).

23 Donis *Trattato della musica scenica* war mir nur in den Auszügen, die Solerti in *Le Origini del Melodramma* abdruckt, zugänglich.

24 Saint-Evremonds aus dem Jahre 1677 stammender Brief war den italienischen Illuministen wohlbekannt. So schreibt Pier Jacopo Martello in seiner Abhandlung *Della tragedia antica e moderna* aus dem Jahre 1714: „Tu hai gustata già la *Medea*, che perciò accorderai potersi denominare tragedia perch'e un'imitazione drammatica de'migliori e differisce, come le vostre opere in musica, dall' antica tragedia, perchè in essa parte solamente cantavasi, in questa tutto si canta, e però a questo proposito si può applaudere al sentimento di Saint Evremond: ,I Greci facevano belle tragedie ove qualche cosa cantavano; i Franzesi ne fanno delle cattive, nelle quali cantano tutto'." Zitiert aus Martellos *Scritti critici e satirici*, hrsg. von Hannibal S. Noce (Bari: Laterzá, 1963). S. 273.

land (Wielands „Versuch über das deutsche Singspiel und einige dahin einschlagende Gegenstände") und verebbt erst in den siebziger Jahren des *siècle des lumières* im Gefolge von Glucks Opernreformen und Reformopern.

Schematisch ließen sich etwa drei Hauptspielarten der Befassung mit und Kritik an der Mischgattung ‚Oper' im 18. Jahrhundert ausmachen: die ausdrücklich oder implizit programmatische gelehrte Abhandlung, die Prosa- und Verssatire und die satirische Parodie im Gewand der Oper bzw. (wie bei Goldoni) des Schauspiels. Ehe ich mich meiner eigentlichen Aufgabe, der Inhalts- und Formanalyse des *Teatro alla moda*, zuwende, will ich zur Veranschaulichung dieses Schemas ein paar charakteristische Beispiele für jede dieser Sparten auflisten und kurz kommentieren.

1. Das erste gewichtige und einflußreiche Traktat der genannten Art ist Ludovico Muratoris Schrift *Della perfetta poesia italiana* aus dem Jahre 1706, das deutliche Spuren in Marcellos Pamphlet hinterläßt, ja gleichsam das Modell bildet, an dem die verkehrte Welt des *Teatro alla moda* sich spiegelt[25]. Das fünfte, für unsere Fragestellung relevante Kapitel dieses Werks trägt die bezeichnende Überschrift „De' difetti che possono osservarsi ne' moderni drammi. Loro musica perniziosa a i costumi. Riprovata ancor da gli antichi. Poesia serva della musica. Non ottenersi per mezzo d'essi drammi il fine della tragedia. Altri difetti della poesia teatrale, e vari inverisimili"[26]. Ihm folgt, um nur die wichtigsten Stationen zu nennen, in zehnjährigem Abstand die *Della tragedia antica e moderna* betitelte Abhandlung Pier Jacopo Martellos, deren fünfte ‚Sitzung' das Thema aufgreift und weiterspinnt[27].

---

25 Einstein (Anm. 7) weist in seinem Kommentar ausdrücklich auf diese Parallelen hin.

26 Ludvico Muratori, *Della perfetta poesia italiana* (Mailand: Marzorati, 1972). S. 573-585. Diese Schrift wurde im Jahre 1706 veröffentlicht, lag aber schon seit einiger Zeit im Manuskript vor. Apostolo Zeno bezieht sich auf sie in einem bei Einstein (Anm. 7, S. 108) zitierten Brief.

27 *Della tragedia antica e moderna* (Anm. 24), „Sessione quinta". S. 270-296.

Den Beschluß und Höhepunkt der Reihe, in die sich auch Metastasios unermüdliche Bemühungen um die Reinhaltung der Gattung – etwa in seinem Schreiben an den Marquis de Chastellux aus dem Jahre 1766[28] – einpassen, bildet zweifellos Francesco Algarottis *Saggio sopra l'opera in musica* (1762), der Furore machte und sehr bald ins Englische, Französische und Deutsche übertragen wurde. (Wieland bezieht sich spezifisch auf ihn und scheint seinen „Versuch über das deutsche Singspiel und einige dahin einschlagende Gegenstände" als Gegenentwurf zu diesem einflußreichen Werk eines Mannes, der mehrere Jahre am Preußischen Hof verbracht hatte, geplant zu haben[29].) Hier feiert der Klassizismus mit Hilfe der uns aus Winckelmanns „Gedanken über die Nachahmung der griechischen Werke in der Malerei und Bildhauerkunst" (1755) und Lessings *Laokoon oder über die Grenzen der Mahlerey und Poesie* (1766) her vertrauten Begriffskorsetts Triumphe. Gefordert wird freilich von diesem Kenner nicht eine auf die Bildhauerei als die prototypische Kunst der Griechen bezogene und von dort auf die Malerei und Dichtung übertragene „edle Einfalt" und „stille Größe", sondern, in klarer Erkenntnis der Künstlichkeit und Komplexität des Phänomens ‚Oper', die harmonische Verknüpfung der heterogenen Teile:

> Di tutti i modi che, per creare nelle anime gentili il diletto, furono immaginati dall'uomo, forse il più ingegnoso e compito si è l'opera in musica. Niuna cosa nella formazione di essa fu lasciata indietro, niuno ingrediente, niun mezzo, onde arrivar si potesse al proposto fine. E ben si può asserire che quanto di più attrattivo ha la poesia, quanto ha la musica e la mimica, l'arte del ballo e la pittura, tutto si collega nell'opera felicemente insieme ad allettare i sentimenti, ad ammaliare il cuore e fare un dolce inganno alla mente[30].

---

28 Brief vom 29. Januar 1766 in Pietro Metastasio, *Opere*, hrsg. von Mario Fubini (Mailand: Ricciardi, [o. J.]). S. 756-761. In englischer Fassung in *The Essence of Opera* (Anm. 19), S. 100-104. Metastasio stand auch mit Algarotti im regen Briefwechsel.

29 Algarotti war besonders angetan von Karl Heinrich Grauns Oper *Montezuma*, die er 1755 in Berlin gesehen hatte. Er lobte vor allem die Wahl des exotischen Stoffes. Siehe Algarotti (Anm. 8). S. 442.

30 Ebenda. S. 435. Algarottis Herablassung diesem Genre gegenüber erhellt aus dem in diesem Absatz verwendeten ästhetischen Begriffsapparat, in dessen Zentrum das diletto, also das sinnliche Vergnügen, steht.

Das hier, bei aller offensichtlichen ‚condescension' gegenüber dieser zweitrangigen, weil letztendlich auf das sinnliche Vergnügen abzielenden Kunstform als Idealzustand postulierte Gleichgewicht zwischen Dichtung, Musik und ihren Hilfskünsten im Rahmen der Oper wurde allerdings bald wieder gestört; denn seit etwa 1810 brach sich bei E. T. A. Hoffmann und Carl Maria von Weber eine neue, zugleich aber altvertraute Opernkunstauffassung Bahn, derzufolge die Musik als gekrönte Kunst die *padrona* zur *serva* der Dichtung spielen sollte. Dieser einschneidende Paradigmawechsel erfolgte jedoch ohne Zwischenschaltung einer satirisch-parodistischen Phase, was sich unter anderem daraus erklären mag, daß sich die Norm – will heißen: das Normale – weit weniger zur parodistisch-satirischen Behandlung eignet als das, was die einmal gesetzten Grenzen überschreitet. (Von Gluck-Parodien schweigt die Geschichte, wenngleich einzelne Stellen in Diderots fiktivem Dialog *Le Neveu de Rameau* durchaus in diesem Sinne gedeutet werden könnten.)

2. Die Prosa- und Verssatire als Parodie der gelehrten Abhandlung nimmt innerhalb der Geschichte der Kritik an der Oper zwar einen wichtigen, aber weniger gewichtigen Platz ein. In der Tat stellt Marcellos Versuch den absoluten Höhepunkt der ziemlich sporadischen Entwicklung dieses Genres dar, die Einstein zufolge mit zwei aus dem fünften Jahrzehnt des siebzehnten Jahrhunderts stammenden, aber erst 1695 veröffentlichten Arbeiten des Malers Salvator Rosa einsetzt[31] und sich mehr schlecht als recht über Boileaus indirekt gegen Lully gerichtete Vers-Epistel „Fragment d'un Prologue d'Opéra" (1713) bis zum dritten Buch von Wielands *Geschichte der Abderiten* (1781 als Buch erschienen) erstreckt, in deren fünftem Kapitel eine im antiken Schilda veranstaltete Aufführung der *Andromeda* des Euripides „und

---

31 Siehe Einstein (Anm. 7). S. 104.

was sich dabei Possierliches zutrug", eher amüsant als bissig geschildert wird[32].

Bei dem unmittelbaren und starken Echo, das *Il Teatro alla moda* in Italien fand, und der nachhaltigen Wirkung, die es daselbst ausübte, mag es verwundern, daß es im restlichen Europa, im Gegensatz zu Algarottis Traktat, fast gänzlich unbekannt blieb und erst 1872 ins Französische[33], 1916 ins Deutsche[34] und gar erst 1948 zum ersten Mal ins Englische[35] übertragen wurde. Schuld daran mag bei aller Klischeehaftigkeit der dargestellten Zustände vor allem der Umstand sein, daß das Werk unendlich viele Anspielungen auf lokale Ereignisse und örtliche Gegebenheiten enthält, die nur dem Einheimischen vertraut gewesen sein dürften. Zu allem Überfluß wird in den Abschnitten, in denen die Gesangsvirtuosinnen und ihre Mütter zu Worte kommen, durchwegs der schwierige Bologneser Dialekt verwendet[36].

An Schlagkraft mit dem *Teatro alla moda* messen können sich eigentlich nur Joseph Addisons Auslassungen über den Fremdkörper ‚Oper' in einem halben Dutzend Beiträgen zu der von ihm begründeten und herausgegebenen Wochenzeitschrift *The Spectator* aus dem Jahre 1710, welche die hitzige Debatte um weitere Nuancen berei-

---

32 Christoph Martin Wieland, *Ausgewählte Werke in drei Einzelbänden: Romane*, hrsg. von Friedrich Beißner (München: Winkler, 1964). S. 716-721. Das Kapitel trägt die Überschrift „Die *Andromeda* des Euripides wird aufgeführt. Großer Sukzess des Nomophylax, und was die Sängerin Eukolpis dazu beigetragen. Ein paar Anmerkungen über die übrigen Schauspieler, die Chöre und die Dekoration".

33 Ernst David veröffentlichte seine Version des Textes 1872 in der Zeitschrift *Le Menestrel* und 1880 mit ausführlicher Einleitung als Buch (Paris: Fischbacher).

34 Einstein (Anm. 7).

35 Reinhard G. Paulys Übertragung erschien in der Zeitschrift *Musical Quarterly* 34 (1948), S. 371-398, und 35 (1949), S. 85-105. Eine weitere englische Fassung der Kapitel „A' poeti" und „A' compositori di musica" von der Hand Oliver Strunks findet sich in dessen *Source Readings in Music History: From Classical Antiquity Through the Romantic Era* (New York: Norton, 1950), S. 518-531.

36 Siehe vor allem das Kapitel „Alle cantatrici" und den Abschnitt „Madri delle virtuose ...". Wie aus Wiels Katalog (Anm. 5) hervorgeht, stellten die Bologneser Sängerinnen ein disproportional großes Kontingent für die Opernhäuser Venedigs im frühen 18. Jahrhundert.

chern. War bei Marcellos Satire als selbstverständlich vorauszusetzen, daß die daselbst zur Sprache kommenden Opern bzw. deren Zerrbilder auf italienische Texte komponiert und von italienischen Sängern in deren Muttersprache gesungen wurden, so kam hier hinzu, daß die italienische Oper in England Importware war, die sich, wie sich bald genug herausstellen sollte, nicht ohne weiteres assimilieren ließ. Es kam zu einer von Addison mit beißendem Witz geschilderten rückläufigen Entwicklung, in deren Verlauf zunächst der Versuch unternommen wurde, die fremdsprachigen Texte zu übersetzen, mit dem Ergebnis, daß diese sinnentstellt wurden, unsinnig anmuteten (nach dem Motto „Nothing is capable of being well set to music that is not nonsense"[37]) oder aufgrund des unweigerlich resultierenden *contre-sens*[38] mit der Musik in Konflikt gerieten[39].

Die zweite Stufe dieser Entwicklung schuf, so Addison, eine ungleich größere Verwirrung:

> The next step to our refinement was the introducing of Italian actors into our opera, who sung their parts in their own language, at the same time that our countrymen performed theirs in our native tongue. The king or hero of the play generally spoke in Italian, and his slaves answered him in English; the lover frequently made his court and gained the heart of his princess in a language which she did not understand. One would have thought it very difficult to have carried on dialogue after this manner without an interpreter between the persons that conversed together, but this was the state of the English stage for about three years[40].

---

37 *The Spectator*, No. 18 vom 21. März 1710.

38 Der Begriff *contre-sens* spielt in der Musik-, d. h. vor allem der Opernkritik des 18. Jahrhunderts eine nicht unwesentliche Rolle. Rousseau widmet ihm einen aufschlußreichen Artikel in seinem *Dictionnaire de Musique* aus dem Jahre 1764.

39 Der in Anm. 37 zitierte Brief Addisons behandelt dieses Thema im unmittelbaren Anschluß an die These „Nothing is capable of being well set to music that is not nonsense" unter dem Motto: „This maxim was no sooner received but we immediately fell to translating the Italian operas, and as there was no great danger of hurting the sense of those extraordinary pieces, our authors would often make words of their own which were entirely foreign to the meaning of the passages they pretended to translate".

40 Aus dem gleichen Brief. Die Praxis ist noch heute relativ weit verbreitet, etwa bei *Boris Godunoff*, dessen Titelrolle von Schaljapin bis Nicola Rossi-Lemeni vielfach im

Auf der dritten und letzten Stufe schließlich schlug das Groteske dieses Zwischenstadiums gänzlich ins Absurde um, indem nunmehr der italienische Originaltext die Oberhand gewann und der Inhalt der auf der Bühne gezeigten Opern für das englische Publikum virtuell zu einem Buch mit sieben Siegeln wurde: „At length the audience grew tired of understanding half the opera; and therefore to ease themselves entirely of the fatigue of thinking have so ordered it at present that the whole opera is performed in an unknown tongue." Was den über das Paradoxale dieses Zustandes mit Recht verwunderten Satiriker zu der treffenden Bemerkung veranlaßt: „I cannot forbear thinking how naturally an historian who writes two or three hundred years hence, and does not know the taste of his wise forefathers, will make the following reflection: ‚In the beginning of the eighteenth century the Italian tongue was so well understood in England that operas were acted on the public stage in that language.'"[41]

3. Die Gattung der Opernsatire/Opernparodie in künstlerischer, d. h. musiktheatralischer Einkleidung entstand wie die *opera buffa* aus dem Intermezzo. Obwohl, wie Einstein berichtet, schon 1712 das *Dirindina* betitelte *melodramma* eines gewissen Girolamo Gigli im Umlauf war[42], ist Marcellos Groteske als wirklicher Ahne dieses Genres anzusehen, das dem *Teatro alla moda* als wahrer Fundgrube von Typen, Situationen und Gebräuchen des Opernbetriebs das ganze achtzehnte Jahrhundert hindurch und darüber hinaus bis hin zu Hofmannsthal/Strauss's *Ariadne auf Naxos* zutiefst verpflichtet war[43].

Original vorgetragen wird, während die übrigen Sänger in ihrer westlichen Muttersprache singen.
41 Gänzlich fremdsprachige Aufführungen sind in letzter Zeit an ersten Opernhäusern recht häufig zu verzeichnen. Bei Mozarts italienischen Opern gehört die Darbietung der Originalfassungen wenigstens an den besseren deutschen Bühnen beinahe zum guten Ton.
42 Hierzu Einstein (Anm. 7). S. 105.
43 In der *Ariadne auf Naxos* wird freilich das Zwischenspiel (Intermezzo) durch ein Vorspiel ergänzt.

Einen Katalog der zahllosen diesbezüglichen Produkte zu erstellen wäre aufwendig und in diesem Rahmen wenig sinnvoll. Erwähnt werden soll neben Goldonis *Impresario delle Smirne* lediglich Metastasios *Impresario delle Canarie*, ein zweiteiliges Zwischenspiel zur berühmten *Didone abbandonata* aus dem Jahre 1724[44], sowie Raniero de Calsabigis, von Florian Gassmann vertonte *Opera seria* – so lautet der Titel –, eine *commedia per musica* (im Untertitel) in drei Akten aus dem Jahre 1769[45]. Und wer kennte nicht den *Schauspieldirektor*? Dessen für uns viel relevanteres Gegenstück, der Prolog zu der von Giuseppe Gazzaniga vertonten Don Juan-Oper *Don Giovanni o sia Il convitato di pietra*, dem unmittelbaren Vorgänger von Mozart/Da Pontes *Don Giovanni*, ist längst in Vergessenheit geraten, weil das *dramma giocoso* des großen Meisters dieses, literarisch gesehen, krude Machwerk ein für allemal aus dem Repertoire verdrängt hat[46].

Das für die Nachwelt verbindlichste, weil immer wieder neuinszenierte und neubearbeitete Exemplar der Gattung ist freilich fern von Italien entstanden und dem heutigen Italiener höchstens auf dem Umweg über die Aufführungen eines deutschen Ablegers am Mailänder Piccolo Teatro bekannt. Es handelt sich um John Gays *Beggar's Opera*, ein von John Pepusch musikalisch eingerichtetes Produkt der leichteren Muse, das 1728 in London aus der Taufe gehoben wurde. Diese „Newgate Pastoral" war so erfolgreich, daß sie, wie ein zeitgenössischer *wit* spöttelte, Gay „rich" und den Impresario Rich „gay" machte. Als Parodie auf die Oper Händels, deren Anfänge Addison zwei Jahrzehnte früher miterlebt und sarkastisch kommentiert hatte, bedient sich dieses Werk der eingespielten Opernmechanismen als Folie für die von ihm propagierte und mit ihr zum Zuge kommende

---

44 Der Text dieses Intermezzos ist abgedruckt im *Teatro di Pietro Metastasio*, hrsg. von Riccardo Bacchelli (Turin: Edizione RAI, 1962). S. 91-96 und S. 111-116.

45 Der Text ist abgedruckt in *Italian Opera Librettos 1640-1770*, hrsg. von H. M. Brown (New York: Garland Press, 1984), ohne Paginierung.

46 Zu diesem *Don Giovanni* vor *Don Giovanni* siehe vor allem Stefan Kunzes Buch *Don Giovanni vor Mozart* (München: Fink, 1972). Dort auch der Text der Oper von Bertati/Gazzaniga samt dem als *Capriccio drammatico* bezeichneten Vorspiel.

Scherz, Satire, Parodie oder tiefere Bedeutung? 187

einheimische Gattung der Balladenoper. Wir wollen an dieser Stelle nicht auf die ausgesprochen parodistischen Aspekte der *Beggar's Opera* eingehen[47], sondern beschränken uns darauf, die satirische Komponente, die in dem vom Verfasser als „Introduction" bezeichneten Prolog zutage tritt, anhand einiger, schon bei Marcello vorgegebener Beispiele zu illustrieren. Ich zitiere zunächst die dem Bettler als dem Inszenator des theatralischen Vergnügens in den Mund gelegte Stelle im Wortlaut:

> This piece I own was originally writ for celebrating the marriage of James Chanter and Moll Lay, two most excellent ballad singers. I have introduced the similes that are in all your celebrated operas: the swallow, the moth, the bee, the ship, the flower, etc. Besides, I have a prison scene, which the ladies always reckon charmingly pathetic. As to the parts, I have observed such a nice impartiality to our two ladies that it is impossible for either of them to take offense. I hope I may be forgiven that I have not made my opera throughout unnatural, like those in vogue, for I have no recitative. Excepting this, as I have consented to have neither prologue nor epilogue, it must be allowed an opera in all its forms[48].

Die spürbaren Anklänge an spezifische Einzelheiten des acht Jahre zuvor erschienenen *Teatro alla moda* sind so groß, daß man vermuten könnte, daß Gay das Werk des Italieners gelesen oder aus zweiter Hand davon gehört hatte, obwohl es hierfür, soweit ich weiß, keinerlei dokumentarische Belege gibt. Da es sich bei den sachlichen Übereinstimmungen meist um weithin kursierende *topoi* handelt, ist eine solche Voraussetzung ohnedies nur bedingt gegeben.

Um drei besonders auffallende Entsprechungen zu nennen: die Kritik an der gewiß zum Teil vom Usus der petrarkistischen Sonetten-Dichter herzuleitenden Manie, in den Arien passende und unpassende Gemeinplätze wie Pelion auf den Ossa zu stürzen, gehört zweifels-

---

47 Am auffallendsten ist die Händel-Parodie im Air XX, „March in *Rinaldo* with Drums and Trumpets" zu den Worten „Let us take the road./ Hark, I hear the sound of coaches./ The hour of attack approaches./ To your arms, brave boys, and load!".
48 John Gay, *The Beggar's Opera*, hrsg. von Edgar V. Roberts (Lincoln: University of Nebraska Press, 1969). S. 5f. Ich kann und muß es mir in diesem Zusammenhang ersparen, auf Brechts *Dreigroschenoper* als Parodie dieser Parodie einzugehen. Ich habe das Verhältnis der beiden Werke in meinem Aufsatz „Brecht's Victorian Version of Gay: Imitation and Originality in the *Dreigroschenoper*" (*Comparative Literature Studies* 7 [1970]. S. 314-335) ausführlich behandelt.

ohne zu den *topoi* der Opernsatire. Marcello selbst schreibt im Abschnitt „A'poeti" seines Traktats:

> L'ariette non dovranno aver relazione veruna al recitativo, ma convien fare il possibile d'introdurre nelle medesime per lo più *farfalletta, mossolino, quagliotto, navicella, companetto, gelsonimo, violazotto, cavo rame, pignatella, tigre, leone, balena, gambaretto, dindiotto, capon freddo,* etc., etc. Imperciocchè in tal maniera il poeta si fa conoscere buon filosofo distinguendo co' paragoni le proprietà degli animali, delle plante, de fiori, etc.[49]

In der *Beggar's Opera* finden sich dementsprechend in einem völlig falschen dramatischen, musikalischen und sozialen Kontext Verse wie

> If love the virgin's heart invade,
> How like a moth the simple maid
> Still plays about the flame (Air IV)

und

> Virgins are like the fair flower in its luster,
> Which in the garden enamels the ground;
> Near it the bees in play flutter and cluster,
> And butterflies frolic around.
> But, when once plucked, 'tis no longer alluring,
> To Covent Garden 'tis sent (as yet sweet),
> There fades and shrinks, and grows past all enduring,
> Rots, stinks, and dies, and is trod under feet. (Air VI)

Noch gegen Ende des „tintenklecksenden Säkulums" setzt sich die Oper, wenn auch nurmehr ironisch, mit dieser rhetorischen Frage auseinander – so zum Beispiel Da Ponte in *Così fan tutte,* wo sich vor allem Don Alfonso über diese manieristische Praxis mokiert („E la

---

49 *Teatro,* S. 9f. Siehe hierzu in Metastasios *Impresario delle Canarie* (Anm. 44) den folgenden Austausch zwischen Nibbio und Dorina:

> Nibbio: Ma questo è un grand-errore:
>   Il poeta mi scusi. E dove mai
>   Si può trovar occasion più bella
>   Da mettere un'arietta
>   Con qualche ‚farfaletta' o ‚navicella'.
> Dorina: Dopo una scena tragica
>   Vogliono certe stitiche persone
>   Che stia male una tal comparazione.
> Nibbio: No, no, comparazione: in questo sito
>   Una similitudine bastava:
>   E sa quanto l'udienza rallegrava. (S. 114)

fede delle femmine/ come l'araba fenice;/ che vi sia ciascun lo dice,/ dove sia nessun lo sa"[50]), während die beiden Damen, besonders die sich hochdramatisch gebärdende Fiordiligi („Come il scoglio immoto resta/ contr'ai venti e la tempesta"[51]), sich ihrer fleißig und unverzagt bedienen.

Auch die Gefängnis-Szene, die zum eisernen Bestand der Oper als Parodie-Objekt gehört und in der sich z. B. Brechts Mackie Messer von seiner allerbesten Seite zeigt, hat bei Marcello ihren Platz[52]. Sie wird zusammen mit anderen *accidenti dell'opera* wie *stili, veleni, lettere, caccie d'orsi, e di tori, terremoti, saette, sacrifizi, saldi, pazzie* und den besonders beliebten Gartenszenen, in denen unentwegt geschlafen und geträumt wird, der Aufmerksamkeit des Textdichters empfohlen und in ihrer völligen Unsinnigkeit wie folgt beschrieben:

> Se si trovassero in una prigione marito e moglie, e l'uno andasse a morire dovrà indispensabilmente restar l'altro per cantar un' arietta, la quale dovrà essere d'allegre parole per sollevar la mestizia del popolo, e per fargli comprendere che le cose tutte sono da scherzo[53].

Was schließlich die „nice impartiality of the parts" anbetrifft, die es den „two ladies" – der *prima donna* und der *seconda donna* – unmöglich machen soll, sich vernachlässigt zu fühlen, so gehört auch sie zu den klischierten Zügen der Operngeschichte und -satire und ist bei Marcello vorgeprägt. Im Abschnitt „Alle cantatrici" heißt es nämlich:

> Se la virtuosa facesse da seconda donna, pretendera dal poeta d'uscire in scena prima, e, ricevuta la parte, numererà le note e le parole della medesima, e si in caso si accorgesse d'esser inferiore a quella della prima donna, obbligherà poeta e maestro di capella a ragiuargliargela cosi di parole come di note, avvertendo di non cedergli punto nello strascico della coda, nel belletto, nei, trillo, passi, cadenze, protettore, papagallo, civetta, etc. (S. 28)

---

50 #2 (Terzett).

51 #4 (Rezitativ und Arie). Dazu als heiter-frivoles Gegenstück Despinas Arie „E amore un ladroncello,/ un serpentello è amor" (#28).

52 Sowohl Gay als Brecht/Weill konzipierten ihre Gefängnis-Szene als Medley. In der *Beggar's Opera* umfaßt sie zehn Airs (LVIII-LXVII).

53 *Teatro*. S. 10. Gefängnis-Szenen erlebten ihre Renaissance in der revolutionären und nachrevolutionären Befreiungsoper. Was wäre Beethovens *Fidelio* ohne eine solche?

Marcello und Gay berufen sich mehr oder minder direkt auf den berüchtigten Dauerstreit zwischen Faustina und Cuzzoni, den eitlen und überheblichen Sängerinnen, die zuerst in Venedig miteinander auftraten und später in London gleichzeitig gastierten[54]. Die Praxis des *tit for tat* war unter den Vokalvirtuosen der Zeit so weit verbreitet, daß Rezepte entwickelt und den Librettisten als Vademecum verschrieben wurden, um diese vor einem möglicherweise für die *stagione* tödlichen *faux pas* zu bewahren. So schrieb der damals in England ansässige Giuseppe Riva ziemlich unverblümt an seinen Freund und Gönner Muratori:

> If your friend thinks of sending a specimen here, I must warn him that in England people like very few recitatives, thirty airs, and one duet at least distributed over the three acts. [...] For this year and the next there must be two equal parts for Cuzzoni and Faustina. Senesino takes the principal male character, and his part must be heroic. The other three male parts should be arranged proportionately song for song in the three acts and entrusted to the two women. If the subject demands three women, a third woman may be employed, as there is a third singer here to take the part[55].

Dieses Beispiel steht durchaus nicht vereinzelt da, sondern läßt sich durch Heranziehung ähnlicher Stellen bei Marcello selbst[56], in den Memoiren Goldonis[57] und anderswo fast beliebig vermehren. Im übrigen sündigt Gays Reform-Antioper, das Muster der von Addison so heftig befehdeten Händel-Oper nachahmend, auch darin, daß sie wie diese, aber wohl in parodistischer Absicht, eine Vielzahl von, wenn

---

54 Nach Wiel (Anm. 5), S. 48, geschah dies erstmals in Carlo Francesco Pollarolos am Teatro S. Gio. Grisostomo aufgeführten Oper *Ariodante*.

55 Zitiert von R. A. Streatfeild in seinem Aufsatz „Handel, Rolli, and Italian Opera" (*Musical Quarterly* 3 [1917]. S. 428-445). Der Originaltext findet sich bei Sesto Fassini, „Il melodramma italiano a Londra ai tempi del Rolli" in *Rivista Musicale Italiana* 19 (1912), S. 617, Anmerkung.

56 *Teatro*. S. 33: „La maggior parte della compagnia dovrà esser formata di femmine: e se due virtuose contendessero la prima parte, farà l'impresario comporre al poeta due parti eguale d'arie, di versi, di recitativo, etc., avvertendo che il nome d'ambedue sia pure formato della medesima quantità di sillabe".

57 Siehe hierzu Goldonis Bericht über eine Soirée in Venedig in seinen *Mémoires* (Kapitel 28). Siehe Goldonis *Opere*, hrsg. von Filippo Zampieri (Mailand: Ricciardi, 1954). S. 55.

Scherz, Satire, Parodie oder tiefere Bedeutung? 191

auch zum Glück angenehm kurzen, Musikstücken, die allerdings nicht durch Rezitative verbunden, sondern durch Prosa-Dialoge getrennt sind, wie Perlen aneinanderreiht. Die *Beggar's Opera* weist insgesamt nicht weniger als fünfundsechzig, meist zweistrophiger Balladen auf[58].

Beim *Teatro alla moda*, dem wir uns jetzt, nachdem die komparatistische Arbeit geleistet ist, ausschließlich zuwenden wollen, interessieren, so scheint mir, vor allem drei Faktoren: 1. der Aufbau des Werkchens, das der Verfasser ‚with tongue in cheek' dem „compositore del libretto presente", d. h. sich selber, widmet[59], 2. die dem Dichter innerhalb des Verbundes, als welchen sich das präsumptive Gesamtkunstwerk gibt, zugestandene Rolle und 3. die rhetorischen Mittel, deren sich Marcello zu seinen satirisch-parodistischen Zwecken bedient.

Gehen wir von dem Modell der in vieler Hinsicht verbindlichen Abhandlung Francesco Algarottis aus, zu der Marcellos Satire gleichsam ein antizipatorisches Gegenstück bildet, so ergibt sich, wenn man die Reihenfolge, in der die einschlägigen Sujets behandelt werden, als Maßstab verwendet, wozu man allerdings nur mit gewissen Einschränkungen berechtigt ist, die folgende Hierarchie der Werte: 1. die Dichtung („Del libretto"). 2. die Musik („Della musica"), 3. der Gesang („Della maniera di cantare e del recitare"), 4. der Tanz („Dei balli"), der freilich nur sehr kurz behandelt wird, und 5. das Bühnenbild („Delle scene"). Hinzu kommt als 6. und letzter, aber vom Verfasser ausführlich und mit großem Engagement behandelter Gegenstand der Theaterbau („Del teatro"), der in der Literatur der Opernsatire sonst nirgends vorkommt[60]. Daß der Abschnitt über die Dichtung zwar an

---

58 In der *Dreigroschenoper* ist im Gegensatz hierzu die Anzahl der Nummern stark reduziert.
59 *Teatro*. S. 5: „A voi, o mio dilettissimo compositore del libretto presente, questo mio libretto consacro. [...] Frattanto, o indiviso mio amico, prendete a grado questo mio dono, come presentatovi da chi senza di voi non può vivere, e state sano, se non volete vedermi ammalato".
60 Besonders gepriesen wird die klassizistische Kunst des Architekten Palladio.

erster Stelle steht, quantitativ aber am schlechtesten abschneidet, ist auffällig, aber letzten Endes verständlich; denn Algarotti, der seiner Abhandlung zwei nur zum Teil ausgeführte, als exemplarisch gedachte *argomenti* beifügt[61], hält es für selbstverständlich, daß der Text im Mittelpunkt der Oper und somit auch der kritischen Befassung mit derselben steht:

> La prima cosa che vuol essere ben considerata è la qualità dell' argomento, o sia la scelta del libretto, che importa assai più che comunemente non si crede. Dal libretto si può quasi affermare che la buona dipenda o la mala riuscita del dramma. Esso è la pianta dell ‚edifizio', esso è la tela su cui il poeta ha disegnato il quadro che ha da esser colorito dipoi dal maestro di musica. Il poeta dirige i ballerini, i macchinisti, i pittori, coloro che hanno la cura del vestiario, egli comprende in mente il tutto insieme del dramma, e quelle parti che non sono eseguite da lui le ha però dettate egli medesimi[62].

Bei Marcello bleibt rein äußerlich die von Algarotti gewählte Sequenz erhalten, wodurch bei der Lektüre zunächst der Eindruck entsteht, auch die von ihm etablierte Hierarchie der Werte sei die gleiche. Zuerst kommt der Dichter an die Reihe. Ihm folgen der undifferenzierte Komponist/Dirigent und die Virtuosen, wobei symptomatisch ist, daß, während im *Saggio sopra l'opera in musica* sowohl in den Kapitelüberschriften als auch im Text die Betonung stets auf dem Phänomen oder Produkt liegt, bei Marcello der Agent, Produzent und Interpret im Vordergrund steht. Aber der Schein täuscht, zeigt sich doch beim näheren Hinsehen, daß die hier vorherrschende Tendenz subversiv ist. In der im Zerrspiegel eingefangenen ‚verkehrten' Opernwelt sind es nämlich die weiblichen Stars, von denen das Wohl oder Wehe („la bona o la mala riuscita del dramma") abhängt.

Nach den *poeti, compositori di musica, musici* und *cantatrici*, die den Kern der Operntruppe bilden, passiert der von Algarotti, der die soziale Dimension vernachlässigt, dafür aber wie sein Vorgänger Muratori im Sinne des Klassizismus die beabsichtigte Wirkung (Mitleid

---

61 Es handelt sich um einen *Enea in Troia* (Algarotti. S. 481-484), von dem Algarotti sagt, er sei „come in embrione", und eine *Iphigenie en Aulide* (ebenda. S. 485-509), von der es heißt, sie sei „spiegato in ogni sua parte e compito".
62 Algarotti. S. 438.

Scherz, Satire, Parodie oder tiefere Bedeutung? 193

und Furcht bzw. Schrecken) betont[63], konsequent ignorierte Klan von Mitwirkenden und Hilfskräften Revue. Zunächst werden die in den Opernbetrieb integrierten und direkt an der Aufführung beteiligten Individuen und Gruppen – an ihrer Spitze der Impresario, der bei Metastasio, Goldoni[64] und Calsabigi ins Sperrfeuer der Kritik gerät – durchgchechelt. Ihm folgen in immer kürzer werdenden Abschnitten die in ihrer Eigenschaft als Techniker und Maschinisten willkommenen Bühnenbildner[65] sowie die in Venedig damals als französische Importware eher geduldeten als bewunderten Tänzer und die zunächst nur in den Intermezzi agierenden Buffonisten.

Daran schließen sich die Vertreter anderer ehrlicher Gewerbe – so die Schneider, Pagen und Statisten, darunter der dem Leser vom Titelkupfer her vertraute Theaterbär, von dem Reinhard Pauly wohl zurecht behauptet, er symbolisiere im *Teatro alla moda* durchgehend „the exaggerated importance ascribed to all matters of equipment" und erwecke durch seine ständige Wiederkehr in Gesellschaft des Löwen und des Erdbebens den Eindruck, er sei der Protagonist der Oper[66]. Die Souffleure, Theaterdiener und Kopisten vervollständigen das Team, zu dem sich schließlich auch noch Handwerker, Logenschließer und der Theaterwirt, der die bunte Gesellschaft mit Getränken freihalten soll, gesellen.

---

63 Bei Muratori (Anm. 26), S. 573, ist von *purgar* und *migliorar* sowie von *compassione* und *terrore* die Rede.

64 In Goldonis *Impresario delle Smirne* tritt außerdem noch ein Agent (*senale*) mit dem Namen Nibio auf.

65 In dem sehr lesenswerten Kapitel seines Buches *La Vita e l'opera letteraria del musicista Benedetto Marcello* (Rome: Modes, 1909) über das *Teatro alla moda* (S. 101-134) zitiert Enrico Fondi einen Brief des Librettisten Pariati aus dem Jahre 1716, in welchem die Superstar-Rolle der Brüder Galli-Bibiena bei der Ausstattung der Oper *La Favorita* betont wird (S. 110f.).

66 Pauly hat völlig recht, wenn er sagt: „The figure of the theater bear is used by Marcello symbolically throughout his work to represent the exaggerated importance ascribed to all matters of equipment. The bear is constantly represented as being more important than the opera's text or music". *The Musical Quarterly* 34 (1948). S. 375.

Aber auch mit der Charakterisierung dieser untergeordneten Chargen hat sich der lange Atem des Satirikers Marcello nicht erschöpft. Die Reihe kommt nämlich auch an die Parasiten, unter denen die Advokaten, Gönner und Mütter, denen ganz am Ende des *Teatro alla moda* noch ein paar deftige Seiten gewidmet werden, eine besonders wichtige Rolle spielen. Neben dem Chor, der bekanntlich in der venezianischen Oper durch Abwesenheit glänzte, fehlt eigentlich nur das Publikum – von den Diplomaten in ihren Logen bis hin zu den Gondoliers, die das Privileg des freien Eintritts dazu benutzten, den Sängern und Sängerinnen entweder frenetischen Beifall zu spenden oder sie auf grobe Art auszupfeifen bzw. -johlen.

Worauf läuft dies alles hinaus? Wird bei Muratori, Algarotti und *tutte quante* der Dichter als die Sonne, um die sich die großen Planeten und kleinen Monde des Opernweltalls drehen, dargestellt, so macht ihn der Satiriker Marcello zum wahren *ultimus inter pares*, der allen denjenigen, die zu ihm aufblicken und ihn als Quelle ihrer schöpferischen oder nachschöpferischen Kraft verehren sollten, den Hof macht und zu Gefallen sein muß[67]. Das geht so weit, daß sich der Komponist ihn vom Theaterdirektor als Teil seines Honorars wie eine Sache schenken läßt: „Pretenderà il compositore moderno dall'Impresario (oltre l'onorario) il *regalo* d'un poeta da potersene servire a suo modo"[68]. Ein Mann ohne Einfluß und ohne künstlerisches Rückgrat, wird er zum Spielball der Kräfte, die er heraufbeschworen hat und lenken sollte. Als armer Hund, der sich mit einem Almosen abspeisen läßt, muß er sich während der langen Theaterferien sein Brot sauer mit untergeordneten und eines *poeta vates* unwürdigen Tätigkeiten verdienen[69].

---

67 „Visiterà spesso la prima donna, imperciocchè per ordinario dipende da questa l'esito dell' opera buono o tristo. [...] Visiterà il maestro di capella [...] Farà cerimonie con suonatori, sarti, orso, paggi, comparse, etc., raccomandando a tutti l'opera sua, etc., etc., etc." *Teatro*. S. 11f.
68 Ebenda. S. 17.
69 Ebenda.

Scherz, Satire, Parodie oder tiefere Bedeutung? 195

Wenn in diesem Multiversum bzw. Diversum überhaupt jemand die Zügel in der Hand hat, so ist es keinesfalls der Dichter, der doch, wie der Magen in der Fabel, die Menenius Agrippa in Shakespeares *Coriolanus* erzählt, „the storehouse and the shop of the whole body" sein sollte[70], sondern die *prima donna*, der zu allem Überfluß auch noch die Regie übertragen wird: „La prima donna insegnerà l'azione a tutta la compagnia"[71]. Es ist ein Wunder, daß bei diesem Tohuwabohu eine Aufführung überhaupt zustande kommt.

Bei den im *Teatro alla moda* – eigentlich: *Opera in musica alla moda* – dargestellten Zuständen ist es verständlich, daß kein wirklicher Poet gesucht wird, sondern ein Stümper, Handlanger und blutiger Laie, der möglichst wenig vom Metier versteht („Dirà bensì di aver corsi gli studi tutti di matematica, di pittura, di chimica, di medicina, di legge, etc., protestando che finalmente il genio l'ha condotto con violenza alla poesia"[72]) und von Tuten und Blasen (d. h. von Musik und Literatur und deren technischen Voraussetzungen) keine Ahnung hat[73]. Alle seine Kenntnisse bezieht er aus zweiter Hand, wie der Librettist Maccario im *Impresario delle Smirne*, der den Kastraten Carluccio darum ersucht, ihm schleunigst „un Metastasio, un Apostolo Zeno, delle opere del Pariati, una raccolta di drammi vecchi, e sopratutto un buon rimario" zu verschaffen[74].

Auch hier ahmt, wie Oscar Wilde uns lehrt, das Leben die Kunst nach, berichtet doch Lorenzo Da Ponte in seiner nicht eben von Genauigkeit strotzenden Autobiographie wie folgt von einem Besuch bei Giovanni Bertati:

---

70 *Coriolanus* I. S. 139f.
71 *Teatro*. S. 28.
72 Ebenda. S. 6.
73 Umgekehrt darf natürlich auch der Komponist, im Gegensatz zu seinen antiken Kollegen, von Literatur nichts verstehen: „[...] avvertendo egli ancora [...] di non intendersi punto di poesia, imperciocchè tale intelligenza parimente conveniva a' musici antichi [...] li quali [...] erano poeti eccellentissimi non meno che musici, ed il moderno compositore deve usar ogni studio per allontanarsi da quelli". Ebenda. S. 17.
74 Goldoni (Anm. 17). S. 544.

Mi domando il mio nome. [...] Pare colpito da un fulmine. Mi domando in un'aria molto imbarazzata e confusa in che cosa potea servirmi, ma sempre fermandosi sulla porta. Quando gli dissi ch'avea qualchecosa da communicarli, trovossi obbligato di farmi entrar nella stanza, il che fece però con qualche renitenza. Mi offrì una sedia nel mezzo della camera; io m'assisi senza alcuna malizia, presso alla tavola, dove giudicai dall'apparenze ch'ei fosse solito a scrivere. Vedendo me assiso, s'assise anch'egli sul seggiolone e si mise destramente a chiudere una quantità di scartafacci e di libri, che ingombravano quella tavola. Ebbi tuttavia l'agio di vedere in gran parte che libri erano. Un tomo di commedie francesi, un dizionario, un rimario e la grammatica del Corticelli stavano tutti alla destra del signor poeta; quelli che aveva alla sinistra non ho potuto vedere ehe cosa fossero. Credei allora d'intendere la ragione per cui gli dispiaceva di lasciarmi entrare[75].

Das von Marcello mit einem lachenden und einem weinenden Auge gemalte Porträt des Operntextdichters stellt, so müssen wir folgern, einen Mann ohne Eigenschaften dar, der sich aus Faulheit oder Ignoranz damit begnügt, vorhandene Texte, von denen er eine umfassende Sammlung besitzt, allein oder im Tandem zu bearbeiten bzw. auszuplündern[76]. Auf Bitten des Komponisten und der Sänger läßt er sich im Handumdrehen dazu herbei, einzelne Arientexte zu streichen oder sie durch andere, unpassende zu ersetzen[77]. Im gedruckten Libretto läßt er dann, um seinen Ruf als Dichter zu retten, die entsprechenden Stellen durch Anführungsstriche markieren[78].

---

75 Lorenzo Da Ponte, *Memorie, libretti mozartiani* (Mailand: Garzanti, 1976). S. 163f.

76 *Teatro*. S. 9: „Sarà provveduto poi di gran quantità d'opere vecchie, delle quali prendera soggetto e scenario, ne cambierà di questi ehe il verso e qualche nome de' personaggi, il che farà parimente nel trasportar drammi dalla lingua francese, dalla prosa al verso, dal tragico al comico, aggiungendo o levando personaggi secondo il bisogno dell'impresario. Farà gran brogli per compor opere, ne potendo altro far, si unirà con altro poeta e verseggiandolo insieme con patto di partire il guadagno della dedica e della stampa."

77 *Teatro*. S. 10: „Se qualche personaggio per convenienza dell'opera fosse scarso di parte, gliene aggiungera subito che ne venga richiesto o dal virtuoso o dal di lui protettore, avendo sempre preparato qualche centinaio d'ariette per poter cambiare, aggiungere, etc., non trascurando di riempire il libro de'soliti versi oziosi segnati con virgolette."

78 *Teatro*. S. 8: „Non importa che il soggetto dell'opera sia istorico; anzi essendo state trattate tutte le storie greche e latine degli antichi Latini e Greci, e da più scelti Italiani del buon secolo, appartiene al poeta moderno l'inventare una favola [...]" Die überwiegende Mehrheit der von Wiel (Anm. 5) registrierten Opern behandeln mitunter obskure, antike und mittelalterliche Stoffe. Erfundene Stoffe tauchten nur selten

Als Anti-Aristoteliker wie er im Buche steht darf er sich weder ernsthafte Gedanken über die Stoffwahl machen[79] noch jemals mit Absicht (*a intenzioni*) vorgehen, sondern muß alles dem Zufall (*capriccio*) überlassen[80]. Und statt die Einheiten des Ortes, der Zeit und der Handlung, die ihm heilig sein sollten, einzuhalten, beachtet er einzig und allein die des Theaters, für das er arbeitet, die der wirklichen Dauer der Vorstellung und die des Ruins des Theaterdirektors:

> Avverta però di non trascurare la solita esplicazione degli tre punti importantissimi d'ogni dramma: il Loco, il Tempo e l'Azzione. Significando il Loco: nel tal teatro; il Tempo: dalle due di notte alle sei; l'Azzione: l'esterminato del Impresario[81].

Dieser Karikatur eines Menschen, der Hanswurst und Hans-Dampf-in-allen-Gassen ist, stellt Marcello in den folgenden Abschnitten seiner Satire würdige Ebenbilder zur Seite und erreicht so Schritt für Schritt sein Ziel: die Enthüllung einer karnevalistischen Welt inmitten des Karnevals und, was noch schwerer wiegt, die Demaskierung von Larven, hinter denen sich keine tiefere Bedeutung verbirgt, sondern nur Eitelkeit, Selbstsucht und Habgier[82]. Er tut dies nicht allein durch den Inhalt seiner Schrift, sondern auch mit Hilfe formaler und stilistischer Mittel, die abschließend kurz zur Sprache kommen sollen.

---

auf. Algarotti (Anm. 8) geht auf die Frage der Stoffwahl ein und äußert sich skeptisch in Bezug auf mythologische und historische Sujets: „La verità si è che tanto co' soggetti cavati dalla mitologia quanto dalla storia vanno quasi necessariamente congiunti di non piccioli inconvenienti" (S. 440). Er rät den Operndichtern, exotische Stoffe zu behandeln: „[...] gli converra prendere un'azione seguita in tempi o almeno in paesi da' nostri molto remoti ed alieni, che dia luogo a più maniere di maraviglioso, ma sia ad un tempo semplicissima e notissima" (S. 441).

79 Und wenn er mit seinem Text irgendeine Absicht verfolgt, soll er diese den Mitwirkenden und Ausführenden verheimlichen: „Ma si guarderà di non dargli ad intendere cosa veruna dell'intreccio dell'opera, perchè la virtuosa moderna non deve intenderne punto". *Teatro*. S. 11.

80 Ebenda. S. 8: „Tutto il rimanente [bei der Stoffwahl] adunque serà un invenzione a Capriccio" und an vielen anderen Stellen.

81 Ebenda.

82 Man darf nicht vergessen, daß es den Venezianern damals vom Senat verboten war, ohne Maske im Theater zu erscheinen. Über die „usanze veneziane" gibt Wiel (Anm. 5) im Schlußteil seines langen Vorworts (S. XLIX-LXXX) Auskunft.

Im Gegensatz zu den seriösen Abhandlungen eines Muratori und Algarotti, in denen systematisch vorgegangen wird und für Impromptus und Improvisationen kein Platz ist, wirkt das *Teatro alla moda* skizzenhaft und wie aus dem Ärmel geschüttelt. Über weite Strecken hin herrscht das Prinzip der lockeren Fügung, weil der Verfasser die Welt der venezianischen Oper seiner Zeit so darstellen will, wie er sie mit seiner nicht eben rosigen Brille sieht: als eine in sich selbst gespaltene und ungeordnete, der es an innerer Logik mangelt. So bedient er sich unentwegt des *non sequitur* als einer rhetorischen Waffe. Mit dessen Hilfe gelingt es ihm denn auch tatsächlich *ad oculos* zu demonstrieren, daß das Gewebe aus Ursachen und Wirkungen, welches als Grundmuster sinnvollen Lebens und sinnvoller Kunst gilt, zerrissen ist.

In seiner bewußt verqueren Gebrauchsanweisung wimmelt es dementsprechend nur so von falschen *imperciocche's, acciocche's* und *però's* wie in dem Satz: „Nello stile del dramma non dovrà il poeta moderno porre molta fatica, riflettendo che dev'essere ascoltato ed inteso della moltitudine popolare, che però ad effetto di renderlo più intelligibile ometterà li soliti articoli, userà gl'insoliti lunghi periodi [...]."[83] Dieser Satz unterstreicht übrigens auch die Tendenz dieses Lehrbuchs *à rebours*, seine hinterhältigen Zwecke durch Verbote (nach dem Muster: du darfst nicht ...) statt durch Gebote (nach dem Muster: du sollst ...) zu erreichen. So heißt es gleich zu Anfang des *Teatro alla moda* doppelzüngig: „In primo luogo non dovrà il poeta aver letti, ne legger mai, gli autori antichi Latini o Greci", was mit dem anachronistischen *non sequitur* „imperciocchè nemeno gli antichi Greci o Latini hanno mai letti i moderni" begründet wird[84].

Auch bedient sich der Satiriker Marcello mit Vorliebe des stereotypen, alle Glieder der Kette nivellierenden und durch ein alle Möglichkeiten offenlassendes „etc." abgeschlossenen Katalogs, der häufig

---

83 *Teatro.* S. 9.
84 Ebenda. S. 6.

ins Absurde umschlägt. So heißt es im Kapitel „Agl'Impresari" einmal:

> Avuto dal poeta il libretto, anderà, prima di leggerlo, a visitare la prima donna, pregandolo di volerlo sentire; nel qual caso alla lettura di detto libro dovranno intervenire, oltre alla virtuosa, il di lei protettore, l'avvocato, i suggeritori, qualche portinaro, qualche comparsa, il sarto, il copista dell'opera, l'orso, il cameriero del protettore, etc.[85]

Und im gleichen Kapitel wird ihm geraten, mit den Dekorationsmalern, Schneidern und Tänzern einen Vertrag zu schließen, „kraft dessen er ihnen für die Oper eine bestimmte Summe zugesteht, ohne sich viel um ihre Leistung zu kümmern, da er sich ganz und gar auf seine Primadonna, die Intermezzi, den Theaterbären, die Gewitter und das Erdbeben" verlassen könne[86].

Ohne das Arsenal der rhetorischen Mittel auch nur halbwegs erschöpft zu haben, brechen wir ab; denn bekanntlich ist kein Genre – auch das literatur- und opernwissenschaftliche – schlechter als das langweilige. Vor allem der Parodie und Satire wird man am ehesten gerecht, wenn man sie unmittelbar genießt. Ich kann nur hoffen, daß, obgleich es meine Aufgabe war, das *Teatro alla moda* nach philologischen Gesichtspunkten in seine Bestandteile zu zerlegen, ich dem Leser den Geschmack an der Lektüre dieses ebenso spritzigen wie witzigen *libretticio* nicht verdorben, sondern ihren Appetit angeregt habe. Mir selbst wird es nach diesem kapriziösen Intermezzo gewiß leichter fallen, in der ernsthaften librettologischen Arbeit fortzufahren.

---

85 Ebenda. S. 32.
86 Einstein (Anm. 7). S. 59. Im Original: *Teatro*. S. 33.

Von Ballhorn ins Bockshorn gejagt
Unwillkürliche Parodie und unfreiwillige Komik in Ambroise Thomas' *Mignon* (1989)

> Goethe dit quelque part, dans son roman de *Wilhelm Meister*, qu'un ouvrage d'imagination doit être parfait ou ne pas exister. Si cette maxime sévère était suivie, combien peu d'ouvrages existeraient, à commencer par *Wilhehn Meister* lui-même.
> (Alfred de Musset[1])

> Die bis zur lächerlichen Fratze entstellte hochpoetische Gestalt der Goetheschen Mignon in der Oper von Thomas hat mein ästhetisches Gefühl immer derart empört, daß ich mir nicht soviel Objektivität wahren konnte, die Vorzüge des Darstellers vor der Scheußlichkeit und Verzerrtheit des dichterischen Objektes, wie es in der Oper vorliegt, zu trennen.
> (Hugo Wolf[2])

In seinem Beitrag zum Symposium über die Literaturoper, welches das Bayreuther Forschungsinstitut für Musiktheater im Sommer 1980 veranstaltete, scheint Carl Dahlhaus stillschweigend vorauszusetzen, daß es sich bei den textlichen Vorlagen für Werke dieser Art (seit Maeterlinck/Debussys *Pelléas et Mélisande* und Wilde/Strauss' *Salome*) stets um dramatische Gebilde handle[3]. Dies trifft zwar in der Mehrzahl der Fälle zu; doch gibt es in der Geschichte der Oper erheblich mehr Ausnahmen, als diese Faustregel vermuten läßt. Bei ihnen handelt es sich teils um Epen (man denke an die zahllosen Ariost-Opern barocker Komponisten einschließlich Händels), teils um Romane (von Verdis *La Traviata* und den *Manon Lescaut*-Opern Masse-

---

1   Aus dem *avant-propos* zu den *Comédies et Proverbes* (1856). Zit. bei Fernand Baldensperger, *Bibliographie critique de Goethe en France*, Paris 1907, 145.
2   „Abschied an Bertha Ehm" (*Wiener Salonblatt*, 3. Mai 1885) in *Hugo Wolfs musikalische Kritiken*, hg. von Richard Batka und Heinrich Werner, Leipzig 1911, 83.
3   „Zur Dramaturgie der Literaturoper", in: *Für und wider die Literaturoper*, hg. von Sigrid Wiesmann, Bayreuth 1982, 147-163.

nets und Puccinis bis hin zu Brittens *Turn of the Screw*) oder Novellen (von Bizets *Carmen* und Offenbachs *Les Contes d'Hoffmann* bis zu Brittens *Death in Venice*), zum geringen Teil aber auch um Gedichte (Brittens *Peter Grimes* nach George Crabbes *The Borough*). In Fällen dieser Art – das versteht sich von selbst – erfordert die Bearbeitung bzw. Transposition der Vorlage ganz besonderes dramaturgisches Geschick, da der Librettist gezwungen ist, zwei Gattungsgrenzen statt einer zu überschreiten.

Mit einer solchen Doppelbearbeitung, Ambroise Thomas' *Mignon* – im November 1866 an der *Opéra Comique* uraufgeführt und neben Gounods *Faust* und Bizets *Carmen* die erfolgreichste französische Oper des 19. Jahrhunderts[4] –, will ich mich im folgenden befassen. In diesem Fall kommt erschwerend hinzu, daß es sich nicht einfach um die Dramatisierung eines in der gleichen Sprache verfaßten Textes handelt, sondern dieser die Übertragung des Urtextes aus einer Zunge in die andere vorausgeht, das Unternehmen also gewissermaßen im dreifachen Sinne komparatistisch ist[5].

Obwohl es sich bei *Mignon* um ein letztes Endes musikdramatisch verfehltes Werk handelt, das dem Kenner der literarischen Vorlage, d. h. also vor allem dem deutschen Publikum, verdächtig, wenn nicht gar anstößig erscheinen muß, wie Hugo Wolfs als Motto verwendete Kritik beweist[6], ist es bedauerlich, daß diese melodisch so einfallsreiche *opéra lyrique*[7] heute nicht mehr im weltweiten Repertoire steht.

---

4   Insgesamt bisher über 3000 Aufführungen in Paris.

5   Als unmittelbare Vorlage diente Carré und Barbier wahrscheinlich die Übersetzung von Théophile Gautier dem Jüngeren, die 1861 in zwei Bänden erschienen war. Den Begriff der *littérature doublement* (noch nicht *triplement*) *comparée* brachte Basil Munteano in die methodologische Debatte innerhalb der Vergleichenden Literaturwissenschaft ein.

6   Das Lied der Mignon nannte Hugo Wolf „eine triviale Chansonetten-Melodie im parfümierten Salonkleide mit langer Schleppe". ([Anm. 2], 2.)

7   Zur *opéra lyrique* siehe die weiter unten (Anm. 10) zitierte Diss. von Morton Achter sowie das Kapitel „Opéra Comique, Operetta and Lyric Opera" in Donald J. Grout, *A Short History of Opera*, New York 1947, und die dort angegebene Sekundärliteratur. In ihrer *Histoire de l'Opéra-Comique: La Seconde Salle Favart 1840-*

Es lohnte sich vielleicht, sie auszugraben. Zum Glück liegt eine ausgezeichnete Platteneinspielung durch das Philharmonia-Orchester unter der Leitung von Antonio de Almeida mit Marilyn Horne in der Titelrolle vor, an die man sich halten kann[8]. Soweit sich feststellen läßt, ist übrigens der Text der Oper, für den die neben Scribe erfolgreichsten Librettisten der Zeit, Michel Carré und Jules Barbier, verantwortlich zeichnen, noch nie eingehend analysiert worden[9]. Die einzige mir bekannte ausführliche musikwissenschaftliche Untersuchung stammt von Morton Achter, der im Jahre 1972 an der University of Michigan eine *Felicien David, Ambroise Thomas and French „opéra lyrique", 1850-1870* betitelte Dissertation schrieb[10]. Ich betrete also operngeschichtliches Neuland. Die hier vorgelegte vergleichende Studie wird sich auch dadurch auszeichnen, daß sie sowohl die ‚Singspiel'-Fassung als auch die Rezitativ-Fassung berücksichtigt[11].

Ehe ich mich meiner eigentlichen Aufgabe zuwende, möchte ich einige Überlegungen literar- bzw. rezeptionsgeschichtlicher Art anstellen, um zu erklären, wie es dazu kam, daß ein prototypischer Bildungsroman wie *Wilhelm Meisters Lehrjahre* überhaupt zum Vorwurf einer französischen Oper werden konnte. Dabei ist zu beachten, daß es sich um einen in der Operngeschichte einmaligen Versuch handelt, Goethes Werk (genauer gesagt: einen Teilaspekt desselben) dem Musiktheater zu überliefern. Ausgehen muß man von der Tatsache, daß es

---

1887 (Paris 1892) verwenden Albert Soubies und Charles Malherbe den Ausdruck „œuvre de demi-caractère". Siehe Bd. II, 81, des vom Genfer Verlag Minkoff veranstalteten Reprints.

8 Es handelt sich um eine 1978 hergestellte Einspielung für Columbia Masterworks auf vier Platten.

9 Mir lag die in der Lilly Rare Books Library in Bloomington (Indiana) aufbewahrte zweite Auflage des Textes (Paris: Calmann-Levy, [o. J.]) vor.

10 Erhältlich durch University Microfilms in Ann Arbor (Michigan). Eine kurze Zusammenfassung aus der Feder des Autors findet sich in *Dissertation Abstracts International* 33 (1972), 2406-a.

11 Bei dem in Anm. 9 genannten Text handelt es sich um die ursprüngliche *opéra comique*-Fassung des Librettos. Der Text der in der Columbia Masterworks-Aufnahme zur Verwendung kommenden Rezitativ-Version liegt der Einspielung bei.

durchwegs Mignon und der Harfner waren, die die Aufmerksamkeit der Kritik innerhalb und außerhalb Deutschlands erregten, während der Roman als Ganzes durchaus keinen ungeteilten Beifall fand[12]. In Frankreich, wo *Die Leiden des jungen Werthers* bei ihrem Erscheinen Furore machten und den Maßstab setzten, der bei der Beurteilung aller nachmaligen epischen Produktionen des Verfassers anzulegen war, empfand man die *Lehrjahre* kaum als sensationell. Dieser Roman galt als typisch deutsch und viel zu abstrus, um den französischen Geschmack zu treffen. Schon Madame de Staël, deren 1810 erschienene Schrift *De l'Allemagne* als Barometer der literarischen Meinungsbildung im Frankreich der Restauration zu gelten hat, war geteilter Meinung über das Buch, das ihr August Wilhelm Schlegel so warm empfohlen hatte. „*Wilhelm Meister*", so heißt es im 28. Kapitel des zweiten Teils, „est plein de discussions ingénieuses et spirituelles; on en ferait un ouvrage philosophique du premier ordre s'il ne s'y mêlait pas une intrigue du roman, dont l'interêt ne vaut pas ce qu'elle fait perdre"[13].

Das Urteil der Herrin von Coppet ist symptomatisch und wird durch Aussagen mehrerer bedeutender Dichter unter ihren Landsleuten bestätigt. So nennt Prosper Mérimée den Roman Goethes „un étrange livre où les plus belles choses du monde alternent avec les enfantillages les plus ridicules" und stellt ergänzend fest: „Dans tout ce qu'a fait Goethe, il y a un mélange de génie et de niaiserie allemande."[14] Und der einflußreiche Kritiker Jules Janin schrieb Anfang 1830: „Ce *chef-d'œuvre*, au dire des Allemands, est pour nous un confus

---

12 Zur Rezeptionsgeschichte innerhalb Deutschlands siehe vor allem den von Klaus Gille herausgegebenen Band *Goethes „Wilhelm Meister": Zur Rezeptionsgeschichte der „Lehr- und Wanderjahre"* (Königstein im Ts. 1979). Die wichtigsten Zeugnisse sind im Erläuterungs- und Dokumentenband zu den *Lehrjahren*, den Ehrhard Bahr im Reclam-Verlag herausgab (1982), abgedruckt.
13 Zit. aus Mme de Staëls *De l'Allemagne*. Nouvelle édition abrégée, par André Monchoux, Paris 1956, 250.
14 Zit. bei Baldensperger (Anm. 1), 146.

assemblage d'aventures triviales, de personnages ignobles, de mysticisme sans intelligence et sans frein."[15]

Erst 1866 – man beachte das Datum: im selben Jahr machte Thomas' *Mignon* ihre theatralische Aufwartung – wurde in Frankreich der erste ernsthafte Versuch einer objektivierenden literarkritischen Darstellung gemacht, und zwar durch Emile Montegut, der in der *Revue des Deux Mondes* einen umfassenden, „Philosophie de *Wilhelm Meister*" betitelten Aufsatz veröffentlichte, in welchem er die ästhetische mit der moralischen (sprich: bürgerlichen) Komponente der *Lehrjahre* in Einklang zu bringen suchte[16].

Fast einhellige Zustimmung fand in Frankreich die ‚romantische' Seite des Romans, die von Mignon und dem Harfner verkörpert wird. Diese Begeisterung war, wenn auch nicht schrankenlos, in der deutschen Kritik vorgebildet. Hatte Schiller dem älteren Freunde und Briefpartner gegenüber gewisse moralische Bedenken angemeldet, aber gefunden, daß sie durch Goethes Kunst der Darstellung ästhetisch aufgehoben seien[17], so äußerte Friedrich Schlegel in seiner *Athenaeums*-Rezension aus dem Jahre 1798 voller Bewunderung[18]:

> Alles, was die Erinnerung und die Schwermuth und die Reue nur Rührendes hat, athmet und klagt der Alte wie aus einer unbekannten, bodenlosen Tiefe von Gram und ergreift uns mit wilder Wehmuth. Noch süßere Schauer und gleichsam ein schönes Grausen erregt das heilige Kind, mit dessen Erscheinung die innerste Springfeder des sonderbaren Werkes plötzlich frey zu werden scheint.

Während aber in Deutschland Romantiker wie Novalis sehr bald gegen Goethe zu Felde zogen, schlug jenseits des Rheins die Begeiste-

---

15 Zit. bei Baldensperger, *Goethe en France: Etude de Littérature Comparée*, 2., durchges. Aufl., Paris: [o. J.]; repr. New York 1973, 177.

16 Die Arbeit erschien in der November/Dezember-Nummer des Jahres 1863 auf S. 178-203 und wurde 1882 in den Sammelband *Types littéraires et fantaisies esthétiques* aufgenommen.

17 „Wie schön gedacht ist es, daß Sie das praktisch Ungeheure, das furchtbar Pathetische im Schicksal Mignons und des Harfenspielers von dem theoretisch Ungeheuren, von den Mißgeburten des Verstandes ableiten, so daß der reinen und gesunden Natur nichts dadurch aufgebürdet wird." Schiller an Goethe am 2. Juli 1796.

18 Aus *Athenaeum: Eine Zeitschrift*, (1798) im Repr. Stuttgart 1960, 329f.

rung für die androgyne Gestalt der – ursprünglich: des[19] – Mignon hohe Wogen. Nannte Hardenberg die Lehrjahre abschätzig „einen *Candide* gegen die Poesie gerichtet" und mokierte sich über das „von Avanturiers, Comoedianten, Maitressen, Krämern und Philistern" bevölkerte Werk[20], so stellte Madame de Staël den „personnages [...] plus spirituels que signifiants" und den „situations plus naturelles que saillantes" die Figur der Mignon gegenüber, die ihrzufolge den eigentlichen Reiz des Romans ausmachen[21]:

> [Elle] est mystérieuse comme un rêve; eile exprime ses regrets pour l'Italie dans des vers ravissants que tout le monde sait par coeur en Allemagne: „Connais-tu cette terre où les citronniers fleurissent, etc." [...] On ne se peut pas représenter sans émotion les moindres mouvements de cette jeune fille; il y a je ne sais quelle simplicité magique en elle, qui suppose des abîmes de pensées et de sentiments; l'on croit entendre gronder l'orage au fond de son âme lors même que l'on ne saurait citer une parole ni une circonstance qui motive l'inquiétude inexprimable qu'elle fait éprouver.

Damit war für die Rezeption und literarische Verwertung dieser Gestalt in Frankreich der Boden geebnet. Zahlreiche Übertragungen und Nachbildungen des Zitronen- und Orangenliedes, das den Schlüssel zum Wesen Mignons zu bieten schien[22], wurden hergestellt, und der holländische Maler Ary Scheffer verfertigte seit 1838 stark idealisierende und ins Madonnenhafte stilisierte ‚Porträts' des Mädchens, die ungeheuer populär waren und, wenn man den Verfassern der *Histoire de l'Opéra-Comique* Glauben schenken kann, eine wichtige Inspirationsquelle für die Librettisten Carré und Barbier waren[23]. („La

---

19 Die geschlechtliche Zwitterhaftigkeit Mignons wird in Goethes Roman durchwegs betont. So heißt es in II 4 (S. 97 der Artemis-Ausgabe): „[Wilhelm] konnte nicht mit sich einig werden, ob er sie für einen Knaben oder für ein Mädchen hielt." Diese Doppelbödigkeit (*Est-ce une fille, est-ce un garçon?*) bleibt in *Mignon* erhalten.
20 Zit. in den *Erläuterungen und Dokumenten* (Anm. 12), 328.
21 *De l'Allemagne* (Anm. 13), 250f.
22 Hierzu in Baldenspergers *Bibliographie critique de Goethe en France* (Anm. 1) ein kurzer Katalog auf S. 80f.
23 „Les librettistes, disait-on, avaient admiré le *Mignon* d'Ary Scheffer et ils etaient inspirés des tableaux du peintre plus que de ceux du poète." *Histoire de l'Opéra-Comique* (Anm. 7), II 88. Zu Ary Scheffer und seinen Bildern *Mignon regrettant sa*

Mignon d'Ary Scheffer", schrieb Théophile Gautier im Jahre 1858, „est tellement acceptée qu'elle s'est substituée peu à peu à la création de Goethe"[24].) Bei diesen rezeptionsgeschichtlichen Gegebenheiten war es also ganz natürlich, daß gerade in den sechziger Jahren und als Pendant zum sentimentalischen *Faust* Gounods, der in Deutschland bekanntlich als *Margarete* kursiert, der Plan einer Mignon-Oper in das Blickfeld französischer Librettisten und Komponisten geriet.

Übersetzungen der *Lehrjahre* gab es schon seit Beginn des Jahrhunderts – so die stark gekürzte und auf den französischen Hausgebrauch zugeschnittene Fassung C. F. Sevelings aus dem Jahre 1802, in der Wilhelm in Alfred umgetauft wird und Mignon als Fanfan auftritt[25]. 1829 legte ein gewisser Roussenel die ersten wort- und sinngetreuen *Années d'apprentissage* vor, denen 1834 eine von der Baronin A. de Carlowitz hergestellte Version folgte. Aber erst mit Gautier fils, einem der bedeutendsten Interpreten deutscher Literatur um die Jahrhundertmitte, trat der entscheidende Vermittler auf den Plan[26]. Übrigens scheint der Text, den Ambroise Thomas vertonte, keine Auftragsarbeit gewesen zu sein. Ursprünglich war das Werk zur Aufführung im *Théâtre-Lyrique* bestimmt, dessen Publikum ein letales Ende akzeptiert hatte, wie es die vieraktige Urfassung Carrés und Barbiers tatsächlich vorsah[27]. Für diese Lösung (nicht: Fassung) entschied man sich vielfach in deutschen Opernhäusern.

---

patrie und *Mignon aspirant au ciel* s. Marthe Kolbs Buch *Ary Scheffer et son temps 1795-1858*, Paris 1937, bes. 343-345.

24 Gautiers Übersetzung der *Lehrjahre*, von der sich in den Vereinigten Staaten ein einziges, durch Fernleihe nicht erhältliches Exemplar befindet, war mir leider unzugänglich.

25 Baldensperger (Anm. 1) druckt auf S. 142f. einen Teil des Vorwortes ab.

26 Mitte der zwanziger Jahre unseres Jahrhunderts sollte seine Übersetzung dreier Novellen Achim von Arnims auf André Breton und den Surrealismus eine nachhaltige Wirkung ausüben.

27 In ihrer *Histoire de l'Opéra-Comique* (Anm. 7) berichten Soubies und Malherbe, die Urfassung des Librettos befinde sich in ihrem Besitz: „Toutefois, si le dénouement s'est quelque peu modifié, jamais plus il n'est revenu à son terme logique, à la mort de l'héroïne, telle que l'avaient présentée les librettistes dans une version primi-

Giacomo Meyerbeer, den dieser Stoff zu interessieren schien und der die Gestalt der Mignon in der Musik zu einem von Henri Blaze de Bury verfaßten dramatischen Pastiche *La Jeunesse de Goethe* zur Geltung bringen wollte, fand die Darstellung der beiden Textdichter nicht seriös genug und machte Änderungsvorschläge, auf die Carré und Barbier aber nicht eingingen[28].

Gounod, dessen *Faust* sie selbst textiert hatten, fand den Gegenstand „trop sérieux" und drang vergebens auf weitere Auflockerung[29]. Erst beim dritten Anlauf gelang es also dem Paar, ihre Dichtung an den Mann zu bringen – freilich auch diesmal unter Opfern, die das Endprodukt der gemeinsamen Bemühungen aus literarischer Sicht vielfach als unfreiwillige Parodie erscheinen lassen. Was Bizet fünf Jahre später dank großer Zähigkeit erreichte[30], blieb den Verfassern der *Mignon* versagt; denn seit der Uraufführung und, wenigstens in Frankreich, *forever after* knüpfen Wilhelm und sein Schützling zum guten Ende das Eheband, und Lothario schließt sich ihnen als Dritter im Bunde an.

Damit sind wir an das Ende der mangels zureichender Dokumentation unvollständigen Vorgeschichte der *Mignon* gelangt und können zur Analyse des Textes und seiner Funktion im musiko-dramatischen Kontext übergehen. Zunächst einige Bemerkungen zur Stoffwahl bzw. Gattungsaffinität. Daß ein Bildungsroman von der Art des *Wilhelm Meister* sich nicht mir nichts dir nichts veropern läßt, wird jedem Leser einleuchten. Das soll natürlich nicht heißen, daß der Roman musi-

---

tive dont le manuscrit est, par le hasard des circonstances, devenu notre propriété" (92).

28 Hinweise bei Baldensperger (Anm. 1), 151f. Die Publikation der Gesamtausgabe von Meyerbeers Briefen ist leider noch nicht bis zu dem hier in Frage kommenden Zeitpunkt gelangt. Entsprechende Angaben in H. W. Blaze de Burys Buch *Meyerbeer et son temps*, Paris 1865.

29 Nach einem bei Baldensperger (Anm. 1, 152) zitierten Auszug aus *La Presse* vom 17. Mai 1866.

30 Siehe hierzu Ludovic Halévys Darstellung *La millième représentation de „Carmen"*, in der Zeitschrift *Le Théâtre* (Januar 1905).

kalisch keine Anknüpfungspunkte bietet; denn die Lieder der beiden ‚romantischen' Gestalten, die bei unterschiedlichen, über die Handlung verstreuten Gelegenheiten vorgetragen werden, boten vor allem – aber keineswegs nur – deutschen Komponisten reichlich Gelegenheit, ihre Kunst spielen zu lassen, wobei „Kennst du das Land" sowohl quantitativ als auch qualitativ am besten abschnitt[31]. Mit diesen Liedern, die Goethe vom Vortragenden jeweils mit der Harfe (Harfner) oder Zither (Mignon) begleiten läßt, ist jedoch kaum ein Handlungsgerüst erstellt, das dramaturgisch stichhält[32].

Recht verwunderlich ist in diesem Zusammenhang die Tatsache, daß Thomas sich die Gelegenheit entgehen ließ, mehr Lieder Mignons und des Harfners in seine Oper einzubauen. Freilich wäre, wenn er dies getan hätte, die musikalische Präponderanz der beiden Rollen so stark gewesen, daß sie die Oper beherrscht und damit das geforderte relative Gleichgewicht der Stimmen gestört hätte. ‚Wörtlich' übernommen wurde eigentlich nur das Paradestück Mignons (Act I, #4[33]) aus dem dritten Buch der *Lehrjahre*, zu dessen Vortrag Goethe dem künftigen Komponisten genaue Anweisungen gibt[34]. Ihm kommt in

---

[31] Ein kurzer Katalog der Vertonungen findet sich unter dem Stichwort *Wilhelm Meister* im dritten Bande (695) von *Grove's Dictionary of Music and Musicians*, 5. Aufl., hg. von Eric Blom, New York. Mit den Vertonungen Schuberts, Schumanns und Hugo Wolfs befaßt sich Jack M. Stein in einem in der Zeitschrift *Comparative Literature* 22 (1970) publizierten Aufsatz.

[32] Johanna Lienhard hat den Liedern Mignons eine 1982 im Artemis-Verlag (Zürich) erschienene literarkritische Monographie (*Mignon und ihre Lieder, gespiegelt in den „Wilhelm-Meister"-Romanen*) gewidmet.

[33] Die Nummernbezeichnung folgt der 1901 bei G. Schirmer in New York erschienenen Ausgabe des Klavierauszugs. Sie bezieht sich auf die gängige Fassung und erstreckt sich nicht auf die Nummern 17 und 18 der früheren Fassung, die der 1866 bei Menestrel in Paris erschienene Klavierauszug mitberücksichtigt.

[34] „Sie fing jeden Vers feierlich und prächtig an, als ob sie auf etwas Sonderbares aufmerksam machen, als ob sie etwas Wichtiges vortragen wollte. Bei der dritten Zeile ward der Gesang dumpfer und düsterer; das ‚kennst du es wohl?' drückte sie geheimnisvoll und bedächtig aus; in dem ‚dahin, dahin!' lag eine unwiderstehliche Sehnsucht, und ihr: ‚Laßt uns ziehn!' wußte sie bei jeder Wiederholung dergestalt zu modifizieren, daß es bald bittend und dringend, bald treibend und vielversprechend war." Ob Thomas diese Beschreibung kannte?

der Oper eine noch zentralere Bedeutung zu, weil es gewissermaßen leitmotivisch verwendet wird.

Höchstens zwei weitere Nummern der Oper gehen auf liedhafte Vorlagen im Roman zurück: das *chanson* Lotharios („Fugitif et tremblant") in der Introduktion, das auf die zwei eng miteinander gepaarten Lieder des Harfners in II 13 („Wer nie sein Brot mit Tränen aß" und „Wer sich der Einsamkeit ergibt") zu verweisen scheint, und das Duett „Légères Hirondelles" (Act I, #5), welches dem in den *Lehrjahren* ausdrücklich als Duett bezeichneten Zwiegesang „Nur wer die Sehnsucht kennt" in IV 11 abgelauscht sein mag, inhaltlich aber nur vage mit diesem verbunden ist[35]. Mignons *„styrienne"* „Je connais un pauvre enfant" (Act II, #10), die dem Ton und der Atmosphäre nach auf Desdemonas *canzone del salice* in Verdis *Otello* vorausweist, läßt sich kaum auf „Heiß mich nicht reden, heiß mich schweigen" (V 16) beziehen, einem „Gedicht", von dem gesagt wird, Mignon habe es „mit großem Ausdruck einigemal rezitiert, der Drang so mancher sonderbarer Ereignisse" habe aber den Erzähler bislang daran gehindert, es mitzuteilen. Das Engelslied aus dem achten Buch („So laßt mich scheinen, bis ich werde") konnte schon deshalb in der Oper keine Verwendung finden, weil dort die im Tod vollendete Trennung des irdischen und überirdischen Teils der verklärten Gestalt nicht vollzogen wird. An seine Stelle tritt im uneigentlichen Sinne das Gebet im dritten Akt (Finale, #16), in dem die hier orthodox katholische Frömmigkeit der Heldin, auf die im Roman eine einzige Stelle verweist, pastos aufgetragen wird[36].

Vom melo-dramaturgischen Standpunkt aus gesehen geschickt war es, daß Carré und die bei Goethe artistisch nur mäßig begabte Philine, von der es in III 3 heißt, sie habe in Melinas Truppe das Kammer-

---

35 Mein Bezugspunkt ist durchwegs der im Artemis-Goethe (Bd. 7) wiedergegebene Text von Goethes Roman.

36 Während die Mignon der Oper wiederholt zum Gebetbuch greift, wird bei Goethe nur einmal (II 6) darauf hingewiesen, sie gehe „in die Messe [...], wohin [Wilhelm] ihr einmal folgte und sie in der Ecke der Kirche mit dem Rosenkranze knien und andächtig beten sah".

mädchen gespielt[37], und die im Roman recht zweideutige Liedchen zum Besten gibt[38], in eine gefeierte Schauspielerin (sprich: Sängerin) verwandelt haben, die die Titania im *Sommernachtstraum* spielt. Sie brilliert in der schwierigen Koloratur-Arie „Je suis Titania, la blonde" (Act II, Finale, #12c), mit der sie nicht erst in der Oper selbst, sondern schon in der Ouvertüre ihre Rivalin Mignon aussticht[39]. Was aber sollte Thomas mit Figuren wie Wilhelm, Laertes und Friedrich anfangen, die sich in den *Lehrjahren* keinesfalls musikalisch gebärden, in *Mignon* aber dazu verpflichtet sind, ihr vokales Scherflein beizutragen?

Bei den zwei Nebenfiguren, die jeweils mit einer kleinen Nummer im Stil des Rokoko (Laertes' „*madrigal*" „Belle, ayez pitié de nous" [Act II, #8] und Fredericks Rondo-Gavotte „Me voici dans son boudoir" [Act II, #10b]) zu Worte kommen, ist dieser Umstand wenig gravierend[40]. Doch ist es für den Unterschied zwischen der *opéra comique*- und der *opéra lyrique*-Fassung charakteristisch, daß in ersterer Laertes als Rhetor auftritt, der zwar versucht, „[de] désapprendre toutes les sottises dont messieurs les poètes m'ont bourré la cervelle" (9), aber dauernd Rückfälle erleidet und in einem fort deklamiert und rezitiert[41].

Problematischer liegt der Fall bei Meister selbst, der in den *Lehrjahren* zwar wie in der Oper (dort unmotiviert) als Dichter auftritt, in dieser Eigenschaft aber in den *Lehrjahren* nur Unwesentliches, in

---

37 Im *Hamlet*, an dessen Stelle in der Oper äußerlich der *Sommernachtstraum* tritt, spielt sie die Königin im Schauspiel.

38 So singt sie zur Begleitung des Harfners die Melodie „Der Schäfer putzte sich zum Tanz", dessen Text der Erzähler den Lesern vorenthält, „weil sie es vielleicht abgeschmackt oder wohl gar unanständig finden könnten" (II 11); und später (V 10) trägt sie das frivole Liedchen „Singet nicht in Trauertönen" vor.

39 In der Handlung unterbricht ihre Stimme als störendes Echo wiederholt das trauliche Beisammensein Wilhelms und Mignons.

40 Fredericks Rolle wurde bei der Uraufführung von einem Tenor gesungen. Seit der Londoner Aufführung des Jahres 1870, bei der Madame Trebelli-Bettini den Frederick sang, gilt sie als Hosenrolle.

41 Er tritt sogar kurz als Theseus auf und zitiert aus dem *Sommernachtstraum*.

Mignon jedoch gar nichts produziert. Goethe sieht in ihm, wie in der Frau Melina, einen „Anempfinder"[42], dem es wohl für immer versagt sein wird, Schöpferisches zu leisten. Dies wird unter anderem dadurch versinnbildlicht, daß Mignon „ihn am Arm [hält] und ihm die Hand leise wegzuziehen" versucht, als er den Vertrag mit Serlo „mechanisch" unterzeichnet (III 5)[43]. In der Oper ist, musikalisch gesehen, seine Rolle so weit aufgestockt, daß ihm in jedem der drei Akte eine Solonummer zufällt, wodurch nicht so sehr seine dramatische als seine melo-dramatische Funktion, die der Konvention tenoraler Territorialansprüche entspricht, gekennzeichnet wird.

Mit dem Hinweis auf die separat erschienene Urfassung des *Mignon*-Textes „en trois actes et cinq tableaux" ist indirekt die Frage nach der Authentizität des Librettos gestellt worden, die uns jetzt näher beschäftigen soll. Es wäre anhand einiger charakteristischer Beispiele zu zeigen, wie gerade bei Literaturopern die Abweichungen vom Modell von Stufe zu Stufe der melo-dramatischen Bearbeitung gravierender werden und sich der eigentliche künstlerische Schwerpunkt zusehends vom Literarischen ins Musikalische verschiebt. Das läßt sich bei *Mignon* besonders leicht demonstrieren. Auch hier führen nämlich die Verkürzungen, die bei der Verwandlung von Dialogen in Rezitative unumgänglich sind, zu Verzerrungen, weil Lücken in der zum Verständnis der Handlung notwendigen Kette von Ursachen und Wirkungen entstehen. Einbußen im szenischen Aufbau, im Text und in den Regiebemerkungen sind, wie die folgenden Vergleiche beweisen sollen, hierfür verantwortlich.

Was die Struktur bzw. die dramaturgische Gestaltung der Oper *Mignon* anbetrifft, so zeigt sich die Tendenz zur Verknappung, über die sich die Verfasser von Operntextbüchern schon immer beschwert

---

42 *Wilhelm Meisters Lehrjahre*.
43 Ebd. V 4.

haben[44], vor allem in der Gestaltung des Schluß-Aktes. So wurde auch hier, gleichsam im letzten Durchgang, ein Szenenkomplex, den Philine beherrscht und für den es in den *Lehrjahren* keinerlei Vorbild gibt, kurzerhand gestrichen. Durch diese Gewaltmaßnahme wird das Gleichgewicht zwischen Protagonistin und Antagonistin einigermaßen wiederhergestellt und vom Schluß her gesehen die Oper *Mignon* wirklich zu einer Mignon-Oper. Im Zuge dieser dramaturgisch und von der Motivation her begrüßenswerten Einsparungen wurde die Darstellerin der Philine eines vokalen „Schaustücks", der „forlana" „Paysanne ou signora" (#17 alter Zählung) beraubt.

Bei Opern des Singspiel-Typs bildet der gesprochene Dialog bekanntlich einen wichtigen und letzten Endes unentbehrlichen Bestandteil der melodramatischen Handlung, und seine Kenntnis muß zum Verständnis der Vorgänge unbedingt vorausgesetzt werden. Leider sündigen in der Praxis Opernregisseure und -dramaturgen bei der Inszenierung gerade in dieser Hinsicht insofern, als sie die gesprochenen Partien zwar selten völlig ausmerzen (das geschieht höchstens bei Platten-Einspielungen), sie aber als Eselsbrücken zwischen Gesangsnummern behandeln, die je kürzer desto besser sind. Dabei wird häufig übersehen, daß gerade in solchen Gesprächen das Publikum oft über die Vorgeschichte der Handlung unterrichtet wird, von der es im musikalischen Kontext nichts oder viel zu wenig erfährt. Man denke an *Die Zauberflöte*, wo man sonst kaum herausfindet, was es mit der Feindschaft zwischen Sarastro und der Königin der Nacht eigentlich auf sich hat, oder an *Carmen*, wo man erst neuerdings zurecht auf die *Opéra comique*-Version zurückgreift.

In *Mignon* ist die Verstümmelung des Dialogs in der Rezitativ-Fassung um so peinlicher, als eine Nabelschnur das Werk mit seinem literarischen Vorbild verbindet. Bei der Umpolung der *Opéra comique* in eine lyrische Oper fielen nicht nur einzelne Stellen, die spezifisch auf

---

44 Im Bereich der deutschsprachigen Oper haben z. B. E. T. A. Hoffmann („Der Dichter und der Komponist") und Hofmannsthal (im Hinblick auf *Tristan und Isolde*) hierüber Klage geführt.

die *Lehrjahre* hinweisen, sondern auch ganze von Carré und Barbier frei erfundene Szenen dem Rotstift zum Opfer. So verzichtete man in der *opéra lyrique*-Fassung wohlweislich darauf, die vierte Szene des ersten Aktes (S. 8-15 des bei Calmann-Lévy erschienenen Textes) so breit auszuspinnen, wie dies in der Urfassung geschieht, weil es hier, musikalisch gesehen, hauptsächlich darauf ankam, Wilhelms „*rondeau*" „Oui, je veux par le monde" (#2) zu motivieren. Der gedruckte Text bringt ein farcenhaftes und mit billigen Wortwitzen gespicktes Gespräch zwischen Wilhelm und Laertes, das sich um das zähe Hühnchen und den sauren Wein dreht, die ihnen das Wirtshaus bietet. Auch entfiel, zusammen mit dem Szenen-Komplex um Philine im dritten Akt, die Szene 7 des gedruckten Textes, in der Laertes seinem Freund Wilhelm ausführlich über die Geschicke der Schauspieler-Gesellschaft seit dem Brand des gräflichen Schlosses berichtet und die Präsenz der Truppe in Italien (genauer gesagt: am Garda-See) begründet[45].

Von den anfangs beibehaltenen Bezügen zu Goethes Roman entfiel in der für heutige Aufführungen verbindlichen Fassung zum Beispiel der Bericht des Laertes über sein eheliches Mißgeschick[46] und der Hinweis auf die nicht eben reibungslos verlaufene Übersiedlung der Truppe ins Schloß[47]. Im Verhältnis zu den von Carré und Barbier bzw. Thomas für nötig befundenen strukturellen Eingriffen in die Substanz der *Lehrjahre* mögen dies Kleinigkeiten sein; doch ist ihre Wirkung kumulativ und selbst bei anscheinend so belanglosen Details wie der Anspielung auf die im Schloß zu veranstaltenden Aufführungen in dem an Philine adressierten Brief des Baron de Rosemberg („Ma toute belle, pour fêter dignement le passage du prince de Tiefenbach qui doit s'arrêter quelques jours dans mon château, j'ai pensé à lui donner le plaisir de quelques représentations dramatiques"[48]) nicht zu

---

45 Der Zwang, auch die Versetzung der Hauptpersonen nach Italien glaubhaft zu machen, führt zu Ungereimtheiten in der Motivation.
46 *Lehrjahre* IV 4 und *Mignon* (Textbuch) I 4 (14).
47 *Lehrjahre* III 3 und *Mignon* (Textbuch) II 1 (44).
48 *Mignon* (Textbuch) I 11 (30).

unterschätzen, weil sie die Illusion einer kontinuierlichen Handlung, wenn auch mehr schlecht als recht, aufrecht erhalten. Andere Eingriffe – vor allem solche, die willkürlich gemachte Zusätze Carrés und Barbiers auslöschen und unentschuldbare Schönheitsfehler beseitigen – verkraftet man gerne. So sucht man in der Rezitativ-Fassung zum Glück vergeblich nach der Stelle, an der das Haupt der Zigeuner, hier aus unerfindlichen Gründen Jarno geheißen, die Vermutung ausspricht, Wilhelm wolle die Mignon wie der Ochs von Lerchenau das Mariandl debauchieren und kaufe sie nur deshalb frei[49]. Hier liegt ein Stilbruch vor, der das Geschehen trivialisiert und die idealisierende Tendenz der Oper unterhöhlt.

In den verbalen Bereich gehören – wenigstens bei der Lektüre eines Operntextbuchs – auch die Regiebemerkungen. Diese werden in den gedruckten Libretti, die man vor der Vorstellung liest oder die den Platten-Einspielungen beiliegen, selten im vollen Wortlaut der authentischen Druckfassung des „Büchleins" dargeboten, sondern sind meistens auf ein Minimum reduziert oder durch nicht autorisierte Zusätze oder Striche entstellt. Zwar handelt es sich hierbei vordringlich um Anweisungen des Verfassers an den Regisseur, doch wendet sich der Autor auch an den Leser und, wenigstens indirekt, an den Zuschauer. Daß es bei mangelnder Akribie in der Wiedergabe szenischer Fingerzeige zu folgenreichen Mißverständnissen kommen kann, soll anhand von zwei Beispielen aus dem *Mignon*-Libretto deutlich gemacht werden.

Auf S. 3 der Druckfassung ihres Textes beschreiben Carré und Barbier den auf die entsprechende Szene in Leoncavallos *I Pagliacci* vorausweisenden Auftritt der Zigeuner wie folgt:

> *Entrée des Bohémiens. La bande défile autour du théâtre. Un chariot couvert d'une toile grossière et chargé d'oripeaux de toutes sortes est traîné sur le devant de la scène par deux ou trois zingari en haillons. Jarno est debout sur le chariot.*

---

49 Jarno: Ah! Ah! Il paraît que l'enfant vous plaît ... mon prince, vous voulez me la débaucher.
Wilhelm *avec colère, en saisissant Jarno au collet*: Misérable! Ne souille pas les oreilles de cette enfant par les infames soupçons! (*Mignon* [Textbuch] I 7 [23]).

Mignon, enveloppé d'un vieux manteau rayé, dort sur une botte de paille au fond du chariot. Un groupe de danseurs, le tambour de basque en main, s'élance en scène. Zafari saisit son violon et donne le signal de la danse. Un tambourin et un hautbois l'accompagnent.

Und kurz danach heißt es:

Zafari prélude sur son violon. Une vieille zingara couvre la sol d'un lambeau de tapis. Les œufs y sont déposés par un enfant. Mignon s'éveille à la voix de Jarno et s'avance au milieu du cercle des curieux. Elle tient un bouquet de fleurs sauvages à la main et semble sortir d'un rêve[50].

In dem Text, der der Aufnahme auf Columbia-Langspielplatten beiliegt, wird im ersten Fall einfach gesagt: „Enter some gypsies and peasants." Der Hörer im stillen Kämmerlein, der den Text verfolgt, wird sich also wundern, warum Jarno „approaches the cart and wakes up Mignon".

Viel schwerwiegender, weil auf eine symbolisch verwendete visuelle Motivkette bezüglich und das erste Glied derselben unterschlagend, ist im Textbuch der Einspielung das Fehlen des Hinweises auf das *bouquet de fleurs sauvages* im ersten Zitat. Carré und Barbier borgten diesen Leitgegenstand aus den *Lehrjahren*, wo in II 4 Wilhelm das Bukett (als vorausgenommenes Liebespfand) der Philine auf ihre Bitten hin überläßt, womit es in Goethes Roman sein Bewenden hat. In Thomas' Oper ist das Bouquet zunächst in Mignons Besitz, geht dann an Wilhelm über und gerät vorübergehend an die falsche – nämlich Philines – Adresse. Seine facettenreiche Symbolkraft in bezug auf das Verhältnis Wilhelms zu den beiden Frauen verdichtet sich in der letzten Szene des zweiten Aktes, als Philine, Kunigunde von Turneck *rediviva*, Mignon ersucht, das blumige Andenken aus dem brennenden Schloß zu holen, und diese, die *fleurs flétries et à demi consumées* in der Hand tragend, von Wilhelm gerettet wird.

Wie wir sahen, sind Operntexte, über die deren Urheber im Zuge des Geschehens die ausschließliche Kontrolle verlieren, geschichtlich gesehen fragile Gebilde, deren jeweiliger Status fragwürdig ist und von der Forschung in Relation zu den vorhergehenden und folgenden

---

50 *Mignon* (Textbuch) I 1 (3 und 4).

Stadien der Entwicklung gebracht werden muß. So sind bei der historisch-kritischen Analyse von Libretti zu musiktheatralischen Werken des Typs *opéra comique* die zum Teil gewichtigen Unterschiede zwischen der Dialog- und der Rezitativ-Fassung zu berücksichtigen und aus der Perspektive der vom Komponisten geltend gemachten musikalischen Erfordernisse zu erklären. Aber selbst wenn man sich, wie bei *Mignon*, auf eine rezitativische Fassung einigt und diese aufgrund eines stillschweigenden Konsensus allen Partituren und Klavierauszügen zugrunde legt, bleibt oft ein unauflöslicher Rest oder es kommt zu Diskrepanzen.

Halten wir uns, um diesen Unsicherheitsfaktor augenfällig zu machen, an das zuhandene Beispiel der vorliegenden Einspielung der Oper auf Langspielplatten. Dem Käufer des Albums wird nämlich bei der Inspektion seiner Neuerwerbung auffallen, daß die achte Plattenseite zwei Zusätze enthält: die sogenannte *alerte* – „a new air of Filina (ad lib.) sung by Mme. Volpini in London", wie es in dem von Schirmer verlegten Klavierauszug heißt – und der als „alternative finale to Act III" bezeichnete ursprüngliche Schluß der Oper. Verantwortlich für derartige Abweichungen von der Norm und bei deren Bewertung zu berücksichtigen ist die Tatsache, daß es sich bei solchen Varianten gewöhnlich um Konzessionen handelt, welche die Bühnenpraxis erfordert. Thomas war ein gewiegter Routinier und wußte sich den jeweiligen Umständen geschickt anzupassen.

Selbst bei anerkannten Meisterwerken der Opernliteratur, die seit Jahrzehnten oder gar Jahrhunderten im Repertoire stehen, sind Alternativlösungen im Früh- oder sogar im Spätstadium ihrer Bühnengeschichte keine Seltenheit. So gibt es von *Don Giovanni* eine sowohl an das Publikum als an das Opernpersonal Konzessionen machende Wiener Fassung, in der die komische Nebenhandlung erweitert wird[51]. (Sie konnte sich allerdings nicht durchsetzen.) Und Streichungen sind

---

51 Mozart komponierte außerdem nachträglich je eine Arie für Donna Anna und (im Austausch gegen ein für den Wiener Tenor zu schweres Stück) eine Arie für Don Ottavio.

bei der Aufführung bzw. Einspielung von umfangreichen Opern wie *Tristan und Isolde* oder den *Meistersingern* gang und gäbe. Doch würde es ein Opern-Intendant kaum dulden, daß sein Chef-Regisseur das Steuermannslied im *Fliegenden Holländer* oder die Arie des Sängers im *Rosenkavalier* ausmerzt, weil die Partie zufällig nicht besetzt werden kann. In *Mignon* hingegen kann, so will es die Partitur, die Bravour-Arie der Filina gestrichen werden „if the singer is unable to execute the Polonaise"[52].

Die musiktheatralische Laufbahn der Thomas'schen *Mignon* zeigt in ihrer ersten, entscheidenden Phase eine auffallend starke Tendenz zur Verkürzung der Handlung durch Eliminierung bzw. Substituierung einzelner Szenen, Nummern oder Nummernteile. Dabei blieb allerdings der Kern erhalten, wie dies vierzig Jahre zuvor bei Rossinis *Guillaume Tell*, der schließlich nur noch eine Rumpf-Existenz führte, der Fall war[53]. Diesen zum Teil durch die Einsprüche der Kritik beschleunigten Raffungsprozeß charakterisieren Soubies und Malherbe wie folgt[54]:

> Pour la partie musicale, la critique aperçut d'abord des points d'ombre et les signala; ils disparurent peu à peu. De la deuxième représentation on pratiqua des coupures dans le second acte; d'autres venaient par la suite, comme au premier acte le rondo que chantait Wilhelm à son entrée, et le ballet qui précédait la danse de Mignon [sic]. Le second tableau du troisième acte avec sa forlane chantée et dansée, avec sa scène cruelle de la rencontre de Philine avec Mignon, avait déplu à quelques-uns. Le rédacteur de la „Revue et Gazette musicale" notamment, plein d'admiration pour le grand trio du précédent tableau, écrivait: „Combien j'eusse préféré rester sous l'impression de mon cher trio et de sa simple prière!" Ce vœu musical devait être exaucé. Le dernier tableau, d'abord raccourci, a fini par être complètement supprimé.

Die Kürzungen, die Thomas an der Partitur seiner Oper vornahm oder ins Auge faßte, erstrecken sich teils auf rein instrumentale Partien – ca. 150 Takte werden in der Partitur als entbehrlich bezeichnet –, teils

---

52 So heißt es auf S. 242 des bei Schirmer erschienenen Klavierauszugs.
53 Es wurde vielfach nur der zweite Akt – als Vorspann zu einem Ballett – gegeben. Siehe hierzu meinen Aufsatz „Der Apfel fiel nicht weit vom Stamme: Rossinis *Guillaume Tell*, eine musikalische Schweizerreise?"
54 *Histoire de l'Opéra-Comique* (Anm. 7), II 88f.

auf Chorstellen und teils auf Tanznummern, wahrscheinlich aufgrund des begrenzten vokalen und instrumentalen Fundus kleinerer Bühnen. Unter den *dramatis personae* war es besonders Philine, deren Rolle anscheinend fast nach Belieben gestutzt werden konnte, womit der poetischen Gerechtigkeit ungewollt Genüge getan wird[55]. Weitere Rollen, die mit Duldung des Komponisten in die Lage kommen konnten, eine beträchtliche Einbuße an musikalischer Substanz zu erleiden, waren die des Frederick, der ohnehin nur eine einzige Chance hat, solistisch zu glänzen[56], und die Wilhelms, dessen einzige Arie bei der Pariser Uraufführung wegfiel, wohl weil Léon Achard, der mit dieser Rolle betraute Interpret, ihr stimmlich nicht gewachsen war. Ihren Verlust kann der literarisch versierte Zuhörer leicht verschmerzen, weil hier, den Intentionen des Verfassers der *Lehrjahre* entgegen, der Held, statt geschoben zu werden, selber schiebt und als Brausekopf erscheint, der in die Welt zieht, um sich die Hörner abzulaufen[57]:

> Oui, je veux par le monde
> Promener librement
> Mon humeur vagabonde.
> Au gré de mes désirs
> Je veux courir gaiement.
> Tout m'attire et m'enchante,
> Tout est nouveau pour moi,
> Et je ris et je chante
> Et ne suis que ma loi.

Dies gesungen nicht von einem *rake*, dessen *progress* geschildert werden soll, sondern vom „fils d'un bourgeois de Vienne", der, wie er seinem Gesprächspartner redselig mitteilt, „depuis un an à peine den bancs de l'université" entlaufen ist und „heureux de [ses] vingt ans, fier de [sa] liberté" die Welt durchstreifen möchte. Aber selbst wenn

---

55 Entfallen konnten unter Umständen nicht nur die Polonaise der Titania, sondern auch die Nummer 7 („Alerte...") und ein Teil der Nummer 3 („En ce pauvre monde...").

56 10 B („C'est moi! J'ai tout brisé").

57 Im Textbuch (11) heißt es einleitend: „Je veux parcourir notre vieille Allemagne. Je veux voir la France et l'Italie et semer mon argent sur le sable de toutes les grandes routes." Hier stempelt sich Wilhelm also selbst zum Weltenbummler.

er dieser Arie nicht verlustig geht, ist der Wilhelm, den uns Carré und Barbier bescheren, nur ein schwacher Abklatsch seines Vorbilds im Roman und muß sich mit der eher beiläufigen Rolle eines Hahns im Korbe zufriedengeben. In den *Lehrjahren* ist der junge Meister, bildlich gesprochen, der rote Faden, der, indem er die theatralischen Bildungsstufen durchläuft, diese miteinander verknüpft und sie als Teile eines umfassenden gesellschaftlichen und kulturellen Panoramas erkennen läßt. Bei Thomas und seinen Textdichtern mußte nolens volens die nach dem Prinzip der Steigerung angeordnete Reihe theatralischer Organisationsformen vom Puppenspiel, an dem sich das Kaufmannssöhnchen ergötzt, über die Provinzbühne, an der Mariane auftritt, und die Laienspielgruppe der Bergarbeiter bis hin zu Serlos und Aureliens ambitionierter und künstlerisch disziplinierter Gesellschaft wegfallen. Übrig blieb – freilich ohne den Prinzipal, seine Frau, den Pedanten und das restliche Personal – die Truppe Melinas. Verlustig ging im Zuge der Kürzungen schließlich auch das gesamte adlige Personal (einschließlich des Geistlichen) und mit ihm das Umfeld, innerhalb dessen die ersten Hinweise auf die Turmgesellschaft der *Wanderjahre* und auf die Pädagogische Provinz erfolgen.

Wie der Titel der Oper von Ambroise Thomas vermuten läßt und die anfangs kurz umrissene Rezeptionsgeschichte der *Lehrjahre* jenseits des Rheins verständlich macht, sollte in ihrem Mittelpunkt die geheimnisvolle, zwitterhaft anmutende Gestalt stehen, die schon die deutschen Romantiker zutiefst beeindruckt hatte. Da Mignon, die im Roman ihr Möglichstes tut, dem Theater fernzubleiben, und sich wiederholt weigert, auf der Bühne aufzutreten[58], hier im Kontext einer dramatischen Handlung erscheinen sollte, mußte ihre Rolle umfunktioniert, d. h. vor allem psychologisch glaubhaft gestaltet werden. Alles, was sie tat, mußte nun ausreichend motiviert werden; nichts durfte unentschieden oder unerklärlich bleiben. Der damit verbundene Hang

---

58 In V 1 der *Lehrjahre* wird berichtet, man hätte sie nicht dazu bereden können, eine Rolle zu übernehmen, oder auch nur, wenn gespielt wurde, auf das Theater zu gehen.

zur Veräußerlichung und Vergröberung war so folgenreich, daß die Figur fast in ihr Gegenteil verkehrt und letztlich zur Karikatur ihrer selbst gestempelt wurde. Diese Behauptung soll anhand einiger besonders markanter Veränderungen erhärtet werden.

Man beachte zunächst, daß das bei Goethe zwölf- bis dreizehnjährige, in seiner körperlichen Entwicklung weit zurückgebliebene Mädchen bei Thomas postpubertär ist, ja als Carmen in Kleinformat in Eifersucht gerät und in einem Wutanfall die Brüsseler Spitzen an einem Kleide, das sie von Philine ohne deren Wissen geborgt hat, zerreißt[59]. (Die Mignon der *Lehrjahre* durchläuft die Stufe der Weiblichkeit, die mit ihrem wohlweislich von Carré und Barbier übergangenen Besuch in Wilhelms Schlafzimmer erreicht wird, sehr schnell in Richtung auf eine angelische Transzendenz[60].) Innerlichkeit und Weltentrückung gibt es in der Oper bei ihr nur noch im Traum- oder Ohnmachtszustand, wo sie ihrem Vorbild bei Goethe am nächsten kommt.

Während die Mignon der *Lehrjahre* sich gerade dadurch auszeichnet und rätselhaft wirkt, daß sie spontan und scheinbar ohne zureichenden Grund handelt, so daß ihr weder psychologisch noch tiefenpsychologisch beizukommen ist, stellen uns Carré und Barbier eine Figur vor Augen, deren Bewußtsein ihr Unterbewußtsein überspielt, die reflektiert – Goethe stellt sie wohlweislich nie vor Spiegel![61] – und die sich mitunter sogar dazu versteigt, wie die Marschallin im *Rosenkavalier* zu philosophieren („Demain, dis-tu? Qui sait où nous serons

---

59 Mignon ist übrigens eine Mezzo-Partie, was musikalisch gesehen darauf hindeutet, daß sie kein weiblicher Cherubino ist.

60 Siehe hierzu V 12 und 13 des Romans und die vom Arzt in VIII 3 versuchte Erklärung.

61 Eine Monologstelle wie „C'est là que tout à l'heure, en souriant à son miroir/ elle écoutait Meister! Je ne voulais rien voir! Je ne voulais rien entendre! Hélas et cependant je n'ai pu m'en défendre .../ Pardonne, cher maître!/ Voici le fard qui la rend belle .../ Eh bien! Si j'essayais de me farder aussi?/ Ma pâleur disparait déjà!/ Mon teint s'anime" wäre bei Goethe undenkbar. In den *Lehrjahren* (II 5) bemüht sich Mignon ganz im Gegenteil, die Röte, die sie für Schminke hält, von ihren Wangen abzureiben.

demain?/ L'avenir est à Dieu, le temps est dans sa main"[62]). Statt der Mignon, deren Naivität, erst im Jenseits aufgehoben, sich dem *homme moyen sensuel* als Weltfremdheit manifestiert, agiert bei Thomas eine Sentimentale, deren pseudochristliches Mitleidsbedürfnis gegenüber den Zigeunern, denen sie glücklich entronnen ist, aus der Sicht des Verfassers der *Lehrjahre* völlig *out of character* ist:

Mignon [zu den Zigeunern]:	Vous dont j'ai partagé
	la honte et la misère, adieu!
[zu einem Kind]:	Toi, pauvre enfant, sois un jour
	protégé par cette médaille!
[zu Jarno]:	Et toi dont la colère
	m'a si souvent fait peur, hélas!
	Adieu! Mignon ne t'en veut
	pas![63]

Auch auf der sprachlichen Ebene haben die Textdichter der *Mignon* in bezug auf die ‚Heldin' der Oper Unheil angerichtet und das von Goethe in den *Lehrjahren* gezeichnete Profil entstellt. Heißt es bei Goethe ausdrücklich, es falle ihr schwer, sich auszudrücken, sie spreche „sehr gebrochen deutsch" und „nur wenn sie den Mund zum Singen auftat, wenn sie die Zither rührte, schien sie sich des einzigen Organs zu bedienen, wodurch sie ihr Innerstes aufschließen und mitteilen konnte"[64], so hat die Carré/Barbiersche Mignon keinerlei sprachliche Hemmungen, spricht Französisch wie geschmiert und bedarf eigentlich gar nicht mehr der Musik, um sich verständlich zu machen. Schon dadurch, daß sie in einer Oper auftritt, wird die Sonderstellung, die sie und der Harfner (der bei Thomas ausgerechnet Lothario heißt!) in den *Lehrjahren* innehaben, aufgehoben und der qualitative Unterschied nivelliert.

---

[62] Die Stelle erinnert von fern an die philosophische Betrachtung der alternden Geliebten Quinquins am Ende des ersten Aktes der Strauss'schen Oper: „Die Zeit, die ändert doch nichts an den Sachen. Die Zeit, die ist ein sonderbar Ding."

[63] Die Mignon der *Lehrjahre* kann im Gegensatz hierzu ihr ‚Zigeuner'-Leben gar nicht schnell genug vergessen.

[64] So in II 16. Schon in II 4 ist von ihrem „gebrochenen Deutsch" die Rede.

Nun abschließend zur Struktur der Oper und zu dem, was Aristoteles in seiner Poetik *mythos*, d. h. die Verarbeitung der stofflichen Vorlage und die Verknüpfung der Handlungsmomente, nennt. In der heute verbindlichen Standardfassung besteht *Mignon* aus drei Akten, von denen jeder seinen fest umrissenen Schauplatz hat. Der erste Akt spielt in einer deutschen Kleinstadt im Schwarzwald[65], die dem „heiteren Landstädtchen" der *Lehrjahre* entspricht, während die spärliche Handlung des zweiten im Schloß (erste Szene: Boudoir) bzw. Park (zweite Szene: am See) des Baron de Rosemberg, den Pendants zu Goethes gräflichem Schloß, vonstatten geht. Der dritte Akt, zu dem es keine direkte Entsprechung in den *Lehrjahren* gibt, führt uns in eine „*galérie italienne ornée de statues*", in der man unschwer die in der zweiten Strophe von Mignons Lied heraufbeschworene Szenerie erkennt:

> Kennst du das Haus, auf Säulen ruht sein Dach,
> Es glänzt der Saal, es schimmert das Gemach,
> und Marmorbilder stehn und sehn mich an:
> Was hat man dir, du armes Kind, getan?

In etwa bezieht sich die Handlung des ersten Aktes auf das zweite Buch (vor allem auf dessen viertes Kapitel), die des zweiten auf das dritte Buch und die des dritten auf das achte Buch (vor allem auf dessen zweites und neuntes Kapitel) der *Lehrjahre*. Im einzelnen wäre hierzu zu bemerken: Aus ihrer melo-dramaturgischen Sicht konsequent lassen Carré und Barbier die Oper in medias res beginnen, ohne auf die im ersten Buch der *Lehrjahre* ausführlich behandelte Vorgeschichte einzugehen. Braucht es weiterer Beweise, um zu zeigen, wie stiefmütterlich Goethes Held von ihnen behandelt wird? Diese krasse Akzentverschiebung geht so weit, daß bei ihnen Wilhelm nach Mignon auftritt – eine Verschiebung, die Goethe sicher nicht geduldet hätte. Das erregende Moment (nach Gustav Freytags berühmt-berüchtigtem Schema) ist die Weigerung Mignons, sich im Eiertanz, der in den

---

65 Im Textbuch heißt es in den Regiebemerkungen zu I 2 (30): „*Les mêmes, Jarno, zingari, paysans de la Forêt-Noire*".

Lehrjahren später nachgeholt wird[66], zu produzieren, und ihr Loskauf durch den hier pistolenschwingenden Helden[67]. Um der Ökonomie des Ganzen willen, gewiß aber auch, um die Rivalität zwischen Mignon und Philine sogleich ins rechte Licht zu rücken, werden die im Roman parallel geführten Handlungsstränge Mignon/Wilhelm und Wilhelm/Laertes/Philine in der Oper miteinander verquickt.

Aus der Sicht des Lesers der *Lehrjahre* störend und Goethes Absichten durchaus widersprechend, für die melo-dramatische Architektonik jedoch bedeutsam ist das frühe Auftreten des Harfners. Dieser erscheint in der Introduktion, wo sein „*chanson fugitif et tremblant*", auf das er am Ende des zweiten Aktes zurückkommt, in den Kneipchor „Bons bourgeois et notables", der aus Offenbachs *Contes d'Hoffmann* stammen könnte, eingebettet ist. Er geht also Mignons Auftritt voraus, während bei Goethe ein gehöriger Abstand (von II 4 bis zu 11) die beiden in umgekehrter Reihenfolge stattfindenden Auftritte trennt. In Thomas' Oper, wo der Alte, der nicht so offensichtlich geistesgestört ist wie in den *Lehrjahren*[68], bewußt auf der Suche nach seiner angebeteten Sperata (Mignons Mutter) ist, wird also die enge Zusammengehörigkeit der beiden ‚romantischen' Figuren noch stärker betont. Diese werden fast konspirativ zu Partnern und dürfen, nachdem sie schon im ersten Akt gemeinsam ‚geschwälbelt' haben, im zweiten ihren Bund durch ein weiteres Duett („As-tu souffert, as-tu pleuré?", #12b) besiegeln. Ihre bei Goethe in der Schwebe gehaltene Relation wird hier also dingfest gemacht. Dramaturgisch gesehen hat die neue Konstellation zur Folge, daß, während bei Goethe Wilhelm zum *pater familias* wird, der Mignon, den Harfner und schließlich auch Felix wie

---

66 In II 8, wo der Tanz als ein Fandango charakterisiert wird. In der Oper sucht Philine Wilhelms Schützling dadurch zu demütigen, daß sie Mignon dazu auffordert, ihr zuliebe eine Privatvorstellung zu geben.

67 Er tut dies unmittelbar nach seinem Auftritt „*en habit de voyage*" und „*suivi d'un valet qui porte sa valise et son manteau*".

68 Einige diesbezüglichen Stellen der *opéra comique*-Fassung des Textes wurden in der Rezitativ-Fassung ausgemerzt, so daß nicht klar ersichtlich wird, wes Geistes Kind der Harfner ist.

Kinder um sich versammelt, er in der Oper dieser Rolle verlustig geht[69].

Der zweite Akt von Thomas' *Mignon* entfernt sich, von einigen rein äußerlichen Zügen abgesehen, inhaltlich so weit von seinem Modell, dem dritten Buch der *Lehrjahre*, und enthält, musikalisch gesehen, so viele Nummern, die keinerlei Bezug zur Vorlage haben, daß der literarisch engagierte Librettologe ihm kopfschüttelnd begegnen wird. Vor allem das erste Bild, in dem Philine ihre Verführungskünste spielen läßt und Mignon es ihr vergeblich gleichzutun sucht, ist ausgesprochen handlungsarm. Leidet diese Szene unter ihrer Statik, so entfaltet sich in der folgenden eine geradezu hektische Dynamik, ‚angeheizt' durch ein sensationelles Ereignis im Sinne Pixerécourts. Schon der gleich anfangs von Mignon in Betracht gezogene Selbstmord à la Ophelia („Ce flot clair et tranquille/ m'attire à lui./ J'entends parmi les verts roseaux/ votre voix, o filles des eaux") gibt einen Vorgeschmack von dem, was uns späterhin, d. h. nach den Shakespeareschen ‚Roulanden' der Titania/Philine, erwartet. Den Höhe-, geschmacklich gesehen aber den Tiefpunkt, des Aktes bildet der Brand des Schlosses, der dem Stadtbrand der *Lehrjahre*, wie er in V 13 geschildert wird, entspricht. Bei Goethe ist bekanntlich der Harfner, der sich selbst als Pyromane sieht[70], ganz allein für das Unheil verantwortlich, das er, ohne es zu wollen, anrichtet. Geht es ihm doch vor allem darum, den Knaben Felix, vor dem ihn böse Träume gewarnt haben, aus dem Wege zu

---

69 Ehe Felix auf den Plan tritt, fungiert Friedrich „als dritte Person der Familie", welche „Vater" Wilhelm als seine eigene ansieht (III 9). Und in der *opéra-comique*-Fassung des Textes sagt Mignon am Ende zu Lothario: „Pardon! je lui [Wilhelm] devais sa part de mon bonheur!/ vous m'aimez tous les deux, partagez-vous mon cœur".

70 Er singt in IV 1, von Wilhelm belauscht, folgende Zeilen:
Ihm färbt der Morgensonne Licht
Den reinen Horizont mit Flammen
Und über seinem schuld'gen Haupte bricht
Das schöne Bild der ganzen Welt zusammen.

räumen[71]. (Daß das von ihm unabsichtlich gelegte Feuer auch das Gebäude, in dem Serlos Truppe spielt, ergreift, hat im Roman symbolische Bedeutung und ist ein weiteres Signal dafür, daß Wilhelm dem Theater entsagen soll.)

In der Oper ist es die auf Philine eifersüchtige Mignon, die den Brand herbeiwünscht („Ah! que la main de Dieu ne peut-elle sur eux faire éclater la foudre,/ et frapper ce palais et le réduire en poudre,/ et l'engloutir sous des torrents de feu") und den Harfner ungewollt dazu veranlaßt, die Katastrophe herbeizuführen. In der nun folgenden Szene, in der, wie schon berichtet, Wilhelm Mignon unter Einsatz seines Lebens rettet und die einem Reißer entnommen zu sein scheint, erreicht die vergröbernde Tendenz ihren Zenit. Nach solchen theatralischen Gewaltmaßnahmen kann das Ende des Werks nur antiklimaktisch sein.

Der durch Streichung des ursprünglich vorgesehenen fünften Bildes erheblich koupierte dritte Akt, der im Klavierauszug nurmehr sechzig Seiten Partitur umfaßt (statt der 150 Seiten des ersten und der 120 Seiten des zweiten Aktes), ist sowohl dramatisch als musikalisch schwach – ein Zeichen dafür, daß den Librettisten und wohl auch dem Komponisten die Puste ausging. Die im achten Buch der *Lehrjahre* nach dem Tode Mignons enthüllte Vorgeschichte wird hier in Handlung umgesetzt und als gegenwärtiges Geschehen zuende, hier zum Happy End, geführt. Die Szene ist, wie gesagt, Italien. Wobei offen bleibt, wie die *dramatis personae* dorthin gelangt sind. Der Harfner erkennt seinen alten Stammsitz, der seit fünfzehn Jahren verlassen dasteht und ausgerechnet jetzt Wilhelm zum Kauf angeboten wird, wieder. Er überzeugt Mignon mit Hilfe von drei Erbstücken – einem Kästchen, das den Schal ihrer Mutter enthält, einem Ring, den sie als Kind am Finger trug, und einem Stundenbuch –, daß dies ihr Elternhaus und er ihr Vater ist. Nun kann sie ihre Liebe zu Wilhelm frei be-

---

71 Siehe hierzu Mignons Schilderung der Ereignisse in V 13, wo der versuchte Mord an Felix so dargestellt wird, als handle es sich um die Opferung Isaaks durch Abraham.

kennen. Die beiden können getrost heiraten, und wenn sie nicht gestorben sind, so leben sie sicher heute noch.

Im dritten Akt überschlägt sich die unwillkürliche Parodie, die zwar von Anfang an spürbar war, aber von der Musik verdeckt wurde, solange sich die Handlung einigermaßen an das literarische Vorbild hielt. Auch hier erscheint Mignon zum Beispiel im weißen Kleide („Sous ce rayon divin/ et dans ta robe blanche,/ tu m'apparais comme un ange des cieux", sagt Wilhelm), aber nicht um, wie bei Goethe, zu scheinen bis sie werde, sondern eher als noch ahnungsloser Engel, der letztendlich eine gute Partie abzugeben verspricht. Auch bei Thomas stirbt sie, freilich nur metaphorisch gesprochen, um aus dem Scheintod schnell in Wilhelms Armen zu erwachen:

Mignon: Ah!
Wilhelm: Mignon!
Lothario: Ma fille!
Wilhelm: Dieu! Qu'a-t-elle donc?
Mignon: Je meurs!
Lothario: Ah! Sperata!
Wilhelm: Grand Dieu!
Mignon: Je meurs!
Lothario: Non, ne meurs pas, chère enfant!
Wilhelm: Le bonheur est ici maintenant. (Elle revit.)[72]

Was hätte Goethe zu diesem, hier aus der literarischen Perspektive beleuchteten Versuch gesagt, *Wilhelm Meisters Lehrjahre* für das verwöhnte, aber für Geschmacklosigkeit zugängliche Pariser Publikum zu verwursteln? Er, der bei Gounods *Faust* vielleicht ein Auge – oder auch beide Augen – zugedrückt hätte, hätte sich gewiß schon bei der Lektüre des von Carré und Barbier verbrochenen Textes schaudernd abgewandt und das französische Opernwesen verflucht. Wir können ihm dies nachfühlen; und so verwundert es nicht, daß mancher musikalischer Glanzlichter zum Trotz die berühmteste Oper des zu seiner Zeit berühmten französischen Komponisten auf den deutschen Bühnen kein Heimatrecht erworben hat. Diese *Mignon* ist, ähnlich wie

---

72 In der Urgestalt endet die Textfassung der Oper mit Philines großmütigem Verzicht auf Wilhelm.

Thomas Carlyles verballhornte englische Fassung des Romans, ein historisches Kuriosum in der facettenreichen Rezeptionsgeschichte des *Wilhelm Meister*. Zwar war die Oper in Frankreich sehr erfolgreich, doch meldeten sich auch dort schon frühzeitig skeptische Stimmen, die darauf aufmerksam machten, daß das Werk als *opéra lyrique* seinen „goût de terroir" bzw. sein „parfum germanique" verloren habe[73]. Auch hielt es der Referent der *Revue des Deux Mondes*, F. de Lagenevais, für seine Pflicht zu zeigen, „à quel point ce sujet était incompatible avec le théâtre, surtout avec l'*opéra-comique*"[74], und E. Reyer schrieb nach der Uraufführung, das Unternehmen als Donquichotterie anprangernd[75]: „Mignon n'est qu'un souffle, un ombre charmante et poétique dans le roman de Goethe, et il a fallu plus que de l'habileté, presque de l'imagination, pour arrêter ce souffle qui passe, donner un corps à cette ombre qui glisse, et grouper autour de cette fugitive et délicate fiction tous les incidents, tous les personnages d'un drame vivant." Wie hier richtig erkannt wird, besaß Ambroise Thomas offensichtlich keine der beiden geforderten Eigenschaften.

---

73 Ohne Quellenangabe zit. bei Soubies/Malherbe (Anm. 7), 88.
74 Aus dem Feuilleton der *Débats* vom 3. Dezember 1866, zit. bei Baldensperger (Anm. 1), 152.
75 Zit. bei Baldensperger (Anm. 1).

"Die letzte Häutung"[1]
Two German *Künstleropern* of the Twentieth Century: Hans Pfitzner's *Palestrina* and Paul Hindemith's *Mathis der Maler* (1992)

> An ihren Werken sollt ihr sie erkennen[2].
> (Adapted from Matthew 7:16)
>
> Und wenn der Mensch in seiner Qual verstummt,
> Gab mir ein Gott zu sagen [dichten, malen, komponieren], was ich leide[3].
> (Goethe, *Torquato Tasso,* 3432-33, con variazioni)

A "typisch deutscher Gegenstand" (Grimm, 10)[4], the *Künstlerdrama,* or artist-drama, has been the object of many critical reflections by major writers, from Ludwig Tieck ("Correggio") by way of Franz Grillparzer ("Sappho") down to Friedrich Hebbel (345-349)[5], as well as of numerous scholarly surveys and investigations (see Goldschmidt 1-12)[6]; but, strangely enough, its direct offshoot, the *Künstleroper* (artist-opera) has been consistently neglected. In fact, an article by Richard Seebohm (1974), dealing with one of the two works discussed in this essay, may well be the only serious attempt to cope with this neglect, although not systematically[7]. In treating comparatively two

---

1 'The last shedding of the skin', taken from Pfitzner's *Palestrina.*
2 'Ye shall know them by their works.'
3 'And when man falls silent in his torments,
   A God bestowed on me the gift to say [write, paint, compose] what I suffer.'
4 'Typically German subject'. Grimm, in his essay, uses "spezifisch-deutsche [...] Entwicklung" in this sense.
5 Hebbel discusses Carl Gutzkow's play *Der Königslieutenant.*
6 See also the secondary literature to which Goldschmidt refers.
7 I have had no access to Stephan Kohler's essay (1979). John Bokina's essay (1988), which deals with *Palestrina, Mathis der Maler,* and Schoenberg's *Moses und*

twentieth-century exemplars of the genre linked, if subconsciously, by the subtle bond of 'influence', namely, Hans Pfitzner's *Palestrina* (text written between 1910 and 1911; music composed between 1912 and 1915; premiered on 12 June 1917 in Munich) and Paul Hindemith's *Mathis der Maler* (written and composed between 1932 and 1935; premiered on 29 May 1938 in Zurich)[8], I enter virgin territory in a largely unexplored subcontinent: what, in the "Introduction" to my anthology *The Essence of Opera* (Weisstein 1964/1969), I have called the "Poetics of Opera" and what is now generally known as librettology (Weisstein 1982)[9].

Before turning to Pfitzner and Hindemith, however, and to their respective masterpieces – so rarely performed (Pfitzner 1955: 32)[10] but fortunately available in two splendid recordings[11] – I wish first to raise some basic poetological and melo-dramaturgical questions and then, after some rather extensive groundwork, partially to answer them. In addition to *Palestrina* and *Mathis der Maler* I will examine two illustrious models, Goethe's play *Torquato Tasso* and Wagner's opera *Die Meistersinger von Nürnberg*, surely the finest eighteenth- and nineteenth-century specimens, respectively, of the genre[12].

Aron but does not focus on the inspiration-creation scenes, was brought to my attention after I had completed this essay.

8   The librettos of the two operas were published separately by Schott in 1916 and 1935, respectively. In this essay I rely primarily on the bilingual texts included with the recordings listed in note 11.

9   In this essay, I sought to establish the methodological parameters for the study of operatic texts.

10 Regarding the nonreception of *Palestrina* abroad, see Pfitzner's own comments in a lecture (Pfitzner [n. d.]). Few, if any, productions of the two works have been mounted in the United States, which Pfitzner never visited but where Hindemith lived and taught between 1940 and 1953.

11 *Palestrina* was recorded for Deutsche Grammophon by the Symphony Orchestra of the Bavarian Radio under the direction of Rafael Kubelik (with Nicolai Gedda in the title role and Dietrich Fischer-Dieskau as Cardinal Borromeo), and *Mathis der Maler* for Angel Records by the same orchestra and conductor (with James King in the title role and Dietrich Fischer-Dieskau as Albrecht von Brandenburg).

12 As the basis for the English renditions of the German texts in this essay, I have used existing translations of the librettos of three operas. They are, respectively, *Die*

I.

Let us start by inquiring why it is that, especially within the German tradition, the artist-play and, to a lesser degree, the artist-opera occupy such a special niche in the repertory, mostly since the late eighteenth century. Although, historically, the sudden blossoming of such works is undoubtedly connected with the emancipation of the artist, which allowed him to acquire 'heroic' status (Grimm, 10, fn. 1; Borchmeyer, 123), it is hard to fathom the decided preference for dramatic, rather than epic, treatment of the subject; for, as one of the interlocutors in Tieck's lengthy disquisition on Oehlenschläger's *Correggio*[13] puts it with regard to the subspecies *Malerdrama* (painter-play):

> Nun dünkt mir [...] diese Aufgaben, wenn sie gelingen sollen, eignen sich mehr dem Roman, der Erzählung und Novelle, wohl selbst dem Märchen. Denn hier kann der Apparat des Malergewerbes, die Ansicht über die Kunst, die Geräte und Zimmer, Modelle und Studien [Skizzen], sowie alles, was das Talent bedarf und mit ihm zusammenhängt, schicklicher auf interessante Art ausgebreitet und mit der Geschichte selbst lebendig verbunden werden. Das Individuelle, was den Maler zum Maler macht, kann geschildert und alles, was im Schauspiel als überflüssig und störend erscheinen würde, in der erzählenden Darstellung anmutig werden. (Tieck, 276)
>
> (But I think that [...] these tasks, if they are to succeed, are better suited to the novel, the story, and the novella, or even the fairy tale. For there the whole apparatus of the painter's craft, his views on art, the tools and rooms, models and sketches, as well as everything else the talent needs and is linked to, can be more easily and interestingly unfolded and more naturally related to the story itself. The specific traits that make the painter what he is can be delineated, and whatever would seem superfluous and disruptive in a drama would be more graceful in the narrative.)

Once we have acknowledged the fact that such plays exist, we are likely to wonder why this is so; why, when drama is first and foremost a *literary* genre whose means of expression is primarily verbal, did

---

Meistersinger von Nürnberg, translated by Frederick Jameson, revised by Gordon Kember and Norman Feasey, in *English Opera Guide* 19 (London: John Calder, 1983); *Palestrina*, translated by Veronica Slater, libretto included with the Deutsche Grammophon recording (1973); *Mathis der Maler*, translated by Bernard Jacobson, libretto included with the Angel recording.

13 Together with Raphael, Correggio was the pet of late-eighteenth- and early-nineteenth-century German writers and artists.

playwrights choose to focus on artistry in the *visual* medium? That is to say, it is natural for Tasso to exclaim: "Und wenn der Mensch in seiner Qual verstummt,/ Gab mir ein Gott zu sagen, was ich leide"; but for the painter-protagonist of a drama to maintain that a God, or the Muse, has privileged him to *paint* what he suffers lacks conviction. Unless, that is, he can be presented, as it were, in action.

In other words, whereas in the *Dichterdrama* there is a perfect correlation between tenor and vehicle – Tasso actually says what he suffers, while he tells us that his genius permits him to do so – in the *Malerdrama* we are faced with an unholy alliance of the two sister arts that complicates the playwright's task: for like engravers, sculptors, and architects, painters are primarily makers, whose function it is to shape rather than to talk ("Bilde, Künstler, rede nicht!" ["Fashion, artist, do not talk!"]). The dramatist who selects a painter as his hero, however, must engage him in some sort of verbal action by combining the *Schauspiel* with the *Sprechspiel*. What he can do, for example, is to use as his setting the artist's studio complete with easel, canvases, and the tools of his trade; or he can make use of the backdrop to project onto the screen a single masterpiece such as Seurat's "Grande Jatte", which figures so prominently in Stephen Sondheim's musical *Sunday in the Park with George*, or a selection of works epitomizing the oeuvre of an individual or school. If he is very conventional, he may also call for the presentation of living pictures in which works of art are reenacted tableau fashion (see Goldschmidt, 5)[14] – an excellent subject for both pantomime and ballet.

More frequently, the *Malerdrama* shows the protagonist at a crucial or climactic moment of his career, engaged in painting, chiseling, etc. a magnum opus while describing it (*in statu nascendi*), either in a monologue or in conversation with a colleague, friend, connoisseur, patron, or collector. At his own risk, the playwright may alternatively 'by indirection seek direction out', offering, through third parties,

---

14 For a sampling of such auxiliary devices, see Goldschmidt, 5, fn. 3.

assurances of the artist's genius, skill, and reputation. Analogously but, because of the closer ties that link the two temporal arts of literature and music, less tortuously so, a *Musikerschauspiel*, whether devoted to Palestrina[15], Stradella, or Mozart, is bound to intermesh verbal and musical elements by 'quoting' from the composer's works. With this type of *Künstlerdrama*, in fact, we begin to approach opera, or operetta, in its triple capacity as *Sprech-*, *Schau-* and *Hörspiel*.

In contrast to the *Künstlerdrama*, the *Künstleroper* is likely to be most persuasive and aesthetically pleasing if it deals with composers in the throes of inspiration or creation. But even if one accepts this frame of reference, so perfectly suited to opera, whether *seria* or *buffa*, one might object to the lack of verisimilitude that practice dictates and convention justifies. For we either must tolerate, no matter how grudgingly, that people sing while eating (*Falstaff, Macbeth*), loving (*Tristan und Isolde*), fighting a duel (*Eugene Onegin*), or dying (*Aida*) (Auden 1952)[16], or we must honor this behavior in the breach.

Given these qualifications, it is easy to see why history has witnessed the rise of so few *Dichteropern* (who has ever heard of musical dramas featuring Homer, Dante, Shakespeare, Milton, or Goethe, much less Thomas Mann or T. S. Eliot?) and even fewer *Maleropern*. In this respect, *Mathis der Maler* is quite exceptional and seemingly at odds with *Palestrina*: for while Pfitzner's hero generates music like his creator, Hindemith's protagonist works in a medium alien to the composer. What is so striking and so original about Hindemith's handling of this crux is the metamorphic (more accurately, synesthetic) quality inherent in the hero's description of a key panel (the so-called "Engelskonzert" or 'Angelic Concert') at the moment of its inception.

---

15 Pfitzner's 'musical legend' was preceded by at least two other German Palestrina dramas: a play by Samuel Schier (1825) and an opera by Melchior Ernst Sachs (1883). Stradella is the protagonist of an opera by Friedrich von Flotow.

16 The troublesome nature of such conventions has often been noted, most poignantly, perhaps, by Auden.

On the whole, the history of both *Künstlerdrama* and *Künstleroper* (see Goldschmidt, 8)[17] seems to prefer historical personages, most cogently so if, as both Tieck and Pfitzner have observed (see Seebohm, 17)[18], they are quasi-legendary and surrounded by an aura. Given the two works that are the subjects of this essay, this aura is probably more important in an opera than it is in a spoken drama. For if relatively little is known about the hard facts of a person's life, the imagination is free to catch hold of a few salient features and embroider them ad lib to furnish those 'intimations of immortality' that endow their object with a kind of secular sainthood. Rather than being cluttered with trivial detail and smothered in Naturalistic documentation, such 'musical legends' can make do with a kernel of truth, in this case the *Künstlerproblematik*, in whose service the few known biographical facts can be rearranged even to the point of defying their actual chronology. In addition, since many *Künstlerdramen* and *-opern* are distinctly, though perhaps discretely, autobiographical, their *Problematik* can be more easily transferred from the creature to its creator. Thus, in a letter to his master and ducal friend Karl August, Goethe calls his *Torquato Tasso* a "gefährliche Unternehmung" ('dangerous enterprise')[19]; Wagner wages war against the critical philistinism of a Beckmesser-Hanslick; Pfitzner embodies the Futurist in Silla (Kunze, 76)[20]; and Hindemith follows his protagonist into a kind of "innere Emigration" (see Paulding 1976)[21].

---

17 In his dissertation, Wilmsmeier calls the Künstlerdrama a "Sonderfall des historischen Dramas" ('specific case of the historical drama'; quoted by Goldschmidt).

18 Pfitzner, as quoted by Seebohm.

19 Letter dated 6 April 1789 (Goethe *Briefe*, 139).

20 Kunze, noting the chronological paradox inherent in Silla's aspirations, remarks on the ambiguity of his song: "Dort, wo sich die Zukunft zum Werk verdichten möchte, erscheint eine Art Karikatur der 'Zukunftsmusik', ein eigentümlich künstlich Gestückeltes, durch und durch Fragmentarisches." ('Where the future would like to condense in a particular work, there surfaces a kind of caricature of the Music of the Future, something strangely artificial and utterly fragmented.')

21 This is hardly the place to point out the parallels that could easily be drawn between Hindemith's predicament in the years immediately following Hitler's rise to

As two prominent German authors have pointed out, the *Künstlerdrama* should have artistry as its central concern – which is to say that it must actually seek to be a *Kunstdrama*. Thus, in the imaginary dialogue that constitutes the bulk of Tieck's trenchant review of Oehlenschläger's *Correggio*, the friend's critical observation,

> Was kann dem Musiker oder Dichter [...] anders begegnen [...] als jedem anderen Menschen, dass er Glück oder Unglück, Leiden und Freuden erlebt, dass er Händel hat, Frieden stiftet, sich verliebt oder stirbt? Soll er Spieler, Zanker, Verschwender, Geiziger oder Verliebter sein, oder schickt ihm der Dichter seltsame Begebenheiten, Familienverhältnisse, Erkennungen und dergl. zu, so begreife ich immer nicht, warum der Dramatiker alles dergleichen einem Maler aufladet. (Tieck, 273-274)
>
> (What can happen to a composer or poet other than what happens to everybody, namely, that he is happy or unhappy, engages in quarrels, makes peace, falls in love, or dies? Let him be a gambler, trouble maker, spendthrift or miser, or somebody in love, or let the poet get embroiled in strange events, family affairs, recognitions, and the like – I, for one, cannot see why the playwright must burden a painter with this sort of thing.)

elicits the answer: "Das Schicksal des Künstlers [...] soll aus seiner Kunst hervorgehen und mit seinem Talente ein- und dasselbe werden ('the artist's fate [...] should grow out of his art and be one with his talent'). And Hebbel's review of Gutzkow's Goethe play *Der Königslieutenant* specifies:

> Wenn Goethe [in seinem *Tasso*] einen sich unter allen Umständen ergebenden inneren Konflikt zum Gegenstand seiner Darstellung erhob, so kamen seine Nachfolger selten über den zufälligen äußeren hinaus; wenn jener veranschaulicht, wie der Künstler vermöge derselben Eigenschaften, die die Welt an ihm schätzt und die ihn zu dem machen, was er ist, mit der Welt in Widerspruch gerät (und geraten muss), so zeigen diese gern, dass es dem Künstler öfterer, wie dem Gevatter Schneider und Handschuhmacher, an Geld gebricht, dass er sich leicht aus dem Stegreif verliebt und bei solchen Gelegenheiten noch leichter auf solide Väter stößt, die ihn als Schwiegersohn verschmähen [...]. (Hebbel, 345)
>
> (Whereas [in his *Tasso*] Goethe made a deeply ingrained inner conflict the object of his presentation, his successors rarely went beyond the accidental and external one. While Goethe demonstrates how the artist, because of the very qualities that

---

power and the problems facing the opera's protagonist. For Hindemith's ambiguous attitude toward the Third Reich, at least in the early years of the regime, see Paulding. The catalogue of the recent exhibition "Entartete Musik", organized by Albrecht Dömling, illustrates that phase with documents from the Hindemith file of the Berlin Musikhochschule.

the world admires in him and that make him what he is, gets (and is bound to get) into conflict with the world, his imitators show that, like the tinker or tailor, the artist is frequently short of money, easily falls in love and, on such occasions, even more easily encounters stodgy fathers who reject him as a son-in-law.)

Still, even though the major conflict may be internal, some sort of externalization is needed to compensate for the lyrical *Innerlichkeit*, since drama, being a mode of action, requires a plot that hinges on a conflict. The agon most suitable for a *Künstlerdrama* or *-oper*, however, is that between the artist and society. Thus, in a moment of crisis, Tasso finds himself pitted against Antonio, a *zoon politicon* without peer and a liberal dispenser of moral precepts, as well as against the Princess, whose quiet but firm insistence on courtly behavior, on *Sitte*, provides the ethical counterpoint to Tasso's aesthetic hedonism. At the end, he has no choice but to throw himself at the mercy of the Duke's trusted adviser who, though inferior to him as a poet –

> Er, der mit steifem Sinn
> die Gunst der Musen zu ertrotzen glaubt,
> der, wenn er die Gedanken mancher
> Dichter zusammenreiht,
> sich selbst ein Dichter scheint (Goethe *Tasso*, ll. 2129-2132)
>
> (He who stubbornly thinks
> he can force the muses to grant him their favors
> and who, in stringing together
> the thoughts of other poets,
> thinks that he himself is one)

– by far outstrips him as a diplomat: "So klammert sich der Schiffer endlich noch/ Am Felsen fest, an dem er scheitern sollte" (Goethe *Tasso*, ll. 3451-3452; 'Thus, at long last, the sailor clings to the rock on which he was to have foundered').

Accommodation, but at what a price! For it is hard to imagine that a man like Tasso, so eccentric in his behavior as to seem downright pathological, would thrive in any social setting. The opposite is true of Wagner's Walther, an *ingenu* and *Simplicissimus in estheticis* who, tutored by both *Vogel* and Vogelweide[22], now wishes to become a solid *Bürger*. Ignorant of the strict but cumbersome rules that the "hochbedürft'gen Meister" have invented "in ihrer Noten Wildnis"[23] – to compensate for their lost virility ("Sie schufen sich ein Bildnis,/ dass ihnen bliebe der Jugendliebe/ ein Angedenken klar und fest,/ dran sich der Lenz erkennen läßt" [Wagner, III ii; '[They] created an image to recapture their youthful days and freshly preserve the image of past springs']) – Walther is groomed (or shall we say: tamed?) by Sachs and Eva; and, though reluctant at first ("Nicht Meister will ich sein, nein,/ will ohne Meister selig sein" [Wagner, III v; 'Not Master, no!/ A better way to heaven I know']), ultimately allows himself – no Futurist he – to be reconciled with an establishment whose artistic code he will rewrite, not because he is a reformer, but simply because he is young.

No such fairy-tale ending is in store for Pfitzner's and Hindemith's protagonists. Both, although only in their fifties, face old age and a dim future in isolation. Having been eulogized as the 'savior of music' (a sort of Counter-Reformation *Held der Arbeit* [hero of labor]), Palestrina, internalizing his *Problematik*, fades from view with an air of resignation, lost "in musikalischen Gedanken" ('in musical thoughts'), while Mathis, having achieved his *Erdenpensum*, follows Ursula's and Albrecht's example by becoming a recluse, that secular version of the hermit:

Nur kurze Zeit
verbleibt mir, dann ergeht der letzte Ruf.
Mein Geist, zu matt der Kunst zu dienen;
Mein Leib, der schweren Mühen satt, sie beide sollen weit

---

22 The names of three of the historical *Meistersingers* (Kunz Vogelgesang, Konrad Nachtigall, and Niklaus Vogel) could be seen as a parodistic echo of this ornithological coupling of nature with art in Walther's musical education. Wagner, however, did not include Vogel as a character in his opera.

23 'Masters, worn out with the pain of living', 'by heavy cares o'er weighed'.

> von allen Stätten früheren Strebens geduldig
> das Ende erharren[24].
>
> (A short time only
> remains before I receive the last summons.
> My spirit, too faint to serve art,
> and my body, exhausted by hard labor, patiently,
> and far from the scenes of past endeavor,
> wait for the end.) (See Zuelch, 13)

I wish there were space to speculate why it is that all four *Künstlerdramen* and *-opern* in question are set in a century, the sixteenth, that, for social, political, and religious reasons, might well be regarded as one of permanent crisis. Significantly, that crisis is thematized in only two of them (*Palestrina* and *Mathis der Maler*), while in the other pair (*Torquato Tasso* and *Die Meistersinger*) stability reigns, at least so far as the affairs of State and Church are concerned. If we arrange the historical settings provided for the four parts of our tetralogy in chronological order, we arrive at the following sequence:

1. *Mathis der Maler*: "Zur Zeit des Bauernkrieges" (ca. 1525) and "einige Zeit später"[25]. Grünewald lived from ca. 1475 to 1528.
2. *Die Meistersinger von Nürnberg*: "Mitte des sechzehnten Jahrhunderts"[26]. Hans Sachs lived from 1494 to 1576.
3. *Palestrina*: "Die Handlung spielt im November und Dezember 1563, dem Jahre der Beendigung des Tridentiner Konzils"[27]. Palestrina lived from ca. 1515 to 1594.
4. *Torquato Tasso*: Date not specified by Goethe. However, since the action occurs at the point when the poet completes his masterpiece, the *Gerusalemme liberata*, the year must be 1581. Tasso lived from 1544 to 1595.

---

24 Mathis makes this statement shortly before burying symbolic tokens of his art and life in a chest; its rediscovery in the early 1930s seems to have been a source of inspiration for Hindemith. Zuelch describes the contents of that *Truhe*.
25 'In the age of the Peasant Wars' and 'a little while later'.
26 'Middle of the sixteenth century'.
27 'The action takes place in November and December 1563, the final year of the Council of Trent.'

The fact that *Torquato Tasso* cannot be pinned down chronologically is symptomatic, for the work deals with what is, essentially, a conflict that takes place in what Pfitzner calls 'ideal time'. This applies to *Die Meistersinger* as well, albeit only to a certain extent. For one thing, in Wagner's comic grand opera, local color plays an important role and provides the basic elements of a setting whose period is firmly fixed, even though the action itself cannot be assigned to a specific year; for another, a distinct sense of political crisis pervades the concluding portion of the final scene, although Wagner fails to specify the historical circumstances that justify Sachs's apprehensions. (One strongly suspects that Wagner was less concerned with Germany's international relations in the mid-sixteenth century than with Prussia's emergence as a European power and its conflicts with the Second Empire, which culminated in the Franco-Prussian War of 1870-71.) This is perhaps how we should interpret Sachs's famous lines:

>Habt acht! Uns dräuen üble Streich'!
>Zerfällt erst deutsches Volk und Reich
>in falscher welscher Majestät,
>kein Fürst bald mehr sein Volk versteht,
>und welschen Dunst mit welschem Tand
>sie pflanzen uns in deutsches Land.
>Was deutsch und echt, wüsst' keiner mehr,
>lebt's nicht in deutscher Meister Ehr'.
>>Drum sag ich Euch:
>>ehrt Eure deutschen Meister,
>>dann bannt ihr gute Geister!
>Und gebt Ihr ihrem Wirken Gunst,
>>zerging' in Dunst
>>das Heil'ge Röm'sche Reich,
>>uns bliebe gleich
>>die heil'ge deutsche Kunst. (Wagner *Meistersinger*, III iv)
>
>(Take heed! Ill times now threaten all;
>And if we German folk should fall
>And foreigners should rule our land,
>No king his folk would understand,
>And foreign rule and foreign ways
>Would darken all our German days.
>The good and true were soon forgot
>Did they not live in German Masters' art.
>I therefore tell you:

> Honor your German Masters
> And you will skirt disasters;
> And if you hold them dear in heart,
> Even were to vanish
> The fame of the Holy Roman Empire,
> We still would have
> Our sacred German art.)[28]

As regards *Mathis der Maler* and *Palestrina*, in them the artist-protagonist is caught in a recognizable historical situation and ground between the millstones of opposing forces. Palestrina, whose life is entirely devoted to art, is a plaything of forces that, unleashed in response to the threat posed by the Protestants, are at work during the Council of Trent; Mathis, the only activist among our four heroes, becomes temporarily embroiled in military action. Thus while Walther makes his peace with society and Goethe's Tasso, although seemingly 'socialized', is unlikely ever to turn into a *Salonlöwe*, Pfitzner's and Hindemith's heroes end up by turning their backs on society. At this point it may be worth noting that, contrary to Helene Goldschmidt's view, according to which "ein Vollendeter zum Helden [des Künstlerdramas] nicht geeignet ist" ('one who has reached the peak [of his art] is unsuited to be the hero [of an artist-drama]'), only one of the four works in question, and none of their authors, meets the following criterion:

> Das Künstlerdrama ist Drama des Übergangs [...] verfaßt zu einer Zeit, da sich der Dichter seines Ringens, seiner Richtung bewußt wird. Es ist häufig das Drama der etwa Dreissigjährigen, die in ihrem künstlerischen Werdegang eine Krise überstehen, und der Kunstrichtungen, die Klarheit über ihre Ziele zu erlangen streben [...]. Deshalb wählen Dichter, deren künstlerischer Instinkt sie richtig leitet, selber noch ringende Künstler zu ihrem Helden. (Goldschmidt, 4)
>
> (The artist-drama is a drama of transition [...] written at a time when the poet becomes cognizant of his struggle and his aims. It is often the drama of individuals roughly thirty years of age who are going through a crisis in their artistic evolution, and of movements that seek to define their goals [...]. For that reason,

---

28 At this point Sachs seems to be turning into Wagner, who lashes out against the likes of Giacomo Meyerbeer.

writers who are guided by their intuition choose struggling artists as their protagonists.)[29]

When they began to write the works in question, Goethe was forty, Wagner in his late forties, Pfitzner in his forties, and Hindemith in his late thirties. But *retournons à nos moutons*: Wagner's Walther, the only member of the quartet who fits this age category, is presented as a *junger Ritter* (young knight) who, paradoxically, finds himself and his *Richtung* by turning rather abruptly and prematurely from a *Stürmer und Dränger* into a well-tempered *Meistersinger*, which may well signify that, even to begin with, *es nicht weit her war* (there wasn't much) to his artistry. By contrast, Goethe's Tasso, whose historical model finished the *Gerusalemme liberata* at age thirty-six or thirty-seven, has already reached the pinnacle of his career and has little to look forward to except, perhaps, his coronation as *poeta laureatus*. (In his play, Goethe carefully avoids any reference to the hero's age and presents him on such a level of generality that the middle-aged Gustav Gründgens could portray him convincingly in a memorable production at the Düsseldorf Schauspielhaus.)

Confirming, rather, Goldschmidt's complementary view that the Künstlerdrama "mitunter als Rückblick auf eine Entwicklung in den späteren Jahren eines Menschen wie eines Zeitalters auf[tritt]" (Goldschmidt, 4; 'at times takes the form of a retrospective glance cast in a person's or epoch's waning years'), both Palestrina and Mathis are, arguably, men past their prime whose artistry, defying the historical facts, culminates not at the apex of their careers but at a point of decline, thus precipitating what Gustav Freytag called a *fallende Handlung*, a falling action. And thereby surely hangs a tale.

As for *Die Meistersinger*, it could join its twentieth-century descendants in this respect if we consider Hans Sachs, rather than his protégé Walther, the true protagonist, a thesis that, given the thrust of the work and its constellation of characters, is hardly outrageous. For

---

29 Bulthaupt makes a similar observation and offers several reasons why this choice is paradoxical, especially since it presupposes a 'prophecy *post factum*' (306).

like Palestrina and Mathis, the shoemaker-turned-poet is a man past fifty and a widower who, unwilling to share the fate of Gottfried's king ("Mein Kind: von Tristan und Isolde/ kenn' ich ein traurig Stück;/ Hans Sachs war klug und wollte/ nichts von Herrn Markes Glück"; [Wagner *Meistersinger*, III iv; 'My child, of Tristan and Isolde/ I know a grievous tale./ Hans Sachs was wise and wanted/ none of King Mark's luck'])[30], rather cheerfully, though sadly underneath, renounces his *Altersliebe*, Eva:

>   Sachs: Er [Beckmesser] hofft dich sicher zu ersingen.
>   Eva: Wieso denn der?
>   Sachs: Ein Junggesell:
>   's gibt deren wenig dort zur Stell'.
>   Eva: Könnt's einem Witwer nicht gelingen?
>   Sachs: Mein Kind, der wär' zu alt für dich.
>   Eva: Ei was zu alt? Hier gilt's der Kunst:
>   Wer sie versteht, der werb' um mich.
>   Sachs: Lieb Evchen! Machst mir blauen Dunst? (Wagner *Meistersinger*, II iv)
>
>   (Sachs: He [Beckmesser] hopes to win you by his singing.
>   Eva: A man like that?
>   Sachs: A bachelor.
>   Eva: Might not a widower succeed?
>   Sachs: My child, he'd be too old for you.
>   Eva: Ah, what? Too old? It's art that counts;
>   And all who sing are free to woo.
>   Sachs: Dear Eva! Are you teasing me?)

The fact that two or, if you will, three of these *Künstlerdramen* revolve about mature or even senescent artists is hardly accidental; and one is tempted to seek the cause for this anomaly in the artistic outlook of their 'fathers'. In this connection, it may be well to remember that, more often than not, the older we get, the more we long for conservation and the less we propagate innovation. What we want in our sunset years is the preservation of values rather than their destruction.

To begin with *Palestrina* and its creator: an archconservative, Pfitzner was a sworn enemy of the avant-garde, which, in the person of Ferruccio Busoni, eminent composer and author of *Neue Ästhethik*

---

30 The historical Sachs wrote a play on the subject.

der Tonkunst[31], he attacked, though on slippery grounds, in his pamphlet "Futuristengefahr" (Pfitzner 1926: 135-223)[32]. In his opera, a mild and rather ambiguous version of the 'music of the future' – hardly that which, since 1908, had been preached and practiced by the poet Marinetti and his Bruitist accomplices – is promoted by Palestrina's pupil Silla. Several decades earlier Silla had gone to Florence to join Count Bardi's Camerata in order "sich dort [zu] befrei'n zur Einzelexistenz" ('there to free myself for an existence of my own'), while his friend Ighino, Palestrina's son and an advocate of polyphony, had stayed behind:

> Du weißt, ich bin so weit zurück
> im klugen Denken gegen dich,
> weiß deiner Frage nicht Bescheid.
> Das eine doch empfinde ich:
> die liebliche Gemeinsamkeit
> von guten Menschen unter sich
> ist doch das Schönste allezeit. (Pfitzner *Palestrina*, I i)
>
> (You know I am so far behind you
> in wise thinking that I can't answer your question.
> But one thing I feel [strongly]:
> the lovely communion of good people among themselves
> is always the most beautiful thing.)

Palestrina himself occupies a position more or less in the middle of the spectrum, halfway between the Florentine progressives and the reactionaries of the Roman curia who, led by the Pope, seek to reinstate Gregorian chant. A more enlightened view is offered by Cardinal Borromeo, who wants to persuade the composer to save polyphony by pressing it into the service of the 'intelligible word' (see Kriss; Weinmann)[33]. (In an earlier version of the text, written by Therese Rie, one of Pfitzner's silent and unacknowledged collaborators, the role of

---

31 Busoni's short treatise – actually a collection of aphorisms – was written in 1906 and published in 1910.

32 Pfitzner's essay was penned and published in 1916.

33 For details concerning the deliberations on music at the Council of Trent see Weinmann, especially p. 3, where this notion is epitomized in the phrase "ut verba ab omnibus percipi possent" ('so that the words could be understood by everyone'; quoted from the official protocol). See also Kriss.

Cardinal Novagerio was assigned to the fanatic Cardinal Geronimo, a Savonarola type. After ordering all musical scores burned:

> So lohten zu Florenz die Scheiterhaufen.
> So möcht' ich sie noch einmal lodern sehen,
> des Menschtums Verderben zu verzehren,
> das ihrer Sinne Gift und ihrer Seelen
> Verdammnis ist und Schande der Musik[34].

> (Thus the stakes burned in Florence;
> and thus I should like to see them burn again,
> in order to consume, once again, human depravity,
> which is poison to their senses, damnation
> to their souls, and the disgrace of music.)

Geronimo is swiftly converted when he hears the strains of Palestrina's Mass – a Saul turned into a Paul.)

Hindemith's opera, too, is a plea for moderation in the social, although not overtly in the artistic, sphere. Both Mathis and his patron renounce violence, whether perpetrated by the nobility (first tableau) or the peasantry (fourth tableau, its exact counterpart), and distance themselves from the political turbulence of the age.

To what extent this critique of modernity in *Mathis der Maler* extends to the musical domain is hard to determine, especially for one who, like myself, lacks the requisite musicological training. One might surmise, for example, that the strident music of the "Temptation of St. Anthony" in the sixth tableau, which, psychologically, reflects the mental anguish of an artist procreating the panels of his altarpiece literally *in tormentis*, is, aesthetically, a protest against that emancipation of dissonance that, in the eyes of neoconservative music makers, the Hindemith of the early nineteen-thirties clearly among them, was bound to result from the radical theories advanced in Arnold Schoenberg's 'Method of Composition with Twelve Tones'[35]. What has been

---

34 Therese Rie's sketch is reproduced in the appendix to Adamy and in Wamlek-Junk.

35 I am grateful to my colleague, David Neumeyer, for having discussed this matter with me and for having given me some excellent hints. In his *Bildmonographie* of Hindemith, Schubert notes in regard to Hindemith's *Unterweisung im Tonsatz*:

convincingly demonstrated by such scholars as the Italian musicologist Armando Plebe (1962) is the decided affirmation of tonality (the dialectic of consonance and dissonance) represented by both *Mathis der Maler* and the *Unterweisung im Tonsatz*. In the operatic realm, accordingly, there seems to exist a most striking parallel between the case of Pfitzner and that of Hindemith and Schoenberg.

Whether the critique of Modernism that is built into *Palestrina* and *Mathis der Maler* applies, in the latter work, to the visual arts as well is hard to fathom, since Hindemith – partly for cogent personal and historical reasons but partly also *faute de mieux*[36] – chose a painter as

> Seine [Hindemith's] Theorie hat in ihrer beabsichtigten 'natürlichen' Grundlegung nicht nur den Widerspruch der Musiktheoretiker herausgefordert [...] sondern Hindemith begab sich zudem mit seinem Verständnis vom Wirken der Tonverwandtschaften [...] ausdrücklich in Opposition zur Schönbergschule. Mit seiner Analyse von Schönbergs zwölftönigem Klavierstück op. 33a [...] will er die Musik durch das Analyse-Ergebnis unausgesprochen als 'chaotisch' bloßstellen. (96)
>
> (In its intended 'natural' basis, not only did [Hindemith's] theory raise objections among the musicologists [...] but with his notion of the effect of tonal relationships [he] directly attacked the Schoenberg school. With his analysis of Schoenberg's twelve-tone *Klavierstück*, op. 33, he implicitly denounced that music as being 'chaotic'.)

36 Hindemith's most illuminating discussion of that issue occurs in the essay "Zur Einführung", which he wrote for the program issued on the occasion of the opera's world premiere in Zurich (reprinted both in the booklet that accompanies the Angel recording and in Briner et al., eds.). This candid preface includes the sentences:

> Dieser Mensch, mit der denkbar höchsten Vollkommenheit und Erkenntnis seiner künstlerischen Arbeit begnadet, dafür aber offenbar von allen Höllenqualen einer zweifelnden, suchenden Seele geplagt, erlebt mit der ganzen Empfänglichkeit einer solchen Natur am Beginn des 16. Jahrhunderts den Einbruch einer neuen Zeit mit ihrem unvermeidlichen Umsturz der bisher geltenden Anschauungen. Obwohl er die folgenschweren Kunstleistungen der angehenden Renaissance voll erkennt, entscheidet er sich in seiner Arbeit doch zur äussersten Entfaltung des Überlieferten [...].
>
> (This person, endowed with the highest possible perfection and the recognition of his [own] creative genius but clearly suffering from the pangs of a doubting and searching soul, experiences with a sensitivity that is characteristic of such an individual in the early sixteenth century, the onset of a new age with its inevitable transvaluation of all values. Although he is fully cognizant of the great artistic achievements to be made by the budding Renaissance, he decided, in his own art, to take traditional values to their limit [...].)

his protagonist without being, himself, equipped to deal authoritatively with art-historical questions. Thus one might argue, though speciously, that the Nidhart of the Isenheim altarpiece was, historically, an early exponent of Teutonic Mannerism and painted in a style that, according to Wilhelm Worringer in one of his most influential books[37], was Gothic and, hence, ideally suited to serve as a model for twentieth-century Expressionism. But to characterize Hindemith's Mathis as an avantgardist *avant la lettre* would miss the mark; for what the composer undoubtedly aimed at in the portrayal of his hero was to show his craving for versimilitude enhanced by a newly awakened social consciousness rather than, *pace* Worringer, a more subconscious than conscious stylistic and artistic volition. What Hindemith brings to the fore is the hero's sympathy for the plight of the common man as expressed in his choice of blatantly realistic models for Christ and the Virgin Mary, which is so offensive to the Church. As the Pope's representative in Mainz, the *Domdechant* Lorenz von Pommersfelden, states bluntly:

> Das Kapitel ist gegen den Maler da.
> Einen kranken Bettelmann stellt er uns als Heiland
> Hin. Für uns ist ein Heiliger kein Bauer.
> Und die Gottesmutter war keine Weisenauer
> Kuhmagd. (Hindemith *Mathis*, II iv)[38]
>
> (The Chapter is opposed to this painter here,
> who portrays our Savior as a sick beggar.
> To us, a saint is not a peasant,
> and the Virgin Mary was no milkmaid
> from Weisenau.)

By contrast, *Die Meistersinger* was originally intended as a parody of *Tannhäuser,* that 'musical legend' of a *Neutöner* who comes to grief

---

37 *Formprobleme der Gothik* (1911) expands some of the views originally presented in Worringer's epoch-making 1908 dissertation, *Abstraktion und Einfühlung*.
38 Tableau II, iv. In "Zur Einführung", Hindemith expressly refers to Grünewald's Karlsruhe "Crucifixion" and his Stuppach "Madonna". The slim corpus of Grünewald's works is conveniently reproduced in Burkhard: the Isenheim altarpiece (plates 9-44), Karlsruhe "Crucifixion" (plates 51-55 and 58-62), and Stuppach "Madonna" (plates 45, 46 and 48).

and is saved only by a woman's love and divine intervention, two distinctly conservative forces. To quote from Wagner's "Mitteilung an meine Freunde" (1851):

> Wie bei den Athenern ein heiteres Satyrspiel auf die Tragödie folgte, erschien mir auf jener Vergnügungsreise [to a Bohemian spa] plötzlich das Bild eines komischen Spieles, das in Wahrheit als beziehungsvolles Satyrspiel meinem "Sängerkrieg auf der Wartburg" sich anschliessen konnte. Es waren dies "die Meistersinger von Nürnberg" mit Hans Sachs an der Spitze. (Wagner 1983: 259)

> (Just as in Athens the tragedy was followed by a humorous satyr play, so during [a recent] pleasure trip I suddenly had the idea of writing a comedy perfectly suited as a comic companion piece to my *Tannhäuser*. That comedy was *Die Meistersinger von Nürnberg,* led by Hans Sachs.)

Although most emphatically a champion of Walther's *Naturtalent*, Wagner sought to reconcile the extremes of Beckmesser's involuntary futurism, which clashes with his ultra-conservative stance as a *Merker*, with the stale though loving routine of his fellow Masters. At the eye of the storm Sachs, the deft manipulator and puppeteer (or *Drahtzieher*, to use Wagner's own double entendre), aims at matching the old with the new by making Walther's art palatable to his colleagues and their art palatable to Walther. (I tend to believe, idiosyncratically, that there is more than a trace of irony in the artistic triumph of the aristocratic parvenu; for what other reason could Wagner, the *literatus*, have had for making the text of the *Preislied* [contest song] so striking an example of Baroque allegorical excessive ornamentation [*Schwulst*], complete with ponderous hyperboles and syntactical involutions, that the plagiarist Beckmesser is bound to misquote and, hence, misinterpret it?)

In *Torquato Tasso* – to conclude our fourfold examination – the resolution of the conflict between old and new takes place solely on the social level; artistically, the hero of this *Künstlerdrama* is 'on target', emulating the past both in style and content. His choice of antiquated subject matter, in fact, shows him to be a *Ritter von der traurigen Gestalt* (knight of the sad figure; see *Tasso*, IV iv; Borchmeyer,

128)[39], and his adulation of Virgil, symbolized by the transfer of the laurel wreath from the latter's herm to his own head, shows him to be an individual talent almost too profoundly steeped in tradition.

Tackling yet another important aspect of our topic: the writers, critics, and scholars who have dealt with the problematic aspects of the *Künstlerdrama* have, by and large, agreed that attention should be focused on the aesthetic rather than the psychological dimension of this genre and, more directly, on specific works of art. If, that is to say, the *Künstlerdrama* is to be regarded as a branch of the *Geschichtsdrama* (history play), it is perfectly natural to see the work, or *Frucht* – in the sense of the quotation from Matthew 7:16, "Ye shall know them by their fruits", that serves as an epigraph to this essay – placed at its center; artistic *Schöpfung* (creation) thus corresponds to historical *Handlung* (action), since the relationship of works to deeds parallels that between artists and men of action.

It is hardly surprising, therefore, that works of art, and frequently masterpieces, tend to play a prominent role in this genre of dramas and operas. Thus in *Torquato Tasso* the protagonist's masterpiece serves as a focal point and provides a major topic of conversation as the moment of its completion approaches. Goethe has arranged things in such a way that Tasso's greatest triumph, still limited to the intimate circle of the Court at Ferrara, coincides with and helps to precipitate a grave personal and social crisis. As a result the poet, having surrendered his manuscript, wants to have it returned so he can complete it elsewhere[40].

---

39 See especially lines 2633-2639, beginning with the words "Bescheiden hofft' ich, jenen grossen Meistern/ Der Vorwelt mich zu nahn" ('In all modesty, I hoped to become worthy of the great masters of the past'). In his chapter on *Tasso*, Borchmeyer notes that Tasso's imagination is "noch ganz vom Geist des ritterlichen Mittelalters erfüllt" (I, 128; 'still fully imbued with the spirit of the knightly Middle Ages') and subsequently speaks of his "anachronistischer Traum einer engen Verbindung von 'Held' und 'Dichter'" ('anachronistic dream of a close linkage between "hero" and "poet"').

40 Unlike Palestrina and Mathis, who fashion their masterpieces in a creative frenzy, which explains why these are "wie aus einem Guss" ('of a piece'), Tasso is an "ewig

In a fifth example of *Künstlerdrama*, Grillparzer's *Sappho*, art plays a different role. The protagonist's oeuvre, which is lyrical rather than narrative and thus less likely to include a decided masterpiece, is of markedly secondary importance. The author explains, "Es lag in meinem Plane, nicht die Mißgunst des Lebens gegen die Kunst zu schildern, wie in *Correggio* oder *Tasso*, sondern die natürliche Scheidewand, die zwischen beiden befestigt ist" (Grillparzer [n. d.], 177) ('It was part of my plan to portray not life's envy of art, as happens in *Correggio* and *Tasso*, but the natural wall that separates the two'). Whereas Goethe chose not to adduce quotations from Tasso's epic, Grillparzer has Sappho recite one of her own poems – oddly enough, for reasons that seem somewhat frivolous: "Ich konnte der Versuchung nicht widerstehen, die zweite der beiden übrig gebliebenen Oden Sapphos, die mir zu passen schien, in dem Stücke, das ihren Namen führt, aufzunehmen, damit man mir doch nicht sagen könnte, es sei gar nichts von ihrem Geiste darin" (ibid.[41]; 'I was unable to resist the temptation of including the second of Sappho's two surviving odes – which I found suitable – in the work that bears her name, so that I could not be accused of having failed to instill some of her spirit into it').

Die Meistersinger, focusing on a municipal song contest and *Fest*, abounds with works in the making, in rehearsal, and in performance (Walther's *Freiungslied* and *Preislied*, David's St. John's Day *Sprüchlein*, Beckmesser's dissonant serenade, and two communally chanted chorales, for example) that are fairly modest in scope and do not qualify as masterpieces, even though, dramaturgically speaking, the *Preislied* comes fairly close to functioning as such. Things are different in Pfitzner's 'musical legend' and Hindemith's *Oper in sieben Bildern*. For just as Tasso's verse epic may be regarded as *ein Stück in*

Unbehauster" ('eternally homeless one'), whose "skrupulöses Feilen" ('scrupulous polishing') stands in the way of organic perfection (Borchmeyer, 125).

41 *Sappho* was originally conceived as a libretto for the composer and conductor Joseph Weigl.

die Ewigkeit verpflanzte Zeit (a piece of time translated into eternity), Palestrina's *Missa Papae Marcelli* and Grünewald's Isenheim altarpiece must be viewed as *zwei in die Zeit verpflanzte Stücke Ewigkeit* (two pieces of eternity translated into time). All three works, by Pfitzner's standards, have their permanent place in a transcendent order (see Kunze, 76)[42]. In so far as, unlike Goethe, both Pfitzner and Hindemith focus on the act of creation, they invalidate Helene Goldschmidt's claim that it is impossible, "das tiefste künstlerische Erlebnis, den eigentlichen Schaffensakt des Künstlers, zur Darstellung zu bringen" (Goldschmidt, 45; see also Seebohm, 27; 'to represent artistically the deepest artistic experience, i. e., the creative moment itself') – one more proof of their analogousness.

II.

After this lengthy preamble, I now turn to the pragmatic portion of this essay: a comparative analysis and interpretation of the scenes from *Palestrina* and *Mathis der Maler* in which, in Pfitzner's case, the *Schaffensakt* (act of creation) and, in Hindemith's case, the *Empfängnis* (conception) or *Zeugungsakt* (procreative act) are paraded before our eyes. In the *Komponisten-Oper* this moment of creative inspiration is conveyed through the binary relationship between and mutual illumination of music and literature (the visual elements of Pfitzner's "Engelkonzert" are of secondary importance); in the *Maler-Oper* the visual component is essential, perhaps paramount.

Palestrina

In an essay written on the occasion of the fifteenth anniversary of the premiere of *Palestrina*, Pfitzner spoke eloquently of his desire to write an opera in which the *Kunstwerk* rather than the *Künstler* would occupy center stage. Contrasting *Torquato Tasso* with his own 'musical legend', he noted,

---

42 Kunze's essay deals with this notion and its applicability to the *Musikalische Legende in drei Akten*.

[In *Torquato Tasso*] spielt das Werk des Künstlerhelden so gut wie gar keine Rolle, der Held ist der Künstler als Figur im Leben, dessen Konflikte als menschlich wie die der anderen gezeigt werden, nur gefärbt, gesteigert, verfeinert durch die Mitgift seiner Natur. [...] Ein anderes ist's, wenn es sich nicht um den Künstler, sondern um das Werk dreht, wenn der Künstler als der notwendige, einzige und einmalige Erzeuger desselben dargestellt, nur seine Mission bedacht werden muß. Hier ist der Gesichtswinkel ein anderer, aus dem der Künstler gesehen wird, das Problem ist ein anderes – die Form muß eine andere werden, denn alles spielt in einem anderen Stockwerk: der Held ist das Werk, was nicht bluten kann. Seine Gegenspieler müssen demgemäß sein. Der Titel [meiner Oper] könnte [deshalb] gerade so gut lauten: *Die Marcellusmesse*. (Pfitzner 1967: 8)

([In *Torquato Tasso*] the work of the artist-hero plays a distinctly minor role. Here the protagonist is the artist [seen] as an individual whose conflicts are shown to be typically human, although colored, enhanced, and ennobled by his talent. [...] The matter is different when the focus is on the work itself, and when the artist is portrayed as its necessary, sole, and unique creator, so that only his mission counts. Here the perspective from which the artist is viewed is different and so is the entire *Problematik*. In consequence thereof, the form must be different as well, since everything is shifted to a higher level; for the true hero is the work, which cannot bleed and whose antagonists are of another sort. Accordingly, the title of my opera could just as well be *Missa Papae Marcelli* [*Pope Marcellus Mass*].)

From the very start Pfitzner, who, paradoxically, considered the *text* rather than the *music* of his *Hauptwerk*[43] to be his greatest artistic achievement (Pfitzner 1955: 44; 1979), envisaged *Palestrina* as triadic. Acts I and III were to be the outer panels of the triptych, depicting the world of the mind, and Act II (the center panel) that of history. In a letter to Artur Eloesser, dated 14 November 1910, he described his '*Festspiel*-in-the-making' (Adamy, 31)[44] in the following terms:

Ich habe in diesem Sommer den ersten Akt der "musikalischen Legende" *Palestrina* fertig geschrieben. [...] Ich weiß noch nicht, ob ich [sie] je vollenden kann [...] Daß es drei Akte sind, weiß ich; was im dritten vorgeht, weiß ich genau, wo der zweite und dritte Akt spielen, weiß ich auch, ebenso die ganze Stimmung, die

---

43 "Dasjenige Werk jedoch, welches in Wahrheit eine große Dichtung genannt werden kann, ist der *Mathis*. Wie es kommt, daß das größte Werk eines Komponisten eine Dichtung ist, das, weil es zugleich einen seiner musikalischen Höhepunkte darstellt, sein eigentliches Lebenswerk genannt werden muss [...]." ('The work, however, which can truly be called a great poem is *Mathis* [*der Maler*]. How is it possible that the finest work of a composer is a literary one that, because it also happens to be a musical masterpiece, must be considered his greatest artistic achievement?')
44 It seems plausible that Pfitzner considered *Palestrina* to be his *Parsifal*.

Signatur des Inhaltes, aber den 'realen' Tatsacheninhalt des zweiten Aktes weiß ich noch nicht. (Pfitzner 1944: 303)

(This summer I have completed Act I of my "musical legend" *Palestrina*. [...] I don't know whether I'll ever finish it. [...] I know that it has three acts and also what happens in the third one. I also know the settings for Acts II and III, as well as the prevailing mood and the 'signature' of the content. But I'm still uncertain as to what will 'actually' happen in Act II.)

In the way it was conceived and executed, *Palestrina* seems to defy dramaturgical common sense; and precisely therein lies the rub. For the actual highlight, the creation of the Mass under angelic guidance, occurs in the latter portion of Act I and is followed, anticlimactically, by the protagonist's falling asleep and being discovered in that state of mental paralysis at the end of a span that, symbolically, represents the progression of natural time from dusk to dawn. The second act, bathed in the glaring light of reason and cold intellect, lets us witness the final session of the Council of Trent, whose participants, all dignitaries of the Church, are unaware of the fact that, while they are still haggling over the issue, Palestrina has already written his Mass. The tone, accordingly, is ironic[45] (Abendroth, 1935).

Act III, which brings the news that the *Missa Papae Marcelli* has been performed and that its author has been rehabilitated after a period of disgrace and incarceration (contrary to historical fact), is so peaceful, even subdued, that, instead of being a triumphant celebration of Palestrina the man and the artist, the scene is replete with an air of resignation. Broken in body if not in spirit, Palestrina is now presumably in his dotage and surely incapable of savoring, let alone exploiting or enhancing, his success. A 'treuer Diener seines Herrn' (and of his music masters), he is depicted in an introspective mood:

---

45 Pfitzner elaborates on this point in a letter to Felix Wolfes dated 22 August 1915: "Das ist ja gerade der Witz, daß die Sache mit der Messe so behandelt wird, als Nebensache, als Dreck. Längst ist sie fertig, über alle Köpfe weg, gegen den Willen des Autors selbst sozusagen, und die großen Leute streiten sich noch herum und glauben es zu machen." ('The point is exactly that the affair of the Mass is treated offhandedly as a joke. It was completed some time ago, over everybody's head, and almost against the artist's will. But the bigshots are still quarrelling among themselves, in the belief that *they* are engineering it.')

"Er setzt sich auf den Stuhl an die Orgel und versenkt sich, leise spielend, in musikalische Gedanken, den Blick über die Tasten hinweg ins Weite gerichtet." ('He seats himself at the organ and plays softly, wrapped in deep musical thoughts and looking beyond the keys into the distance.') This is hardly a pose suited to an artist at the apogee of his career or in the thrall of apotheosis[46].

As we turn to the crucial sequence (I, iii-vi) that culminates in Palestrina's creative vision and its immediate artistic translation, we must realize that Pfitzner, although fully conversant with the historical facts on which he based his text – I hesitate to say 'libretto' – chose not only to condense, but also to reshuffle, the data to suit his purpose[47]. Accordingly, he specifies the time span covered by the action of his opera as follows: "Die Handlung spielt im November und Dezember 1563, dem Jahre der Beendigung des Tridentiner Konzils. [...] Zwischen dem ersten und zweiten Akt liegen etwa acht Tage, zwischen dem zweiten und dritten etwa vierzehn Tage." ('The action takes place in November and December 1563, the final year of the Council of Trent. [...] Approximately one week elapses between Acts I and II, and two weeks between Acts II and III.')

In line with this drastic foreshortening, he rearranged some of the basic dates in the life of Palestrina, who was born around 1525, married in 1545, composed his *Missa Papae Marcelli* around 1560, lost his first wife in 1580, and died as *maestro compositore* and Chapel Master of St. Peter's in 1594. In contrast, Pfitzner's hero was born approximately ten years earlier[48], has lost his wife an unspecified

---

46 This kind of presentation easily lends itself to parody, at least of the involuntary kind, such as we have in Hanns Johst's Expressionist play *Der Einsame* and, as parody of the parody, in Brecht's *Künstlerdrama, Baal*.

47 In preparation for writing the text for *Palestrina*, Pfitzner consulted the histories of the Council of Trent by Paul Sarpi and Sforza Pallavicini.

48 In the stage directions for Act I, iii, Pfitzner describes Palestrina as a man who "die fünfzig leicht überschritten [hat] und, zumal an den Schläfen, leicht ergraut ist" ('is slightly over fifty years of age and greying, especially at the temples').

number of years ago, writes the Mass in 1563, and will live for another thirty years.

The opera's plot can be summarized as follows: Lukrezia's death, precipitated or, at least, hastened by her husband's dismissal from Papal service[49], has temporarily blocked Palestrina's creative vein and has led to an impasse marked by a mental condition that might be considered a Schopenhauerian version of *melancolia*. As Ighino explains to Silla, who does not fathom why it should be so hard for a famous man like his teacher to bear "sein kleines Kreuz":

> Hast Du vom Leid der Welt noch nicht gehört,
> Davon die Dichter sagen,
> Man geht und weint, weil man geboren ist.
> Ich glaub im Vater ist etwas davon. (Pfitzner *Palestrina*, I ii)
>
> (Haven't you heard of the sorrows of the world,
> to which the poets refer?
> One lives and weeps because one has been born.
> Father, I think, has a touch of that.)

Shortly after Ighino utters these words, Cardinal Borromeo berates Palestrina for being too indulgent with Silla. Palestrina halfheartedly admits his skepticism concerning the young radicals who, embracing a vague progressive ideal, are, in his opinion, bent on wrecking "die Kunst der Meister vieler hundert Jahre,/ Geheimnisvoll verbündet durch die Zeiten" ('the art that masters have built through the centuries in a mysterious alliance'). Borromeo counters these plaintive

---

49 [...] Ein Menschenalter schuf und schuf er Werke
In unvermindert wunderbarer Stärke,
Bis daß ihn endlich traf der schwerste Schlag,
Bis meine Mutter auf der Bahre lag. [...]
Da ward es still in ihm und leer.
Seit ihrem Tode schrieb er keine Note mehr.

(For a whole generation, he created one work after another
with wonderfully undiminished power,
until the heaviest blow fell on him
and my mother lay dead.
Since she departed he is silent and barren,
and hasn't written a single note.)

Ighino, in Act I, ii, implies that Palestrina had been dismissed from service because Papal singers were supposed to remain celibate.

words with a long 'sermon' in which, disabusing Palestrina of this notion, he shows the real danger to lie not in the relatively harmless machinations of the Camerata[50] but in the very bosom of the Church, where polyphonic music is being threatened with extinction. He tells his protégé of his own efforts to stem the tide, which had proved futile until the Emperor himself came to his rescue by writing a letter urging the Pope to preserve "aus grosser Meister Zeit/ Das wohlerfund'ne Alte,/ Weil es den Geist der Frömmigkeit/ Erwecke und erhalte" ('all that is well made/ in masterpieces from the past,/ since it awakens and upholds/ the spirit of piety'); he then pleads with Palestrina to create a masterpiece whose entire style and action (*Stil und Haltung*) could serve as a chaste model for all sacred music[51].

Persisting in his existential despair, Palestrina remains indifferent to the plea and, at first, ignores Borromeo's appeal to the dead Masters, whom the Cardinal describes as lamenting the threatened loss of their works along with those of their illustrious successor. Emulating the theatrical manager in the prologue to Goethe's *Faust* ("Gebt Ihr Euch einmal für Poeten,/ So kommandiert die Poesie" ['If you call yourselves poets, you should have poetry at your beck and call']), Borromeo instructs Palestrina to perform the task with which he has charged him; but he is vehemently rebuffed and leaves in a huff. In spite of its apparent rejection, however, the message has sunk in, and as the symbolic *noche oscura* descends, Palestrina's mind begins to ponder the issue. Searching for a solution, the composer vainly appeals to the portrait of Lukrezia, at whose death the wellspring of his creativity had dried up; receiving no answer, he moves, a second Faust, to the brink of suicide.

Precisely at this point *his* Easter bells – the voice of the Masters with its hollow ring – come to the rescue. Nine in number, these male muses make their ghostly appearance and urge him to fulfill his

---

50 The reference to Count Bardi's Florentine circle is, of course, anachronistic.
51 It is somewhat ironic that the salvation of music is accomplished at the price of its subservience to language, i. e., through artistic self-abnegation.

Erdenpensum, the duty that "der alte Weltenmeister,/ Der ohne Namen ist; der gleichfalls untertan/ Uraltem Wort am Rand der Ewigkeit" ('the old Master of the world,/ who has no name [and] is just as subject/ to the primeval word on the edge of eternity') has imposed on him[52]. Touched by these familiar echoes from the past, Palestrina once again feels the pain that signals the onrush of inspiration and, bucking his own conscious will, prepares to undergo one more, his last, artistic metamorphosis. (As the Masters, who watch him closely and comment on the miraculous transformation, soothingly explain to him: "Die Wachstumsschmerzen sind's!/ Es kommt vom Werden./ Die letzte Häutung – s'ist die Mutation." [Pfitzner *Palestrina*, I v; 'These are growing pains caused by becoming – the last shedding of the skin, a transformation.'].)

Ready at last to do the Masters' bidding[53], Palestrina hears the strains from the "Kyrie" and "Sanctus" of the *Missa Papae Marcelli* as sung by the angelic choirs that have replaced his artistic forebears (see Rectanus, 139-141). They are shortly joined by Lukrezia, who steps out of her portrait to surround him once again, though only briefly, with her encompassing love. In a state of quasi-mystical rapture,

---

52 Borromeo has asked Palestrina specifically to place "der höchsten Spitze Kreuzesblume/ [...] auf der Töne Wunderdom" ('the crowning glory [...] of music's wondrous cathedral'). This metaphorical treatment of music as flowing architecture, derived from German Romantic thought, is endemic throughout the opera.

53 Only two of the nine Masters who appear to him are identified in the libretto. They are Josquin Des Prez ("Josquin, du Herrlicher") and Heinrich Isaac ("Tedesc' Enrico nannt' ich dich"). Judging by Pfitzner's stage directions – "Sie sind in verschiedenen – spanischen, niederländischen, italienischen, deutschen, französischen – Trachten und scheinen aus verschiedenen Jahrhunderten der vor-Palestrinaschen Zeit zu stammen. Der älteste, etwa 13. Jahrhundert, ist durch eine Erscheinung im Mönchskleid repräsentiert." ('They are dressed in various national costumes – Spanish, Dutch, Italian, German, French – and seem to hail from different centuries preceding the age of Palestrina The oldest [tradition] is represented by a figure in monastic garb.') – the group probably includes Guillaume Dufay, Johannes Okeghem, and Tomas Luis de Victoria, as well as the half-legendary Arcadeel (Arcadelt), whom the composer mentions in a letter to Therese Rie dated 30 May 1909 (quoted in Adamy, 26). My colleague George Buelow of Indiana University also suggested Alexander Agricola, Jacob Obrecht, Pierre de la Rue, and Antoine Busnois (the Burgundian).

Palestrina "ergreift mechanisch die Feder" and "läßt sie nicht wieder aus der Hand" ('mechanically picks up the pen' and 'does not put it down') until the entire piece is finished[54]. Naturally, for reasons of dramatic economy, Pfitzner does not quote either the Latin text or the music of the Mass in its entirety, but wisely limits himself to offering a condensed, one might say 'collagistic', version that ends verbally, though not musically, with the "dona nobis pacem" of the second "Agnus Dei". In lieu of a perfect synchronicity between words and tones, we thus have a symbolically foreshortened construct in which the text and the music are no longer *deckungsgleich* (mirror images)[55].

Having witnessed these events, we, the spectators, sense that we have been the privileged observers of a creative act that was not so much an overflow of the imagination as a transfer from one link in the Great Chain of Being to another, an outpouring, not so much of the Holy Ghost as of holy music. Although it is perfectly appropriate for the protagonist of a *Künstleroper* to be shown in the act of composing, it is less readily apparent why he should sing while composing. However, since, on the one hand, the creation of a musical score is a visible rather than an audible activity (unless the composer hums to himself or works things out at the piano) while, on the other, the agents of operatic action are human voices, sung speech, in the form of a recitative-like running commentary on the work-in-progress, seems to be fully justified on artistic grounds. The fact that the real Palestrina was a singer is surely coincidental; for unlike his historical model, the protagonist of the 'musical legend' is a chorus-master long past the age at which he could serve as a *Sängerknabe*!

---

54 The latter part of Act I, iv, increasingly resembles, in both language and action, the conclusion of the scene "Nacht" (roughly lines 720-807) in Goethe's *Faust, der Tragödie erster Teil*, just as the conclusion of scene vi, with its angelic choirs, parallels the scene "Bergschluchten" of *Faust II*.

55 In the libretto (Schott edition), the disparity is graphically manifested by the use of double columns (21-23).

Mathis der Maler
How did Hindemith come to choose the story of a painter, a topic seemingly so much against the generic grain, as the basis for his opera? Hindemith had previously worked with Gottfried Benn on the oratorio *Das Unaufhörliche* and found this joint effort to his liking (see Fehn[56]). Now that he was considering an opera, he once again turned to Benn for help. The poet was perfectly willing to oblige, and even during the final months of the Weimar Republic, whose collapse, accentuating the poet's and composer's ideological differences, made further collaboration impossible, they discussed a number of possibilities; Benn leaned toward a contemporary subject and Hindemith toward a historical one (see Fehn, 67)[57]. One of the subjects that Hindemith rejected was Knut Hamsun's early novel *Viktoria*, mainly because the composer was a little apprehensive with regard to topics "die schon einmal in einer anderen Kunstgattung eine gute Lösung gefunden haben" (Hindemith 1982: 149; 'that have been solved satisfactorily in another medium')[58].

More to the point, and better suited to the subgenre, was an opera set in medieval Germany that would provide opportunities to use music in a cogently dramaturgical function. As Hindemith put it in a letter to Benn:

> Könnte man nicht an einem alten Beispiel zeigen, wie kulturell kolonisiert wird? [...] Ich dachte an die St. Galler Klosterschule zu Karls des Großen Zeit. Darüber gibt es mancherlei Geschichten, aus denen sich eine Handlung bauen ließe; und da die Leute auch die ersten Anfänge der Musikkultur ins barbarische Germanien

---

56 Benn's correspondence with Hindemith, as well as Hindemith's correspondence with his publishers, has been edited by Fehn.

57 Benn wrote to Hindemith on 15 September 1932: "In einer Zeit, wo so neue interessante Dinge sich prägen, historisch sein, ist das gut?" (67; 'To be historical in an age in which new and interesting developments are in the offing, is that good?'). The interest in historical subjects at that time was by no means limited to Hindemith, but is characteristic of the writers of both *Exil* and *Innere Emigration*, especially the novelists. For details concerning two projects, a "Weizengeschichte" and the "Fragment eines Singspiels", in which the Rönne figures would have been resuscitated, see Fehn's notes and commentary.

58 Letter to Benn dated 20 August 1932.

gebracht haben, ließe sich auch musikalisch viel machen, mit Anwendung der Gregorianischen Gesänge. (Hindemith 1982: 149)[59]

(Couldn't one, using an old example, show how cultural colonization occurs? [...] I was thinking of the monastic school of St. Gallen at the time of Charlemagne. That subject has been treated in several stories, from which a plot could be constructed. And since these people brought the rudiments of musical culture to barbarian Germany, there are a lot of musical possibilities, for instance through the use of Gregorian chant.)

But as Hindemith complains in a letter to his publishers, Benn did not find that subject sufficiently attractive, largely, one assumes, because of the ironic stance toward Germany and the Germans that is implied by the tone of the resumé Hindemith sent him[60] (Hindemith 1982: 154). Nor could they agree on two other subjects that they must have discussed concurrently. Gutenberg, one of the possibilities, Hindemith rejected because he thought the inventor of the printing press to be "ein ziemlich trockner Herr" ('a rather dry gentleman') who would be hard to make it aesthetically viable. Grünewald, the other historical figure, brought to his attention by an editor of the Schott-Verlag, pleased him more. He resisted at first, however, mainly because Grünewald was a painter, and he did not wish to run into the same problems that had plagued Franz Schreker, who had set a bad example in his *Maleroper, Die Gezeichneten*:

Grünewald wäre gut, wenn er nicht gerade Maler wäre. Wesen und Zweck einer Oper um [ihn] könnte doch nur die Malerei sein und man käme ja nicht drum herum, den Mann in Begeisterung malen zu lassen, ein für die Musik sehr dürftiges und für meine Begriffe komisches Motiv. Erinnern Sie sich an *Die Gezeichneten*, wo die exaltierte Dame vor der Staffelei in Verzückung gerät? Etwas Ähnliches müßte wahrscheinlich auch hier passieren. (Hindemith 1982: 155)

(Grünewald would do well if he weren't a painter. The essence and purpose of an opera about him could only be painting, and one couldn't help but let the man paint with enthusiasm. Musically speaking, that is a scanty and, in my opinion, downright humorous motif. Do you remember *Die Gezeichneten*, where the high-

---

59 From the same letter. By a strange coincidence, this opera would have featured the introduction of the Gregorian chant which, by way of a historical *Rückgriff* (backward glance), figures so significantly in *Palestrina*.

60 In a letter to his publishers dated 10 October 1932, Hindemith observes dryly: "Benn funkt eben gar nicht. Er kommt vor lauter Überkritik zu nichts." ('Benn doesn't spark at all. He remains totally barren with all his excessive criticism.')

strung lady waxes ecstatic before the easel? Something of the sort probably would have to happen here as well.)

After tentatively shelving this project and flirting briefly with Ernst Penzoldt, he turned again to Grünewald (see Schubert, 78), determined now to proceed. Unable to find a congenial librettist, he himself took up the pen and wrote to his colleague Gian Francesco Malipiero (Hindemith 1982: 156): "Ich selbst bin gerade sehr mit einer Oper beschäftigt. Veranlaßt durch die ewige Not mit den Dichtern mache ich jetzt endlich den Text selbst und [...] hoffe, daß er brauchbar wird." ('Right now, I am hard at work on an opera. Having had a lot of trouble with authors, I finally decided to write my own libretto and hope that it will be fitting.') He labored mightily for well over two years, completing the final version of the libretto only in June 1935 – barely two months before he finished the score (Briner et al., eds., 140)[61]. His procedure was quite unlike the one used for *Palestrina* or, for that matter, Wagner's *Ring des Nibelungen*, in which publication of the texts preceded that of the music by several years.

The following excerpt from a letter written by Ludwig Strecker of the Schott-Verlag in the wake of Hindemith's oral presentation of an intermediate version of the text is especially interesting in this context:

> Er ist so gefangen von dem Stoff, von der ihm vertrauten Atmosphäre und der Größe des Vorwurfs, der Parallele der damaligen Zeit mit der unsrigen und vor allem mit dem einsamen Künstlerschicksal, daß er mit einer Begeisterung und persönlichen Teilnahme schaffen wird wie noch nie [...]. Vor allen Dingen [ist er] wie erlöst, daß er den Text zu seiner Musik schreiben kann und nicht umgekehrt; und da er in der ganzen Anlage dies berücksichtigt, so erwarte ich mir etwas sehr Erfreuliches. (Schubert, 80, fn. 39)[62]
>
> (He is so caught up in the subject, in the familiar atmosphere, the greatness of the theme, the parallels between the two ages and, most important, the artist's lonely existence, that he will work with unprecedented enthusiasm and great personal *engagement*. [...] He is especially relieved to know that he can furnish the text for

---

61 Briner et al. provide a detailed chronology of the genesis of both text and music of the opera.

62 The letter is dated 4 August 1933. "Vertraute Atmosphäre" (familiar atmosphere) must refer to the Rhein-Main area in which both Grünewald and Hindemith were at home.

his music, rather than the other way round; and since he takes this fact into account in his overall plan, I foresee excellent results.)

In this somewhat exceptional case, then, the *musica*, or at least a fair portion thereof, preceded the *parola*. This, in addition to Hindemith's untried talents as a writer, helps to explain why the text of *Mathis der Maler* cannot be judged fairly as a verbal construct in its own right. Let us also keep in mind that, while Hindemith was planning his opera, he was also writing a piece of purely instrumental music, the *Mathis der Maler* symphony, commissioned by Wilhelm Furtwängler and premiered on 12 March 1934 in Berlin[63]. In fact, large segments of that profoundly moving orchestral work were subsequently incorporated into the opera – all of the "Engelskonzert", much of the "Grablegung", and part of the "Versuchung des Heiligen Antonius" (Wohlke, 11-12, 52-60)[64].

The structure of *Mathis der Maler* underwent a number of changes before Hindemith settled on a pattern satisfactory to him. A detailed history of the evolution of the libretto remains to be written, but the sketches and summaries reproduced in Andres Briner's monograph *Paul Hindemith* permit us to pry into the artist's workshop. For example, in a preliminary version, the painter's vision, not yet distinctly creative, occurs in the central (fourth) *Bild* rather than in the penultimate sixth and shows Mathis, not as the St. Anthony, but as the St. Sebastian of the Isenheim altarpiece. In an intermediate version, probably dating from late 1933, the sixth *Bild*, the only one outlined in detail, closely resembles the one that ultimately replaced it but with one basic difference: in the earlier version the protagonist is not paralyzed by his creative vision, functioning as little more than an *appa-*

---

[63] I owe thanks for a great deal of information about this period in Hindemith's life to Professor Bernhard Heiden of the School of Music at Indiana University, who was then studying with Hindemith. Professor Heiden also owns a copy of the program of the concert at which the symphony was introduced; it contains a brief analysis by the composer.

[64] Wohlke discusses the exact relationship between the symphony and those portions of the opera into which it has been interpolated.

reil enregistreur, but is an energetic Mathis who walks through the landscape of Grünewald's "Temptation" and "Conversation" panels: "Es ist dunkel. Im Hintergrund wird eine phantastische Landschaft sichtbar [...]. Mathis wandelt in der Kleidung des Antonius durch die Landschaft. Die verschiedensten Figuren kommen, ihn zu versuchen. Erst Fabelwesen wie in Grünewalds Bild, dann die Personen der Oper selbst" (see Briner et al., eds., 125). ('It is dark. In the background, a fantastic landscape comes into view. [...] Dressed in St. Anthony's garb, Mathis traverses the scene. A motley crew of figures comes to tempt him – at first fantastic creatures, as in Grünewald's painting, and then the opera's *dramatis personae*'.) In this earlier version, the order of allegory and vision was reversed. As Briner notes, psychologically the earlier solution was much less compelling because the allegory represents a state of consciousness that is still relatively close to the surface, whereas the visions, being projections of the subconscious, originate on a much deeper level.

The definitive text of the sixth tableau, to which I now turn in conclusion, offers a series of kaleidoscopic visions tied to the *Schaffensakt*, thereby not only justifying, but fairly crying out for, a comparison with the analogous segment of *Palestrina*. Set in the Odenwald, the scene shows Mathis and Schwalb's daughter, Regina, on the final leg of their flight, which began at the end of the fourth tableau with the peasants' defeat and the death of Regina's father on the battlefield. Regina is exhausted and haunted by the dreadful experience; and the painter, her second father, seeks to soothe her pain. As she lies down to rest on his outspread cloak, he puts her to sleep, not with a fairy tale or a lullaby, but by vividly describing what is to be a *Tafel*, with explicitly musical motives perfectly matching her mental state:

> Alte Märchen woben
> Uns fromme Bilder, die ein Widerscheinen
> Des Höheren sind. Ihr Sinn ist dir
> Fern. Du kannst ihn nur erahnen.
> Und frömmer noch reden

> Zu uns die Töne, wenn Musik, in Einfalt hier
> Geboren, die Spuren himmlischer Herkunft trägt. (Hindemith *Mathis*, VI i)[65]

(Old fairy tales wove
us pious pictures that are reflections
of a transcendent realm. Their meaning is
obscure to you; you can only sense it.
And the sounds speak to us
even more piously when the music, in innocence here born,
shows traces of its heavenly origin.)

What Mathis describes in the twenty-six lines that follow is, fittingly enough, a panel of the Isenheim altarpiece, the so-called "Engelkonzert", whose instrumental transcription, doing double duty as a Prelude to the opera and as the first movement of the symphony, is quoted extensively during his narration. This music constitutes the 'objective correlative', or signature tune, for Regina's essence (her *Wesen*). She identifies with it and, being drawn into the charmed angelic circle, chimes in with Hindemith's version of "Es sungen drei Englein süßen Gesang" ('Three angels sang a sweet song') from Franz Magnus Böhme's *Altdeutsches Liederbuch* (Wohlke, 16)[66].

Let us remember that what Mathis creates in this sequence are not paintings already in existence and on exhibit – he is, after all, not in his studio but in the middle of a forest – but canvases *in statu inspirandi*. In so arranging his text, Hindemith circumvents the cliché of the *Malerdrama* or *Maleroper* that he had condemned in his earlier comments on Franz Schreker. By logical extension, the actual *Schaffensakt* occurs after an interval of several months or years ("einige Zeit später", according to the direction given in the *Studienpartitur*), for as Ursula tells Regina at the beginning of the seventh, and final, tableau:

> Als er zurückkam,
> Ergoß sich in unbändigem Strom sein Schaffen. Im wirren
> Taumeln des Höhersteigens gebar er Tat um Tat, nahm
> Unmenschlichen Laufs die Gipfel des Tuns, entreißt

---

65 Music, as described in this passage, seems to function as a kind of *biblia pauperum*.

66 In both operas, period style and flavor take the place of local color.

> Fast dem Schöpfer Geheimnisse des Gebärens, die ihren
> Raffenden Entdecker blenden. (Hindemith *Mathis*, VII i)
>
> (When he returned,
> his creativity was unleashed as if in a torrent. In the mounting chaotic
> frenzy of this ascent he was in a productive fever, scaled
> the summit of his activities with uncanny speed, and almost snatched
> from the Creator the secret of parturition,
> which blinds the rapacious discoverer.)

In contrast to *Palestrina*, *Mathis der Maler* allows for an indeterminate period of gestation to intervene between the conception and the execution of the pictorial masterpiece, during which the visions are gradually absorbed and the pictorial ensemble takes shape in the artist's mind.

In the first segment of the *Bildbeschreibung*, the account of Mathis's painting, though suffused with interpretative matter, is rather straightforward, and the narrator causes the beholder's eye to travel from one point of the angelic triangle to the other in an order that is somewhat idiosyncratic but, on the whole, compelling:

> Der eine geigt
> Mit wundersam gesperrtem Arm,
> Den Bogen wägt
> Er zart, damit nicht eines wenigen Schattens Rauheit
> Den linden Lauf trübe. Ein andrer streicht
> Gehobenen Blicks aus Saiten seine Freude.
> Verhaftet scheint der dritte dem fernen Geläute
> Seiner Seele und achtet leicht des Spiels. Wie bereit
> Er ist, zugleich zu hören und zu dienen! (Hindemith *Mathis*, VI i; see fig. 1)
>
> (One plays the fiddle
> with a stiffly held arm
> and moves the bow delicately,
> so as to keep the least shadow of roughness
> from marring its gentle action. Another, with uplifted eyes,
> strokes his joy from the strings.
> A third seems spellbound by the distant chimes
> of his soul and pays scant attention to his playing. How eager
> he is to hear and serve concurrently!)

In this opening portion of the narrative, sight, movement, and sound are correlated in such a way as to alternate rather than intersect; in its sequel, however, sight and sound interpenetrate to create a synesthetic fusion:

Fig. 1: Detail from the "Engelkonzert". From the Isenheim altarpiece at Colmar, France.

Ihr Kleid selbst musiziert mit ihnen.
In schillernden Federn schwirrt der Töne Gegenspiel.
Ein leichter Panzer unirdischen Metalls erglüht
Berührt von Wogen des Klanges wie vom Beben
Bewegten Herzens, und im Zusammenklang viel
Bunter Lichterkreise wird aus kaum gehörtem Lied
Auf wunderbare Weise sichtbares Formenleben[67]. (Hindemith *Mathis*, VI i)

(Even their dress joins in the music-making.
The interplay of sounds whirrs in irridescent plumes.
A light coat of armor made of unearthly metal glows,
touched by the waves of sound as by the throbbing
of an excited heart. And in the harmony of many
bright circles of light a barely audible song
turns miraculously into the visible life of forms.)

In the concluding portion, the synesthesia that characterized the middle section is replaced by another kind of *symphonein*, in which art and religion enter into an alliance with music and prayer that leads to an ecstatic epiphany:

Wie diese ihr klingendes Werk verrichten,
So beten andre. Mit weichen Füßen treten
Sie auf weicheren Stufen der Töne, und du
Weißt nicht: musizieren, die Gebete dichten,
Oder hörst du der Musikanten Beten?
Ist so Musik Gebet geworden, hört lauschend zu
Natur. Ein Rest des Schimmers solcher Sphären
Mög' unser dunkles Tun verklären[68]. (Hindemith *Mathis*, VI i; see also Plebe, 227)

(As these perform their melodious task,
others pray. With soft feet they step on
softer steps of sound; and one
cannot tell whether those who write prayers make music
or whether one hears the musicians' prayers.
When music has thus been transformed into prayer, nature listens
attentively. May a vestige of the glowing of such spheres
transfigure our dark doings.)

---

67 The phrase "kaum gehörtem Lied" ('barely audible song') may indicate that Regina has 'entered' the picture and is fully at one with its content.

68 "Weichere Stufen der Töne" seems to allude to music's technical vocabulary. Plebe, in referring to Hindemith's penchant for tonality (227), speaks of his preference for "Stufengänge armonici" ('harmonic step-progression').

At this point Regina, who has joined Mathis with two lines from the song ("Die Welt ist erfüllt von göttlichem Schall,/ Im Herzen der Menschen ein Widerhall" ['The world resounds with divine sound,/ an echo in the hearts of men']), quietly (*unbemerkt*) disappears and yields the stage to an allegory, or 'morality', which unfolds in a setting that, as the stage directions note, constitutes "ein Bild nach der Art süddeutscher Maler" ('a picture in the style of South German painters'), perhaps in the style of Albrecht Altdorfer and the *Donau-Schule*[69] (Hindemith *Studienpartitur* 1965: 416, fn. 5). Mathis now exchanges his role as narrator for that of participant and, as long as Hindemith's version of the *Everyman* story lasts, lies on the ground "in der Gestalt des Hl. Antonius", verbally interacting with the transposed *dramatis personae* – all, that is, except Regina and Riedinger[70].

Within the allegory, which takes the symmetrical form of a triptych, the focus is clearly on Ursula, the person nearest and dearest to Mathis' heart, who appears in the triple role of Beggar, Harlot, and Martyr. This progression echoes, by synopsizing, the major facets of her relationship with the painter. The central panel in which she figures is flanked by Luxury (*Gräfin*) and Power (*Pommersfelden*) on the left and Science (*Capito*) and War (*Schwalb*) on the right. Unlike the visions that follow, this preliminary vision will not be recorded in a tangible work of art; for such works, if genuinely felt, result wholly from anxieties experienced in the abyss of a mind wracked by its own aesthetic hubris:

> Der ärgste Feind sitzt in dir
> Selbst. Ist dir die Gabe, Dinge zu sehen, sieh'
> Nicht zu genau hin.
> Kannst du denken, denke nicht zu Ende.
> Bezwinge dich, Letztes zu erfühlen.
> Kannst du dich nicht bescheiden, stößt dich zurück
> Das Leben, die Hölle nimmt dich auf. (Hindemith *Mathis*, V ii)

---

69 "Auch hier wie auf alten Bildern" ('Here, too, as in old pictures').

70 Regina, who is the figure closest to Mathis, is excluded from the allegory even in the sketch, where Riedinger still has a part (see Briner et al., eds., 125).

(Your worst enemy is within yourself.
If you have the gift of seeing,
don't look too closely.
If you can think, don't think things through.
Subdue excessive feelings.
If you don't learn to be modest, life will cast you out
and Hell take you in.)

Having passed through the inferno of his pictorial imaginings, Mathis-Anthony rebounds and finds himself translated into a third panel of his still-to-be-created masterpiece[71], the conversation with Albrecht-Paulus who, gently raising him from the ground and inviting him to an animated conversation, reconstructs approximately the scene of the altarpiece ("ungefähr die Szene des Altarbildes")[72] (see Waddell, ed., 47-50). Their extended dialogue (during which, in contrast to the earlier outline of the plot [Briner et al., eds., 125], Mathis-Anthony is a listener rather than an interlocutor) revolves around the artist's, specifically Grünewald's, true vocation. At its conclusion the two speakers, presumably retransformed into their proper selves, find themselves once again in broad daylight and at the very spot where we left them at the end of the second tableau: "Die Landschaft verwandelt sich abermals. Man sieht im hellsten Morgenlichte die Stadt Mainz und den Rhein" ('The landscape changes once more, as the city of Mainz and the Rhine become visible in broad sunlight'). One cycle has now been completed and, as the Cardinal and the painter sing in unison, "Dem Kreis, der uns geboren hat, können wir/ Nicht entrinnen, auf allen Wegen/ Schreiten wir stets in ihn hinein" ('We cannot escape from the circle/ into which we were born,/ for we enter it wherever we go'), the curtain falls over the penultimate tableau.

In the seventh and final *Bild*, Albrecht, who has withdrawn from the world, just as Ursula, in her own way ("Mitten im Treiben will ich

---

71 The fourth panel, "Grablegung", which adumbrates Regina's death and Mathis's abdication, is musically circumscribed but not envisioned.
72 "The Life of St. Paul, the First Hermit" was penned by St. Jerome, and "The Life and Affairs of Our Holy Father Anthony" by Athanasius. Their encounter is described by Jerome and summarized in Jacobus de Voragine's *Golden Legend*, entry for 10 January.

ausharren,/ Will geben und helfen./ Bis zum letzten starren/ Gedanken will ich mich enteignen" [Hindemith *Mathis*, IV iii; 'I will persevere in the midst of life's hustle and bustle,/ will give and help,/ yielding myself up to the last breath']), has withdrawn from hers, pays a final visit to Mathis who, at his patron's departure, is preparing for voluntary exile in anonymity. His *Erdenpensum* accomplished and his creative powers drained, the painter buries the symbolic tokens of his life and art in a chest, enacting a farewell that completes the double analogy, matching the corresponding actions of the woman he loved and the man who protected him. (No such parallel prevails in Pfitzner's opera, since Borromeo, its Albrecht figure, can hardly be regarded as a partner, much less a double. Although a patron and friend, he remains the 'other'. Furthermore the role of Ighino is incompatible with that of Ursula: at the end of the 'musical legend', Ighino 'deserts' his father and runs out into the street to celebrate Palestrina's belated triumph.)

In both *Palestrina,* whose protagonist survives to enter history, if only as a somewhat hazy legendary figure, and *Mathis der Maler,* whose protagonist plunges into anonymity and resurfaces only after a long hiatus, the work takes precedence over its maker, and the *Personenkult* of the Renaissance is replaced, though in varying degree, by a *Werkkult* that spurns excessive individualism. What both Pfitzner and Hindemith proclaim through their respective masterpieces might be subsumed under the familiar acclamation, modified to suit the circumstances: Palestrina and Grünewald are dead; long live the *Missa Papae Marcelli* and the Isenheim altarpiece!

Works cited

Abendroth, Walter. *Hans Pfitzner.* Munich: Langen-Müller, 1935.
Adamy, Bernhard. "Das *Palestrina*-Textbuch als Dichtung". *Symposium Hans Pfitzner Berlin 1981: Tagungsbericht.* Ed. Wolfgang Osthoff. Tutzing: Schneider, 1984. 59-65.

Auden, W. H. "Some Reflections on Music and Opera". *Partisan Review* 19 (1952): 10-18.
Bokina, John. "Resignation, Retreat, and Impotence: The Aesthetics and Politics of the Modern German Artist-Opera". *Cultural Critique* (Spring 1988): 157-195.
Borchmeyer, Dieter. *Die Weimarer Klassik: Eine Einführung*. Frankfurt a. M.: Athenäum, 1980. 123-128.
Briner, A., D. Rexroth, G. Schubert, eds. *Paul Hindemith: Leben und Werk in Bild und Text*. Zurich: Atlantis/Mainz: Schott, 1988.
Bulthaupt, Heinrich. *Dramaturgie des Schauspiels*. Vol. 3. Oldenburg/Leipzig: Schulz, 1902.
Burkhard, Artur. *Matthias Grünewald: Personality and Accomplishment*. Cambridge, MA: Harvard UP, 1963. Rpt. 1976.
Busoni, Ferruccio. *Neue Ästhetik der Tonkunst*. Leipzig: Insel, 1910.
Fehn, Ann Clark, ed. *Gottfried Benn: Briefwechsel mit Paul Hindemith*. Wiesbaden: Limes, 1978.
Goethe, Wolfgang von. *Briefe der Jahre 1786-1814*. Zurich: Artemis, 1949.
—. *Torquato Tasso: Ein Schauspiel*. Stuttgart: Reclam, 1962.
Goldschmidt, Helene. *Das deutsche Künstlerdrama von Goethe bis R. Wagner*. Weimar: Duncker, 1925.
Grillparzer, Franz. "Anmerkungen". *Sämtliche Werke*. Eds. Peter Frank, Karl Poinbacher. Vol. 1. Munich: Hanser, 1960. 1307-1310.
—. "*Sappho*: Entwurf eines Briefes an Müllner" (1818). *Sämtliche Werke*. 5th ed. Ed. August Sauer. Vol. 18. Stuttgart: Cotta, [n. d.] 173-178.
Grimm, Reinhold. "Dichter-Helden: *Tasso, Empedokles* und die Folgen". *Jahrbuch für deutsche Gegenwartsliteratur* 7 (1977): 7-25.
Hebbel, Friedrich. *Sämtliche Werke*. Historisch-kritische Ausgabe. Ed. R. M. Werner. Vol. 11. Berlin: Behr, 1903. 345-349.
Hindemith, Paul. *Briefe*. Ed. Dieter Rexroth. Frankfurt a. M.: Fischer Taschenbuch, 1982.
—. *Mathis der Maler: Oper in sieben Bildern*. Studienpartitur. Mainz: Schott, [n. d.].
—. "Zur Einführung". Rpt. Andress Briner. *Paul Hindemith*. Zurich: Atlantis; Mainz: Schott, 1971. 136-138.
Kohler, Stephan. "Der Komponist als Opernheld: Zur Gattungstradition von Pfitzners *Palestrina*". *Programmheft der Bayerischen Staatsoper*, 1979.

Kriss, Rudolf. *Die Darstellung des Konzils von Trient in Hans Pfitzners "Musikalischer Legende"* Palestrina. Munich: Selbstverlag, 1962.

Kunze, Stefan. "Zeitschichten in Pfitzners *Palestrina*". Ed. Wolfgang Osthoff. *Symposium Hans Pfitzner: Berlin 1981. Tagungsbericht.* Tutzing: Schneider, 1984. 69-82.

Paulding, James E. "*Mathis der Maler*: The Politics of Music". *Hindemith-Jahrbuch* 5 (1976): 102-122.

Pfitzner, Hans. "Der zweite Akt *Palestrina*: Ein Vermächtnis und eine Abwehr". *Mitteilungen der Hans Pfitzner-Gesellschaft* 19 (1967): 5-10.

—. "Futuristengefahr". *Gesammelte Schriften.* Vol. 1. Augsburg: Filsner, 1926. 185-223.

—. "Mein Hauptwerk: Ein Beitrag zur Hamburgischen Neuinszenierung von 1937". Rpt. *Programmheft der Hamburgischen Staatsoper*, 18 Nov. 1979.

—. "*Palestrina*: Ein Vortrag über das Werk und seine Geschichte". *Reden, Schriften und Briefe: Unveröffentlichtes und bisher Verstreutes.* Ed. Walter Abendroth. Berlin: Luchterhand, 1955. 23-34.

—. *Palestrina: Musikalische Legende in drei Akten.* Studienpartitur. Ed. Joseph Keilberth. Mainz: Schott, [n. d.].

—. "Philosophie und Dichtungen in meinem Leben" (1914). *Reden, Schriften und Briefe: Unveröffentlichtes und bisher Verstreutes.* Ed. Walter Abendroth. Berlin: Luchterhand, 1955.

Plebe, Armando. "Il problema del linguaggio melodrammatico nel *Mathis* di Hindemith". *La Rassegna Musicale* 32 (1962): 224-232.

Rectanus, Hans. *Leitmotivik und Form in den musikdramatischen Werken Hans Pfitzners.* Würzburg: Triltsch, 1967.

Schubert, Giselher. *Paul Hindemith: Bildmonographie.* Hamburg: Rowohlt, 1981.

Seebohm, Richard. "Triumph und Tragik des Künstlertums: Die Stellung von Pfitzners *Palestrina* in der Geschichte des deutschen Künstlerdramas". *Mitteilungen der Hans Pfitzner-Gesellschaft* 32 (1974): 10-35.

Tieck, Ludwig. "*Correggio* von Oehlenschläger". *Kritische Schriften.* Vol. 4. Leipzig: Brockhaus, [n. d.]. 270-312.

Waddell, Helen, ed. *The Desert Fathers.* London: Constable, 1936.

Wagner, Richard. *Die Meistersinger von Nürnberg.* Complete Vocal and Orchestral Score. New York: Dover, 1976.

—. "Mitteilung an meine Freunde". *Dichtungen und Schriften.* Ed. Dieter Borchmeyer. Vol. 6. Frankfurt a. M.: Insel, 1983.

Wamlek-Junk, Elisabeth. *Hans Pfltzner und Wien: Sein Briefwechsel mit Victor Junk und andere Dokumente.* Tutzing: Schneider, 1986. 169-181.

Weinmann, Karl. *Das Konzil von Trient und die Kirchenmusik.* Leipzig: Breitkopf & Haertel, 1919.

Weisstein, Ulrich. *The Essence of Opera.* New York: Free Press, 1964. Paperback ed., New York: Norton, 1969.

—. "Librettology: The Fine Art of Coping with a Chinese Twin". *Komparatistische Hefte* 5/6 (1982): 23-42.

Wilmsmeier, Wilhelm. *Camoens in der deutschen Dichtung des 19. Jahrhunderts.* Diss. Erfurt, 1913.

Wohlke, Franz. *Mathis der Maler.* Berlin-Lichterfelde: Lienau, 1965.

Worringer, Wilhelm. *Abstraktion und Einfühlung.* Munich: Piper, 1908.

—. *Formprobleme der Gothik.* Munich: Piper, 1911.

Zuelch, Werner K. *Grünewald: Mathis Gothardt-Neithardt.* 2nd ed. Munich: Münchner Verlag, [n. d.].

Between Progress and Regression
The Text of Stravinsky's Opera *The Rake's Progress* in the Light of its Evolution (1992)

> You know how justly esteemed Da Ponte is for his libretto of *Don Giovanni*. The result of the collaboration between Auden and Kallman is, in my opinion, as good if not better.
> (Igor Stravinsky)[1]

I.

Auden/Kallman/Stravinsky's opera *The Rake's Progress,* premiered on September 11, 1951, at the Teatro La Fenice in Venice[2], has long (and justly) been regarded as a classic of twentieth-century musical theater and as a prime example of neoclassical opera in the epic vein[3]. It is one of the very few contemporary examples of the genre which have entered the international repertory[4]; and at least four complete recordings, three of them conducted by the composer, have been issued

---

1 From Stravinsky's conversation with Emilia Zanetti, published in conjunction with the Venice premiere as part of a pamphlet entitled *Guida al "The Rake's Progress"*. A German version of the interview appeared in *Musik in der Zeit: Igor Stravinsky* (Bonn, 1952); it was reprinted in Bertolt Brecht/Kurt Weill, *Die Dreigroschenoper* – Igor Stravinsky, *The Rake's Progress*, ed. Attila Csampai and Dietmar Holland [Csampai/Holland] (Hamburg: Rowohlt/Ricordi, 1987), 244-248; here: 246.

2 The production, mounted by Carl Ebert, was conducted by the composer. The cast included Elisabeth Schwarzkopf, Jennie Tourel, Hugues Cuenod, and Robert Rounseville.

3 The 'epic' quality of Stravinsky's work for the theater, understood in the Brechtian sense, is the subject of Carl Dahlhaus' essay "Igor Strawinskijs episches Theater" in: *Beiträge zur Musikwissenschaft* 23 (1981), 163-188. *The Rake's Progress* figures on pp. 179-181.

4 I was fortunate enough to see several performances of the work in productions mounted by the Opera Theater of the School of Music at Indiana University in Bloomington.

over the years[5]. Whatever one may think of its artistic worth[6], there can be little doubt that, in spite of its highly controversial nature, the piece, viewed as a whole[7], offers a rare instance of the successful fusion – or, more aptly, combination – of three arts and, as such, is matched perhaps only by Hofmannsthal/Strauss' *Der Rosenkavalier*, which, being a sort of companion piece, harks back to a Hogarth series as well[8].

Given the unique place which *The Rake's Progress* – stylistically, a curious but deliberately contrived mixture of progressive and conservative/reactionary tendencies, especially in the musical realm[9] –

---

5   An annotated discography is found on pp. 313f. of Csampai/Holland.

6   The title of a program note written for the 1964 recording of *The Rake's Progress* reads, characteristically: "The Composer's View, in which the Author Asks for a Moratorium on Value Judgments". The text of this note, included in the booklet accompanying this Columbia recording, is reproduced in the Cambridge Opera Handbook on Stravinsky's opera that was edited by Paul Griffiths [Griffiths] (Cambridge: Cambridge University Press, 1982), 2-3. The booklet also offers similarly critical reflections ("Looking and Thinking Back") by Chester Kallman.

7   Wholeness, in this case, does not signify 'total work of art' in the Wagnerian sense, which Stravinsky vehemently rejected, but in the modern sense of a montage-like assemblage of divergent elements. In his conversations with Emilia Zanetti (Csampai/Holland, 247), the composer confessed: "I have always been interested in the opera but utterly dislike the music drama, [which] cannot generate a tradition. It is, rather, the total absence of form; and I am totally indifferent to art that is non-canonic." (My transl., U.W.)

8   *Der Rosenkavalier* is based on Hogarth's *Marriage-à-la-mode,* as well as being indebted to sundry French literary sources. For the Hogarth connection, see Mary E. Gilbert, "Painter and Poet: Hogarth's *Marriage-à-la-mode* and Hofmannsthal's *Der Rosenkavalier*" in: *Modern Language Review* 64 (1969), 818-827. – For comparative treatments of the Hogarth connections in both operas see especially: Joseph Kiermeier-Debre, "Wie Bilder laufen lernen: Hogarths Graphik-Zyklen und ihre poetischen Um-Malungen durch Hugo von Hofmannsthal und W.H. Auden" in: *Maske + Kothurn* 31 (1985), 203-218, and Frieder Busch, *"The Rake's Progress* von Hogarth zu Strawinsky" in: *Scholastic Midwifery: Studien zum Satirischen in der englischen Literatur 1600-1800,* ed. Jan E. Peters (Tübingen: Narr, 1989), 139-166.

9   In this respect, the following excerpt from Stravinsky's program note (fn. 6) is symptomatic:

>   Can a composer re-use the past and at the same time move in a forward direction? Regardless of the answer (which is 'yes'), this academic question did not trouble me during the composition, nor will I argue it now, though the supposed back-

occupies in the cultural landscape of our century, it is not surprising that a rich crop of secondary literature concerning it has shot up in the four decades which have passed since it first reached the boards which, proverbially, signify/symbolize the world. In my modest, and limited, contribution to this *Festschrift* honoring Professor Ulla-Britta Lagerroth, who has done so much for the institutionalization of the Comparative Arts in Sweden, I shall not aim at offering a survey or providing a *bibliographie raisonée* of the scholarly endeavors seeking to shed light on the work from different angles. Rather, in order to stake my claim for adding a fresh voice to the large chorus, I shall begin, *ex negativo*, by briefly explaining what I want to avoid, so as not to duplicate work already done.

First of all, then, in what follows I shall not make a musical analysis of *The Rake's Progress* – a task for which I am not qualified, at any rate – along the lines suggested by such experts as Wolfgang Burde, Deryck Cooke, Harald Kaufmann, Roman Vlad, and Eric Walter White[10]. On the other side of the ledger, I shall refrain from indulging in a strictly literary or *literaturhistorisch* interpretation of the text, such as John G. Blair and Monroe K. Spears, among others, have already undertaken[11]. Nor will I trespass on Barbara Engelbert's terri-

---

ward step of The Rake has taken on a radically forward-looking complexion when I have compared it with some more recent progressive operas.

10 Wolfgang Burde, "Zur Musik in Strawinskys *Rake's Progress*" in: W. B., *Strawinsky: Eine Monographie* (Mainz: Schott, 1982); as reprinted in Csampai/Holland, 296-301; Deryck Cooke, "*The Rake* and the 18th Century" in: *The Musical Times* 103 (1962), 20-23; Harald Kaufmann, "Ausverkauf der alten Oper: Notizen zu Strawinsky" in: H. K., *Spurlinien* (Vienna: Lafitte, 1969), as reprinted in Csampai/Holland, 289-295; Roman Vlad, "Culmination and End of Neo-Classicism: *The Rake's Progress*", chapter XIX of R. V., *Stravinsky*, tr. Frederick Fuller, third ed. (London/New York: Oxford University Press, 1978), 165-172; and Eric Walter White, *Stravinsky: The Composer and his Work* (Berkeley/Los Angeles: The University of California Press, 1969), 412-428. Some of the Russian sources, especially Tchaikovsky's influence on Stravinsky, are discussed in the volume *Stravinsky Retrospectives*, ed. Ethan Haimo and Paul Johnson (Lincoln: University of Nebraska Press, 1987).

11 See chapter VI ("Opera: *The Rake's Progress*") of John G. Blair's book *The Poetic Art of W. H. Auden* (Princeton: Princeton University Press 1965), 154-184, and

tory as regards her very useful and illuminating comparison between Auden's poetological reflections on opera and his own librettological practice[12]. This will not keep me, however, from pointing out that Engelbert has gone about her, perfectly legitimate, business without realizing, or demonstrating, that Auden's melo-dramaturgical views are highly eclectic and show him to be a past master of the hallowed cliché. (For the rest, it should be noted that these reflections, often taking the form of brilliant quips and neatly phrased aperçus, would seem to be a direct outgrowth, or byproduct, of the work on the libretto of *The Rake's Progress*[13].)

Finally, and still speaking in the literary vein, I shall refrain from dwelling on the exact nature and scope of Auden's collaboration with Chester Kallman, which Stravinsky at first grudgingly tolerated but later welcomed[14]. As regards the division of labor between them, at any rate, Auden himself furnished concrete and detailed evidence in a

---

chapter IV of Monroe K. Spears' monograph *The Poetry of W. H. Auden: The Disenchanted Island* (New York: Oxford University Press, 1963), 262-289.

12 See section B ("Audens Operntheorie: Seine Auffassung von der Musik im allgemeinen, der Oper im besonderen, dem Wesen des Librettos [und] der Opernübersetzung") in: Barbara Engelbert [Engelbert], *Wystan Hugh Auden (1907-1973): Seine opernästhetische Anschauung und seine Tätigkeit als Librettist* (Regensburg: Bosse, 1983), 36-132, and the application to *The Rake's Progress* on pp. 173-210. My essay "Reflections on a Golden Style: W. H. Auden's Theory of Opera" was published in *Comparative Literature* 22 (1970), 108-124.

13 The principal source of information about Auden's views on opera is his text "Some Reflections on Music and Opera", which exists in different versions. Originally published in the British journal *Tempo* (No. 20, Summer, 1951), its 'classic' formulation is that found in *The Partisan Review* 19 (1952), 10-18, as reprinted in *The Essence of Opera*, ed. Ulrich Weisstein [Weisstein] (New York: Norton, 1969), 354-360. See also "Notes on Music and Opera" in: W. H. A., *The Dyer's Hand and Other Essays* (London: Faber and Faber, 1963), 465-474.

14 In a letter dated January 16, 1948, Auden announced that he had "taken in a collaborator, an old friend of mine in whose talents I have the greatest confidence": Stravinsky, *Selected Correspondence [Corr.]*, ed. Robert Craft (New York: Knopf, 1982), 304. Stravinsky met Kallman for the first time on April 5, 1948, and, in Craft's words, "was immediately won by his intelligence and sense of humor". (Quoted from "The Poet and *The Rake*", an essay included in *W. H. Auden – A Tribute*, ed. Stephen Spender (London, 1974), 149-155.)

letter to Stravinsky's associate, Robert Craft[15]; yet, as Paul Griffiths shrewdly maintains, "it is extremely doubtful [...] whether anyone would be able to detect the two voices without being told which is which"[16]. Taking this cue, I shall, exceptions duly noted, treat the jointly written libretto, though not, of course, the Scenario which preceded it, as being, for all practical purposes, homogeneous.

Downplaying, though by no means ignoring, the various approaches catalogued above, I shall, in the first segment of my paper, trace the genesis of the *Rake* text chronologically from the moment of inception to the completion of the libretto. The, astonishingly brief, time span covering both the gestation and the execution of the opera's literary foundation can be divided into three stages, namely

a) the phase extending from the moment of inspiration to the first meeting between composer and poet (May to early November, 1947);

b) the phase during which the Scenario was jointly redacted (November 11 to 18, 1947)[17];

c) the phase which saw the expansion and transformation of the Scenario into the libretto (late November, 1947, to March, 1948).

These preliminary but necessary steps having been taken, I shall proceed to my principal task, which is that of comparing the two texts[18] –

---

15 The letter, written on February 10, 1959, was first published in the volume *Stravinsky in Pictures and Documents*, ed. Vera Stravinsky and Robert Craft (New York: Simon & Schuster, 1978). It is reprinted, though not quite accurately, in Griffiths, 14. See the corrections presented in chapter X of Stephen Walsh's book *The Music of Stravinsky* (London: Routledge, 1988). For a brief account of the initial difficulties in the collaboration see Kallman's retrospective glance in the libretto booklet mentioned in fn. 6.

16 "The Makers and Their Work" in: Griffiths, 14. In his essay "Translating Opera Libretti" (*The Dyer's Hand*, 483) Auden speaks of his collaboration with Kallman in terms of a "corporate personality".

17 The Scenario is reproduced in Igor Stravinsky and Robert Craft, *Memories and Commentaries* [*Memories*] (New York: Doubleday, 1960), 167-176. In his essay "A Note on the Sketches and the Two Versions of the Libretto" (Griffiths, 18-30, specifically 20 and 27), Craft offers a few corrections to that text.

Scenario and libretto – with the intention of showing what changes were made for what reasons, and what esthetic conclusions can be drawn from the numerous modifications which, so Stravinsky claimed[19], were largely Auden's work[20].

The moment of incitation arrived on May 2, 1947, when Stravinsky, a permanent resident of the United States since 1939, visited an exhibition of English art at the Chicago Art Institute and found himself engrossed by William Hogarth's eight-part series dating, roughly, from 1733[21]. In chapter III of *Memories and Commentaries*, responding to a question posed by his *adlatus* – "How did you come to choose *The Rake's Progress* as the subject?" – he stated: "Hogarth's paintings immediately suggested a series of operatic scenes to me. I was [...] readily susceptible to such a suggestion, for I had wanted to compose an opera in English ever since my arrival in the United States" (154). He waxed more eloquent in his conversation with

---

18 The comparison is not entirely unprecedented, as Barbara Engelbert offers a scene-by-scene description relating Hogarth's engravings, the Scenario and the Libretto to each other (157-173). But she does so rather mechanically and without addressing the question from a broader critical perspective.

19 In his conversation with Emilia Zanetti (Csampai/Holland, 246), Stravinsky maintains that Auden was responsible for [all?] deviations from Hogarth's 'plot': "Die Varianten zur Handlung Hogarths sind ihm [Auden] zuzuschreiben". At the same time, he claimed [out of false modesty or courtesy?] that the Scenario, too, was the work of the English poet: "In einer Woche schrieb er mir den Entwurf zur Handlung". – This, naturally, raises the perennial problem encountered in any attempt to determine the exact share of composers and librettists in the writing of operatic texts whenever, as in *Don Giovanni* and *Die Zauberflöte*, no documentation is available. The written exchanges between Verdi and Boito, on the one hand, and Strauss and Hofmannsthal, on the other, are exceptions that prove the rule.

20 By using the collective "we" – "our subject", "our fable", etc. – in an article he wrote for the New York *Herald Tribune* of February 8, 1953, entitled "New Stravinsky Opera: *The Rake's Progress* to have its American Premiere on Saturday", Chester Kallman, on the other hand, takes it for granted that theirs was a true collaboration.

21 It is not quite clear whether Stravinsky was inspired by the paintings, as he maintains, or by the engravings on which the paintings were based, as both Auden and Robert Craft assert. – For information about Hogarth see Ronald Paulson, *Hogarth's Graphic Works*, red. ed. in two volumes (New Haven/London: Yale University Press, 1970) and the same author's *Hogarth: His Life, Art, and Times* in two volumes (New Haven/London: Yale University Press, 1971).

Emilia Zanetti. Once again fording a question ("Welche Art Anruf, *provocatio*, kam Ihnen aus den Stichen Hogarths? War er visueller oder logisch-dramatischer Art?") he, an "Augenmensch" par excellence[22], asserted:

> Bühnenmäßiger Art vor allem. In der Kunst Hogarths berührte mich vor allem der Charakter des Theatermäßigen, der sich wunderbar auf die Bühne übertragen läßt; ein Charakter, der sich in jener Neigung zur Erzählung mittels einer Reihe von Bildern mit einer bestimmten Moral offenbart, die ich wahren wollte. Deshalb habe ich [...] den ursprünglichen Titel der von mir ausgewählten Bilderreihe beibehalten[23].

Auden, who thought that "any visual art is so different from music that you have almost to start again"[24], felt that only two of the pictures constituting Hogarth's series – The Brothel [#2] and Bedlam [#8] – were suited for dramatic ends because, on the whole, it had been the artist's "main concern [...] to make a series of pictures satirizing various aspects of life in eighteenth-century London" in which it is the hero's "only function [...] to give [...] a certain unity by appearing in them all"[25]. (It can be assumed, but not proved, that the rejection, in principle, of the other settings was Auden's choice, and that it was relatively easy to convince Stravinsky of its justness.) This is not to say, however, that the remaining *tableaux* simply fell by the wayside; for the librettists borrowed many other features, including some of the principal characters, from their pictorial model using, and reshaping, them for their own melo-dramaturgical ends. Thus Rakewell's guard-

---

22 The appeal to the sense of vision suited an artist like Stravinsky, who, throughout his career, excelled in writing music for the ballet. Thus, in discussing the genesis of *L'Histoire du Soldat*, he wrote in his *Autobiography* of 1936: "I have always had a horror of listening to music with my eyes shut, with nothing for them to do."

23 Csampai/Holland, 244. In the same interview, he justified his choice of *La carriera* (*Laufbahn*, career) *d'un libertino* as the Italian title of his opera by referring to the ambiguity of 'progress' understood in the double sense of *Fortschreiten* and *Fortschritt*.

24 From an unpublished BBC Third Programme talk on *The Rake's Progress* broadcast on August 28, 1953, as quoted in Engelbert, 152.

25 W. H. Auden, "The Mythical World of Opera", *Times Literary Supplement* [*TLS*] of November 2, 1967, 1038. Kallman, too, regarded the Hogarth series as a mere 'framework'.

ian angel, Sarah Young, became Anne Truelove, and the old, one-eyed widow whom Tom is seen marrying in Plate #5 was scotched in favor of Baba the Turk. Thus only the distinctly Mephistophelian double, Nick Shadow[26], has no precedent in the Hogarth sequence, which Auden tartly described as a "bourgeois cautionary tale"[27], but completes the trinity of *dramatis personae* in the Morality Play, as an eighteenth-century version of which the playwright came to regard his libretto[28]. (One should note in passing that, as Gabriel Josipovici has pointed out, Stravinsky was, as it were, on intimate terms with the Devil, whom he and his librettist Charles-Ferdinand Ramuz had put to excellent use in their post-World War I *Story of a Soldier*.)

A thematic link with *L'Histoire du Soldat* is also provided by the fiddle, which, in the latter work, the Devil acquires from the Soldier in exchange for the book that functions both as a safe and as a daily register of the Stock Market[29]. As a musical instrument, the violin is, naturally, an ideal operatic prop, especially, that is to say, if it acquires dramaturgical significance. In fact, one of the details in Hogarth's final *tableau* is a blind man playing a one-string fiddle. It immediately caught the eye of the composer, whose first letter to Auden included the suggestion: "As the end of any work is of importance, I think that

---

26 The linkage with Goethe's Mephisto figure shows up in a number of ways, most strikingly perhaps in the various asides (*ad spectatores*) which Shadow addresses to the audience.

27 As Auden put it in a contribution to the February, 1953, issue of *Harper's Bazaar*, "The Rake's Progress, as depicted by Hogarth, is a bourgeois cautionary tale; its twin is the story of the virtuous apprentice who is never late for work, saves his pennies and finally marries the master's daughter. Wine, Women, and Cards are to be avoided, not because debauchery is wrong in itself but because it lowers the bank balance. Chastity is the child of economic Abstinence." (165)

28 "If he [Tom Rakewell] was to have any mythical resonance, though settings, costumes and diction might be eighteenth-century, he would have to be an embodiment of Everyman and the libretto a mixture of fairy story and medieval morality play"; *TLS*, 1038.

29 "C'est un livre, je vais vous dire,/ qui se lit tout seul: il se lit pour vous./ On n'a qu'à l'ouvrir, on sait tout./ C'est un livre, c'est un coffre-fort./ On n'a qu'à l'ouvrir, on tire dehors [...]/ Des titres! Des billets/ de l'or." Quoted from *L'Histoire du Soldat/ Die Geschichte vom Soldaten* (St. Gallen: Tschudy Verlag, 1961), 10.

the hero's end in an asylum scratching a fiddle would make a meritorious conclusion to his stormy life. Don't you think so?" (*Corr.* I, 299). Auden considered the notion of an "Asylum finale" to be quite apropos but, broadening the perspective, wondered whether it might not be appropriate to have the motif "run through the story" (ibid., 300).

In the end, the violin, though not altogether dropped, was – at whose instigation? – reduced to the minor role which it plays in Hogarth's series, figuring only in the stage directions for III, 3, which call for "a blind man with a broken fiddle, a crippled soldier, a man with a telescope and three old hags". Thus the tie with *L'Histoire du Soldat* was broken, at least in this respect; and, what is worse from the melo-dramaturgical point of view, the plan, not specifically mentioned by either the composer or his librettists, to present Tom Rakewell as the New Orpheus was aborted in favor of a design to depict him as the New Adonis. Yet, as Auden observes, the effort, though ultimately in vain, had not been wasted; for it was precisely that tangential figure which had excited the composer's imagination: "In the opera he actually wrote there is no such figure, but as a sidelight on the way the creative mind works the anecdote has interest."[30]

Having found a subject entirely to his liking, Stravinsky began to cast about for a suitable librettist – one, that is to say, who would be willing (and able) to re-create in his own medium, language, a period style, just as he, the composer, casting a wider net and using less stringent historical analogies, would recapture, in a blatantly modern way, a musical tradition extending from Monteverdi by way of Handel to Mozart – his key witness – and beyond him all the way to Donizetti and Verdi[31]. His friend and Hollywood neighbor Aldous Huxley was

---

30 *TLS*, 1038.
31 There is no room in this paper for discussing the wide, willed, and provocative discrepancies between the music, on the one hand, and the text, the situations and the characters, on the other, which would lend themselves to a fruitful comparison with similarly ironic features in Brecht/Weill's *Dreigroschenoper*. Good examples of musical irony in *The Rake's Progress* are furnished by Anne Truelove's Stravinskyan (*Oedipus Rex*) *cabaletta* "I go to him" in I, 3, and, less stridently but no less effec-

consulted and warmly recommended W. H. Auden, the forty-year-old English poet/playwright then living in New York. Having enthusiastically responded to an overture made, on Stravinsky's behalf, by Ralph Hawkes[32], co-owner of the publishing house to which the composer entrusted all his scores, Auden was contacted by the Maestro, who, in a letter dated October 6, 1947, enjoined him to prepare "the general outline for a work consisting of two acts, maybe five [should read: seven] scenes (five for the first act and two for the second act)". (Eventually, i. e., after a realignment proposed by Auden[33], *The Rake's Progress* was to have three acts of three scenes each, although Stravinsky preferred, at times, a two-act version in which the caesura falls after II, 2[34].) Neither the Choreographic Divertissement at the end of Act I mentioned in Stravinsky's first letter nor the Aristophanic parabasis, modelled perhaps on a similar feature in T. S. Eliot's Aristophanic melodrama *Sweeney Agonistes*, to which Auden refers in his answer, came to fruition.

With musical considerations uppermost in his mind – for Stravinsky the rule *prima la musica e poi le parole* invariably took precedence over its opposite, *prima le parole e dopo la musica*[35] – the composer stipulated the use of a chamber music ensemble and seven vocal soloists (as against the ten Hawkes had suggested). In generic terms he made it plain that he wanted to write "not a musical drama [à la Wagner] but just an opera with definitely separate numbers connected by

---

tively so, the references to the Countess's first aria from *Le Nozze di Figaro* in which Tom's aria "Vary the Song" in II, 1, is instrumentally embedded.

32 Stravinsky's correspondence with Hawkes is found in Volume III of his *Selected Correspondence*.

33 On January 28, 1948, Auden wrote to Stravinsky: "Voici Acte II. It seemed best to transfer the auction scene to Act III, as that is where the time interval occurs"; *Memories*, 161.

34 Information given in Griffiths, 12. Eric Walter White corroborates the fact by stating that "this was the arrangement usually followed at Glyndebourne, for example" (416, fn. 1).

35 In his "Reflections on *The Rake's Progress*" (*The Score* 9 [1954], 27) Robert Craft calls Stravinsky a "'music first' composer".

spoken (not sung) words of the text because [he] want[ed] to avoid the customary operatic recitative"[36]. In pursuing this goal, he instructed Auden to prepare "a free verse preliminary for the characters (arias, duets, trios, etc.) as well as for a small chorus"[37]. In so doing, he treated his librettist-to-be as a mere "versifier with whom he could collaborate in writing songs, an unusal starting point for an opera". No wonder that Auden, with tongue in cheek, dubbed himself his *"syllabiste"*[38].

This, then, was the solid musical rock on which Auden's verbal edifice was to be erected according to the composer's blueprint. Indeed, if Stravinsky had had his way, as fortunately he did not (or not altogether), the verses the English poet submitted to him would hardly have appealed to a literate audience, as is actually the case, but would have merely served as a "private letter to the composer" which, "having had their moment of glory, the moment in which they suggest to him a certain melody", would have become "as expendable as infantry is to a Chinese general" by "effac[ing] themselves and cease to care what happens to them"[39].

The pre-Scenario phase of the genesis of *The Rake's Progress* ended when, having received Auden's favorable reply, dated October 12, 1947, Stravinsky invited him to California for an intensive work-

---

36 As it turned out, Stravinsky did not stick by this decision but freely and, from a melo-dramaturgical vista, significantly employed both *recitativo secco* (especially for Nick Shadow, the most 'prosaic' character in the cast) and *accompagnato*, as well as occasionally treating prose passages *arioso* style. As for the librettist's stance with regard to the two types of opera, see Auden's remarks: "Stravinsky wished to write an opera of the Mozart kind [...] This suited us fine since for a beginner it is technically easier to write a libretto for such conventions than a music drama of the Wagnerian type"; *TLS*, 1038.

37 Quoted in Igor Stravinsky and Robert Craft, *Themes and Episodes* (New York: Knopf, 1967), 96. The quotation continues: "I simply gave all priority to verse, hoping that we could evolve the theatrical form together and that it would inspire Wystan to dramatic poetry."

38 An undated letter by Auden, written in November, 1947, was sent "du syllabiste au compositeur"; *Corr.* I, 303.

39 Quoted in Weisstein, 359.

ing session. Auden gladly accepted the invitation and arrived on November 10. In *Memories and Commentaries*, the composer offers the following account of their *modus operandi* during this long initial encounter:

> Auden arrived at night [...] Early the next morning we began work on *The Rake's Progress*. Starting with a hero, a heroine and a villain, and deciding that these people should be a tenor, a soprano and a bass, we proceeded to invent a series of scenes leading up to the final scene in Bedlam that was already fixed in our minds. We followed Hogarth closely at first and until our own story began to assume a different significance.
>
> Mother Goose and the Ugly Duchess were Auden's contribution, of course, but the plot and the scene of action were worked out by the two of us together, step by step. We also tried to coordinate the plan of action with a provisional plan of musical pieces, arias, ensembles and choruses. Auden kept saying "Let's see now [...] ah ah ah [...] let's see [...] ah ah" and I the equivalent in Russian, but after ten [actually: eight] days we had completed an outline which is not radically different from the published libretto. (156f.)

The choice of the still generic triad of types – hero/tenor, heroine/soprano and villain/bass or, as Auden arranged them in their conceptual order, protagonist, antagonist/double and redeemer[40] –, being dictated by both musical and literary considerations, proves that the two artists worked hand-in-glove from the start; but Stravinsky's contention, mindlessly echoed in the critical literature[41], that the "outline [= Scenario] is not radically different from the published version" is a gross over-simplification, as shall be demonstrated in the final segment of this essay.

Another question, which, due to the lack of *prima facie* evidence, cannot be satisfactorily resolved, concerns the authorship of the Sce-

---

40 "So as Faust is accompanied by Mephisto, Tom Rakewell acquires a certain Nick Shadow. Now we had at least continuous roles for two singers. [...] As a counter for Nick Shadow we provided our hero with a guardian angel, Anne Truelove" (*TLS*, 1038). With the subsequent introduction of the Ugly Duchess/Baba the Turk, the foursome of major *dramatis personae* was complete. What has so far been ignored in the secondary literature is the fact that just as Shadow is Rakewell's *alter ego*, so both musically and dramatically Baba is the inverted mirror image, or caricature, of Anne Truelove.

41 Engelbert, 172, for example.

nario as reproduced on pp. 167-176 of *Memories and Commentaries*[42]. For a time I thought that the French passages, mostly dialogue, of which large chunks reappear almost verbatim in the libretto, had been written by Stravinsky, who, having spent a quarter of a century in the *Suisse Romande* and subsequently in France, was surely fluent in that language. But considering the fact that, as Stravinsky stated in his conversation with Emilia Zanetti (246), Auden "*schrieb* den Entwurf der Handlung in einer Woche" (italics mine; U.W.), and that some of Auden's letters to him are wholly or partly couched in somewhat halting French[43], I am now inclined to believe that the composer can be credited with the fourth column, which, under the general heading "Number", provides musical instructions such as "bruits choriques", "marche militaire", and "danse choquante", as well with the English labels "serenade", "nursery rhyme", and "lullaby" in the third column, entitled "Action" but actually concerned with dialogue. In neat separation of the co-authors' artistic functions, the remainder of the Scenario – Column 1 ("Place"), concerned with setting; Column 2 ("Characters"), concerned, oddly enough, with plot; and the bulk of Column 3 – would then be Auden's share at this initial stage of their collaboration.

In order to convey a notion of how this division of labor works, I reproduce the information which the Scenario provides for I, 3, of *The*

---

42 A critical analysis of some aspects of the Scenario, with some emendations and corrections, was provided by Robert Craft in his essay "A Note on the Sketches and the Two Versions of the Libretto" in: Griffiths, 18-30, esp. 27ff.

43 Thus the undated letter of November, 1947, reads as follows: "Je crois que ce sera mieux si c'est un oncle inconnu de l'hero [sic] au lieu de son père qui meurt, parce que comme la richesse est tout à fait imprevue, et la note pastorale n'est pas interrompue par le [sic] douleur, seulement par la présence sinistre du villain. En ce cas, la *girl* possèdera un père, pas un oncle. Etes-vous en accord? Je tiendrai silence pour Oui". (*Corr.* I, 303). Stravinsky wrote several letters to Auden (November 25 and December 5, 1947, for instance) in French. 'Multilingual', or at least cross-cultural, communication between Stravinsky and his literary collaborators was not unusual. See, for example, the 'Franco-Russian' exchange of views with Ramuz during their work on *L'Histoire du Soldat*.

Rake's Progress, i. e., the scene in which Anne Truelove announces her intention to follow her fiancé to London:

PLACE	ACTION
Same as Sc. 1.	She speaks of getting no letters, fears
Winter Night.	Hero has forgotten her and announces
Full moon.	her intention to run away from home to
	London to find him.
CHARACTERS	MUSIC
Girl comes out	Orch. recit. &
of house dressed	sop[rano] aria[44].
in traveling clothes.	

In due time, we shall see what changes were wrought in the Scenario on its way toward emerging as the libretto almost exactly three months later[45]. But prior to embarking on the actual comparison between the 'sketch' and the finished 'canvas', we must continue, and complete, our account of the creative process. In a letter written shortly after his return to New York, Auden proposed a modification in I, 1 by suggesting that the illness of Tom's father, which, in the Scenario, precipitates Rakewell's departure for London, be replaced by the death of an uncle, at whose country cottage Anne – presumably an orphan – was originally depicted as dwelling. (The text of this letter is reproduced in footnote 43.) This change, in turn, necessitated the substitution, on stage, of a father for that uncle. This dramaturgical manoeuver was designed a) to heighten the surprise effect and b) to have the pastoral mood of the scene broken less by the need for compassion than by the sudden arrival of the villain. Stravinsky readily accepted the proposal and even congratulated Auden on his "bonne trouvaille" (*Corr.* I, 303).

---

44 *Memories*, 169.

45 According to the correspondence, the text of Act I was completed by January 16, that of Act II by January 28, and that of Act III by February 9, 1948. Sometime in March of that year it was shown to Auden's literary mentor, T. S. Eliot, who "noted one split infinitive and one anachronism" (Stravinsky in: *Memories*, 162). Having composed the Prelude to III, 2 (the graveyard scene) in December, 1947, i. e., before he had received any of Auden's text, Stravinsky began working on the score in the pre-established order of numbers in May, 1948, and completed it on April 7, 1951, five months before the Venice premiere.

As a comparison between the Scenario version of this segment and its equivalent in the libretto verifies, Auden's plan entailed a fairly substantial revision of the entire scene. Here, then, is the original synopsis:

> Villain explains how his coach has stuck in mid. of lane. Uncle invites him in. Girl goes to fetch wine. They drink. Villain proposes toast to the Future and says he can foretell it. Girl asks him to tell hers. He does so in the manner of a Baroque Delphic Oracle. Egged on by girl, reluctant Hero asks his future. A brief silence. Villain whistles. (Villain: "read it!".) Hero reads letter announcing illness of father. "I must get to London." (167)

In the "Character" column, the Villain's whistling and his invitation to the reading, the stage direction "Servant enters with letter for Hero" explicates the concurrent action. Here, then, in contrast to the libretto version, the Villain is not himself the harbinger of the news but functions as an operator who cleverly works behind the scenes[46]; and Anne is spared the embarrassment of finding herself, if only figuratively, in the clutches of the Devil. The revision of this scene also had its musical consequences in so far as, in keeping with the change, Auden replaced the, still unwritten, text for the "bass aria with soli comments" (= the vocal realization of the Baroque Delphic Oracle) provided for in the jointly written sketch by Shadow's straightforward prose account of the late uncle's life and business career. Compensating for this loss and saving the musical substance provided for in the Scenario, Stravinsky transformed the narrative into an *arioso* passage beginning with the words "Fair lady, gracious gentlemen"[47].

Apart from Auden's letter of January 28, 1948, which is not included in the *Selected Correspondence*, and to which I shall refer at some length in the final section of my paper, the correspondence between composer and librettist offers but one further example of a major change in substance. The two writers having cemented the parallel with Goethe's *Faust* in the churchyard scene (III, 2) by letting

---

46 For Kallman's role in the rewriting, see the second paragraph of the author's comments in "Looking and Thinking Back" (footnote 6).

47 See pp. 17-20 of the piano-vocal score issued by Boosey & Hawkes in New York.

Shadow/Mephisto[48] remind Rakewell/Faust of their, previously concluded, pact ("A year and a day have passed away/ Since first to you I came./ All things you bid I duly did/ And now my wages claim."), they felt, naturally, urged to offer tangible proof of its existence. Thus in I, 1 of the libretto we now have the following dialogic recitative:

Shadow: All is ready, Sir.

Rakewell: Tell me, good Shadow, since born and bred in indigence, I am unacquainted with such matters, what you are accustomed to receive.

Shadow: Let us not speak of that matter until you know better what my services are worth. A year and a day hence we will settle our account and then, I promise you, you shall pay me no less than what you yourself acknowledge to be just[49].

The two other references to the libretto which occur in the correspondence between the composer and the poet concern matters of prosody and versification. In both instances, Stravinsky asked Auden for the kind of minor favor that is often requested in the collaborative enterprise which is the writing of an opera. In the first case, the desire was to have "four new lines of same length and rhythm to fit with the already existing music" for the conclusion of the chorus of Roaring Boys and Whores in the Brothel scene (I, 2)[50]. Auden willingly complied by submitting the stanza "While food has flavor and limbs are shapely/ And hearts beat bravely to fiddle or drum,/ Our proper employment is reckless enjoyment/ For too soon the noiseless night will come". And roughly one month later the two artists exchanged views

---

48 In his contribution to *Harper's Bazaar*, Auden calls Shadow a "Mephisto disguised as Leporello".

49 In his letter dated February 9, 1948, Auden speaks of sending along "the last act (& an insert for Act I to explain Act III, scene 2)" (*Corr.* I, 304.) There would seem to be a direct reference to lines 1649ff. of Goethe's *Faust, der Tragödie erster Teil*, beginning with the lines:
Faust: Und was soll ich dagegen dir erfüllen?
Mephisto: Dazu hast du noch eine lange Frist.

50 Letter to Auden of November 17, 1948, and the latter's reply of November 23, 1948; *Corr.* I, 306f.

on Baba's contrastive part in the trio with Tom and Anne which forms the climax of II, 2[51].

This, then, is the sum total of textual changes that are touched upon in the Stravinsky/Auden correspondence[52]. The other, more far-reaching because structurally and 'psychologically' significant, modifications, to be discussed in the second half of this paper, were not the subject of a written dialogue between the composer and his librettist – the term used here in the singular since Kallman and Stravinsky do not seem to have directly communicated in that way, if at all – must therefore be deduced from the text itself or extracted from Auden's and Kallman's published statements. For the rest it is evident that the comparisons which follow are *punktuell* and far from exhaustive, especially in the details.

II.

From the firsthand information about the revisions in the Hogarth 'plot' which is currently at our disposal it is clear that the chief impulse for the major corrections resulted from the librettists' assessment of the status and mental disposition of the hero. Mainly because they felt that Tom Rakewell's character was rather "stale, flat and unprofitable", they concluded that "the subject as it [was] in Hogarth [was] not really very interesting for a contemporary opera"[53]. That, in this particular context, Auden should have used the term "contemporary" strikes one as being anomalous since he had been specifically charged with furnishing a period-style text – which was 'updated' largely by

---

51 The discussion on that subject is evidenced in letters dated October 18, 1949 (Stravinsky to Auden), October 24, 1949 (Auden to Stravinsky), and November 15, 1949 (Stravinsky to Auden, and Auden to Stravinsky). Auden's suggestion that Baba's rhythm should be more irregular and her tempo of utterance faster (*Corr.* I, 310) did not fall on deaf ears. Stravinsky effusively thanked his librettist for the "brilliant versified version of Baba's interfering recitative" (ibid., 311).

52 Some subsequent minor changes are mentioned by Craft in: Griffiths, 29f.

53 From Auden's BBC talk, as quoted in: Engelbert, 153.

adding a good dosage of post-Kierkegaardian Existentialism in order to supply a philosophical basis[54].

Once we drop the word "contemporary", however, we come much closer to Auden's true meaning; for as he puts it in his contribution to *Harper's Bazaar*,

> Hogarth's Rake [...] is not a demoniacally passionate man like Don Giovanni but a self-indulgent one who yields to the temptation of the immediate moment. Consequently, in the engravings the decor is more significant than the protagonist. In an opera this is impossible, for music is, par excellence, the expression of subjective activity; a character in opera can never appear the victim of circumstance; however unfortunate, he or she is bound to seem the architect of fate[55].

Speaking, once again and even more pointedly, of Hogarth's rather pale persona, the English poet explained, fourteen years later: "Hogarth's Rake is a purely passive figure, whose role is to succumb to whatever temptation, lust, boredom, money, and so forth, he is led into next. This filled us with dismay, for, as I said, passive characters cannot sing"[56]. Something had to be done, accordingly, to strengthen Rakewell's will and to give him at least a modicum of 'pluck'. (Aptly enough, the effect of his upgrading was enhanced by diminishing the strength of Anne Truelove's character[57].)

Several devices were used to bring about the desired change and to persuade the audience that here, after all, was a viable melo-dramaturgical subject, though perhaps not of the purest water. In musical terms, for instance, the addition of a full-fledged aria in I, 1 was aimed at showing that the hero was decidedly his own man and to a certain

---

54 Auden's views on the esthetics, and poetics, of opera must be seen in conjunction with his reading of Kierkegaard, an English version of whose *Either/Or* he reviewed in the May 15, 1944, issue of the American journal *The New Republic* (683-685).

55 Auden surely has a point when asserting that the abdication of the Will, such as is preached, and practiced, in Wagner's *Tristan und Isolde*, rarely figures as the central problematic in operatic discourse.

56 *TLS*, 1038.

57 In the Scenario, Anne is shown to be self-confident and highly assertive, as when, in II, 1, she scorns Rakewell: "False one, what of your vows to me?" In the libretto, however, she is merely "a soprano" excelling by the "sheer invariable goodness of her simple soul" (Chester Kallman in "Looking and Thinking Back").

extent responsible for his actions. While at the equivalent place in the Scenario, after both Girl and Uncle[58] have left him 'solus', Rakewell meekly "walks about [the] garden, humming [the] melody of the [preceding] duo" until "his voice trails off into silence" (167), in the opera he – as it turns out, ironically – manifests the Triumph of his Will by bursting into a declaration of faith, first in a recitative beginning with Luther's Protestant credo "Here I stand" and continuing with the aria "Since it is not by merit/ We rise or we fall" (I say 'ironically' because the piece turns out to be a eulogy of Fortune "that governs us all").

In an equally, or perhaps even more, significant way, the voluntarist bolstering of the hero was accomplished through the breaking up of a pattern that looms large in the Scenario. There Rakewell's sloth is underscored by repeated manifestations of boredom taking the form of yawns, such as are totally absent from the libretto[59]. Thus in the passage from I, 1 cited above, the silence into which his voice "trails of" is punctuated by that semiotic gesture which, serving as an acoustic leitmotif, accompanies him in II, 2 and II, 3 as well. By way of emphasizing the contrast between the two hostile partners, the Villain of the Scenario cultivates a whistle articulating his decided sense of superiority in their, at least initially, uneven power struggle. Thus in I, 1, when he appears as if out of nowhere, he attracts Rakewell's attention in precisely that manner; but, characteristically, in III, 1 (the cemetery scene) his whistling abruptly stops when the hero, having gained moral strength by appealing to a future that his opponent can never have, finally wins the upper hand:

(Villain sings with defiant despair of the future of a love he can never have.)
Hero: "Assez. Joue." (They play at dice. Villain loses.) Hero: "Eh bien, siffle."

---

58 In the libretto, the Father, having sent Anne into the house, engages in a sternly moralistic dialogue with Rakewell.
59 In the libretto, boredom is presupposed in Rakewell's aria "Vary the song. O London, change" (II, 1).

(Silence.) Hero: "Siffle." (Silence.) Hero: "Siffle." (Villain sinks into the grave. The clock finishes its striking.)[60]

(Not so parenthetically, it should be noted, at this point, that the librettists modified the conclusion of this scene in a thematically significant way, for while in the Scenario the reasons for Tom Rakewell's commitment are not clearly spelled out, in the libretto Shadow/Mephisto actually calls the curse of insanity upon him[61], and, in so doing, facilitates, and dramaturgically motivates, the transition to the final scene of the opera and Rakewell's 'translation' to the realm of myth.)

The scenically effective yawn/whistle dichotomy of the Scenario having been scrapped, apparently at Kallman's suggestion[62], the collaborators replaced it, for patent structural and thematic reasons, by the "old fairy-story trick of the three wishes"[63], which, to quote Auden once again, mark "the stages of [Rakewell's] flight from reality"[64]. Placed in the order of their appearance, they are 1) "I wish I had money" (I, 1); 2) "I wish I were happy" (II, 1); and 3) "I wish it [the dream of being able to change stones into bread[65]] were true". How-

---

60 The directions in the "Numbers" column are slightly confusing in this portion of the scene in so far as Rakewell's concluding *arioso* "Let it strike. Le temps ne m'effraye plus" (174) is assigned to a Bass.

61 Shadow's last lines ("To reason blind shall be your mind./ Henceforth be you insane") are linked to Sorge's curse in Act V of *Faust, der Tragödie zweiter Teil* (ll. 11497ff.): "Die Menschen sind im ganzen Leben blind,/ Nun, Fauste, werde du's am Ende". The two statements are thematically analogous in the sense that Faust's blindness, like Rakewell's insanity, are blessings on the symbolic/allegorical level.

62 "To think back to the writing of the *Rake* libretto is, for me, to re-experience the euphoria in which we worked. I myself was drawn into the collaboration casually, almost accidentally. When Auden returned from California with the outline that he and Stravinsky had constructed for the opera, he showed it to me: and I made some slight criticism: I found the placing of Shadow as a character too vague, and that yawn that summons him the first time too likely to resemble a soundless note in the remote reaches of the typical opera house." ("Thinking and Looking Back")

63 From Auden's BBC talk, as quoted in: Engelbert, 175. Similarly Kallman in "The New Stravinsky Opera", as quoted ibid., 157.

64 *Harper's Bazaar*, 165. Auden continues, by way of explanation: "The real world from which he flies but can never forget is represented by Ann[e] Truelove."

65 In the Scenario, the fantastic apparatus which the Villain wheels in is designed to make "gold out of sea-water". It is, then, an alchemistic rather than a Utopian process

ever, the matter is by no means as simple as all that; for the issue is somewhat clouded by the fact that a fourth wish – that of being reunited with Anne – crops up in III, 2[66]. This triad of wishes, whose realization in no way depends on the hero's own will, should be reviewed in the light of concepts which Auden invokes in his letter of January 28, 1948:

> Have made a few slight alterations in our original plot in order to make each step of the Rake's Progression unique, i. e.,
>
> Bordel – Le Plaisir   = physical pleasure
> Baba   – L'acte gratuit   = freedom of will (human plane)
> La Machine – Il désir de devenir Dieu = omnipotence (divine level)[67]

One should keep in mind that in this version of the plot outline sensual pleasure (I, 2) has been substituted for the craving for wealth (I, 1) as marking the first stage in the hero's trajectory. As the lack of consistency in handling the problem indicates, the three wishes were a makeshift device, although it cannot be denied that they vastly improve the way in which Auden and Stravinsky had, by anticipation, solved the problem in their Scenario. There the wishes figure only in the churchyard scene and, in addition to emerging too late to have a

---

that is set in motion for Rakewell's benefit. As Auden notes in his contribution to *Harper's Bazaar*, "one Hogarth engraving" – it happens to be the fifth, set in the debtor's prison – "is concerned with the Philosopher's Stone". Needless to say that both activities may be linked to New Testament miracles worked by Christ, namely the changing of water into wine at the wedding of Cana (John: 2) and the feeding of the three thousand with a few loaves and fishes (John: 6). In the context of *The Rake's Progress*, these are temptations "to do good by magic without having to change" (Auden's BBC talk, as quoted in: Engelbert, 181). Here Auden may refer to Matthew 4: 3, where the tempter says to Jesus: "If thou be the Son of God, command that these stones be made bread."

66 This occurs in connection with the card game, which, in the Scenario, was still a game of dice. Shadow broaches the subject by egging on Rakewell: "Come, try./ Let wish be thought and think on one to name./ Your wish, in all your fear, could rule the game/ Instead of Shadow." That wish also comes true when, at the end of the scene, Tom, remembering Anne's words "A love that is sworn before Thee can plunder Hell of its prey", exclaims: "I wish for nothing else./ Love, first and last, assume eternal reign."

67 *Memories*, 161. The gratuitous act may be loosely defined as the Dada version of an important Existentialist category. Its absurdist leaps without faith are illustrated by Lafcadio in André Gide's novel *Les Caves du Vatican*.

striking effect on the action, form the nucleus of a question-and-answer game that is limited to the verbal plane:

Hero: Je m'ennuie.
Villain: Qu'est-ce que vous désirez maintenant? Le plaisir?
Hero: Non.
Villain: La gloire?
Hero: Non.
Villain: La puissance?
Hero: Non.
Villain: Quoi donc?
Hero: Le passé ... (Memories, 161)

Independently of each other, Auden and Kallman later realized that, while they had done their level best to 'make ends meet', they had not gone far enough in their attempt to rid their subject of the 'epic' or tableau character which typifies the drama of open form. Ten years after the fact Kallman frankly acknowledged their defeat by stating:

> Tom gave us other troubles. As a Hogarth figure he is exclusively acted upon, all the way from brothel to bedlam. Modeling clay can't sing, and a singing Rake was what we wanted: so we endowed him with three wishes, both to suggest that he had a little will of his own, and to accentuate the sinister quality that the subject seemed to call for. That he does sing, and convincingly so, can be counted as a success for the librettists, too, I think. It must be admitted, though, that placing our tenor between Shadow, who rather triggers the wishes he too wickedly grants, and Anne, the voice of Good Pursuant, neat as the pattern is, leaves this protagonist almost as passive as his Hogarth original. ("Looking and Thinking Back")

Auden, by contrast, rather than being apologetic, resorted to a ruse by claiming that, actually, he had saved the day by presenting the hero as a psychiatric case. As he wrote in his article in *Harper's Bazaar*, "Rakewell is a man to whom the anticipation of experience is always exciting and its realization in actual fact always disappointing; temperamentally, therefore, he is a manic-depressive, elated by the prospect of the future and disgusted by the remembrance of the recent past"[68]. And in "The Mythical World of Opera" he echoed this view, though somewhat more cautiously, by stating: "As compensation, not altogether satisfactory, for Tom's passivity, we decided to make him a manic-depressive one moment up in the clouds, the next down in the

---

68 *Harper's Bazaar*, 165.

dumps. This would at least give his role some musical variety"[69]. Even if his diagnosis came close to the medical truth, which it does not[70], Auden's argument would strike one as being casuistic; for what unsuspecting audience would guess that this was what the librettists had had up their sleeves?

Given the fact that Stravinsky aimed at, and largely succeeded in, writing a neoclassical opera steeped in a modern idiom, it is puzzling that Auden/Kallman, rather than emulating this tendency, furnished a text which, though being period-style in a strictly linguistic sense, turned increasingly 'Romantic' as the libretto unfolded. Corresponding to Auden's desire to map the course of Rakewell's "flight from reality", it acquired a new dimension as the authors unfurled the flag not so much of *Verfremdung* (= alienation understood in the abrasive, Brechtian sense) as of *Entfremdung* (= a more gentle and gradual weaning from reality). The melo-dramaturgical program which Kallman spelled out in his article in the New York *Herald Tribune* on the occasion of the *Rake's* American premiere[71] was more or less in tune with Auden's notion of opera as a genre privileged to depict the impossible or improbable sides of life:

> The librettist need never bother his head, as the dramatist must, about probability. A credible situation in opera means a situation in which it is credible that someone should sing. [...] No opera plot can be sensible, for people do not sing when they are feeling sensible. The theory of "Music-drama" presupposes a libretto in which there is not one sensible remark[72].

One of the most cogent arguments in favor of making opera a locus for the "secondary world" – Auden's term – stems from the pen of

---

69 *TLS*, 1038. By "musical variety" Auden seems to mean something like the musical equivalent of "himmelhochjauchzend, zu Tode betrübt".

70 Identified by Emile Kraepelin, manic-depressive insanity is marked by the alternation between mania (in Auden's fuzzy definition: euphoria) and depression.

71 The apparently garbled version of Kallman's statement quoted in: Engelbert, 188, reads as follows: "The Fantastic is no problem. Music also allowed us to indulge the fantastic side of our fable. [...] But [by?] the immediacy of music, these elements (the supernatural and fantastic) became real on being presented."

72 Quoted in Weisstein, 358. In *TLS*, 1038, Auden opines that "no opera plot can be sensible".

Ferruccio Busoni, with whose *New Esthetic of Music* (1907), a harbinger of things to come, the English poet was probably familiar. There we are informed that

> opera should avail itself of the supernatural and unnatural as the only realm of phenomena and feelings suitable to it. In this way, it could create a world of make-believe that reflects life in either a magic or a distorting mirror, and which aims at showing something that is not to be found in real life[73].

Indeed, after a close reading of the libretto for *The Rake's Progress* one might well be persuaded that, rather than being a moralistic text, as some critics have foolishly maintained[74], it is more closely akin to Surrealism, whose founder and high priest, André Breton, boldly announced in his 1924 Manifesto: "Je crois à la resolution future de ces deux états, en apparence si contradictoires, que sont le rêve et la réalité, en une sorte de réalité absolue, de surréalité, si l'on peut ainsi dire."[75] The ingredients of the mix Breton considered most likely to produce the desired disorientation, as a result of which the *merveilleux*, which, according to him, is "toujours beau" (29), will manifest itself, are, to name only the ones that are most relevant to Stravinsky's opera, the worlds of children, fairy-tales, myth and insanity, used both singly and in combination[76].

Let us, then, by way of conclusion, briefly examine the scope and dramatic function of these complexes with a view toward establishing the difference in their treatment in the Scenario and the libretto. A perusal of the Scenario from this perspective, that is to say, reveals that

---

73 Quoted in Weisstein, 266, in the editor's translation.

74 See, for example, Engelbert, 173: "Auden verfolgt mit diesem Libretto ein didaktisches Konzept, wie aus seiner inhaltlichen Bestimmung und der Moral am Ende deutlich wird."

75 André Breton, *Les Manifestes du Surréalisme* [...] (Paris: Editions du Sagittaire, 1946), 28.

76 The marvellous finds its most cogent expression in narrative prose. Good 'Surrealist' plays are rare, although they do exist, both in the Romantic period and in the twentieth century. Jean Cocteau's drama *La Machine infernale* (1932), which may be regarded as an elaboration of or extrapolation from Cocteau/Stravinsky's opera-oratorio *Oedipus Rex* (1927), offers a good example of how the three realms of the fantastic can be integrated and put to perfectly legitimate dramatic – and even tragic – ends.

the original outline includes only scattered attempts to achieve some sort of coherence in that respect. Thus, firstly, we have the Ugly Duchess, drawn from Lewis Carroll's 'Kunstmärchen' *Alice in Wonderland* but later replaced by the grotesque figure of Baba the Turk. Secondly, we have the still nameless Madam of the brothel regale Rakewell with a nursery rhyme as she leads him out of the parlor to seal what Auden calls his "loss of innocence"[77], and thirdly the lullaby with which Anne puts Tom to sleep in his last abode, which is Bedlam. But that is all. In fact, the only pattern within the domain of the fantastic that emerges from the Scenario is one of myth – the Adonis/Venus relationship. But, taken by itself, myth, no matter how fantastic its trappings, can hardly qualify for the label 'Surrealistic'.

Turning from the Scenario to the libretto, we notice that there the flight from reality is much more clearly articulated. This is especially true of the 'infantilism' to which the hero finds himself increasingly drawn. Thus Mother Goose of nursery-rhyme fame[78] was substituted for the Madam of the Scenario; and that lady's innocuous ditty gave way to a choral riddle song suffused with sexual innuendos. As the stage directions specify, "the chorus forms a lane with the men on one side and the women on the other, as in a children's game. Mother Goose and Rakewell walk slowly between them to a door backstage." The text of this "Lanterloo" chorus so enthralled Stravinsky that it directly inspired him to provide a truly congenial musical setting for it[79]. The childhood pattern is rounded out by the demented Rakewell's

---

77 Auden's contention that "from the Rake's point of view, this [...] is going to be an initiation, a loss of innocence" (BBC talk, as quoted in: Engelbert, 160) may well apply to Hogarth's series and to the Scenario; but in the libretto the sexual rite, seen in a much more positive light, betokens the acquisition of a new innocence, a Paradise Regained.

78 In English slang, to goose means to engage in sexual intercourse.

79 "I think he [Auden] was inspired, and in any case he inspired me. At the business level of the collaboration he wrote 'words for music', and I wonder whether any poet since the Elizabethans has made a composer such a beautiful gift of them as the 'lanterloo' dance in our opera." From Stravinsky's "Tribute to a Librettist" (1965) in: Griffiths, 4.

singing a ballad-tune ("With roses crowned, I sit on the ground") "to himself in a childlike voice".

As a means of intertwining the various strands of surreality in *The Rake's Progress*, the two writers decided further to heighten the dreamlike atmosphere surrounding the events which seal the hero's fate. Like Breton and his cohort, they insisted, in purely esthetic emulation of Freud's theories, then hotly contested, that dreams are ideally suited for bringing about the aimed-for fusion of reality and fantasy. Quite in this vein, the initiation rite in the brothel concludes with Shadow's truly Mephistophelian send-off: "Sweet dreams, my master. Dreams may lie,/ But dream. For when you wake you die."[80] And the granting of Rakewell's third, Utopian, wish is, in the libretto, prefigured by an identical dream which Shadow imposes on the sleeping protagonist[81].

From all the indications given in this essay, as well as from the many signs which the librettists have posted along the way, one can draw certain conclusions about their attitude to and their approach toward the subject which Igor Stravinsky had asked them to rework into a libretto. Just as the title and content of Hogarth's series, that is to say, are to be seen as an ironic reflection on John Bunyan's Puritan epic, *The Pilgrim's Progress*, so what Auden and Kallman did to *The Rake's Progress* is also to be viewed as an ironic reflection on the eighteenth-century model. For while the surface action of the twentieth-century opera they helped to concoct actually shows the hero's progress toward decadence and death, on the symbolic (and 'Surrealistic') level we note a progress through regression, a return to and

---

80 Like numerous other lines or phrases in the libretto, this one is reminiscent of T. S. Eliot. In addition, it reminds one of the concluding portion of the second "Studierzimmer" scene in *Faust I*, more specifically Mephisto's instruction to the chorus of *Geister*: "Er schläft! So recht, ihr luft'gen, zarten Jungen!/ Ihr habt ihn treulich eingesungen." (Ll. 1506f.)

81 "Return" and "repetition", for instance, are the keywords in the crucial dialogue between Shadow and Rakewell in the churchyard (III, 2). Philosophically, *The Rake's Progress* might well be seen, and discussed, as a treatise on Time (past, present, and future), its loss and its recovery.

recovery of the past, whether historical or mythical, that perfectly 'jibes' with Stravinsky's intention of being, concurrently, conservative and experimental.

What is Romantic Opera?
Toward a Musico-Literary Definition (1994)

> Wie das zeitliche Einschränken [...] hat das
> sachliche Einschränken [...] etwas Gewaltsames:
> es ignoriert die Lebensfülle[1].
>
> (Like the temporal limitation, the limitation in
> subject matter is somehow contrived;
> it ignores life's plenitude.)
>
> The Romantic movement made the opera composers
> specialists because it took its opera more seriously
> than did the eighteenth century[2].

I.

A collective volume devoted to Romantic drama would be sadly deficient if it failed to consider the kind of multimedia stage work which, as the second motto indicates, became paradigmatic in various countries for various lengths of time during the first half of the nineteenth century. Hence the need for an essay like the present one, an attempt to develop some basic criteria, pinpoint the chief representatives and identify the handful of works that might qualify as paragons of melodramatic Romanticism viewed from a supranational vantage point. Throughout, my aim will be methodological rather than historical, although I am not foolish enough to wish to ignore chronology; for to do so would be tantamount to abandoning the justified view of Romanticism as a cultural phenomenon that is as unique as it is *unwiederholbar*, and acknowledging implicitly the existence of a perennial or categorial Romanticism that may surface randomly at any

---

1 Werner Braun, Das *Problem der Epochengliederung in der Musik* (Darmstadt: Wissenschaftliche Buchgesellschaft, 1977), p. 39. – All translations in this essay are my own.
2 Alfred Einstein, *Music in the Romantic Era* (New York: Norton, 1947), p. 103.

given time or place. (In committing this perspectival error, I would be as penny-wise as the cultural historian who claims, pound-foolishly, that in so far as music is, by definition, a Romantic art, all opera is, at least partly, Romantic.)

Since the Comparative History of Literatures in European Languages, to which this essay and the volume in which it appears belong, is truly international and interdisciplinary[3], I am honor-bound to focus on the dialectic of indigenous and universal traits which characterizes the Romantic age above all ages. Thus we shall find, to no one's surprise, that E. T. A. Hoffmann turned to Carlo Gozzi as a principal source of literary inspiration ("Der Dichter und der Komponist"), that Carl Maria von Weber emulated French opera in *Der Freischütz*, that the 'Parisian' Rossini drew on Schiller (*Guillaume Tell*), and that Hector Berlioz availed himself of resources provided by Goethe, Beethoven, and Weber (*Symphonie fantastique*) – not to mention the supposedly neo-Romantic Verdi[4], who took from Victor Hugo (*Ernani*, *Rigoletto*) what his native tradition was unable to supply[5].

One can see that such a dense web of musical, literary, and musico-literary interrelationships is hard to disentangle, and that any sustained effort to dissolve the whole into its parts and reassemble those is likely to require an intense joint effort by representatives of *Musik-* and *Literaturwissenschaft*. I cannot hope to accomplish in a handful of pages what would require a monographic treatment; but perhaps I can measure the vacuum that exists in this respect. As far as I know, no lite-

---

3 The principle of interdisciplinarity was established, at my request, in conjunction with the volume *Expressionism as an International Literary Phenomenon* (Budapest and Paris: Akadémiai Kiadó & Didier, 1973), the first in this series. – A shorter German version of the present study, translated from the original English, appeared in the volume *Einheit in der Vielfalt: Festschrift für Peter Lang zum 60. Geburtstag*, ed. Gisela Quast (Bern: Lang, 1988), pp. 568-588.

4 See chapter XVI of Einstein's book (footnote 2 above), where the bulk of French, German, and Italian operas produced in the second and third quarters of the nineteenth century are dealt with under that label.

5 For whatever reasons, Verdi seems to have found Alessandro Manzoni's historical tragedies *Il conte di Carmagnola* (1820) and *Adelchi* (1822) unsuitable.

rary scholars or critics have made a move in this direction; and few music historians have tackled the problem systematically. Thus valid solutions are as rare as the proverbial Phoenix, and most authors of books or articles with appropriate titles fail to rise from the ashes of the fire they themselves have set.

Thus, to mention a few recent examples, Palmiro Pinagli's book *Romanticismo di Verdi*[6] offers no explanation whatever of the intended meaning of the key word in its title; and Peter Conrad's controversial *Romantic Opera and Literary Form* – "gepriesen viel und viel gescholten" – is equally opaque in this respect[7]. Wherever we look, labels are loosely attached (as in *Early Romantic Opera*, a series edited by Philip Gossett and Charles Rosen and reproducing the scores of works by Bellini, Donizetti, Rossini, Meyerbeer, and Halévy[8]) or designed to justify the making of strange bedfellows (as in Edward J. Dent's posthumously published Messenger Lectures on *The Rise of Romantic Opera*[9]).

No clearcut sense of what constitutes Romantic opera emerges from most general surveys of music history, most of which suffer from the handicap of being organized according to composers rather than works. Thus in his widely used and, on the whole, admirable *Music in Western Civilization*[10], Paul Henry Lang treats German

---

6 Palmiro Pinagli, *Romanticismo di Verdi* (Florence: Vallecchi, 1967).

7 Peter Conrad, *Romantic Opera and Literary Form* (Berkeley: Univ. of California Press, 1977).

8 The series was published by the Garland Press of New York. No explanation for the title is given by the editors.

9 Edward J. Dent, *The Rise of Romantic Opera*, ed. Winton Dean (Cambridge: Cambridge Univ. Press, 1976). "The purpose of these lectures is to study Romantic opera. The composers whom I select as typical Romantics are Weber and Bellini. You might expect me to talk to you about Donizetti, Wagner, Verdi and perhaps Berlioz; but I may tell you at once that I do not intend to discuss any of these directly at all" (p. 7). In his paper on "The Romantic Spirit in Music", *Proceedings of the Musical Association, 59th Session, 1932-1933* (Leeds: Whitehead & Miller, 1933), pp. 85-95, Dent also identifies Weber as the Romantic composer *par excellence*.

10 Paul Henry Lang, *Music in Western Civilization* (New York: Norton, 1941).

Romantic opera – meaning primarily Weber – as a transitional phenomenon in chapter XV ("The Confluence of Classicism and Romanticism"), offers three sections on opera ("The Grand Opera", "Italian Opera", "German Opera" [Marschner and Lortzing]) in chapter XVI, brackets Wagner with Berlioz in chapter XVII ("From Romanticism to Realism"), and handles Verdi alongside Brahms and Bizet in chapter XVIII ("Counter Currents").

Historians of opera, too, have largely failed to suggest a distinct, and discernible, pattern. Often they altogether avoid the issue (at least as far as the Table of Contents, the most widely used guide for reading a book, is concerned) by scattering the relevant information. As the respective *indices nominum et rerum* demonstrate, this is true of Donald Grout's standard *A Short History of Opera*[11], of *The Opera: A History of its Creation and Performance 1600-1941*, a book co-authored by Wallace Brockway and Herbert Weinstock[12], as well as of the only history of the libretto written in English, Patrick J. Smith's *The Tenth Muse*[13]. The easy way out, which brings no solution, is that preferred by Anna Amalia Abert in her contribution to *Musik in Geschichte und Gegenwart*, where the section on Romantic Opera, so designated, is preceded by a section called "Von den Anfängen bis gegen 1800" and followed by one called "Nachromantische Oper bis zur Gegenwart"[14].

Even where, as in Alfred Einstein's *Music in the Romantic Era*, the focus is entirely on our subject, the distribution of pertinent materials is open to challenge. Thus chapter X ("Romantic Opera") is duly concerned with the German branch but inexplicably concludes with a subsection entitled "Parisian Opera: Meyerbeer". Berlioz is grouped with Mendelssohn, Schumann, Liszt, Brahms, and Bruckner in chapter XI

---

11 Donald Grout, *A Short History of Opera* (New York: Columbia Univ. Press, 1947).

12 Wallace Brockway and Herbert Weinstock, *The Opera: A History of its Creation and Performance 1600-1941* (New York: Simon & Schuster, 1941).

13 Patrick J. Smith, *The Tenth Muse* (New York: Knopf, 1970).

14 The article appears in volume X of *Musik in Geschichte und Gegenwart* (Kassel: Bärenreiter, 1959), and the relevant section in columns 35-59.

("Symphonic and Chamber Music"), and Wagner appears, together with Verdi and the Italian *bel-cantists*, in chapter XVI under the heading "Universalism within the National II: Neo-Romantic Opera". There all of Wagner's and Verdi's works for the musical stage (down to *Parsifal* and *Falstaff*) are sheltered under one umbrella.

Einstein's justification for including Meyerbeer in the chapter on Romantic Opera is paradoxical; for, as he puts it rather gingerly, "[t]he 'Romantic' side of this Parisian opera is revealed primarily in the choice of material" (p. 120), that is to say it is chiefly thematic and, hence, literary[15]. This indicates that Meyerbeer's Romanticism is half-baked, and that there could be, at the other end of the scale, an equally half-baked operatic Romanticism that qualifies solely on account of the inherent musical qualities. We have reached a crucial point in our discussion; for as it turns out, the majority of operas commonly called 'Romantic' would seem to be, in one way or the other, impure. Music historians, at any rate, seem to have been agonizingly aware of this dilemma; and Einstein is by no means the only scholar to have pointed to this glaring discrepancy. Thus Paul Henry Lang opines that E. T. A. Hoffmann's *Undine*, thought to be a veritable prototype of the genre, is "romantic in [its] subject matter", while the music is "still in a vein nearer to the classic than to the Romantic"[16]; and Grout maintains that in contrast to Bellini's melo-dramatic products, in which "romanticism pervades the music as well", Donizettis's operas "are romantic only in their librettos"[17].

---

15 The literary-thematic approach to Romantic opera simply will not do. It would result in vastly enlarging the body of such works, for instance by including most or all of the works discussed by Jerome Mitchell in his book *The Walter Scott Operas* (Tuscaloosa: Univ. of Alabama Press, 1977).

16 Lang, p. 796.

17 Grout, p. 341. Paul Henry Lang, on the other hand, states with regard to Bellini and Rossini: "They are not at all the Romantic figures we have known in their literary form, but the music that surrounds them – Italian to the core – is romantic." (*Music in Western Civilization*, p. 834)

As these observations suggest, the canon of Romantic operas *pur sang* is likely to be small if both literary and musical criteria are applied. Perhaps the only way of settling the issue and obtaining a halfway satisfactory result is to limit oneself voluntarily to works for the musical stage that are Romantic in a programmatic sense, while staying within a historically viable framework, i. e., approximately the second to fourth decades of the nineteenth century[18]. In order to identify the canonic works, one must scrutinize relevant statements made by composers and librettists with a view toward joint creative endeavors along the suggested lines. I shall do so in the second, pragmatic part of this essay. But the question "Which are the Romantic operas?" cannot be answered until after the one that precedes it, and which furnishes the title of my presentation – "What is Romantic Opera?" – has been solved.

In order to accomplish this task, I shall have to identify those central features which, at the hub of Romantic aesthetics at large, may enable me to separate the genuine product from those operatic creations which are flawed through compromise with existing traditions and conventions. According to my scheme of values, there are two of these, both compatible with the notion of organicism which, as the evidence suggests, is firmly embedded in Romantic thinking on art.

---

18 I personally do not share the defeatism which inheres in Werner Braun's complacent statement (*Das Problem der Epochengliederung in der Musik*, p. 39): "Von den beiden genannten Beispielen für den verallgemeinernden Sprachgebrauch, 'Barock' und 'Romantik', ist letzteres hier das bessere, weil es nach neuerer allgemeiner Überzeugung keinen romantischen Epochenstil in der Musik gegeben hat und weil demzufolge auch die Grenzen dieser 'Epoche' sehr unterschiedlich gezogen werden." ('Of the two examples cited above for the generalizing usage, i. e., "Baroque" and "Romanticism", the latter is more appropriate in so far as, according to a consensus fairly recently arrived at, there is no Romantic period style in music and because, for that very reason, the borderlines of that epoch are drawn in several different ways.') In literature, which precedes music by approximately a decade, the Romantic era, viewed from a supranational perspective, can be said to extend from, roughly, 1795 to, roughly, 1830. Those readers who wish to pursue the latter question are urged to consult *Die europäische Romantik*, ed. Ernst Behler (Frankfurt: Athenäum-Verlag, 1972) and, for the semantic aspect, *'Romantic' and Its Cognates: The European History of a Word*, ed. Hans Eichner (Toronto: Univ. of Toronto Press, 1972).

To be specific: the demands I have in mind encompass 1) a merger of composer and playwright, taking the form of *Doppelbegabung* and 2) the unification of text and music (as well the other contributory arts) in the total work of art. It goes without saying that the *Gesamtkunstwerk* envisaged by the proponents of this theory entails the breaking up of the pattern common to both the *Singspiel* and the serious *Nummernoper,* i. e., a more or less regular alternation of spoken dialogue or recitative with detachable arias and ensembles, and its replacement by a more closely woven fabric, the through-composed opera, in which transitions are gradual and the flow of the melo-dramatic action uninterrupted[19]. If these are to be the yardsticks by which the romanticality of an opera is to be measured, Italian works of the *bel canto* type are immediately ruled out, as are the Hugoesque *melodrammi* of Verdi's early middle period. To be sure, Verdi, champion of the *parola scenica*[20], moved in the direction of the integrated opera; but he did so much later in his career and reached his goal only with *Falstaff,* a work hardly qualifying as Romantic.

Having thus, in a mood of puristic fervor and with one possible exemption still to be discussed (Rossini's *Guillaume Tell*), eliminated Italian opera from the canon, I seem to be rapidly moving toward the conclusion, regrettable in view of the comparative nature of this enterprise, that Romantic opera is, by and large, German opera. Such a conclusion would be premature, however, in so far as the evidence will show that at least one eminently French composer, Hector Berlioz, will figure significantly in my account – not as a composer of works specifically written for the musical stage but as the author of *sympho-*

---

19 There are various intermediate stages between the two extreme solutions. Finales, for example, tend to grow in some of Mozart's operas to encompass nearly half an act; and the use of tableaux and 'scenes' may enhance the continuity of the melo-dramatic action.

20 This is a term which frequently surfaces in Verdi's letters to Antonio Ghislanzoni concerning the text of *Aida*. It demonstrates the composer's interest in the correlation between word and tone in a scenographic sense.

nies dramatiques analogous to the *drames symphoniques* conceived and executed by Richard Wagner, his admirer *outre-Rhin*[21].

At this juncture, and before entering into a discussion of the specifics of Romantic opera, I must raise a theoretical problem that has dogged historiographers of early-nineteenth-century culture: the apparent paradox constituted by the fact that while, on the one hand, music (from Hoffmann to Schopenhauer and beyond[22]) is regarded as the perfect vehicle for expressing soul states and, hence, the condition to which all the other arts aspire, "what unites the various currents that make up the Romantic era", on the other, "is a general literary orientation"[23]. The contradiction dissolves if one calls to mind, as a close observer of the scene cannot fail to do, that the Romantic artist, like the Expressionist after him, tended to shy away from pure abstraction and wanted his creations, whether verbal or not, to convey meaning, if only on the emotional and spiritual level, thus conjoining the tangible with the intangible. Another justification for this union of contraries is provided by the Romantics' desire to reconstitute the lost Paradise, that as yet undifferentiated state in which, according to some modern observers[24]. the arts existed in the prelapsarian age. (Kleist, who tackles the question of lost 'grace', both in the theological and aesthetic senses, in his essay "Über das Marionettentheater" [1801],

---

21 In the final chapter of his book *La Musique aux temps romantiques* (Paris: Alcan, 1930), Julien Tiersot succinctly states: "Le drame musical de Wagner, c'est donc la continuation normale de la symphonie dramatique de Berlioz." ('Wagner's musical drama, then, is the logical continuation of Berlioz's dramatic symphony.')

22 One need only think of the Symbolists, one of whose principal aims was to bring poetry closer to music. The last line of Verlaine's poem "Art Poétique", "et tout le reste est littérature" ('and all the rest is literature'), succinctly defines that goal.

23 Lang, p. 808. In "Der Dichter und der Komponist", E. T. A. Hoffmann juxtaposes "die unnennbare Wirkung der Instrumentalmusik" with the latter's need, in opera, "ganz in das Leben [zu] treten" and "seine Erscheinungen [zu] ergreifen" ('the unnamable effect of instrumental music [...] to enter life fully [... and] cover its entire range').

24 The Tübingen Romanist Kurt Wais, for example, postulates an initial fusion of the arts in an expanded lecture published under the title *Symbiose der Künste* (Stuttgart: Metzler, 1937).

unmasks this yearning as Utopian.) In so far as the Romantic composers, all the way down to Wagner, clearly exalted the role of music in their operas by assigning it a loftier role, the two conceptions – that of music as the supreme art and that of the need for a *Gesamtkunstwerk* – can be reconciled. Accordingly, the notion which we encounter at the hub of Romantic thinking about opera is equally remote from the two extremes, that is to say, from the unfettered sensuousness advocated by Stendhal, who stresses the insignificance of words in opera by treating the lyrics as mere vehicles for vocal pyrotechnics[25], and from the programmatic literalism into which Berlioz's symphonic poems deteriorate in the hand of Liszt, Tchaikovsky, and Richard Strauss[26].

In the treatment of my chosen subject, as in any other humanistic pursuit, history, theory and criticism go hand in hand[27]. It is, therefore, my duty to complement the brief theoretical observations on the topic "What is Romantic Opera?" with a somewhat more elaborate attempt to test the qualification of certain operatic works for admission to the exclusive club with its strict charter. Predictably, I begin my tour of inspection by assessing the role of E. T. A. Hoffmann, whose creative and critical activities in both music and literature uniquely qualify him, true *Doppelbegabung* that he is, to serve both as a model and convenient point of departure. His decisive, though in some ways inconclusive, role was aptly summarized by Friedrich Blume, who notes with apprehension:

> Enttäuschen auch Hoffmanns eigene Kompositionen die Erwartungen, die von seinen ästhetischen Ansichten her an sie zu stellen waren [...] so ist es doch unzweifelhaft E. T. A. Hoffmann gewesen, der den Musikbegriff in der Romantik für Deutschland und von da aus auch für Frankreich geprägt und der das romanti-

---

25 Relevant passages can be found in his *Vie de Rossini* (Paris: Boulland, 1824).

26 An interesting discussion of this problem is offered by Jacques Barzun in the chapter "Program Music and the Unicorn" of his book *Berlioz and the Romantic Century* (New York: Columbia Univ. Press, 1969), I, pp. 169-198.

27 I am referring to the by now classic distinction made by Wellek/Warren in the fourth chapter ("Literary Theory, Criticism, and History") of their *Theory of Literature* (New York: Harcourt Brace, 1949), pp. 29-37.

sche musikalische Denken und Empfinden für ein Jahrhundert entscheidend beeinflußt hat[28].

(Even though Hoffmann's compositions disappoint the expectations to be placed on them judging by his aesthetic views [...] there can be no doubt it was he who defined the essence of musical Romanticism for Germany and, by extension, for France, and who decisively influenced Romantic musical thinking and feeling for a century.)

The two works we need to scrutinize, however briefly, are the dialogue "Der Dichter und der Komponist" and the opera *Undine*.

Conceived in 1809 as a "nicht zu lange[r] Aufsatz, der über die Forderungen, die der Komponist an den Dichter einer Oper mit Recht macht, sprechen würde" ('an essay of moderate length concerned with the demands which the composer of an opera could justly make of his librettist')[29], "Der Dichter und der Komponist" was written four years later and first published in the *Allgemeine Musikalische Zeitung*[30]. Augmented by a frame, it was subsequently included in the first volume of the collection of novellas and short prose pieces entitled *Die Serapions-Brüder*. Rather than offering a detailed analysis of the piece – still a *desideratum* in spite of Aubrey Garlington's essay[31] – I shall emphasize those features which I have already singled out as being symptomatic for Romantic opera, namely 1) the desired unity of composer and librettist, 2) the notion of the total work of art in which all ingredients are smoothly blended, and 3) the replacement of the 'numbers' opera by the through-composed work for the musical stage.

Regarding the *Personalunion* of poet and musician, Ludwig – Hoffmann's spokesman in the dialogue[32] – clearly presents it as desir-

---

28 Article "Romantik" of *Musik in Geschichte und Gegenwart*, XI, col. 787.

29 From Hoffmann's letter to the editors of the *Allgemeine Musikalische Zeitung* dated July 1, 1809, as reprinted in *E. T. A. Hoffmanns Briefwechsel*, ed. Hans von Müller and Friedrich Schnapp (Munich: Winkler, 1967), I, p. 293.

30 The piece was published in two installments on December 8 and 15, 1813.

31 Aubrey Garlington, "E. T. A. Hoffmann's 'Der Dichter und der Komponist' and the Creation of German Romantic Opera", *The Musical Quarterly*, 65 (1979), pp. 22-45.

32 The one-to-one relationship is confirmed by identical wording in Hoffmann's letter to his friend Hitzig dated November 30, 1812 (*Hoffmanns Briefwechsel*, I, p. 357).

able but concurrently notes that only in rare instances (and surely not in his own case) will composers have the technical skill and the necessary patience to commit their thoughts to paper in poetically proper, i. e., metrical language. The musician will thus almost invariably turn to the man of letters (in this instance, Ludwig's friend Ferdinand), asking him to furnish the needed text, with the seemingly inevitable result that their collaboration ends in frustration and fails to achieve the envisaged symbiosis. To be sure, the composer may on occasion conceive of his work in one piece, though characteristically in a timeless moment "zwischen Wachen und Schlafen"[33]; but the organization of the verbal material, a tedious process at best, would entail the dissipation of the original model. Consequently, the resulting opera would be a bastard child in whose blood the humors of language and music are unevenly mixed.

As for the relation between words and tones, it is evident that unlike Weber and Wagner, his fellow laborers in the vineyard of Romantic opera, Hoffmann gives preferential treatment to the music. As Ludwig puts it in the opening portion of the dialogue,

> Ja, um noch bestimmter meine innere Überzeugung auszusprechen: in dem Augenblick der musikalischen Begeisterung würden [dem Komponisten] alle Worte, alle Phrasen ungenügend, matt, erbärmlich vorkommen und er müßte von seiner Höhe herabsteigen, um in der unteren Region der Worte für das Bedürfnis seiner Existenz betteln zu können. Würde aber hier ihm nicht bald, wie dem eingefangenen Adler, der Fittich gelähmt werden und er vergebens den Flug zur Sonne versuchen? (P. 81)

> (To express my innermost conviction even more strongly: at the moment of musical inspiration, all words and phrases would seem inadequate, weak and pitiful to the composer, who would have to descend from his height in order to beg for the bare means of existence in the lower realm of words. Would he not, like the captive eagle, find his wings paralyzed as he vainly strove to soar upwards toward the sun?)

He further downplays the significance of the text as a vehicle of expression (or meaning) by stressing, in anticipation of Hofmannsthal[34],

---

33 Hoffmann, *Die Serapions-Brüder*, p. 80.
34 I think specifically of Hofmannsthal's preface to *Die ägyptische Helena*.

the melo-dramaturgical significance of scene and situation. In his opinion, the composer

> hat es wirklich nötig, ganz vorzüglich bemüht zu sein, die Szenen so zu ordnen, daß der Stoff sich klar und deutlich vor den Augen des Zuschauers entwickele. Beinahe ohne ein Wort zu verstehen, muß der Zuschauer sich aus dem, was er geschehen sieht, einen Begriff von der Handlung machen können. (P. 92)
>
> (must be doubly careful to arrange the scenes in such a way that the action unfolds clearly and distinctly before the eyes of the beholder. While barely able to comprehend the text, the latter must be in a position to construct the action from the events unfolding on the stage.)

Especially illuminating, because symptomatic of Hoffmann's transitional place in the history of music and opera, are Ludwig's views on the intermixture and patterning of the verbal and musical ingredients. While, on the one hand, the author's fictional *alter ego* nowhere advocates the practice of alternating spoken dialogue and fixed musical numbers, customary in the *Singspiel*[35], he seems unwilling, on the other, to go much beyond the kind of unification of the elements that is present in *opera seria* in its high tragic mode as exemplified in Gluck's operas on mythological subjects. Both he and Ferdinand seem to take it for granted that serious operas consist of arias, duets, tercets, and the like, even though they do not find this mode to be fully satisfactory[36]. Hemmed in by convention, they seem to wish to do away with it, one hand taking what the other hand is giving. In actual practice, both Hoffmann and Weber, seasoned conductors steeped in the French repertory, followed the hallowed precedent.

If we pursue the comparison between the theoretical notions on Romantic opera conveyed in "Der Dichter und der Komponist" and

---

35 For Hoffmann's scathing remarks on the kind of *Singspiel* produced by Ditter von Dittersdorf see p. 91 of *Die Serapions-Brüder*. His reviews of various exemplars of this genre are found in his *Schriften zur Musik/Nachlese*, ed. Friedrich Schnapp (Munich: Winkler, 1963), *passim*.

36 Hoffmann's admiration for Gluck, whom in "Der Dichter und der Komponist" he calls "herrlich", is second to that for no other composer, barring Mozart.

Hoffmann's "Zauber-Oper" *Undine*[37], we quickly realize that there are as many discrepancies as there are parallels. Before taking that route, we should call to mind that Hoffmann read Friedrich de la Motte-Fouqué's fairy-tale by that name shortly after its publication in 1811; already in the following year he made plans to use it for an opera. Since, like his double in the dialogue, he did not trust his own skills as a librettist, he asked his friend Hitzig to suggest a suitable collaborator. As it turned out, that collaborator was to be the poet himself; and on August 15, 1812, overjoyed by this prospect, Hoffmann initiated a correspondence by submitting to Fouqué an extended sketch of the projected work now lost in which he marked the distribution of musical numbers[38].

Fouqué completed the libretto in October, 1812, and Hoffmann composed the music between July, 1813, and August, 1814. However, for a variety of reasons the premiere at the Berlin Königliches Schauspielhaus did not take place until two years later (August 3, 1816). In so far as "Der Dichter und der Komponist" was written while Hoffmann was at work on *Undine* – to be precise: between October 3 and 16, 1813, that is to say after the completion of the music for Act One –, we are justified in treating these works as two sides of a coin, the ideal and the real. For while the dialogue portrays Romantic opera in glowing colors, though not without a dash of skepticism, the completed opus mirrors the need for compromise on several fronts.

---

37 Hoffmann himself called *Undine* "Zauber-Oper", rather than a 'romantische Oper', as if he wanted to indicate, by means of this generic designation, that this was not the paradigm envisaged in "Der Dichter und der Komponist".

38 Writing to Fouqué on August 15, 1812, Hoffmann observes: "Sie haben, Herr Baron, eine ausführliche Skizze der Oper, wie ich sie mir vorzüglich rücksichts der historischen Fortschreitung denke, verlangt, und nur dieses konnte mich bewegen, die Beylage auszuarbeiten, welche Szene für Szene das Historische, so wie den musikalischen Gang des Stücks nach einzelnen Nummern darlegt". ('You have asked me, my dear Baronet, to furnish a detailed sketch of the opera such as I envisage it, especially with regard to the plot progression. Only that request could move me to prepare the enclosed outline, which describes, scene by scene, the unfolding of the action, as well as the musical progression of the piece from number to number'.) (*Hoffmanns Briefwechsel*, I, p. 347)

First of all, as regards the text, the desirable union of poet and composer failed to materialize – not surprisingly if one considers the strictures imposed in "Der Dichter und der Komponist". Fortunately, in this case Hoffmann, himself a writer of the first rank, managed to enlist the services of the author whose story he had decided to adapt. Although, on the whole, their collaboration seems to have been harmonious, the evidence shows that they did not always see eye to eye. Matters were further complicated by the fact that, as subsequently in Weber's case, the Royal *Intendant*, Count Brühl, proposed additional changes, one of which was made only after Hoffmann's death. One thing is clear: in a number of cases, the composer modified texts submitted by Fouqué or furnished entirely new ones from his own pen[39]. Thus, to a certain degree the text of *Undine* is a joint creation, with most of the credit for the dramaturgy, including the actual distribution of numbers, going to Hoffmann, and most of the credit for the verbal *Gestalt* going to his literary compeer.

Secondly, as I have already noted, Hoffmann's *Undine*, like Weber's *Der Freischütz*, falls far short of being a through-composed opera. It contains a fair, though not excessive, amount of spoken dialogue and even in its tone (which is serious but popular) seems to corroborate Dent's view that, in spite of all programmatic statements to the contrary, "[German] Romantic opera was derived from comic opera and not from *opera seria*".[40] – Thirdly, and perhaps most glar-

---

39 His own contributions to the text are included in the volume *Schriften zur Musik/ Nachlese*, pp. 814-820, under the heading "Ergänzungen, Abänderungen und Regieanweisungen zu Fouqué's Operntext der *Undine*" ('Additions, Modifications and Stage Directions for Fouqué's *Undine* Libretto'). More practical considerations speak out of the following passage from a letter to Hitzig dated November 30, 1812: "Ich finde durchaus im Texte nichts zu ändern und nur der gemeinen Bretter und des gemeinen neidischen ärgerlichen Volks wegen, was sich gewöhnlich darauf bewegt, werde ich vielleicht noch eine Arie für die Berthalda wünschen müssen" ('I see no reasons for making any changes in the text. Still, solely on account of the wretched stage and the wretched, invidious folk which usually treads it, I would like to request an additional piece for Berthalda') (*Hoffmanns Briefwechsel*, I, p. 358).
40 Dent, *The Rise of Romantic Opera*, p. 15.

ingly, theory and practice clash on the level of subject matter. For Hoffmann's mouthpiece in "Der Dichter und der Komponist" the preferred Romantic subject is exotic in the most literal sense of the word, that of "having the charm or fascination of the unfamiliar; strangely beautiful, enticing"[41]. According to Ludwig, the exotic serves as a channel for the intrusion of the marvellous (*das Wunderbare*) into the world of everyday reality[42]. As an exemplary *Stoff* he cites that of Carlo Gozzi's dramatic fairy tale *Il Corvo* (The Raven), a detailed outline of whose plot forms part of the dialogue.

Undine, however, while stressing the interplay of natural and supernatural elements within a fairy-tale framework, is essentially an opera of the folk (based on a *Volks-* rather than a *Kunstmärchen*) and, like *Der Freischütz*, with its more ominous overtones, does not exemplify the high fantastic mode[43]. Both operas, it might well be said, smack somewhat of the *Biedermeier*, the most striking operatic incarnation of which is found in the operas of Lortzing, including his *Undine*[44].

What all these confrontations of theory and practice amount to is an awareness that Hoffmann's vision of Romantic opera was Utopian, and that Jean Chantavoine correctly assessed the situation when he stated:

---

41 This is the definition offered by Webster's *Collegiate Dictionary*.

42 Ludwig distinguishes clearly between what one might call the 'high exotic', where the lofty mood is maintained throughout, and what might be called the 'low exotic' of the *commedia dell'arte* and the *opera buffa*, where strangeness intrudes into the *Alltagswelt*.

43 I fully agree with Garlington's conclusion that "Hoffmann's critical speculations remain his major contribution to the efforts of creating German Romantic opera", the "*Undine* was not to be the success, much less the vindication, of his theories that he must have desired", and that the immediate popular success of *Der Freischütz* "appeared to turn German Romantic opera into pathways not consistent with Hoffmann's lofty conceptualization of Romanticism" (Garlington, in *The Musical Quarterly*, p. 42).

44 Paul Henry Lang has good reasons for calling Lortzing "the embodiment of the German petty bourgeois of the times" (*Music in Western Civilization*, p. 841).

> Ainsi se trouve réalisée en partie cette unité que le romanticisme littéraire de Tieck, de Jean-Paul (pour ne pas parler de Hoffmann, qui n'y est pas arrivé dans sa propre *Undine*) envisageait comme le caractère essentiel de l'opéra nouveau. On n'y trouve encore, en effet, ni l'union du librettiste et du compositeur en une seule personne (sauf chez Lortzing, contemporain mais non représentant du romantisme), ni la suppression du dialogue parlé qui subsiste dans *Freischütz*, dans *Oberon*, dans [Marschner's] *Hans Heiling*[45].

(Thus the unity the German literary Romanticism of Tieck and Jean Paul – not to mention Hoffmann, who did not attain it in his *Undine* – envisaged as the essential character of the new opera was achieved, but only in part. Actually, one finds as yet neither the fusion of librettist and composer in one person (except for Lortzing, who was a contemporary but not a representative of Romanticism) nor the suppression of the spoken dialogue, which lives on in *Der Freischütz*, *Oberon*, and [Marschner's] *Hans Heiling*.)

What goes for Hoffmann, wrongly accused of having written a highly critical review of *Der Freischütz*[46], goes also for Weber, enthusiastic reviewer of *Undine*[47]. Since Weber is universally recognized as the Grand Master of (German) Romantic Opera, and, in addition, has been widely written about, I do not need to go into detail concerning his role and historical position; nor do I intend to repeat what I have said about *Der Freischütz* in a different context[48]. What is needed is a brief but pithy comparison between his and Hoffmann's melo-dramaturgical theory and practice.

Weber, the melo-dramaturgist, emerges most forcefully in "Tonkünstlers Leben", those "Fragmente eines Romans" which, written between 1809 and 1820, convey, partly in dialogue form and partly

---

45 Jean Chantavoine, in Jean Chantavoine & Jean Gaudefroy-Demombynes, *Le Romantisme dans la musique européenne* (Paris: Michel, 1955), p. 102.

46 Still cited as his work in some recent books but unmasked by Wolfgang Kron in his study *Die angeblichen 'Freischütz'-Kritiken E. T. A. Hoffmanns* (Munich: Huebner, 1957). The text of the reviews in question is reprinted in *'Der Freischütz': Texte, Materialien, Kommentare*, ed. Karl Dietrich Grawe (Hamburg: Rowohlt, 1981), pp. 104-114.

47 Reprinted in Weber's *Sämtliche Schriften*, ed. Georg Kaiser (Leipzig: Schuster & Loeffler, 1908), pp. 127-135.

48 My lecture on the *Freischütz* libretto, delivered at the Fourth McMaster Colloquium on German Literature, has been published in *The Romantic Tradition: German Literature and Music in the Nineteenth Century*, ed. Gerald Chapple, Frederick Hall, and Hans Schulte (Lanham: Univ. Press of America, 1992).

through parodies, his views of and opinions about music both classical and contemporary[49]. The section which most closely corresponds to "Der Dichter und der Komponist" is the fifth chapter, especially the portion dating from 1817 (that is, from the time when Weber was in the early stages of work on *Der Freischütz*). Its key sentence runs as follows:

> Es versteht sich von selbst, daß ich von der Oper spreche, die der Deutsche und Franzose will, einem in sich abgeschlossenen Kunstwerke, wo alle Teile und Beiträge der verwandten und benutzten Künste ineinanderschmelzend verschwinden und auf gewisse Weise eine neue Welt bilden[50].

> (It is obvious that I am talking of the kind of opera that is congenial to the German and the Frenchman alike, that is to say, an organic, self-sufficient work of art in which the parts and elements contributed by the various arts constitute a new cosmos and lose their proper identity.)

How much importance Weber attached to this credo is shown by the fact that he literally quotes it (omitting "und Franzose") in his review of *Undine*, published that same year. A second source of crucial information about Weber's conception of the *Gesamtkunstwerk*, less familiar than "Tonkünstlers Leben", is constituted by two conversations with A. C. Lobe which took place in the early twenties[51]. There Weber elaborates on the characteristic notions of *Hauptelement*, *Hauptcharakter* and *Haupt(klang)farbe*, techniques and devices aimed at rendering the total work of art more cohesive.

As for Weber's actual practice, illustrated by *Der Freischütz*, that alleged paragon of Romantic opera writ large[52], it, too, clashes with the theory. Thus, like his fellow composer-conductor, the Dresden

---

49 "Tonkünstlers Leben" is included in *Sämtliche Schriften*, pp. 437-503. It has been discussed by Steven P. Scher in *Comparative Literature Studies*, 15 (1978), pp. 30-42, and by Steven Cerf at the above-mentioned symposium.

50 Weber, *Sämtliche Schriften*, p. 469.

51 The conversations are reprinted in *'Der Freischütz': Texte, Materialien, Kommentare*, as well as in *Carl Maria von Weber in seinen Schriften und in zeitgenössischen Dokumenten*, ed. Martin Hürlimann (Zurich: Manesse, 1973), pp. 217-250.

52 *Der Freischütz* appears as a 'Romantic opera' both in the *Klavierauszug* and on the title page of the textbook issued for the premiere of the opera, but not on the *Theaterzettel*.

Kapellmeister did not author his own libretto but engaged the service of the hack writer, Friedrich Kind, with whom he collaborated and on whom he imposed (literally speaking) a fair number of more or less significant changes[53]. Nor is *Der Freischütz* a through-composed opera but a work that is heavily interlarded with prose dialogue, *Melodram* and quasi-recitative (as in the *Wolfsschlucht* scene), some of it cut in most performances. It is a *Nummernoper*, each of the sixteen units labelled as such forming an entity by itself. Yet there are instances of closer integration, such as the bracketing of different musical forms in a given number (#13, "Romanze, Rezitativ und Arie"), and signs of greater continuity, such as the fading out of the waltz in #3 and the spilling over of the *Volkslied* in #14.

Weber has further enhanced the flexibility of the melo-dramaturgical scheme by softening the rigid outlines of standard pieces. Thus, in accordance with his notion of "deklamatorisches Anschmiegen" ('declamatory snuggling')[54] he has strengthened the expressiveness of Max's "Rezitativ und Arie" (#3, after the waltz) and Agathe's "Szene und Arie" (#8) by alternating moods – in stark contrast to #4 (Kaspar's *Lied*) and #7 (Ännchen's *Ariette*), where the retention of the stereotypical form is justified because we deal with standard patterns in the German tradition. A similar conflict, less clearly resolved, arises with regard to the labeling of the individual numbers which, in the case of Hoffmann's *Undine*, were consistently Italianate. In the piano-vocal score, Weber throughout uses designations like *aria, scena* and *tercetto*; but in the full orchestral score he Germanizes these technical terms (*Arie, Szene, Terzett*), an operation which in some instances (*Romanze, Kavatine*) entails an (intended?) modification of their meaning. Unlike Hoffmann, he juxtaposes such conventional foreign superscriptions with unequivocally German ones (*Walzer, Lied, Volks-*

---

53 Including the omission of the opening scenes, these changes are detailed in my contribution to the Fourth McMaster Colloquium.
54 Weber's formulation as recounted by Lobe (*'Der Freischütz': Texte, Materialien, Kommentare*, p. 158).

lied, Jägerchor), thereby establishing an equilibrium between indigenous and imported features and concurrently demonstrating that his *Freischütz* is part *opera seria* (based on Franco-Italian models as well as harking back to *Fidelio* and the Sarastro strain in Mozart's *Zauberflöte*) and part *Singspiel* and German *Volksoper*.

Without wishing to extend the discussion of Weber's operatic Romanticism unduly, I should like to call attention to Franz Grillparzer's harsh treatment of *Der Freischütz* in a fragmentary review, a parody, a satirical *Avertissement*, and some very serious reflections on the relationship of music and language[55]. The Viennese playwright and would-be librettist for Beethoven[56] castigates that ingratiating piece as a work whose creator has overindulged in the superficial art of tone painting in the vain hope of making the score more natural. Having discussed the aesthetic properties congenial to the two media, Grillparzer concludes the theoretical portion of his essay – the only one to have been written or, at any rate, to have survived – with the following sentences pillorying Weber's attempt to take musical Romanticism to its counterproductive extreme:

> Was folgt aus dem allen, wird man fragen? Soll Musik aufhören, bezeichnend sein zu wollen? Soll sie in der Oper nicht streng dem Text folgen? Soll sie nicht streben, den Verstand zu befriedigen? Es folgt daraus, daß die Musik vor allem streben soll, das zu erreichen, was ihr erreichbar ist; daß sie nicht [...] das aufgeben soll, worin sie allen Redekünsten überlegen ist; daß sie nicht streben müsse, aus Tönen Worte zu machen; daß sie, wie jede Kunst, aufhöre, Kunst zu sein, wenn sie aus der in ihrer Natur gegründeten Form herausgeht. [...] daß so wie der Dichter ein Tor ist, der in seinen Versen den Musiker im Klang erreichen will, ebenso der Musiker ein Verrückter ist, der mit seinen Tönen Dichter an Bestimmtheit des Ausdrucks es gleich tun will; daß Mozart der größte Tonsetzer ist und Maria Weber – nicht der größte[57].

---

55 All these pieces are reproduced in Grillparzer's *Sämtliche Werke*, ed. Peter Frank and Paul Pörnbacher (Munich: Hanser, 1964), vol. III, "Ausgewählte Briefe, Gespräche, Berichte". The fragmentary review appears on pp. 885-888, the parody ("*Der wilde Jäger*, Romantische Oper") on p. 21, das *Avertissement* on pp. 72f., and the serious reflections, under the heading "Über die Oper", on pp. 897-900.

56 The work in question is *Melusina*, a "Romantische Oper in drei Aufzügen". The text, set to music by Conradin Kreutzer, is reprinted in Grillparzer, I, pp. 1167-1202.

57 Grillparzer, III, p. 888.

(What's the upshot of all this?, people will ask. Should music desist from wanting to designate? Should it follow the text slavishly? Should it strive to satisfy the reason? The upshot is that, most of all, music should strive to attain what is proper to it; that it should not abandon that in which it excels the verbal arts; that it should not attempt to make sounds into words; that, like every art, it ceases to be art as soon as it oversteps its natural boundaries; [...] that, just as the poet who seeks to rival the composer is a fool, so the composer who seeks to equal the poet by trying to express specific ideas is a madman; that Mozart is the greatest composer, and [Carl] Maria [von] Weber is – not the greatest.)

Historically speaking, Grillparzer, in mounting this attack, assumes a puristic stance which in some ways approximates the position defended in "Der Dichter und der Komponist".

While it goes without saying that an essay entitled "What is Romantic Opera?" cannot ignore the art of Richard Wagner without being rightly accused of criminal negligence, the issue at stake in the present context would be muddled if I were to survey that composer's entire output, especially given the fact that Wagner's artistic career extends well beyond the outer limits of European Romanticism conceived in a strict historical sense, making him a contemporary of Brahms rather than Schumann, much less Weber. Thus, with a heavy heart, I must refrain from entering into a discussion of *Tristan und Isolde* (1859), the apogee of that perennial Romanticism to which Chantavoine refers in connection with the Master of Bayreuth[58]. Instead, I shall focus on *Der fliegende Holländer* (1841) as the work which, in more ways than one, brings operatic Romanticism *a la tedesca* to a quintessential climax.

To create the right atmosphere for such a discussion, I should like to remind the reader that Wagner, especially in his twenties and thirties, was an ardent admirer of Hoffmann and Weber (the maker of *Der Freischütz*, not of *Euryanthe* – about which latter he has a few nasty things to say[59]). When a Paris production of Weber's masterpiece was in the offing in 1841 (the *Holländer* year!) he wrote two essays, one in

---

58 Chantavoine, p. 294.

59 The critique of *Euryanthe* occupies the better part of a long paragraph in the essay "Die deutsche Oper" (1834), in Wagner, *Gesammelte Schriften* (fn. 60), pp. 8f.

anticipation of the performance and the other, in its wake, as a report to the German public[60]. Describing the opera, in Weber's sense, as "ein vollkommenes, sowohl dem Gedanken als der Form nach in allen seinen Teilen wohlgegliedertes Ganzes" ('a whole which, in all its parts, is well articulated both in form and content'), he denounced its transformation into Grand Opera. He sounded his note of warning in view, and in spite, of the fact that it was no other than Hector Berlioz, the only French composer likely to stand "auf der Höhe eines solches Versuchs" ('capable of tackling such a task') (p. 19), who had been commissioned to adapt the work, supply the mandatory recitatives, and procure the music for the balletic interludes[61].

Throughout his life, Wagner esteemed E. T. A. Hoffmann, whose work, both creative and critical, he emulated on many occasions[62]. To mention only the most obvious instances of such borrowing: taking his clue (or so it would seem) from "Der Dichter und der Komponist", he based one of his early operas, *Die Feen* (1834), on one of Gozzi's dramatic fairy-tales[63]; and shortly after the completion of *Der fliegende Holländer* he furnished, at the request of a hack composer named Dessauer, a detailed scenario based on Hoffmann's "Die Bergwerke zu Falun", a novella which, as Marc Weiner has shown in a recent essay, had an impact on several of his works[64]. Since this was not a labor of love but an *Auftragsarbeit* commissioned on the strength of *Le Vaisseau fantôme* (the text, but not the music), he arranged the

---

60 "*Der Freischütz*: An das Pariser Publikum" and "*Le Freischütz:* Bericht nach Deutschland" are both reproduced in Wagner's *Gesammelte Schriften*, ed. Julius Kapp (Leipzig: Hesse & Becker, [1914]), VIII, pp. 7-41.

61 The music for the ballets was taken from various works by Weber and included the famous "Aufforderung zum Tanz".

62 For a more detailed survey see Linda Siegel's essay "Wagner and the Romanticism of E. T. A. Hoffmann," *The Musical Quarterly*, 51 (1965), pp. 597-613.

63 The work on which *Die Feen* was based is *La donna serpente*. Curiously enough, Brahms considered writing an opera on Gozzi's *Il re cervo*, to which Hans Werner Henze turned in his *König Hirsch*.

64 Marc Weiner, "Richard Wagner's Use of E. T. A. Hoffmann's 'The Mines of Falun'", *Nineteenth-Century Music*, 2 (1982), pp. 201-214.

material in such a way as to suit operatic convention by subdividing the action into the usual arias, ensembles, and finales[65]. Had he adapted the story for his own use, he would hardly have resorted to this technique; for thus to perpetuate the antiquated *Nummernoper* would have meant a step backwards for one who had embarked on a journey to the *Gesamtkunstwerk*.

Now that the preliminaries, aimed at demonstrating that the young Wagner was an adept of Romanticism and its chief representatives in the field of melo-drama, are out of the way, let us look at *Der fliegende Holländer* as a late bloom of Romantic opera. This is how the work was designated on the playbill issued in connection with its premiere at the Königlich-Sächsisches Hoftheater in Dresden on January 2, 1843. Wagner, who uses the same label in a letter to Schumann dated November 3, 1842, where he refers to the recently completed piece as an opera, "einem ganz anderen Genre, dem rein romantischen [angehörend]" ('[belonging] to a totally different genre, the purely Romantic')[66], subsequently applied it to *Tannhäuser* and *Lohengrin* as well, largely, one assumes, with reference to their subject. But already in his lengthy "Mitteilung an meine Freunde", composed in 1851, he viewed the whole matter with considerable skepticism. Without repudiating the 'Romantic' triad, he states defensively, equating 'romantische Oper' with 'Grosse Oper':

> Der Richtung, in die ich mich mit der Konzeption des *Fliegenden Holländers* schlug, gehören die beiden ihm folgenden dramatischen Dichtungen, *Tannhäuser* und *Lohengrin*, an. Mir ist der Vorwurf gemacht worden, daß ich mit diesen Arbeiten in die, wie man meint, durch Meyerbeers *Robert der Teufel* überwundene und geschlossene, von mir mit meinem *Rienzi* bereits selbst verlassene Richtung der 'romantischen' Oper *zurück*getreten sei. Für die, welche mir diesen Vorwurf machen, ist die romantische *Oper* natürlich eher vorhanden als die *Opern*, die nach einer konventionell klassifizierenden Annahme 'romantische' genannt werden. Ob ich von einer künstlerisch formellen Absicht aus auf die Konstruktion

---

65 "*Die Bergwerke zu Falun*: Entwurf zu einer Oper in drei Akten" is found in Wagner's *Gesammelte Schriften* (fn. 60 above), VI, pp. 55-67, an English version thereof in the appendix to Weiner's article.

66 Richard Wagner, *Sämtliche Briefe*, ed. Gertrud Strobel and Werner Wolf (Leipzig: VEB Deutscher Verlag fur Musik), II (1970), p. 170.

Toward a Musico-Literary Definition 323

von 'romantischen' Opern ausging, wird sich herausstellen, wenn ich die Entstehungsgeschichte jener drei Werke genau erzähle[67].

(The genre which I initiated with the conception of *The Flying Dutchman* also includes my two subsequent operas, *Tannhäuser* and *Lohengrin*. I have been told that with these works I have regressed to the level of the so-called 'romantic' opera which I myself had already left behind with my *Rienzi*, and which found its culmination in Meyerbeer's *Robert le Diable*. In the eyes of those who make this reproach, the *romantic opera* pre-existed operas which, according to the conventional classification, are called 'Romantic'. Whether, aesthetically speaking, I deliberately meant to create 'romantic' operas will come to light once I describe the genesis of these three works.)

In later years he ceased, for tactical reasons, to bestow this weighty epithet on the three works that precede *Der Ring des Nibelungen*[68]. So much for the name of the many-splendored thing that is 'romantisch' – and now to its nature, both in the stage of inception and execution. Let us briefly trace the genesis of *Der fliegende Holländer*, so as to demonstrate how Wagner's conception of the work changed due to his growing awareness of the pragmatics of show business. The original outline, a sketch written in French[69] and sold, under some pressure, to the manager of the Paris Opéra, composed by Louis Philippe Dietsch and performed on November 9, 1841 under the title *Le Vaisseau fantôme ou Le Maudit des mers*, "opéra fantastique en deux actes" – was intended as a curtain raiser in which the unity of action was to have been preserved almost in the manner of Greek tragedy. As Wagner states in his autobiography:

Ich faßte den Stoff [...] für einen einzigen Akt zusammen, wozu mich zunächst der Gegenstand selbst bestimmte, da ich auf diese Weise ihn ohne alles jetzt mich

---

67 Richard Wagner, *Dichtungen und Schriften*, ed. Dieter Borchmeyer (Frankfurt: Insel-Verlag, 1983), VI, p. 237.
68 In letters to Liszt dated November 25, 1850, and February 18, 1851, he still uses the expression "drei romantische Opern"; but a letter to his publishers of August 23, 1851, merely refers to "drei Operndichtungen".
69 So far unpublished, it will appear in the *Dokumentenband* to *Der fliegende Holländer* in Richard Wagner, *Sämtliche Werke* (Mainz: B. Schott's Söhne, 1970ff.), under the editorship of Carl Dahlhaus.

anwidernde Opernbeiwerk auf den einfachen dramatischen Vorgang zwischen den Hauptpersonen zusammengedrängt geben konnte[70].

(Due to the kind of subject matter this was, I decided to concentrate the action into a single act since, dispensing with the usual operatic claptrap, which now disgusts me, I was thus able to focus narrowly on the simple dramatic development involving the major characters.)

Wagner never dropped this notion altogether, even though the first plot outline in German indicates a division into three acts that is retained in both 'versions' of the score[71]. As the observation contained in a letter to Cäcilie Avenarius "Wir gaben die Oper in drei Aufzügen, so daß sie den ganzen Abend füllte" ('We gave the opera in three acts, so that it filled the entire evening')[72] suggests, he regarded the tripartite scheme as artificial and as going against the very grain of his original plan. Indeed, an uninterrupted performance of *Der fliegende Holländer* can be accomplished after minor surgery along the orchestral seams which separate the acts. Productions which treat the work as an 'Einakter in drei Aufzügen' have been fairly common in recent years; and some prominent stage directors have cast the action either in the form of Senta's dream (Harry Kupfer in Bayreuth, successfully) or that of the Steuermann (Jean Pierre Ponelle and his assistants in New York, San Francisco, and Chicago, unsuccessfully)[73].

Perceived as Senta's dream, the work has its center of gravity and spiritual, though not factual, point of departure in that character's ballad in the second act, which was one of the first (if not the first)

---

70 Richard Wagner, *Mein Leben*, ed. Martin Gregor-Dellin (Munich: List, 1976), p. 193. In a letter to Eugène Scribe (*Sämtliche Briefe*, I, p. 390), Wagner speaks of a "petit opéra en un acte".

71 The incomplete prose sketch, dated 1840, was first published in the *Programmheft* of a production of *Der fliegende Holländer* at the Munich Staatsoper in January, 1981, pp. 88-90. The original version of the score was published for the first time in the *Gesamtausgabe* (see fn. 69 above).

72 Wagner, *Sämtliche Briefe*, II, 204.

73 As the Chicago production demonstrated, interpreting the opera as the Steuermann's dream is extremely awkward as it necessitates 1) the dreamer's sporadic participation in the dreamt action, and 2) the dreamer's awakening at the end to close the frame.

musical number to be written[74]. That Wagner considered this particular piece to constitute the true germ of *Der fliegende Holländer*, which he himself called a "dramatische Ballade"[75], can be deduced from the following passage in his "Bemerkungen zur Aufführung des *Fliegenden Holländers*" ('Remarks concerning the staging of *The Flying Dutchman*', 1852) which seems to justify the oneiric interpretation of the work:

> Die Rolle der Senta wird schwer zu verfehlen sein; nur vor einem habe ich zu warnen: möge das träumerische Wesen nicht im Sinne einer modernen, krankhaften Sentimentalität aufgefaßt werden! Im Gegenteile ist Senta ein ganz kerniges nordisches Mädchen, und selbst in ihrer anscheinenden Sentimentalität ist sie durchaus *naiv*. Gerade nur bei einem ganz naiven Mädchen konnten, umgeben von der ganzen Eigentümlichkeit der nordischen Natur, Eindrücke wie die Ballade vom "fliegenden Holländer" und des Bildes des bleichen Seemannes einen so wunderstarken Hang wie den Trieb zur Erlösung des Verdammten hervorbringen:

---

74 "Als ich [...] noch hoffte, dieses Sujet für die französische Oper bearbeiten zu dürfen, hatte ich bereits einige lyrische Bestandteile desselben poetisch und musikalisch ausgeführt. [...] Dies waren die Ballade der Senta, das Lied der norwegischen Matrosen und der Spuk-Gesang der Mannschaft des 'Fliegenden Holländers'." ('At the time when I still hoped to be able to treat this subject for the (Paris) *Opéra*, I had already executed a few lyrical ingredients of the piece verbally and musically. These were Senta's ballad, the song of the Norwegian sailor and the ghostly chorus of the Flying Dutchman's crew.') (Wagner, *Mein Leben*, p. 212)

75 "Als ich die fertige Arbeit betiteln sollte, hatte ich nicht übel Lust, sie eine 'dramatische Ballade' zu nennen. Bei der endlichen Ausführung der Komposition breitete sich mir das empfangene thematische Bild ganz unwillkürlich als ein vollständiges Gewebe über das ganze Drama aus; ich hatte [...] nur die verschiedenen thematischen Keime, die in der Ballade enthalten waren, nach ihren eigenen Richtungen hin weiter und vollständig zu entwickeln [...]." ('When I pondered the title of the completed work, I first thought of calling it a "dramatic ballad"; for in the course of composing the piece the thematic node quite involuntarily spread like a web over the entire drama, and all that was left for me to do was to develop the various thematic germs contained in the ballad according to the directions suited to them.') Quoted from "Eine Mitteilung an meine Freunde" by Dieter Borchmeyer in his contribution ("*Der fliegende Holländer* – eine 'dramatische Ballade'") to the *Programmheft* (cited in fn. 71), p. 16. – Let us remember that it was Goethe who characterized the ballad as the germ (*Keimzelle*) of the three basic literary modes, the lyrical, the epic, and the dramatic.

dieser äußert sich bei ihr als ein kräftiger Wahnsinn, wie er wirklich nur ganz naiven Naturen zu eigen sein kann[76].

(The role of Senta is easy to interpret; but there is one thing I must insist on: let her dreamy nature not be understood in the sense of a modern, pathological sentimentality. On the contrary, Senta is an extremely healthy Nordic girl; and even in her apparent sentimentality she is truly naïve. Only in such a girl, surrounded by a characteristically Nordic nature, impressions like those generated by the ballad of the 'Flying Dutchman' and the picture of the pale sailor could produce such a strong desire as her drive to redeem the accursed man. In her case, that desire takes the form of a vigorous madness, such as suits truly naïve persons.)

The dream, which *is* the action of the opera unfolding before our eyes, would thus be triggered by, and revolve around, the "Bildnis eines bleichen Mannes mit dunklem Barte, in schwarzer spanischer Tracht" ('the portrait of a pale man with a dark beard, dressed in black Spanish garb') which dominates the setting for Act II; and in the characteristically Romantic interplay between the natural and supernatural spheres the realism of Daland's, Eric's, and Mary's world would be pitted against the fantastic otherworld of the phantom ship and its crew, Senta being the point at which the two spheres intersect.

As regards the unification of the action through the replacement of the *Nummernoper* by the through-composed music drama, Wagner, like Weber before him, has gone only half of the way. For even though in a letter to Ferdinand Heine he claims to have repudiated "den modernen Zuschnitt in Arien, Duette, Finales, etc."[77], the evidence shows that he did so somewhat halfheartedly by combining various traditional numbers (#4, "Lied, Szene, Ballade und Chor", #6, "Arie, Duett und Terzett", and #8, "Duett, Kavatine und Finale" – to name only the most glaring examples) with the aim of cementing the action and achieving greater continuity. Thus, while making considerable progress in the right direction, he ended by striking a compromise. As Carl Dahlhaus so aptly observes, *Der fliegende Holländer*

---

76 Wagner, *Gesammelte Schriften*, IX, pp. 51f. Wagner uses 'naiv' and 'sentimentalisch' in the Schillerian sense, whereas Nietzsche, condemning "Senta-Sentimentalität", obviously does not but introjects the popularized meaning of the term.
77 Undated letter (early August, 1843) in Wagner, *Sämtliche Briefe*, II, p. 314.

ist keine 'Nummern-', sondern eine 'Szenenoper'. Das Verfahren, einzelne Arien, Duette, Ensemblesätze und Chöre zu Komplexen zusammenzufassen, statt sie unverbunden nebeneinanderzustellen [...] erstreckt sich [hier] über das ganze Werk, ohne daß jedoch von einem 'durchkomponierten Musikdrama' die Rede sein könnte[78].

(is no 'numbers' opera but a 'scenic' one. The technique of clamping individual arias, duets, ensembles, and choruses together, instead of merely lining them up, here extends to the entire work without there as yet resulting a through-composed drama.)

As I have previously indicated, it would be regrettable if it turned out that the subgenre under consideration happened to be a *typisch deutscher Gegenstand* without any foreign offshoots or equivalents. An effort should, therefore, be made to establish its internationality.

I am, accordingly, well advised to search abroad and look into other national traditions that might be compatible in one way or another. Failing to discover any worthy subjects in England, Russia or Spain, one will turn to Italy and France for corroborating evidence. To begin with the homeland of opera as we know it: since not the faintest hint of a concerted striving for the unified total work of art which I have portrayed as the culmination of Romantic opera, whether in theory or practice, is discernible in Bellini or Donizetti[79], we would, methodologically speaking, waste our time if we took that much trodden but still hopelessly entangled path.

With the younger Verdi matters are somewhat different in so far as by setting to music two librettos based on plays by the self-confessed arch-Romantic Victor Hugo he would seem to have demonstrated a certain kinship in artistic outlook. On the literary – thematic and

---

78 Carl Dahlhaus, *Richard Wagners Musikdramen* (Velber: Friedrich-Verlag, 1971). From the chapter on *Der fliegende Holländer*, as reprinted in the *Programmheft* (fn. 71), p. 66.

79 In his massive study of *Donizetti and his Operas* (Cambridge: Cambridge Univ. Press, 1982), William Ashbrook conceives of Romanticism in purely thematic, and literary, terms: "Simply put, the basic demand for Romantic melodrama is that the composer give musical coherence and credibility to an intense plot whose denouement is tragic and inevitable" (p. 497). This will hardly do as a criterion for defining Romantic opera.

stylistic – level, the only one likely to yield results[80], an explanation, however tentative and general, is provided by David Kimbell in the chapter on *Ernani*: "Verdi abandoned the distinctive Italian kind of Romanticism, the Romanticism of Church and State, in favour of a Romanticism more lurid in hue and more grotesque in form, a Romanticism fundamentally French."[81] That it was precisely this contrast between the sublime and the grotesque, championed in Hugo's "Preface" to *Cromwell* of 1827, which appealed to Verdi is shown by the following passage from a letter dated December 14, 1850, and addressed to C. D. Marzari, the director of the Teatro Fenice in Venice:

> Putting on the stage a character grossly deformed and absurd, but inwardly passionate and full of love, is precisely what I find the beautiful thing. I chose this subject precisely for these qualities, these original traits, and if they are taken away, I can no longer write music for it. If you tell me that my music can stay the same even with this drama, I reply that I don't understand such reasoning; and I say frankly that whether my music is beautiful or ugly I don't write it by chance, but always try to give it a definite character[82].

Here, then, is Verdi's artistic credo, echoed in so many letters written, throughout his career, to his librettists. For the rest, Verdi being no theoretician but a man of the theater, who cared little for -isms and was solely concerned with achieving the greatest intrinsic effect – in contrast to Puccini, who preferred the extrinsic effects of melodrama – we can probably take him at his word when he writes, almost three decades later, to Opprandino Arrivabene:

---

80 In a book which he shrewdly entitles *Verdi in the Age of Italian Romanticism* (Cambridge: Cambridge Univ. Press, 1981), David R. Kimbell states unambiguously that, melo-dramaturgically speaking, Verdi was not "disposed to dispute [...] that opera was [...] a type of drama in which the ongoing action had to be expressed in self-contained, lucidly architected 'numbers'" (p. 624, with regard to *Rigoletto*).

81 The quotation is drawn from the chapter "Verdi and French Romanticism: *Ernani*" of Kimbell's book (p. 460). Its opening chapter contains a balanced account of artistic and literary life in Italy during the 'Romantic' period.

82 Quoted in English by Kimbell, p. 270. The original text, reproduced in Verdi's *Copialettere*, ed. G. Cesari and A. Luzio (Bologna: Fori, 1913), p. 111, begins as follows: "Io trovo appunto bellissimo rappresentare questo personaggio deforme e ridicolo, ed internamente appassionato e pieno d'amore. Scelsi appunto questo soggetto per tutte queste qualità, e questi tratti originalli; se si tolgono, io non posso più farvi musica."

> I shan't talk about music because I no longer remember any. I only know that I've never understood what music of the past and music of the future mean, just as I've never understood in literature the terms classical and romantic [...].[83]

Seen from our, the 'Romantic', perspective, the case of Rossini is more promising, not so much in view of his prodigious output of *opere buffe*, culminating in that perennial favorite which is *Il Barbiere di Siviglia*, as with regard to *Guillaume Tell*, his last opera and the crowning glory of the final, Parisian phase of his relatively short career. The potentially 'Romantic' nature of Rossini's art had been discerned by Stendhal, the passionate advocate of Romanticism taken in the sense of pure emotionalism, whose *Vie de Rossini*, without so much as breathing the word 'romantic', contains a number of passages in which the composer's perspectivism and the atmospheric quality of his works at their best are eulogized, as in the following excerpt from the chapter on *Tancredi*:

> Si l'on veut arriver [...] à l'idée de l'harmonie dans ses rapports avec le chant, je puis dire que Rossini a employé avec succès le grand artifice de Walter Scott. [...] Comme Rossini prépare et soutient ses chants par l'harmonie, de même Walter Scott prépare et soutient ses dialogues et ses récits par des descriptions[84].

> (If this conception of the relationship between orchestral and vocal music can be made any clearer by analogy, I would suggest that Rossini successfully employs a device invented by Walter Scott. [...] Just as Rossini uses his *orchestral harmony* to prepare the way for and to reinforce his passages of vocal music, so Walter Scott prepares the way for, and reinforces, his passages of dialogue and narrative by means of *description*.)

As for *Guillaume Tell*, which is rightly seen as one of the immediate precursors of Grand Opera, it amply rewards an inquiry into its Romantic properties. Since I have tackled that question, among several others, in an earlier paper[85], I will limit myself to stating that such an

---

83 The letter dates from May 26, 1878. It is quoted in English in *Verdi: The Man in his Letters*, ed. Franz Werfel and Paul Stefan (New York: Fischer, 1942), p. 346.

84 Stendhal, *Vie de Rossini*, transl. by Richard N. Coe (New York: Criterion Books, 1957), p. 57.

85 "Der Apfel fiel recht weit vom Stamme: Rossinis *Guillaume Tell*, eine musikalische Schweizerreise", read at the Berlin *Romanistentag* in October, 1983, and published in the proceedings of the libretto section of that congress: *Oper als Text:*

ascription could well be justified in terms of the literary and musical, although not necessarily in those of the melo-dramatic, tradition. Based on a play by Schiller, which the latter – author of the "romantische Tragödie" *Die Jungfrau von Orleans* and the "Trauerspiel mit Chören" *Die Braut van Messina*, which parallels the verbal operas of Hugo on a much higher artistic plane – characterized as the upshot of an attempt, "einen romantischen Stoff antik zu behandeln" ('to treat a Romantic theme in the ancient manner')[86], *Guillaume Tell* constitutes, musically speaking, a solid link in the chain that extends from Beethoven's Pastoral Symphony by way of *Der Freischütz* to Hector Berlioz, who, in addition to copying the parts of Rossini's score for its publisher, analyzed *Guillaume Tell* in a lengthy essay published in the *Gazette musicale de Paris*[87].

To be brief: while *Guillaume Tell* satisfies few, if any, of the programmatic conditions attached to the Romantic *Gesamtkunstwerk* – Rossini employed no less than four librettists and created a work that strikes one as being monumental without possessing the virtue of unity-in-diversity[88] – certain portions, especially the universally admired second act, manage superbly to generate a mood and an atmosphere that are reminiscent of *Der Freischütz* and *Der fliegende Holländer* at their best. It most certainly served as a model for the towering genius of French Romantic music, that monstrous exception with-

---

Romanistische Beiträge zur Libretto-Forschung, ed. Albert Gier (Heidelberg: Winter, 1986), pp. 147-184.

86 This is what, according to Heinrich Voss, Jr., Schiller said at a party in Weimar. The remark is cited in *Dichter über ihre Dichtungen: Friedrich Schiller*, ed. Bodo Lecke (Munich: Heimeran, 1970), II, p. 462.

87 The essay appeared in the first volume of that periodical, pp. 326-327, 336-339, 341-343, and 249-251. A complete English version is found in *Source Readings in Music History from Classical Antiquity through the Romantic Era*, selected and annotated by Oliver Strunk (New York: Norton, 1950), pp. 809-826.

88 Both Berlioz and Verdi (in a letter to Camille Du Locle of December 8, 1869), while greatly admiring the work, were dismayed by its lack of integration.

in the French ambience[89], whose art E. T. A. Hoffmann (though hardly Weber) would surely have admired. It is to him that we must turn in conclusion, though not in his capacity as an operatic composer in the routine sense. For while works like the opera-oratorio *La Damnation de Faust* and, to a considerably lesser degree, *Les Troyens* (over which the classical spirit of Vergil presides along with the 'romantic' genius of Shakespeare) might do to illustrate certain obvious aspects of Berlioz's Romanticism, it is in the *Symphonie fantastique* of 1830, if anywhere, that we shall find a source of satisfaction.

In the same year in which Hugo's *Hernani* had its turbulent premiere[90] and three years after Delacroix exhibited his monumental "Mort de Sardanapale"[91], Berlioz, the third member of the triumvirate, composed the piece for which he is most widely known[92]. To use the composer's own description, the Fantastic Symphony belongs to the "*genre instrumental expressif,* [which] is most closely related to Romanticism". As Berlioz puts it, by way of explanation, in the "Aperçu sur la musique classique et la musique romantique", from which the above phrase is culled:

---

89 In his *Le Romanticisme dans la musique européenne*, Chantavoine observes (p. 13): "La conception romantique de la musique n'est pas une conception française; Berlioz est une monstrueuse exception, tout-à-fait isolée dans la tradition musical française." ('The Romantic notion of music is not specifically French; and Berlioz was a monstrous and altogether unique exception within the French national tradition.')

90 Berlioz attended an early performance of the play, though probably not its premiere.

91 In 1829 Berlioz wrote a cantata on the subject which earned him the Prix de Rome.

92 The best general introduction to the Fantastic Symphony in English is that provided in the edition prepared by Edward T. Cone (New York: Norton, 1971), which includes the texts of several versions of the composer's programs. Nicholas Temperley's essay "The *Symphonie fantastique* and its Program" (*Musical Quarterly*, 57 [1971], pp. 593-608) is rather disappointing given the fact that the author is editing the work for the New Berlioz Edition.

In the works of Beethoven and Weber a poetic idea is everywhere manifest, but music is wholly in command, with no help from words to give it precise expression: we feel no longer in the theatre, rather a new world opens before us[93]. This certainly will not do as a justification for the so-styled *Symphonie descriptive de Faust* as which the Goethe enthusiast Berlioz and author of *Huits scènes de Faust* seems originally to have conceived the work[94]. In line with the composer's emerging theory, the symphony ultimately took the shape of a "composition instrumentale d'un genre nouveau" which, initially labelled "Episode d'une vie d'artiste (grande symphonie fantastique en cinq parties)" ('instrumental piece of a novel kind [...] episode from the life of an artist [grand fantastic symphony in five parts]')[95], acquired its present title sometime after the composition of the score. What qualifies the Fantastic Symphony as a Romantic 'opera' in our sense is, first of all, the unity of composer and librettist (= author of the literary program)[96]; but, more important still and epitomizing the trend toward integration on all levels, it is the identity of creator and creature in the unnamed protagonist as whose autobiography the work is presented. While initially Berlioz spoke of his hero's experience as taking place on three different levels – internal in the first movement, external in the second and third, and oneiric in the fourth and fifth – he later changed his 'tune' by describing the entire piece as the opium dream of a "jeune musicien d'une

---

[93] The quotation, inaccessible to me in the original French, is culled from Barzun's *Berlioz and the Romantic Century*, I, p. 152. The reference to Weber pertains undoubtedly to *Der Freischütz* (which, like *Fidelio*, Berlioz had recently seen with Wilhelmine Schröder-Devrient in the leading female part), that to Beethoven probably to the Pastoral Symphony.

[94] The designation *Symphonie descriptive de Faust* occurs in a letter to Humbert Ferrand dated February 2, 1829. *Correspondence générale d'Hector Berlioz*, ed. Pierre Citron (Paris: Flammarion) I (1972), p. 232.

[95] The label is supplied in a letter to Humbert Ferrand of April 16, 1830, which offers the first, unpublished program of the symphony. See *Correspondence générale*, I, pp. 319ff.

[96] Like Wagner's *Der fliegende Holländer* which, in the composer's own words, falls short of being "aus einem Guß" ('of a piece'), the Fantastic Symphony lacks the unity of the creative process in so far as certain portions of the music were derived from earlier compositions by Berlioz.

sensibilité maladive et d'une imagination ardente" ('a young musician with a sickly sensibility and a fiery imagination')[97]. More spectacular, because easily apparent and in no need of a programmatic explication, is the introduction of a recurrent melodic phrase embodying the hero's beloved who, being the musical protagonist, is the antagonist of the *drame* which the symphony depicts. Her double function both explains and justifies the use of the term *double idée fixe* which Berlioz attached to this device and which he subsequently modified to *mélodie-aimée* ('melody-beloved')[98].

Described in a letter to Humbert Ferrand which contains the first program of what Berlioz then called "mon roman, ou plutôt mon histoire" ('my novel or, rather, my history')[99] – designations which are not generic but merely indicate that the work is autobiographical – the *Symphonie fantastique*, patterned after Beethoven's Sixth and therefore, as Robert Schumann puts it in his famous analysis, naturally in five 'acts'[100], was later dubbed a "drame instrumental privé du secours de la parole" and thus in dire need "d'être exposé d'avance" ('instrumental drama deprived of all verbal support [...] to be explicated beforehand')[101]. As the composer observes in defending the need for verbal support, "le programme suivant doit donc être consideré comme le texte parlé d'un opéra servant à amener des morceaux de

---

97 References throughout this portion of the paper are to the texts of the various programs as reproduced in the appendix to Wolfgang Dömling, *Hector Berlioz: Die symphonisch-dramatischen Werke* (Stuttgart: Reclam, 1979), pp. 143-149.

98 This term occurs in the third version of the program. See Dömling, p. 149.

99 The phrase is used in the letter to Humbert Ferrand mentioned in footnote 94.

100 "[...] vier Sätze sind ihm zu wenig. Er nimmt, wie zu einem Schauspiel, fünf" ('four movements do not suffice for him; he needs five, as is proper to drama'). Robert Schumann in his essay "Sinfonie von H. Berlioz", published in several installments in the *Neue Zeitschrift für Musik* (1835) and reprinted in Schumann's *Gesammelte Schriften über Musik und Musiker*, ed. Martin Kreisig (Leipzig: Breitkopf & Härtel, 1914) I, pp. 69-90; quotation on p. 71. An English version of this detailed musical analysis based on Liszt's piano version of the symphony is found in Edward T. Cone's edition (fn. 92).

101 Dömling, p. 145.

musique, dont il motive le caractère et l'expression" ('the following program should thus be regarded as the spoken text of an opera aimed at introducing musical numbers whose nature and character it explains')[102]. As the Romantic Mendelssohn wrote *chants sans paroles*, so the Romantic Berlioz produced an opera *presque sans paroles*.

After completing a sequel to the *Symphonie fantastique*, an aesthetically deficient and therefore rarely performed monodrama called *Lélio ou Le Retour à la vie* that requires staging, Berlioz changed his mind and downgraded the significance of the program in words that leave little doubt that, however reluctantly, he had abandoned the Romantic perspective, partly, one suspects, in reaction to the blatantly literary though highly poetic program music cultivated by his friend and admirer Liszt:

> Si on exécute la symphonie isolément dans un concert, cette disposition [on the stage] n'est plus nécéssaire; on peut même à la rigueur se dispenser de distribuer le programme, en conservant seulement le titre des cinq morceaux; la symphonie (l'auteur l'espère) pouvant offrir en soi un intérêt musical indépendant de toute intention dramatique[103].

> (When one performs the symphony in the concert hall, that [theatrical] disposition is unnecessary; at a pinch one could even do without the programme while retaining the titles of the five movements; for the symphony by itself – so I hope – offers sufficient musical interest even without the support of an underlying dramatic intention.)

Thus Berlioz, who, in foisting a story upon his instrumental composition, had taken a decisive step beyond the generalized musical program offered by the Pastoral Symphony and had thus single-handedly created his own brand of Romantic opera-for-orchestra, undermined his success by once again drawing a clear line of demarcation between purely instrumental music, on the one hand, and programmatic music on the other. For the Berlioz of 1855 the *Symphonie fantastique* no longer counted as a total work of art as it had originally been conceived, but as counterpart of Beethoven's Sixth.

---

102 Dömling, p. 145.
103 Dömling, p. 147. Berlioz called *Lélio* a *mélologue* in 1832 but changed the label to the more familiar *monodrame* in the printed edition of 1855.

We have completed our experiment, which was designed to produce examples of Romantic opera in its purest and least adulterated form. After rejecting the thematic approach as well as those definitions which are satisfied with the presence of exclusively literary or exclusively musical qualities alleged to the Romantic, we decided to focus on a view which, programmatically expressed, presupposes a fusion of the contributing arts and calls for the identity of composer and librettist as well as, ideally, the protagonist or perspective. Moving from two opposite poles toward an imagined center, we singled out two works which, while not altogether perfect paragons, come close enough to being exemplary to deserve some kind of recognition: Wagner's *Der fliegende Holländer* in its incipient balladesque form and Berlioz's *Symphonie fantastique* conceived as an opera without words, both implying the presence of dream structures. In the wake of Romanticism conceived as a historical movement, two works on an even higher level of artistic accomplishment round out the picture: Wagner's *Tristan und Isolde*, heavily weighed down by its philosophical luggage, and Strindberg's *Dream Play*, an orchestrated drama which, profoundly indebted to Wagner though hardly to Berlioz, might well be regarded as the apex of Romantic opera generously defined.

Böse Menschen singen keine Arien
Prolegomena zu einer ungeschriebenen Geschichte der Opernzensur (1996)

> „Die Dichter haben ihre beliebteste Ausred' eingebüßt. Es war halt eine schöne Sach', wenn einem nichts eing'fallen ist und man hat zu die Leut' sagen können: ‚Ach Gott! Es ist schrecklich, sie verbieten einem ja alles'. Das fällt jetzt weg."[1]

I.

Dieses Zitat, dem einzigen Stück Johann Nepomuk Nestroys (der am 1. Juli 1848 uraufgeführten *Freiheit in Krähwinkel*) entnommen, welches nicht der staatlichen Zensur unterlag, läßt sich, mutatis mutandis, auch auf die Oper, vorzüglich in den ersten zwei Dritteln des 19. Jahrhunderts, anwenden. Leider ist das vielseitige und kulturgeschichtlich aufschlußreiche Thema der Opernzensur bislang von der Wissenschaft stiefmütterlich behandelt worden. Symptomatisch hierfür ist der, im übrigen ausgezeichnete, Beitrag Klaus Kanzogs zum *Reallexikon der deutschen Literaturgeschichte*, in welchem dem Theater zwar ein eigener, wenn auch relativ kurzer Abschnitt gewidmet ist, die Oper aber völlig leer ausgeht[2]. Soweit ich weiß, gibt es bis heute keine einzige monographische Darstellung der Opernzensur für den deutschen Sprachbereich, während sowohl für Frankreich[3] als auch für

---

1 Johann Nestroy: *Sämtliche Werke*, hg. v. Otto Rommel, Wien 1948 (photostatischer Nachdruck, 1962), Bd. 5, S. 73 (I, 7).

2 Klaus Kanzog: „Zensur", in: *Reallexikon der deutschen Literaturgeschichte*, zweite Auflage, Bd. 4 (Sl-Z), 1984, S. 998-1049. Zur Theaterzensur: § 6 (S. 1015-1018).

3 Victor Hallays-Dabot: *Histoire de la censure théâtrale en France*, Paris 1862 (bis 1850). – Ders.: *La Censure dramatique et le théâtre: Histoire des vingt dernières années (1850-1870)*, Paris 1871.

Italien[4] immerhin einige historische Längsschnitte vorliegen. Es kann im folgenden nicht meine Absicht sein, diese Lücke zu stopfen. Vielmehr geht es mir darum, gleichsam aus der Vogelperspektive eine Typologie zu erstellen und anhand einiger markanter Beispiele zu erläutern.

Einleitend ein paar Bemerkungen zur Problematik der Zensur als solcher sowie einige Hinweise auf die wichtigsten Spielarten derselben. Daß das entweder von der Justiz, der Polizei[5], dem Souverän oder dem Klerus ausgeübte zensorielle Einspruchsrecht sowohl seine juristischen als auch seine ideologischen Seiten hat, wird jedermann einleuchten, wobei in letzterem Fall das repressive Moment betont wird. So dekretierte Napoleon unverblümt: „Zensur ist das Recht, die Manifestation von Ideen zu hindern, die den Frieden des Staates, seine Interessen und seine gute Ordnung verwirren."[6] Eine objektivere, weil juristisch stichhaltige Begriffsbestimmung bringt Olaf von Kruedener in seinem Buch *Die Zensur im deutschen Verwaltungsrecht unter Berücksichtigung des kanonischen Rechts*[7]. Ihm zufolge qualifiziert sich nämlich als Zensur „jeder Verwaltungsakt, der nach inhaltlicher Prüfung der Gesetzmäßigkeit einer Äußerung in formellem Verfahren über die generelle Zulässigkeit [...] ihrer Mitteilung entscheidet", wobei zu beachten wäre, daß es hierbei stets um die Überwachung der menschlichen Äußerung (hier: des Kunstwerks) geht, nicht aber um

---

4 Carlo di Stefano: *La censura teatrale in Italia (1660-1962)*, Bologna 1964 (Documenti di teatro, Nr. 29).

5 Für Preußen war die Polizeizensur für das Theater im Jahre 1851 durch den Polizeipräsidenten von Hinckeldey eingeführt worden und wurde erste 1926 abgeschafft. Eine der amüsantesten diesbezüglichen Episoden betrifft die Uraufführung von Carl Sternheims Komödie *Die Hose* (1911), die zunächst vom Berliner Polizeipräsidenten von Jagow verboten, dann aber aufgrund einer geschickt eingefädelten Intrige von ihm doch zugelassen wurde. Siehe den Bericht des Herausgebers in Carl Sternheim: *Dramen* I, hg. v. Wilhelm Emrich, Neuwied 1963, S. 570f.

6 Zitiert bei Kanzog (Anm. 2), S. 1007, aus H. v. Srbik: *Metternich. Der Mensch und der Staatsmann*, München, 1925, Bd. 1, S. 348. Im Original: Henri Welschinger: *La Censure sous le premier Empire, avec documents inédits*, Paris 1882, S. 29.

7 Berlin: Ebering 1938.

die Überwachung des Menschen (hier: des Künstlers), welche im totalitären Staat, in dem die Zensur durch das Verbot oder gar die Vernichtung von Werken sowie durch die Verfolgung, Verbannung, Einkerkerung oder, im Extremfall, Verbrennung ihrer ‚ketzerischen' Urheber ins Unmenschliche gesteigert wird.

Die Zensur, ganz gleich welche Formen sie annimmt, ist ihrem Wesen nach staatserhaltend, d. h., politisch gesehen, konservativ. Eine progressive Zensur ist schon deshalb rein definitorisch ein Unding, weil sie zwangsläufig in die Forderung münden müßte, sich selber abzuschaffen. Sie befaßt sich nicht, oder wenigstens nicht vordringlich, mit strafbaren Handlungen, sondern mit Darstellungen und Formulierungen, die, weil sie behördlicherseits als anstößig empfunden werden, dem breiten Publikum vorzuenthalten sind. Zu unterscheiden wäre dabei, was die Verfahrensweise anbetrifft, zwischen den im Anschluß an bereits erfolgte Publikationen oder Aufführungen getätigten Verboten (Nach- oder Prohibitivzensur[8]) und der im allgemeinen auf Teilaspekte eines Werkes beschränkten und lediglich die Änderung oder Streichung einzelner Stellen zur Auflage machenden Vor- oder Präventivzensur. Dabei wurde nur ganz ausnahmsweise versucht, die erwünschten Korrekturen selbst vorzunehmen oder auch nur vorzuschlagen[9]. Neben der Globalzensur, die allen Lesern ohne Ansehen der Person den Zugang zu einem bestimmten Werk verwehrte, gab es die selektive Zensur, die eine bestimmte Schicht – gewöhnlich die Leute

---

8 Als Beispiel der zum Verbot führenden Nachzensur sei Victor Hugos Drama *Le Roi s'amuse* (1832) angeführt, auf dem das Libretto von Verdis *Rigoletto* beruht. Die diesbezüglichen Dokumente sind abgedruckt in Hugos *Théâtre Complet*, hg. v. Roland Purnal, Paris 1967: „Préface", S. 1323-1333, und „Procès" (einschließlich von Hugos Plaidoyer in eigener Sache), S. 1663-1687. Aubers *La Muette de Portici* und Rossinis *Guillaume Tell* erlitten ein ähnliches Schicksal.

9 Siehe hierzu folgende Stelle aus der in Anm. 10 erwähnten Denkschrift Hägelins: „Die Zensur ist nicht schuldig, das Anstößige zu korrigieren und statt der von der Zensur verworfenen Stellen einen zulässigen Text einzuschalten oder hinein zu korrigieren. Für solche Dinge hat der Autor zu sorgen; die Zensur verwirft und streicht weg; tut sie etwas mehreres, so ist es bloße Wohltat für den Autor und besondere Beförderung guter Absichten." (S. 66)

von Stand – gegenüber anderen Schichten – gewöhnlich die Ungebildeten – privilegierte. So heißt es in einer österreichischen Zensurvorschrift aus dem Jahre 1810:

> Bei der Beurteilung der Bücher und Handschriften muß vor allem genau unterschieden werden zwischen Werken, welche ihr Inhalt und die Behandlung des Gegenstandes nur für Gelehrte und den Wissenschaften sich widmenden Menschen bestimmt, und zwischen Broschüren, Volksschriften, Unterhaltungsbüchern und den Erzeugnissen des Witzes[10].

So bedurfte über lange Zeitstrecken hinweg der Erwerb bzw. die Ausleihe bestimmter Bücher der behördlichen Genehmigung in der Form eines unter dem Namen erga schedam bekannten Erlaubnisscheines[11]. Und noch gegen Ende des vorigen Jahrhunderts wurde die öffentliche Präsentation eines Stückes, Gerhart Hauptmanns Sozialdrama *Die Weber*, vom Preußischen Oberverwaltungsgericht u. a. deshalb für unverfänglich gehalten, weil das Proletariat, um dessen Sache es hier bekanntlich geht, den Preis für die Eintrittskarten ohnehin nicht zahlen könne[12]. Die von der Forschung arg vernachlässigte künstlerische

---

10 Siehe hierzu, wie wiederholt im folgenden, die als Leitfaden für die Theaterzensur in der Donaumonarchie gedachte Denkschrift von Franz Karl Hägelin aus dem Jahre 1795. Abgedruckt in Carl Glossys Arbeit „Zur Geschichte der Wiener Theaterzensur" in: *Jahrbuch der Grillparzer-Gesellschaft*, Bd. 7 (1897), S. 57-74, hier: S. 65.

11 Eine ähnliche Tendenz innerhalb der zensoriellen Praxis unter dem Zeichen des Doppeladlers, wie auch anderswo im deutschen Sprachraum, verfolgte die Anordnung, derzufolge umfangreiche Manuskripte und Publikationen ungeschoren blieben, weil – wohl mit Recht – angenommen wurde, daß nur Gelehrte sich mit ihnen beschäftigen würden. Die in einer österreichischen Zensurvorschrift vom 14. September 1810 aufgelisteten Formeln für die offiziell verwendeten Zensur-Urteile lauten admittitur, transeat, erga schedam conced. und damnatur (§ 15) sowie toleratur (§ 17). Der betreffende Text findet sich in: Julius Marx: *Die österreichische Zensur im Vormärz*, München 1959, S. 73-76.

12 Das Urteil zitiert in: Gerhart Hauptmann: *Die Weber. Vollständiger Text des Schauspiels, Dokumentation*, hg. v. Hans Schwab-Felisch, Berlin 1963, enthält den bezeichnenden Satz: „Mag, worüber die Parteien streiten, der letzte Platz im Deutschen Theater 1.50 oder 1 M. kosten, jedenfalls sind, wie bekannt, die Plätze im Allgemeinen so teuer und ist die Zahl der weniger teuren Plätze verhältnismäßig so gering, daß dieses Theater vorwiegend nur von Mitgliedern derjenigen Gesellschaftskreise besucht wird, die nicht zu Gewalttätigkeiten oder anderweitiger Störung der öffentlichen Ordnung geneigt sind." (S. 247) Eine genaue Entsprechung hierzu bietet ein Zensurbericht vom 17. Januar 1828, in welchem es um eine Nachahmung bzw. französische Bearbeitung von Schillers *Wilhelm Tell* geht und wo vom Théâtre Fey-

Selbstzensur, wie sie in der Filmbranche – sowohl in der Bundesrepublik als auch in den Vereinigten Staaten – als freiwillige Selbstkontrolle zutagetritt[13], ist eine Variante der Präventivzensur, bei der der Urheber oder die mit der Umsetzung oder Verbreitung seiner Werke befaßten Institutionen im Hinblick auf einen potentiellen Eingriff der Behörde Vorbeugungen treffen, indem sie bestimmte Themen vermeiden, Aussagen entschärfen oder Handlungen umfunktionieren. Das kann auch ex post facto geschehen. So schrieb Schiller am 10. Dezember 1804 an Christian Gottfried Koerner:

> Wenn man in Dresden den *Wilhelm Tell* zu geben gedenkt, so wäre es wohl anständiger, dieses Stück nach derjenigen Bearbeitung, die ich fürs hiesige [will heißen: das Weimarer] Theater gemacht habe, zu geben. Sie ist sehr wesentlich verkürzt und z. B. der ganze fünfte Akt weggelassen, weil wir des Kaisermords nicht erwähnen wollten. Auch sind viele Personen in wenige verwandelt, viele schwürige oder bedenkliche Stellen weggelassen[14].

Eine Art interner, d. h. gänzlich auf den Bereich der Kunst beschränkter Selbstkontrolle stellt die auf einen bestimmten Apparat oder eine bestimmte Einrichtung zugeschnittene Modifizierung eines Werkes dar. Als Beispiele dieser, vor allem für Frankreich charakteristischen Praxis mögen die Hinzufügung des für Paris obligaten Balletts in Wagners *Tannhäuser*, die Ersetzung des gesprochenen Dialogs durch Rezitative in Berlioz' Bearbeitung von Webers *Freischütz* sowie die Berücksichtigung der an der Opéra Comique gültigen Konventionen

---

deau als einer Bühne die Rede ist „qui n'est [...] pas fréquenté par la dernière classe". Zitiert in Herbert Schneider/Nicole Wild: *‚La Muette de Portici'. Kritische Ausgabe des Librettos und Dokumentation der ersten Inszenierung*, Tübingen 1993, S. 194.
13 In der Bundesrepublik Deutschland existiert ein solches Organ, mit dem Sitz in Wiesbaden, seit 1949, in den Vereinigten Staaten schon erheblich länger.
14 Zitiert aus *Friedrich Schiller*, hg. v. Bodo Lecke in der Reihe Dichter über ihre Dichtungen, München 1970, Bd. 2, S. 530. Eine Apologie für die Darstellung eines Königsmordes im 5. Akt seines Schauspiels bietet Schiller in Beantwortung einer Frage aus dem von Ifflands Theatersekretär übersandten Fragebogen vom 7. April 1804. Siehe *Wilhelm Tell. Quellen, Dokumente, Rezensionen*, hg. v. Herbert Kraft, Reinbek 1967, S. 180. Überhaupt ist, wie sich zeigen wird, *Wilhelm Tell* ein *test case* für die Herausarbeitung der Unterschiede zwischen Schauspiel- und Opernzensur.

bei Bizets Gestaltung seiner *Carmen* dienen[15]. Wie sich denken läßt, hängen sowohl die Art als auch die beabsichtigte Wirkung des Zensuraktes von vielen Faktoren ab, die jeweils in Betracht zu ziehen sind. So wäre zu zeigen, inwieweit sich die Opernzensur, um die es uns geht, von der auf das bloße Sprechtheater bezogenen Zensur unterscheidet und die Theaterzensur als solche von der Buchzensur. Da letztere abseits von meinem Thema liegt und an historisch-kritischen Darstellungen derselben innerhalb und außerhalb Deutschlands kein Mangel herrscht[16], brauche ich mich in diesem Rahmen nicht mit ihr zu befassen. Was die Schauspielzensur betrifft, deren Kriterien und Voraussetzungen zum Teil natürlich auch für die Opernzensur gelten, so hat sie ihre eigenen Probleme, weil der Text eines Dramas eigentlich erst durch seine Verwirklichung auf der Bühne zum Leben erwacht. Nur beim sogenannten *closet drama* wird der gravierende Unterschied zwischen (privater) Lektüre und (öffentlicher) Darbietung nivelliert. Aus der Sicht des Zensors erläutert Hägelin den Unterschied zwischen Literatur und Theater wie folgt:

> [Es] versteht sich von selbst, dass die Theatralzensur viel strenger sein [muß] als die gewöhnliche Zensur für die bloße Lektüre der Druckschriften. [...] Dieses ergibt sich schon aus dem verschiedenen Eindruck, den ein in lebendige Handlung bis zur Täuschung gesetztes Werk in den Gemütern der Zuschauer machen muß, als derjenige sein kann, den ein bloss am Pulte gelesenes gedrucktes Schauspiel bewirkt. Der Eindruck des ersteren ist unendlich stärker als jener des letzteren, weil das erstere Augen und Ohren beschäftigt und sogar in den Willen des Zuschauers treten soll, um die beabsichtigten Gemütsbewegungen hervorzubringen, welches die blosse Lektüre nicht leistet. (Anm. 10, S. 58)

Hier ist sinngemäß nicht so sehr an die Texte selbst gedacht als an deren Wirkung auf ein Publikum, mit der sich im Gegensatz zur Kritik

---

15 Zu *Carmen* siehe z. B. Ludovic Halévys Aufsatz „La millième représentation de Carmen" in: *Le Théâtre* (Januar 1905). In englischer Übersetzung bei Ulrich Weisstein: *The Essence of Opera*, New York 1969, S. 223f.

16 Von besonderem Interesse sind, auch was die Theaterzensur anbetrifft, die entsprechenden Abschnitte in Ludwig Leisz: *Kunst im Konflikt: Kunst und Künstler im Widerstreit mit der Obrigkeit*, Berlin 1971 und zwei Bücher von H. H. Houben: *Hier Zensur: Wer dort? Antworten von gestern auf Fragen von heute*, Leipzig: Brockhaus, 1918 und: *Polizei und Zensur: Längs- und Querschnitte durch die Geschichte der Buch- und Theaterzensur*, Berlin 1926.

die Zensur, welche gleichsam eine vorweggenommene öffentliche Kritik ist, ausschließlich befaßt. Da sie im Theater gewöhnlich vor die vollendete Tatsache gestellt wird, gibt es, falls keine Inspektion während der Proben erfolgt, zwar ein Verbot, aber keine Zensur von Inszenierungen[17].

Aus der von ihm als grotesk bezeichneten Tatsache, daß man am „Ende des 18. Jhs. in Wien *Don Carlos*" – wie übrigens die Mehrzahl der Dramen Schillers – zwar „beim Buchhändler kaufen, aber auf der Bühne nur in ‚gereinigter Fassung' sehen konnte", schließt Kanzog, daß man dem gesprochenen Wort behördlicherseits einen „großen Affektwert" beimaß und daß die „Körperlichkeit des Spiels und die Mündlichkeit der Rede" die auf der Bühne gemachten Aussagen erheblich verstärke[18]. Wieviel größer aber ist dieser Affektwert beim gesungenen Wort! Nur so erklärt sich, daß, wie Verdi dem römischen Impresario Jacovacci im Hinblick auf die geplante Aufführung seines *Ballo in maschera* mitteilte,

Gustave III [Eugène Scribes Schauspiel dieses Namens] is allowed in prose, but a libretto on the same subject, to be set to music, is forbidden[19].

Schon drei Jahrzehnte früher hatte ein französischer Zensor in seinem Urteil über einen Vorläufer von Aubers *Muette de Portici* geschrieben:

J'ajouterai que si un pareil ouvrage est pernicieux en tragédie ou en drame, il l'est encore davantage [...] animé par le prestige de la musique[20].

---

17 Daß sich der Staat gelegentlich im zensoriellen Sinne mit Opern-Inszenierungen befaßte, zeigt die von Leisz (Anm. 16) bibliographisch erfaßte Schrift A. Vierbachers und E. Kochanowskis über eine Augsburger *Figaro*-Aufführung im Jahre 1963. Auch die von Joseph Wulf in seiner Dokumentation *Musik im Dritten Reich*, Berlin 1982, S. 305, angeführte Kritik Wilhelm Rodes an Inszenierungen des *Tannhäuser* und des *Fliegenden Holländers* an der Berliner Kroll-Oper ist in diesem Zusammenhang beachtenswert. Man sehe ferner das im Kapitel „Theaterkritik unter Aufsicht" von H. H. Houbens *Polizei und Zensur* (S. 78ff.) erwähnte Verbot der öffentlichen Kritik an den Leistungen des Preußischen Generalmusikdirektors Gasparo Spontini.
18 Kanzog (Anm. 2), S. 1017.
19 Zitiert aus einem Brief Verdis vom 19. April 1859, in: *Verdi. The Man in his Letters*, hg. v. Franz Werfel und Paul Stefan, New York 1942, S. 214.
20 Zitiert bei Schneider/Wild (Anm. 12), S. 198.

Andererseits – und so erklärt sich das widersprüchliche Verhalten der Zensur gegenüber der Gattung ‚Oper' – wird im dramma per musica der durch die Musik zum Teil verdeckte und oft schwer verständliche Text[21] aus dem rationalen, semantisch eindeutigen Bereich, sozusagen durch *guilt by association*, in den sinnlichen Bereich verschoben und, wenn man so will, dadurch verharmlost. So konnte der Zensor Royer in seiner Expertise zum Libretto der *Muette* schlankweg behaupten:

> [...] le seul avantage peut-être de l'opéra que nous examinons c'est que les paroles en sont moins distinctement entendus qu'elles ne l'eussent été à [le Théâtre] Feydeau[22].

Nicht immer verhält sich, wie Hägelin, demzufolge „gemeiniglich im lyrischen Theater [...] keine große Moral angebracht wird"[23], vorauszusetzen scheint, die Musik in der Oper ethisch oder ideologisch neutral. Sie kann z. B., wo sie bei Ouvertüren oder Zwischenspielen zur Anwendung gelangt, durch das Zitieren von Nationalhymnen oder Revolutions-Melodien – etwa der Marseillaise – im Publikum patriotische Sentiments erzeugen; und vor allem die Chöre, die vielfach bei Verdi das Gefühl der Vaterlandsliebe heraufbeschwören, aber der Zensur durch die Lappen gehen, weil sich ihre Assoziationsträchtigkeit nicht beweisen läßt, bieten ein Beispiel für eine gelungene Umgehung derselben.

Wie Kurt Honolka bemerkt:

> Die Zensur in Italien verbot unverhüllte Anspielungen auf der Bühne, aber Verdis Publikum spürte schon heraus, was gemeint war. „Schwören wir! [...] Ich sehe uns alle wie einen einzigen Mann uns erheben" singt der Chor in der frühen Oper *I Lombardi*, „Nun sei das Vaterland mein einziger Gedanke" in der *Giovanna d'Arco*, „Möge dir die *ganze* Welt gehören, mir bleibt Italien" im *Attila*. In der venezianischen Uraufführung der *Battaglia di Legnano* – es geht darin um den Kampf gegen Kaiser Barbarossa, also gegen einen Fremdherrscher – sprang das

---

21 Viele bedeutende Komponisten haben sich zu diesem, für sie und ihre Textdichter so wichtigen Thema geäußert. Von Richard Strauss z. B. gibt es verschiedene Hinweise darauf, daß in Anbetracht des zu erwartenden Verlustes – er schätzte ihn auf etwa ein Drittel des Textes – der Opernkomponist, instrumentell gesehen, kammermusikalisch vorgehen müsse.
22 Zitiert bei Schneider/Wild (Anm. 12), S. 202.
23 Hägelin (Anm. 10), S. 58.

Publikum von den Sitzen und feierte den maestro mit stürmischen Evviva Verdi-Rufen[24].

Präventiv zensuriert werden kann im Theater, einschließlich der Oper, wie schon gesagt nur der fixierte Text, nicht aber die ihn begleitenden und untermalenden Gesten und Gebärden, mit deren Hilfe der Schauspieler – weniger oft der Sänger – dem etwa anwesenden Polizeispitzel leicht ein Schnippchen schlagen kann; denn dieser konnte ja nur das, was er Schwarz auf Weiß besaß, getrost in seine muffige Amtsstube tragen[25]. Wie besonders der Fall Nestroy beweist, gibt es zahlreiche derartig evasive Praktiken. Zum Beispiel verstand sich dieser Dichter-Schauspieler vorzüglich darauf, bei der Unterbreitung von Zensur-Exemplaren seiner Stücke verdächtige oder subversive Passagen durch weniger verfängliche zu ersetzen. Gegen diese offenkundig weit verbreitete Praxis suchte sich die Behörde – sicher vergeblich – zu wehren. So steht im Wiener Zensurkalender unter dem 19. November 1801:

> Da es mehrmals vorgekommen [ist], daß die Schauspieler in den drei Vorstadttheatern die Theaterstücke nicht genau so vortragen, wie solche die Zensurbewilligung erhalten haben, sondern vielmehr jene Stellen, welche abgeändert oder durchgestrichen worden sind, beibehalten, nebst dem aber auch mit zweideutigen und sittenwidrigen Zusätzen vermehren, wird die Polizeidirektion beauftragt, den Unternehmern der Vorstadttheater zu bedeuten, daß derjenige Schauspieler, welcher sich beikommen [läßt], von dem wörtlichen Inhalt des zensurierten Theaterstücks abzugehen, [...] mit einem achttägigen Polizei-Hausarrest bestraft werden würde[26].

Zu den Besonderheiten der Gattung ‚Oper' gehört u. a. auch der Umstand, daß es sich bei ihren Vertretern stets um Mehr- bzw. Gesamtkunstwerke handelt. Dies hat zur Folge, daß bei der kritischen Durch-

---

24 Kurt Honolka: *Kulturgeschichte des Librettos. Opern, Dichter, Operndichter*, Wilhelmshaven ²1978, S. 212f.

25 Hierzu Hägelin (Anm. 10), S. 69: „Gesetzt auch, man hätte den Dialog von allem Schlüpfrigen gereinigt, so können doch noch durch extemporierte Zusätze, Tonlegung und abgesetzte Reden oder Pausen mannigfaltige Zweideutigkeiten gemacht werden." Verschiedene aufschlußreiche Beispiele hierzu in Karl Glossys Dokumentation „Zur Geschichte der Wiener Theaterzensur I (1801-1820)" im *Jahrbuch der Grillparzer-Gesellschaft* 25 (1915), *passim*.

26 Zitiert bei Glossy (Anm. 25), S. 4.

leuchtung eines dramma per musica jeweils zwei Hauptbestandteile – Musik und Text – in Rechnung zu stellen sind. Dieser Aufgabe war jedoch die Zensurbehörde, die keine Musik-Experten beschäftigte, sondern sich ausschließlich auf dem literarischen Parkett bewegte, nicht gewachsen. Fälle einer Präventivzensur von Partituren sind nicht bekannt und stehen auch deshalb kaum zu erwarten, weil die semantische Dimension der Musik als solcher schwer zu erfassen ist. Daher kommt es gegebenenfalls höchstens zur ästhetischen Sippenhaftung, indem der Musik ohne Umschweife unterstellt wird, sie drücke genau dasselbe aus wie der ihr zugrundeliegende Text. Ein besonders krasses Beispiel von zensoriell orientierter Doppelkritik bietet der viel zitierte *Prawda*-Artikel vom 28. Januar 1936, in welchem Musik und Text von Schostakowitschs aufsehenerregender Oper *Lady Macbeth von Minsk* in die Zange genommen werden. Ich zitiere einen Abschnitt des mit der Komposition befaßten Anfangsteiles:

> Eine diensteifrige Musikkritik hebt diese Oper in den Himmel, bereitet ihr einen lärmenden Ruhm. Anstatt daß der junge Komponist sachliche und seriöse Kritik hört, macht man ihm nur begeisterte Komplimente. Den Zuschauer verblüfft von der ersten Minute an das Chaos des absichtlich uneleganten Klangstromes. Fragmente von Melodien, Rudimente musikalischer Phrasen gehen unter, tauchen wieder auf und verschwinden in einem Gepolter, Kreischen und Knirschen. [...] Auf der Bühne ist der Gesang durch Geschrei ersetzt. Ist der Komponist einmal auf der Spur einer einfachen und angenehmen Melodie, verwirft er sie sofort, als ob er sich erschrecke, und wirft sich in das Labyrinth des Chaos, das sich an einigen Stellen sogar in eine Kakophonie verwandelt. Die Ausdrucksfülle, die der Zuschauer verlangt, ist durch tollwütigen Rhythmus ersetzt. Der musikalische Lärm muß die Leidenschaft ausdrücken[27].

Und in diesem Tone geht es weiter. Ihrem totalitär-repressiven Kontext entsprechend, zeitigte diese, angeblich von Väterchen Stalin höchstpersönlich inspirierte, vielleicht sogar entworfene Rezension prompt die gewünschten Folgen; und die zuvor an mehreren Bühnen der Sowjetunion gespielte Oper wurde im Zuge der Nachzensur verboten – und dies keineswegs nur wegen ihrer ‚dekadenten' Musik,

---

27 Ich zitiere aus dem Text des „Chaos statt Musik" betitelten Aufsatzes in deutscher Übersetzung aus dem Programmheft der Wiener Volksoper zur dortigen Inszenierung in der Spielzeit 1991/92.

sondern auch aufgrund der ihr angelasteten Verfälschung der literarischen Vorlage:

> Während unsere Kritik [...] auf den sozialistischen Realismus eingeschworen ist, bietet uns die Bühne in der Schöpfung von Schostakowitsch vulgärsten Naturalismus. Alle seine Kaufleute, sein Volk sind äußerlich und animalisch dargestellt. Die räuberische Kaufmannsfrau, die über Mord zu Reichtum und Macht kommt, ist als ‚Opfer' der bürgerlichen Gesellschaft dargestellt. Dem Roman von Nikolai Leskov wird ein Sinn unterlegt, den er nicht hat. Und das alles auf primitive Weise vulgär.

Selbst in Fällen, in denen vom Standpunkt der Machthaber aus eine Zensurierung von Opernmusik geboten wäre, ergäben sich aus dem zeitlichen Ablauf der Genese von Kunstwerken dieser Art schon deshalb rein faktische Probleme, weil der Komponist mit seiner Arbeit vielfach erst dann beginnt, wenn das komplette Libretto vorliegt. Um zu verhindern, daß ein Teil der Musik vor der Approbation des Textes geschrieben wurde, bestand deshalb z. B. die neapolitanische Zensur um 1820 auf dem Vorlegen des Librettos ein ganzes Jahr vor der geplanten Premiere[28]; und unter Hinweis auf die bereits erwähnte Masaniello-Oper klagte ein Pariser Zensor:

> L'examen de cette pièce, dit-on, est chose pressée. La musique en serait-il faite? Ce serait une grande imprudence. Avant d'y travailler, il faudrait s'assurer que les paroles ont reçu l'approbation requise[29].

Im Schaffen Verdis spielt dieses Problem eine nicht zu unterschätzende Rolle – etwa beim *Rigoletto*, dessen Text am 26. Januar 1851 zur Aufführung freigegeben wurde, dessen Partitur aber schon zwei Wochen später abgeschlossen war. Da die Premiere am 11. März stattfinden sollte, blieb der Zensur, hätte sie sich auch mit der Musik befaßt, nur sehr geringer zeitlicher Spielraum für einen möglichen Eingriff. Übrigens war Verdi bereits in einem früheren Stadium der Entstehung dieser Oper – im Zusammenhang mit der von der Zensur geforderten, ziemlich radikalen Umarbeitung des Textes – auf ein für ihn als Kom-

---

28 „The legal requirement in those days was that a libretto had to be submitted a full year in advance; [but] this requirement frequently had to be overlooked for practical reasons." William Ashbrook in: *Donizetti and his Operas*, Cambridge, England 1982, S. 616, Anm. 202.
29 Zitiert bei Schneider/Wild (Anm. 12), S. 197.

ponisten schwerwiegendes Problem gestoßen, nämlich auf die Notwendigkeit, bereits komponierte Musik im Hinblick auf textliche Änderungen umzuschreiben. Er wehrte sich mit aller Kraft und, wie sich herausstellen sollte, mit Erfolg gegen diese Zumutung und ließ den Präsidenten des Teatro La Fenice, C. D. Marzari, wissen:

> Wenn man mir sagt, daß meine Noten, so schön oder häßlich sie sein mögen, auch zu diesem Drama [will heißen: die unter dem Titel *Il Duca di Vendôme* von Piave erstellte Zweitfassung des Librettos] passen, antworte ich, daß ich solche Argumente nicht verstehe, und sage offen, daß ich meine Noten, so schön oder häßlich sie sein mögen, nicht einfach hinschreibe, sondern immer bemüht bin, ihnen einen Charakter zu geben[30].

Er, der dramatische Komponist par excellence, weigerte sich also standhaft, das, was Rousseau in seinem *Dictionnaire de Musique* als Gegensinn (*contresens*) bezeichnet, zu tolerieren oder gar selbst zu produzieren[31].

Daß die Musik den ihr als Vorlage dienenden Text verfremdend behandeln und mit ihm auf diese Weise in ein dialektisches Verhältnis treten kann, ist operngeschichtlich evident. So ist es etwa für die Untergattung ,Epische Oper', vertreten durch Brecht/Weills *Dreigroschenoper* und Auden/Strawinskys *The Rake's Progress*, charakteristisch, daß über die bloße ironische Brechung hinaus Spannungen, Widersprüche und daraus entstehende Konflikte zwischen den Schwesterkünsten auftreten, die den Zuhörer und Zuschauer verunsichern und ihm interpretatorisch den Boden unter den Füßen wegziehen. Dies ist, so unwahrscheinlich es anmutet, sogar bei einzelnen Standardwerken des Operntheaters der Fall, wie die im letzten Jahrzehnt zum Teil recht heftig geführte Debatte über den Sinn der *Zauberflöte* zeigt, die früher eigentlich nur im Hinblick auf ihre freimaurerische Symbolik hinterfragt worden war.

---

30 Brief vom 14. Dezember 1850, in: *Giuseppe Verdi: Briefe*, hg. und übersetzt von Hans Busch, Frankfurt a. M. 1979, S. 41.
31 Das *Dictionnaire de Musique* wurde 1767 abgeschlossen. Der Artikel „Contresens" in englischer Übersetzung ist abgedruckt in *The Essence of Opera* (Anm. 15), S. 82.

Ich möchte diese Kontroverse, die Attila Csampai in seinem Aufsatz „Das Geheimnis der *Zauberflöte* oder die Folgen der Aufklärung"[32] auf einen Höhepunkt geführt hat, anhand einiger konkreter Beispiele exemplifizieren. Csampais Argumente stellen einen Versuch dar, die ethische Wertskala, die das Textbuch Schikaneders erstellt, in ihr Gegenteil zu verwandeln. Dabei handelt es sich, grob gesagt, um die Dichotomie: hier Sarastro, die Priesterschaft, Pamina und der nicht eben charakterstarke Tamino und da die Königin der Nacht nebst ihren Drei Damen und dem in doppelter Hinsicht schwarzen Monostatos, wozu – gewissermaßen als Neutrale – der Naturmensch Papageno als Vertreter der Immanenz und die Drei Knaben als solche der Transzendenz treten und somit das Bild des Großen Welttheaters abrunden.

Daß hier eine tradierte, aber eindeutig klischierte Deutung vorliegt, beweist ein *close reading* des Dialogs. So tritt im Gespräch zwischen den Drei Damen und Tamino in I, 5 zutage, daß Sarastro ein Dämon ist, der sich in „jede erdenkliche Gestalt verwandeln" kann und Pamina gewaltsam entführt hat. Hier scheint die als Folie zu Schikaneders Libretto dienende, aus dem von Liebeskind und Wieland stammenden „Feen- und Geistermärchen" *Lulu oder Die Zauberflöte* übernommene Grundkonstellation von guter Fee und bösem Zauberer gleichsam als Kehrseite der Medaille auf. Daß Sarastro in der Tat seine dunklen Seiten hat, erhellt aus seinem Bekenntnis gegenüber Pamina: „Zur Liebe will ich dich nicht zwingen,/ Doch geb' ich dir die Freiheit nicht" (I, 18).

In seinem lesenswerten, aber sachlich ungenauen Aufsatz bringt nun Csampai das ursprüngliche Märchenschema unter Heranziehung der Musik ins Spiel, um zu beweisen, daß Mozart in mancher Hinsicht gegen den Strich komponiert und auf diese Weise die Oberflächenstruktur des Textes durch die Tiefenstruktur der Musik widerlegt habe. Der, freilich nur bedingt stichhaltige, Beweis für diese Behauptung wird u. a. durch eine recht eigensinnige Interpretation der Arie Nr. 15

---

[32] W. A. *Mozart*: Die Zauberflöte. *Texte, Materialien, Kommentare*, hg. v. Attila Csampai und Dietmar Holland, Reinbek 1982, S. 9-39.

(„In diesen heil'gen Hallen") erbracht. Csampai stellt nämlich fest, es handle sich hierbei nicht um eine wirkliche Arie, wie der Titel verheißt, sondern um ein Strophenlied, bei dem, im Gegensatz zur Arie, keine Wandlung im Affektbereich stattfinde, sondern durch Wiederholung angedeutet werde, daß kein ethischer Fortschritt erzielt worden ist[33]. Das läßt sich hören; doch daß im Gegenzug Sarastros Antagonistin, ihrer fulminanten Arie mit der halsbrecherischen Koloratur (Nr. 14, „Der Hölle Rache kocht in meinem Herzen") wegen, kategorisch als „leidende Mutter" eingestuft wird, erregt mehr als leises Kopfschütteln.

Recht überzeugend klingt hingegen Csampais unter Hinweis auf die Arie Nr. 13 („Alles fühlt der Liebe Freuden") aufgestellte These, der angebliche Lüstling Monostatos sei in Wahrheit ein Double Papagenos, was Mozart dadurch zu verstehen gegeben habe, daß er auch ihm eine (Pikkolo-)Flöte zuordne und ihn sein Liedchen – um ein solches handelt es sich nämlich trotz der auch dieser Nummer vorangestellten Bezeichnung „Arie" – in einem heiteren und versöhnlichen Ton singen lasse[34]. Es findet also, Csampai zufolge, in der *Zauberflöte* eine Entschleierung des Textes durch die Musik statt, die als Binnenzensur verstanden werden könnte.

II.

Für ein Verständnis meines Überblicks ist es von Vorteil, daß die in der schon erwähnten Denkschrift Hägelins niedergelegten Richtlinien systematisch geordnet und jeweils durch konkrete Beispiele erläutert werden. Der durch jahrzehntelange Praxis bestens mit der Materie vertraute Autor behandelt den Gegenstand in zwei Hauptabschnitten, deren erster dem Inhalt und deren zweiter der sprachlichen Gestaltung gewidmet ist.

---

33 Siehe den Abschnitt „Arie mit Strophen", ebd., S. 30-32.
34 Diese Anweisung findet sich in dem 1791 bei Ignaz Alberti in Wien veröffentlichten Textbuch zur Uraufführung, nicht aber im Text der Rowohlt-Ausgabe.

Bei Hägelin ergibt sich das folgende Schema, wobei zu beachten ist, daß die Reihenfolge der aufgelisteten Punkte kaum zufällig ist und diese sowohl einzeln als auch in Verbindung miteinander auftreten können:
1) „Gebrechen des Stoffes wider die Religion";
2) „Gebrechen des Stoffes in politischer Hinsicht und wider den Staat";
3) „Gebrechen des Stoffes in Absicht auf die Sitten";
4) „Reinigkeit des Dialogs in Absicht auf die Religion";
5) „Gebrechen des Dialogs in Absicht auf den Staat";
6) „Gebrechen des Dialogs wider die Sitten".

Als weiteres, von Hägelin nicht eigens erwähntes oder gar in sein Schema einbezogenes Kriterium ließen sich die ‚Gebrechen gegen die Kunst' bezeichnen. Diese tauchen allerdings nur andeutungsweise am Horizont der zensoriellen Tätigkeit auf, weil sie im Sinne Kants außerhalb der Interessensphäre von Religion, Politik und Moral stehen und daher ruhig der Kritik überlassen werden können. In der Tat ist also „der sogenannte Geschmack in dramatischen Werken [...] kein Gegenstand der Zensur [...], sondern gehört vor den Richterstuhl der Kunst"[35].

Daß die Zensur in der theatralischen Praxis bisweilen aber auch in diesem Sektor tätig war, bestätigt der Fall *Rigoletto* insofern, als die aus Victor Hugos Drama *Le Roi s'amuse* übernommene Figur des

---

35 Zitiert bei Glossy (Anm. 25, S. 15) nach Hägelin. Bei Hägelin heißt es (Anm. 10, S. 57) ausdrücklich: „Nach der Hauptregel soll das Theater eine Schule der Sitten und des Geschmacks sein. Zu wünschen wäre es, dass die dramatischen Autoren dieser wahren Regel, die sie so oft vorpredigen, in der Ausführung allzeit getreu blieben. Allein sie scheinen sich, wenn sie Stücke verfassen, oft zu vergessen. Obige Hauptregel, so weit sie die Sitten betrifft, gehet die Zensur im strengen Verstande an, den Geschmack aber nur insoweit, als er das Schickliche, das Anständige und Vernunftmässige in Absicht auf die Sitten selbst und das Konventionelle oder auch das natürliche und politische Dekorum [...] angeht. Denn der Geschmack ist in verschiedenen Zeiten verschieden, und [es ist] noch nicht ausgemacht, wo der wahre Geschmack wirklich existiert; zumal wo in Deutschland, das aus so vielen kleinen und grösseren Höfen besteht, der wahre Geschmack sich schwerlich an einem Orte fixieren und den Hauptton geben wird."

buckligen Protagonisten ihr ausgesprochenes Mißfallen erregte. Dabei muß man bedenken, daß die Gestalt des Triboulet, genau so wie diejenige des Glöckners von Notre Dame, für den französische Dichter symptomatisch für die im „Préface de Cromwell" entwickelte romantische Ästhetik des Dramas war, in der die Kategorie des Grotesken bekanntlich eine wichtige Rolle spielt[36]. Die auf der Bühne offen zutage tretende Diskrepanz zwischen häßlichem Körper und schöner Seele war für Verdi mit ein Hauptgrund für die Wahl gerade dieses Stoffes. So erklärt sich die Heftigkeit seiner Reaktion auf die Bedenken des Zensors und auf die durch sie veranlaßte Umformung in der von ihm verworfenen Neufassung des Operntextes: „Dazu hat man vermieden, Triboletto häßlich zu machen und mit Buckel darzustellen", schrieb er in dem schon erwähnten Brief an Marzari, und fuhr fort: „Ein Buckliger, der singt? Warum nicht? [...] Wird das Effekt machen? Ich weiß es nicht. Aber wenn ich selbst es nicht weiß, dann kann es auch der nicht wissen, der diese Änderung vorgeschlagen hat."

Was die Darstellung religiöser Themen betrifft, so ist verständlich, daß sie, besonders in den katholischen Ländern, den weltlichen und vor allem den geistlichen Zensoren ein Dorn im Auge war. Doch gab es gravierende Unterschiede in bezug auf die jeweilige Toleranzschwelle. So war man im päpstlichen Kirchenstaat durchweg weit weniger päpstlich als im bourbonischen Neapel, wie Verdi erfahren mußte, als er den *Ballo in maschera* dort zur Aufführung bringen wollte. Auch Hägelin macht kein Hehl aus seiner Abneigung gegen solche Sujets: „Überhaupt können die Religion und religiöse Gegenstände nie ein Stoff theatralischer Vorstellung werden. Die Religion ist zu erha-

---

[36] „La poésie née du christianisme, la poésie de notre temps est donc le drame; le caractère du drame est le réel; le réel résulte de la combinaison toute naturelle de deux types, le sublime et le grotesque, qui se croisent dans le drame, comme ils se croisent dans la vie et dans la création. Car la poésie vraie, la poésie complète, est dans l'harmonie des contraires." Victor Hugo: *Théâtre I* (Anm. 8), S. 425.

ben und zu ehrwürdig, als daß sie durch das profane Theater abgewürdigt werden dürfte" (Anm. 10, S. 59).

Trotz dieses prinzipiellen Einwandes sah auch der habsburgische Zensor sich in Anbetracht der theatralischen Praxis gezwungen, seinen Kollegen gegenüber die Grenzen des auf der Bühne diesbezüglich Tragbaren abzustecken. Unter den Themen, die er aus theologischen Gründen für künstlerisch unverwertbar hielt, figurieren u. a. der Selbstmord und die Ehe, sofern sie als religiöses Sakrament betrachtet wird[37].

Im sprachlichen Bereich erstellt Hägelin eine umfangreiche Liste von Wörtern, Bezeichnungen und Ausdrücken, die er für untragbar hält. Auch wollte er unter dem Zeichen des Doppeladlers keinerlei Redensarten dulden, „die biblischer, katechetischer oder hierarchischer Herkunft" sind, sowie „jeglichen Hinweis auf den christlichen Sündenbegriff" (S. 66). Und Aussagen, „die in den Ton liturgischer Kirchengebete [fallen]", sollten „entweder gänzlich unterlassen oder [zumindest] verbessert werden" (S. 68). Unter dieses Edikt fielen z. B. Ausrufe wie „Jesus Maria", „heiliger Anton" und „allmächtiger Gott" sowie viele andere rein rhetorische und schon längst in ihrem Aussagewert abgeblaßte Floskeln, wie sie im italienischen melodramma gang und gäbe sind. An ihre Stelle traten in der Tat oft unvorbelastete, heidnische Entsprechungen. So wurde aus ‚gran Dio' ‚numi'; und, wie wiederholt im *Rigoletto*, aus ‚Kirche' (chiesa) ‚Tempel' (tempio)[38].

Hierzu zwei charakteristische Beispiele aus der Geschichte der italienischen Oper. Im Jahre 1838 arbeitete Donizetti an einer auf Corneilles Trauerspiel *Polyeucte* basierenden Oper, die im Teatro San

---

37 Auch in einem der Zensurberichte über die *Muette de Portici* wird dieses Thema angeschnitten. Dort heißt es besänftigend: „La cérémonie du mariage religieux au l'acte [...] n'est qu'un effet de théâtre. Tout se passe loin des yeux du spectateur." Zitiert bei Schneider/Wild (Anm. 12), S. 200.

38 So heißt es gleich zu Beginn der Introduzione (Nr. 2.): „Duca: Della mia bella incognita borghese/ Toccare il fin dell'avventura io voglio. Borsa: Di quella giovin che vedete al tempio?" Ich zitiere aus *Giuseppe Verdi: Rigoletto. Texte, Materialien, Kommentare*, hg. v. Attila Csampai und Dietmar Holland, Reinbek 1982.

Carlo in Neapel aufgeführt werden sollte. Doch verbot der Herrscher beider Sizilien die Realisierung des bereits teilweise komponierten Werkes, weil der Titelheld ein Heiliger war[39]. Er hätte sich bei diesem Eingriff in die Freiheit der Kunst auf Hägelin berufen können, der dreiundzwanzig Jahre zuvor geurteilt hatte: „Ebenso wenig können Stücke passiert werden, die irgendeine darin handelnde geistliche Person der katholischen oder auch der protestantischen Kirche enthielten: dieses ist vom Papste an bis auf den geringsten Abbé oder Priester zu verstehen, wozu auch die Klostergeistlichen männlichen und weiblichen Geschlechts" genau so gehören wie etwa Heilige oder Märtyrer (S. 60). Zwölf Jahre später mußte Verdi bei den Vorbereitungen zur Premiere seines *Stiffelio* in Triest ähnliche Erfahrungen machen. Die von der Zensur geforderten Korrekturen am Text führten in diesem Fall, wie Julian Budden ausführt, unter anderem dazu, daß „einige für die dramatische Logik wichtige Verse verändert und dadurch sinnentleert wurden"[40]. Das Schlimmste jedoch war, der gleichen Quelle zufolge, daß es nunmehr in der Schluß-Szene der Oper weder Kirche noch Bibel gab und an die Stelle der Christus-Worte, mit denen der ehebrecherischen Frau vergeben werden sollte (Johannes-Evangelium, Kap. 8), ein moralischer Gemeinplatz trat.

Der auf das Gebiet der Moral, d. h. vordringlich auf das Sexualleben bezügliche Teil von Hägelins Denkschrift ist sehr knapp bemessen und im Verhältnis zu den mit der Religion und der Politik befaßten Teilen denkbar allgemein gehalten – und das aus Gründen, deren der Verfasser sich voll bewußt ist. Hägelin bezeichnet denn auch die im Abschnitt „Gebrechen des Dialogs wider die Sitten" behandelte Materie – vor allem auf der sprachlichen Ebene – als unerschöpflich (S. 70). Hieraus folgert er, daß man „einem Zensoren keine bessere

---

[39] Ashbrook (Anm. 28), S. 133, zitiert einen Brief Donizettis an Antonio Vasselli, in dem es heißt: „Do you know that perhaps my Poliuto will be prohibited now because he is a saint. And I have written half of it. Imagine with what a will [sic] I go on writing."
[40] Julian Budden: *Verdi. Leben und Werke*, übersetzt v. Ingrid Rein und Dietrich Klose, Stuttgart 1987, S. 65.

praktische Regel [auf den Weg] mitgeben könne als folgende Grundsatz-Erklärung: ‚das Publikum muss als eine gesittete, wohlerzogene Gesellschaft angesehen werden, gegen die man die Achtung nicht verletzen darf'" (S. 69). Zu eliminieren oder stark abzuschwächen wären demnach insbesondere alle „schmutzige[n] Ausdrücke, Zoten und Zweideutigkeiten, [...] vor denen die Ehrbarkeit erröten muß" (ebd.).

Einen besonders eklatanten Verstoß gegen dieses Gebot, der von der Zensur entweder nicht bemerkt oder stillschweigend übergangen wurde, stellt die bekannteste Fassung des im deutschen Sprachraum kaum zufällig zunächst als Puppenspiel oder Kasperliade verbreiteten Don-Juan-Stoffes, Lorenzo da Pontes Libretto zu Mozarts *Don Giovanni*, dar, der vielleicht auch deshalb geduldet wurde, weil es sich um einen Text in italienischer Sprache handelt[41].

Wie sich bei sorgfältiger Lektüre herausstellt, gibt es in diesem dramma giocoso viele sexuelle Anspielungen, die Mozart, wenigstens in einem ganz besonders prominenten Falle – dem der Katalog-Arie – genüßlich in Musik umsetzte[42]. Nicht nur sprachlich, sondern auch inhaltlich wird in dieser Oper naturgemäß viel gesündigt. Allerdings kommt kein Ehebruch im heutigen Wortverständnis vor; denn Don Giovanni war mit Donna Elvira, die er so schnöde verlassen hat, zwar verlobt, aber noch nicht verheiratet. Da aber, wie Molière in seinem *Dom Juan* vor Augen führt, die Verlobung in früherer Zeit als ein so festes Eheversprechen galt, daß der sexuelle Vollzug ohne weiteres geduldet wurde, impliziert Don Giovannis Flucht einen Verstoß gegen das Sakrament der Ehe[43]. Andererseits erklärt sich aus dem gleichen

---

41 Zum ganzen Komplex siehe Ulrich Weisstein: „„Per porle in lista'. Da Ponte/Leporello's Amorous Inventory and its Literary and Operatic Antecedents from Tirso de Molina to Giovanni Bertati", in: *Komparatistik. Theoretische Überlegungen und südosteuropäische Wechselseitigkeit. Festschrift für Zoran Konstantinović*, hg. v. Fridrun Rinner und Klaus Zerinschek, Heidelberg 1981, S. 179-198 [Wiederabdruck in diesem Band].

42 Besonders auffallend ist in dieser Beziehung die musikalische Untermalung der Zeilen „Porche porti la gonnella,/ Voi sapete quel che fa".

43 Bei Molière heißt es zum Beispiel: „Sganarelle: Mais, par exemple, de vous voir tous les mois vous marier comme vous faites [...] Dom Juan: Y a-t-il rien de plus

Kontext, warum Don Ottavios Beziehung zu Donna Anna, der er, wenn man E. T. A. Hoffmann Glauben schenkt, gewiß schon beigewohnt hat, die Grenzen des Erlaubten, vielleicht sogar des Schicklichen, nicht überschreitet[44]. Andererseits geht es jedoch um Verführung und versuchte Vergewaltigung – ganz abgesehen davon, daß, wie die Champagner-Arie zeigt, der Protagonist den von Hägelin ausdrücklich tabuisierten epikuräischen Prinzipien huldigt. Daß ein Lebenslauf nach viel Lieb' und Lust in der Hölle endet, ist im Grunde wenig mehr als ein moralisches Pflästerchen, das dem Christenmenschen unter den Zuhörern bzw. Zuschauern die Sache einigermaßen erträglich machen soll.

Daß gerade in der Oper das erotische Element als körperliche Umsetzung der von der Musik entfachten bzw. mit- oder nachvollzogenen Leidenschaften zum Tragen kommt, ist unbestritten. Schon aus diesem Grunde mußte diese Gattung der Zensur verdächtig sein. Umso verwunderlicher ist es z. B., daß Richard Wagners vielfältige Übertretungen des Sittengebots, von wenigen, eher privaten Ausnahmen abgesehen, kaum je die Gemüter erregte[45]. Die Indifferenz des Publikums so-

---

agréable? Sganarelle: Il est vrai, je conçois que cela est fort agréable et fort divertissant, et je m'en accomoderais assez, moi, s'il n'y avait point de mal; mais, Monsieur, se jouer aussi d'un mystère sacré et [...] Dom Juan: Va, va, c'est une affaire entre le Ciel et moi, et nous la démêlerons bien ensemble, sans que tu t'en mettes en peine." (Akt 1, Szene 2). Zitiert aus Ulrich Weisstein: „So machen's eben nicht alle: Da Ponte/Mozarts *Don Giovanni* und die vergleichende Erotik", in: *Elemente der Literatur. Beiträge zur Stoff-, Motiv- und Themenforschung. Elisabeth Frenzel zum 65. Geburtstag*, hg. v. Adam Bisanz und Raymond Trousson, Stuttgart 1980, Bd. 1, S. 94.

44 Siehe hierzu die sattsam bekannte, von Hoffmann in seiner Erzählung *Don Juan* entfachte Kontroverse über den ‚Fall' Donna Annas, beruhend auf der Doppeldeutigkeit des Zeitwortes *piegar* in deren Bericht an Don Ottavio (Nr. 10, „Recitativo accompagnato ed Aria").

45 So spricht Wagners Frau Minna in einem Brief an eine unbekannte Freundin vom 15. Dezember 1861 von Tristan und Isolde als einem „gar zu verliebten und ekligen Paar"; und der Kritiker der *Allgemeinen Musikalischen Zeitung* bemängelt „die Verherrlichung der sinnlichen Lust mit allem aufregenden Apparat" sowie den hier zutage tretenden „trostlosen Materialismus". Beide Zitate aus: *Richard Wagner. Dokumentarbiographie*, bearbeitet von Egon Voss, Taschenbuchausgabe: München 1982, S. 383 und 409.

wie der Zensur gegenüber dem Inzest in der *Walküre*[46], dem Ehebruch in *Tristan und Isolde*, der freien Liebe in *Tannhäuser* und der, wenngleich religiösen, Prostitution im *Parsifal* läßt sich daher, wie ich glaube, nur so erklären, daß diese Verletzungen des moralischen Codes fernab der geschichtlichen Realität auf mythologischer Ebene erfolgen. Wagner hatte nämlich aus seinen Erlebnissen in Dresden die Lehre gezogen, daß man sich, um politisch sicher zu gehen, von der Wirklichkeit ab- und dem Mythos bzw. der Legende zuwenden müsse[47].

Zum Thema ‚Sittlichkeit und Opernzensur' ein paar bezeichnende Beispiele. Im *Rigoletto* z. B. fiel eine ganze Szene aus *Le Roi s'amuse* – nämlich diejenige, in der sich Franz I. seines Schlüssels bedient, um in das Gemach, in das die Entführer Gilda eingesperrt haben, einzudringen – dem Rotstift der präventiven Selbstzensur zum Opfer, weil sie, gegen die gesellschaftliche *convenance* verstoßend, Gefahr lief, von der Zensur beanstandet zu werden[48]. Und noch in unserem Jahrhundert hatte es Richard Strauss bei zwei seiner bekanntesten Opern nicht leicht, der damals von den Hoftheatern ausgeübten Selbstzensur

---

46 Ludwig Leisz (Anm. 16) zitiert eine für diese Auffassung symptomatische Überlegung aus dem Urteil der 6. Strafkammer des Landgerichts 3 in Berlin vom 18. 11. 1921 im Prozeß gegen Arthur Schnitzler wegen der öffentlichen Aufführung seines *Reigens*: „In Wagners *Walküre* spielt die ganze Handlung auf eine geschlechtliche Beiwohnung hin, die man sich als nach Aktschluß stattgefunden zu denken hat. Ähnlich liegen die Dinge bei *Romeo und Julia*. [...] Diese Stücke kann man nicht als unzüchtig bezeichnen wegen des hohen ethischen Wertes, der sie [...] zum Kunstwerk stempelt" (S. 296).

47 Siehe hierzu Wagners ausführliche Darstellung in „Eine Mitteilung an meine Freunde" (1851) in: *Dichtungen und Schriften in zehn Bänden*, hg. v. Dieter Borchmeyer, Frankfurt a. M. 1983, Bd. 6, S. 290ff.

48 Es handelt sich um die Szene III, 2 in Hugos Drama (*Théâtre I*, S. 1418ff.). Vergleiche hierzu Verdis ‚romantische' Lösung am Ende der Nr. 8 im zweiten Akt: „Ah! sappia alcun chi l'ama,/ Conosce appien chi sono,/ Apprenda ch'anco in trono/ Ha degli schiavi amor." Hierzu Verdi selbst an Piave: „Lass' dich nicht zu Änderungen überreden, die die Charaktere, das Sujet und die Situationen verfälschen könnten. Du darfst nur Worte ändern und auch die Stelle, in der Franz mit dem Schlüssel in Biancas Zimmer geht; zumal ich selbst der Meinung bin, daß es angebracht ist, etwas Besseres zu finden." *Rigoletto* (Anm. 38), S. 148.

die Erlaubnis zur Aufführung abzuringen. So erhielt der Operndirektor Gustav Mahler am 15. September 1905 vom Intendanten der Wiener Hofoper die Nachricht:

> Abgesehen davon, daß die Darstellung von Vorgängen aus dem Neuen Testament, insbesondere auf einer Hofbühne, grundsätzliche Bedenken erregt, wirkt die Vorführung einer perversen Sinnlichkeit, wie sie in der Figur der Salome verkörpert ist, sittlich verletzend. Ich möchte mich deshalb aus religiösen und sittlichen Gründen gegen die Zulassung des vorliegenden Operntextes aussprechen[49].

Erst unter Mahlers Nachfolger, Joseph Gregor, konnte dreizehn Jahre später die Wiener Erstaufführung stattfinden.

Im Gegensatz zur *Salome*, wo das ganze Werk mit dem zensoriellen Bann belegt wurde, gab es beim *Rosenkavalier* derartige Schwierigkeiten vor allem bei einer Szene: der des intimen Levers der Marschallin. Hieß es in Hofmannsthals Regieanweisungen ursprünglich – wie noch heute in der Buchausgabe dieser Komödie für Musik – „Octavian kniet auf einem Schemel vor dem Bett und hält die Feldmarschallin, die im Bett liegt, halb umschlungen", so wurde auf den Einspruch des Dresdner Intendanten, Graf Seebach, hin bei der Premiere am dortigen Hoftheater sowie in dem bei Fürstner erschienenen Textbuch „im Bett" kurzweg durch „in der Sofaecke" ersetzt[50]. Graf Seebach monierte übrigens auch – nur zum Teil mit Erfolg – einige schlüpfrige Stellen aus dem erotischen Repertoire des Ochs von Lerchenau[51]. Ferner kann man vermuten, der Dichter habe den zensoriellen Eingriff in die künstlerische Freiheit des Librettisten und Kompo-

---

49 Zitiert bei Leisz (Anm. 16), S. 184.
50 Im *Ingénu libertin ou le marmiton* (1907), der Operette von Louis Artus und Victor Terrasse, die dem *Rosenkavalier* in vieler Hinsicht als direktes Vorbild diente, heißt es noch viel anzüglicher: „Quand le rideau se lève, la Marquise dort encore derrière les courtines closes. Faublas, qui vient de sortir du lit, est dans sa petite culotte et chemisette de cavalier." Die französischen Quellen der Oper behandelt Ulrich Weisstein in seinem Aufsatz: „(Pariser) Farce oder wienerische Maskerade?", in: *Hofmannsthal-Forschungen*, Bd. 9, hg. v. Wolfram Mauser, Freiburg i. Br. 1987, S. 75-102 [Wiederabdruck in diesem Band].
51 Siehe hierzu vor allem den Brief Hofmannsthals an Strauss vom 12. Juli 1910 in: *Richard Strauss/Hugo von Hofmannsthal: Briefwechsel*, hg. v. Franz und Alice Strauss, Zürich 1952, S. 88f.

nisten vorausgeahnt und sich gleichsam antizipierend gerächt, indem er im dritten Akt der vorgeblich im Zeitalter Maria Theresias spielenden Oper die Polizei in ihrer Eigenschaft als Sittenwächter auftreten ließ[52].

Daß die Oper auch ein Politikum ist, wie Kurt Honolka behauptet[53], versteht sich von selbst. Gerade in diesem Bereich, in dem sich Dichtung und Wahrheit eng verquicken, war die Zensur – vor allem die italienische um die Mitte des vorigen Jahrhunderts – im Dienst konservativer Regierungen unermüdlich tätig. Freilich waren die Zensoren im Hinblick auf die in Italien ausgesprochen volksnahe und daher volkstümliche Gattung ‚Oper' vielfach wie Hunde, die zwar viel bellen, aber nur selten beißen; denn letztendlich waren sie meist zu Konzessionen bereit. Theorie und Praxis der Zensur klafften also weit auseinander. Die Leitgedanken einer politisch orientierten Theaterzensur, wie sie ihm vorschwebte, faßte Hägelin wie folgt zusammen:

> Es können in einem monarchischen Staate keine Stücke aufgeführt werden, deren Inhalt auf die Abwürdigung der monarchischen Regierungsform abzielte oder der demokratischen oder einer anderen den Vorzug [...] einräumte oder auch die ständische Verfassung eines Landes herabsetzte. (S. 61)

Es leuchtet ohne weiteres ein, daß Exemplare der Untergattung ‚Historisches Drama' stets im Brennpunkt der zensoriellen Interessen standen[54]. Mit etwas anderen Vorzeichen gilt dies natürlich auch für das Sub-Genre ‚Historische Oper', als dessen erstes Exemplar Claudio Monteverdis Spätwerk *L'Incoronazione di Poppea* (1642) zu gelten hat. Mit geschichtlichen Stoffen befaßte Opern begannen um die Mitte des 18. Jahrhunderts den bis dato dominierenden mythologischen Themen Konkurrenz zu machen und verursachten Kontroversen, die über einen relativ langen Zeitraum hinweg in kritischen Schriften von

---

52 Als Sittenpolizei tritt die Zensur in der Figur des Kommissarius auf, der den Ochs verdächtigt, „ein gottverdammter Debauchierer und Verführer" zu sein.
53 Kurt Honolka (Anm. 24), S. 207-218: „Die Oper, ein Politikum".
54 Zum historischen Drama siehe Herbert Lindenberger: *Historical Drama: The Relation of Literature and Reality*, Chicago 1975 und Friedrich Sengle: *Das historische Drama in Deutschland*, Stuttgart 1974.

Algarotti bis Busoni ihren Niederschlag fanden[55]. Nicht selten kam es unter dem antizipierten Druck der Behörde zu einer Flucht aus der Geschichte, wie bei dem bekehrten Revoluzzer Wagner, der das mit *Rienzi, der letzte der Tribunen* (1840; uraufgeführt 1842) begonnene Experiment bekanntlich nicht fortsetzte – was den scharfsinnigen und -züngigen Musikkritiker George Bernard Shaw nicht davon abhielt, in seiner Schrift *The Perfect Wagnerite* (1888) den *Ring des Nibelungen* als eine allegorische Darstellung der Auseinandersetzung zwischen Kapitalismus und Nihilismus bzw. Sozialismus zu deuten. Während der reifere Wagner in seinen Musikdramen nur kryptopolitisch agierte, gab sich, im Gegensatz zu dessen eher unpolitischem Landsmann Rossini[56], sein Zeitgenosse Verdi (akronymisch: Vittorio Emmanuele, Re d'Italia) in vielen seiner Opern betont politisch.

Im Unterschied zur Zensur des *legitimate drama*, die, wie Hägelin bemerkt, „keine Begebenheiten aus der Geschichte des Erzhauses [...], deren Ausschlag diesen Regenten nachteilig war, z. B. die Empörung der Eidgenossenschaft, die sich dem österreichischen Szepter entzogen hat: item der Schweizerheld Wilhelm Tell; item die Rebellion der Vereinigten Niederlande [...] und dergleichen" (S. 62), zur Aufführung freigeben durfte, begnügte sich freilich die Opernzensur vielfach mit der Anwendung rein kosmetischer Mittel wie der bloßen Versetzung von Ort und Zeit oder dem Wechsel des Namens und Standes der *dramatis personae*.

So wurde im *Rigoletto* der König von Frankreich zum Herzog von Mantua, Guillaume Tell ging in Mailand als Guglielmo Vallace, in Rom als Rodolfo di Sterlinga und in St. Petersburg gar als Carlo il

---

55 Es handelt sich um Francesco Algarottis *Saggio sopra l'opera in musica* (1754) und Ferruccio Busonis *Entwurf einer neuen Ästhetik der Tonkunst* (1907). Auszüge aus beiden Werken finden sich in: *The Essence of Opera* (Anm. 15), S. 69-74 und 264-267.

56 Immerhin schrieb dieser am 12. Juni 1864 an Filippo Santocanale: „Per distruggere poi l'epiteto di codino, dirò per finire che ho vestite le parole di libertà nel mio Guglielmo Tell modo di far conoscere quanto io sia caldo per la mia patria per nobili sentimenti che la investono". *Lettere di G. Rossini* raccolte e annotate per cura di G. Mazzatinti e F. G. Manis, Florenz 1902, S. 271.

Temerario (= Karl der Kühne) in Szene[57]; und *Un ballo in maschera* wurde von Stockholm nach Boston verlegt, weil man nach den kurz zuvor verübten Anschlägen sowohl auf Napoleon III. als auch auf den König von Sizilien die Darstellung eines unmittelbar nach der Französischen Revolution erfolgten Königsmordes – Gustav III. von Schweden war im März 1792 durch einen Revolverschuß getötet worden – für unzumutbar hielt[58].

Als frühes Beispiel einer zumindest unterschwellig politischen Präventivzensur im Opernbereich kann man den Fall von Mozarts ‚commedia per musica' *Le nozze di Figaro* bezeichnen. Ich sage ‚unterschwellig', weil Da Ponte weder in seinen Memoiren[59] noch in seinem Vorwort zum deutschen Textbuch[60] mit der ganzen Wahrheit herausrückt, sondern sich auf die Erwähnung moralischer und ästhetischer Gründe für die am Schauspieltext vorgenommenen Retuschen beschränkt. In diesem Vorwort, in dem der Dichter übrigens nicht auf sein Gespräch mit dem Kaiser eingeht, heißt es diplomatisch:

> Die für dramatische Vorstellungen von dem Gebrauche vorgeschriebene Zeit, eine gewisse bestimmte, in denselben allgemein gewöhnliche Zahl der vorstellenden Personen, und einige andere kluge, in Rücksicht der guten Sitten, des Ortes und der Zuschauer nötige Beobachtungen sind die Ursache gewesen, warum ich dieses vortreffliche Lustspiel nicht übersetzt sondern nachgeahmt oder vielmehr nur einen Auszug davon gemacht habe. (Anm. 60, S. 255)

Wie hochpolitisch im Grunde diese Handlungsweise war, erhellt aus dem kaiserlichen Verbot der Aufführung des Stückes von Beaumarchais im Februar 1785, also ungefähr ein Jahr vor der Uraufführung der Oper, und manifestiert sich u. a. in der Tatsache, daß Da Ponte den großen ideologisch verbrämten Monolog des Figaro in V, 3 von *La*

---

57 Siehe hierzu den im Textbuch zur London Records-Aufnahme der Oper abgedruckten Aufsatz William Weavers.

58 Ich stütze mich bei diesen Angaben auf die Darstellung Kurt Pahlens in seiner Ausgabe des *Maskenball*-Textes, Mainz, München 1986, S. 178ff.

59 Lorenzo Da Ponte: *Mein abenteuerliches Leben*, übs. v. Walter Klefisch, Reinbek 1960, S. 86ff. Dort Näheres (wie zuverlässig?) über Da Pontes Gespräch mit Joseph II.

60 Abgedruckt in *W. A. Mozart: Die Hochzeit des Figaro. Texte, Materialien, Kommentare*, hg. v. Attila Csampai und Dietmar Holland, Reinbek 1982, S. 253.

Folle Journée erbarmungslos zusammenstrich und sich bei seiner Umsetzung der Vorlage auf die intime Thematik der Arie „Aprite un po' quegl'occhi" (Nr. 26, IV, 8) beschränkte.

Gerade im politischen Umfeld der Opernzensur gibt es eine Reihe von Paradoxa, von denen ich abschließend wenigstens eines anhand dreier Beispiele exemplifizieren möchte. Mangels eines konsensfähigen terminus technicus nenne ich es kurzerhand ‚die konservative Behandlung revolutionärer Stoffe'. Mein erstes Beweisstück ist der nachgerade klassische Fall der am 29. Februar 1828 in Paris aus der Taufe gehobenen *Muette de Portici*, deren Brüsseler Premiere im August 1830 bekanntlich Ereignisse auslöste, die entscheidend zur Trennung Belgiens von den Niederlanden beitrugen.

Die Frage, ob es sich bei diesem Werk um eine Revolutionsoper oder um ein proletarisches Trauerspiel mit Musik handelt, muß im Sinne unseres Paradoxes offen bleiben, weil zwar in der steigenden Handlung die politische Spannung zusehends wächst und am Ende des zweiten Aktes (Nr. 11, Finale) mit einem kollektiven *in tyrannos* ihren Höhepunkt erreicht, in der fallenden Handlung aber der Rebellenführer Masaniello, nunmehr ein wirklich Zerrissener, an seiner Sendung zweifelt und von Gewissensbissen geplagt wird. Von einem Mitstreiter als Verräter gebrandmarkt und vergiftet, stirbt er, dem Wahnsinn nahe, genau in dem Augenblick, in dem er, der schwankende Held, sich erneut dazu aufrafft, die Leitung des Aufstandes zu übernehmen.

Wie die erhaltenen Zensurberichte zeigen, war man sich behördlicherseits durchaus bewußt, daß hier ein echtes Dilemma vorlag, entschied sich aber in diesem Fall dazu, das Placet zur Aufführung zu geben, während man es bei einer unmittelbar vorher der Zensur unterbreiteten Bearbeitung des gleichen Stoffes verweigert hatte. Ausschlaggebend für diese Entscheidung waren u. a. die Tatsache, daß in dieser Fassung keine echte Revolution, sondern lediglich ein Aufstand gegen das spanische Joch vor Augen geführt wird, sowie der Umstand, daß der Held für seine Hybris bestraft wird. Und auch der spektakuläre Selbstmord Fenellas wurde vom wohlwollenden Zensor nicht als Todsünde eingestuft, sondern als lässliche Sünde und atypische Handlung entschuldigt[61].

Mein zweites Demonstrations-Objekt ist Rossinis *Guillaume Tell* – im August 1829, also anderthalb Jahre nach der *Muette* uraufgeführt und mit Aubers Oper in mancher Hinsicht thematisch verwandt[62]. Auch dieser, der melodramatische Schwanengesang des italienischen Meisters, wurde, wie Anselm Gerhard berichtet, „ohne Beanstandung genehmigt"[63], nachdem der Vorsitzende der Jury Littéraire et Musical der Pariser Opéra dem Directeur des Beaux-Arts ausführlich über den Text berichtet, Einwände aber nur in estheticis erhoben hatte[64]. Auch diesmal drückte die Zensur ein Auge zu, und zwar vermutlich nicht nur deshalb, weil Rossini an einer kulturpolitischen Schaltstelle saß, sondern auch – und wohl hauptsächlich –, weil der Stoff zwar an und für sich umstürzlerisch, seine Behandlung aber eher konservativ war. Denn eigentlich geht es im *Guillaume Tell* weniger um die Beseitigung eines ganzen Regimes, der Habsburger als mehr oder minder totalitärer Weltmacht, als um die Vertreibung eines kleinen Despoten (Gessler) und um die Wiederherstellung eines Zustandes – will heißen: der Schweizer Idylle –, in dem die Natur zu ihrem Rechte kommt und der Mensch harmonisch in sie eingebettet ist. Die Musik, in welche das Schluß-Tableau der Oper getaucht ist, ist ausgesprochen pa-

---

61 „Le peuple de Naples, fatigué du joug des Espagnols, ne se soulève que contre cette domination étrangère et il n y a dans cette combinaison, rien qui sorte du cercle ordinaire des moyens dramatiques. – Ce soulèvement populaire est promptement réprimé. Le chef Mazaniello périt misérablement empoisonné d'abord et assassiné ensuite par le peuple qui l'avait poussé à la révolte. La mort de Fenella [...] ne peut être regardée comme un suicide dans le sens où nous l'entendons ordinairement. Cet acte d'un désespoir amoureux, sur la scène de l'Opéra, n'entraîne aucune réflexion. Il n'est point pris dans nos manières, il n'y a là aucun danger." Schneider/Wild (Anm. 12), S. 199.

62 Siehe hierzu meinen Aufsatz: „Der Apfel fiel recht weit vom Stamme: Rossinis Guillaume Tell, eine musikalische Schweizerreise?", in: *Oper als Text. Romanistische Beiträge zur Libretto-Forschung*, hg. v. Albert Gier, Heidelberg 1986, S. 147-184.

63 Anselm Gerhard: „Sortire dalle vie communi. Wie Rossini einem Akademiker den *Guillaume Tell* verdarb", ebd., S. 185-220; hier S. 193, Anm. 3.

64 Zitiert ebd., S. 216.

storal; und die entsprechende Regie-Anweisung lautet: „poco a poco si dileguano le nubi, ed il cielo si rasserena".

Hinzu kommt beim *Guillaume Tell*, wie auch in der *Muette* eine ‚romantische' Nebenhandlung, deren, freilich nur angedeutetes, Happy End den im zweiten Akt groß herausgestellten Rütli-Schwur vergessen läßt. In bezug auf diese charakteristisch melodramaturgische Taktik ist Patrick J. Smith, dem Verfasser der einzigen bisher in englischer Sprache erschienenen Geschichte des Librettos, zuzustimmen, wenn er feststellt:

> Problems with censorship probably accentuated [the] tendency to dwell on the personal side of the characters; for a libretto that revolved around love and jealousy would be more likely to pass unscathed than one dealing with freedom or the evils of the aristocracy[65].

Ein ganz explizites Happy End gibt es beim dritten und letzten Glied unserer Reihe, Beethovens einziger Oper, *Fidelio*, einem Hauptvertreter der unter der Bezeichnung ‚Rettungsoper' bekannten, um 1800 florierenden Variante der ‚konservativen Revolutionsoper', von der Spuren noch in der *Muette* zu finden sind. Ihr Erfinder war Jean Nicolas Bouilly, der Verfasser zweier, auf eigenen Erlebnissen beruhender Libretti: *Léonore ou l'amour conjugal* (Musik von Pierre Gaveaux; uraufgeführt am 19. Februar 1798) und *Les Deux Journées* (zu deutsch: *Der Wasserträger*, Musik von Luigi Cherubini und uraufgeführt am 16. Januar 1800). Beide Werke spielen im Leben und Schaffen Beethovens eine wichtige Rolle – ersteres, weil es die Vorlage für *Fidelio* war, und letzteres, weil es auf ihn und viele seiner bedeutendsten Zeitgenossen (darunter auch Goethe) einen unauslöschlichen Eindruck machte.

Die Rettungsoper etablierte sich als Gattung vor allem dadurch, daß sie sich mit dem „Heroismus weiblicher (Fidelio-Leonore) oder

---

65 Patrick M. Smith: *The Tenth Muse. A Historical Study of the Opera Libretto*, New York 1970, S. 194.

männlicher (der Wasserträger) Tugenden"[66] im Umfeld des nachrevolutionären Terrors befaßte und die Menschen- bzw. Gattenliebe als leuchtendes Beispiel des homo humanus dem Haß und den aus ihm entspringenden Rachegelüsten (Pizarro) entgegenstellte, also den politischen Aspekt dem privaten unterordnete. Trotz dieser humanitären und im weiteren Sinne aufklärerischen Tendenz sah sich Bouilly veranlaßt, Schauplatz und Zeitpunkt der Handlung sowie die Namen der Handelnden zu kaschieren; und auch im *Fidelio* finden sich Relikte dieser präventiv verfremdenden Verfahrensweise. So lauten die Regiebemerkungen in der Fassung von 1814 noch immer: „Spanisches Staatsgefängnis, einige Meilen von Sevilla entfernt. Zeit: 18. Jahrhundert".

Relativ wenig bekannt ist der Umstand, daß die Urfassung des *Fidelio*-Textes von der Zensur bemängelt und erst nach „Milderung der krassesten Stellen"[67] genehmigt wurde. Dies erklärt die Verschiebung der Premiere vom 9. September auf den 20. November 1805. Der Theaterwissenschaftler Karl Glossy entdeckte im Wiener Zensurarchiv folgende, auf diesen Vorgang bezügliche Aktennotiz, die ich, mit nur leichten Kürzungen, im Wortlaut zitiere, weil sie ein Bild von den damals der Behörde gegenüber angewandten Taktiken vermittelt:

> Hofsekretär Josef Sonnleithner bittet das am 20. September 1805 erfolgte Verbot aufzuheben, da diese Oper nach dem französischen Original des Bouilly [...] vorzüglich deshalb bearbeitet worden sei, weil die Kaiserin [Marie-Therese von Sizilien] das Original sehr schön gefunden und versichert habe, kein Opernstoff hätte ihr jemals so viel Vergnügen gemacht; zweitens: diese Oper, vom Kapellmeister Paer nach dem italienischen Text bearbeitet, schon zu Prag und Dresden gegeben worden sei; drittens: Beethoven über eineinhalb Jahre mit der Komposition zugebracht habe, auch, da man nicht im geringsten ein Verbot besorgte, bereits Proben gehalten und alle übrigen Veranstaltungen [sic] getroffen worden seien, um diese Oper zur Namensfeier zu geben; viertens: die Handlung im 16. Jahrhundert vorgehe, also gar keine Beziehung [zur Gegenwart] unterliegen könne; endlich fünftens ein so grosser Mangel an guten Opernbüchern besteht, das gegenwärtige

---

66 So Josef von Sonnleithner an den Staatsrat von Stahl am 3. Oktober 1805. Zitiert aus *Ludwig van Beethoven:* Fidelio. *Texte, Materialien, Kommentare*, hg. v. Attila Csampai und Dietmar Holland, Reinbek 1981, S. 88.

67 So Willy Hess in seinem Buch: *Beethovens Oper* Fidelio *und ihre drei Fassungen*, Zürich 1953, S. 18.

aber das rührendste Gemälde der weiblichen Tugend darstelle und der bösgesinnte Gouverneur nur eine Privatrache ausübe[68].

Die Uraufführung der Oper, aufgrund dieses Bouquets von heterogenen Gründen gesichert, fand eine Woche nach dem Einmarsch französischer Truppen in das menschenleere Wien statt und war nur spärlich besucht; was die Absetzung nach insgesamt drei Vorstellungen zur Folge hatte. Der europäische Siegeszug dieses weltlichen Hoheliedes der Gattentreue begann auch nicht mit der Aufführung der zweiaktigen Version von 1806, sondern erst mit der Premiere der Fassung letzter Hand acht Jahre später.

Ich fasse zusammen: mein panoramatischer Überblick über das weite, aber bislang unzureichend kultivierte Feld der Opernzensur ergab, daß es auf ihm, wie bei der Theaterzensur im allgemeinen, typologisch gesehen vier verschiedene Sektoren – den religiösen, den politischen, den moralischen und, eher beiläufig, den ästhetischen – gibt, die innerhalb eines gegebenen Werkes entweder einzeln oder in Verbindung miteinander auftreten. Es zeigte sich ferner, daß die religiöse Komponente in der Geschichte der Opernzensur kaum ins Gewicht fällt und hauptsächlich auf der sprachlichen Ebene zum Tragen kommt. In der Domäne der Politik kam zum Vorschein, daß in der Historischen Oper Handlungen mit ausgesprochen subversiven Tendenzen weitaus seltener sind als im Historischen Drama, wie die Herausbildung des von mir charakterisierten Typs der ‚konservativen Revolutionsoper' einschließlich der sogenannten Rettungsoper beweist. Was die moralische Dimension der Oper anlangt, wird, wie sich herausstellte, in diesem künstlerischen Medium die Sexualität durch ihre Umsetzung in Erotik ästhetisch legitimiert. Ein Problem besonderer Art stellt, in bezug auf die Oper, selten aber in bezug auf die Opernzensur, die von W. H. Auden unter Berufung auf Sören Kierkegaard postulierte ‚ethische Indifferenz der Musik' dar, welch letztere, dieser

---

68 Zitiert von Karl Glossy in: *Zur Geschichte der Theater Wiens I* (1801-1820) (Anm. 25), S. 83f.

Auffassung zufolge, ‚jenseits von Gut und Böse' steht[69]. Bei näherer Betrachtung zeigt sich freilich, daß dies im Grunde nur auf die sogenannte absolute Musik zutrifft, nicht aber auf die im dramma per musica dominierenden Wort-Ton-Verbindungen; denn obschon wir, gleich den von ihm verführten Frauen, bei Don Giovannis Champagner-Arie und seinem Ständchen momentan vergessen, daß er ein Nichtswürdiger und moralisch Verwerflicher ist, lassen uns weder Beethovens Pizarro noch Verdis Jago – ganz zu schweigen von Berlioz', Gounods und Boitos Mephistopheles – auch nur einen Augenblick darüber im Zweifel, welch Geistes Kind sie sind. Auden zutrotze singen also in der Oper böse Menschen zuweilen sehr wohl böse Arien. Für den Zensor sind jedoch Operngestalten, ganz gleich ob sie schön oder häßlich singen, schlecht, d. h. zensuranfällig, nur dann, wenn der Text, den sie singen, nicht aber der Gesang selbst, dessen moralische Qualität die Zensur sich nicht zu beurteilen anmaßt, gegen die behördliche Auffassung von religiöser, politischer oder sittlicher bienseance verstößt. Quod erat demonstrandum.

---

69 Siehe hierzu Audens „Reflections on Music and Opera", in: *Partisan Review*, Januar/Februar 1952, z. B. die Aperçus auf S. 14: „Feelings of joy, tenderness and nobility are not confined to ‚noble' characters but are experienced by everybody, by the most conventional, most stupid, most depraved" und: „Opera [...] cannot present character in the novelist's sense of the word, namely, people who are potentially good and bad, active and passive; for music is immediate actuality, and neither potentiality nor passivity can live in its presence."

Sources

"The Libretto as Literature". *Books Abroad: An International Literary Quarterly* 35/1 (1961): 16-22.

"Cocteau, Stravinsky, Brecht, and the Birth of Epic Opera". *Modern Drama* 5/2 (1962): 142-153.

"Introduction" to *The Essence of Opera*. London/New York: Glencoe/Macmillan, 1964. 1-10.

"Reflections on a Golden Style: W. H. Auden's Theory of Opera". *Comparative Literature* 22/2 (1970): 108-124.

"'Per porle in lista': Da Ponte/Leporello's Amorous Inventory and its Literary and Operatic Antecedents from Tirso de Molina to Giovanni Bertati". Fridrun Rinner/Klaus Zerinschek, eds. *Komparatistik: Theoretische Überlegungen und südosteuropäische Wechselseitigkeit*. Festschrift für Zoran Konstantinović. Heidelberg: Winter, 1981. 179-198.

"Educating Siegfried". *Richard Wagner: Siegfried. National Opera Guide 28*. London: John Calder, 1984. 7-20.

"(Pariser) Farce oder wienerische Maskerade? Die französischen Quellen des *Rosenkavalier*". Wolfram Mauser, ed. *Hofmannsthal und Frankreich*. Hofmannsthal-Forschungen 9. Freiburg i. Br. 1987. 75-102.

"The Little Word *und*: *Tristan und Isolde* as Verbal Construct". Leroy R. Shaw/Nancy R. Cirillo/Marion S. Miller, eds. *Wagner in Retrospect: A Centennial Reappraisal*. Amsterdam: Rodopi, 1987. 70-90.

"Benedetto Marcellos *Il Teatro alla moda*: Scherz, Satire, Parodie oder tiefere Bedeutung?". Ursula Müller/Ulrich Müller, eds. *Opern und Opernfiguren*. Festschrift für Joachim Herz. Anif/Salzburg: Verlag Ursula Müller-Speiser, 1989. 31-57.

"Von Ballhorn ins Bockshorn gejagt: Unwillkürliche Parodie und unfreiwillige Komik in Ambroise Thomas' *Mignon*". Maria Moog-Grünewald/Christoph Rodiek, eds. *Dialog der Künste: Intermediale Fallstudien zur Literatur des 19. und 20. Jahrhunderts. Festschrift für Erwin Koppen*. Frankfurt a. M. et al.: Peter Lang, 1989. 395-414.

"'Die letzte Häutung'. Two German *Künstleropern* of the Twentieth Century: Hans Pfitzner's *Palestrina* and Paul Hindemith's *Mathis der Maler*". Claus Reschke/Howard Pollack, eds. *German Literature and Music: An Aesthetic Fusion: 1890-1989*. Houston German Studies 8. Munich: Wilhelm Fink, 1992. 193-236.

"Between Progress and Regression: The Text of Stravinsky's Opera *The Rake's Progress* in the Light of its Evolution". Bernt Olsson/Jan Olsson/Hans Lund, eds. *I Musernas Sällskap: Konstarter och deras relationer*. En vänbok till Ulla-Britta Lagerroth 19. 10. 1992. Wiken: Förlags AB Wiken, 1992. 355-390.

"What is Romantic Opera? Toward a Musico-Literary Definition". Gerald Gillespie, ed. *Romantic Drama*. Amsterdam/Philadelphia: John Benjamins, 1994. 209-229.

"*Böse Menschen singen keine Arien*: Prolegomena zu einer ungeschriebenen Geschichte der Opernzensur". Peter Brockmeier/Gerhard R. Kaiser, eds. *Zensur und Selbstzensur in der Literatur*. Würzburg: Königshausen & Neumann, 1996. 49-73.

Acknowledgments

Bra Böker AB
Comparative Literature
The Free Press of Glencoe
Hofmannsthal-Forschungen
John Benjamins Publishing Co.
John Calder Publishing Co.
Königshausen & Neumann GmbH
Modern Drama
Peter Lang GmbH
Ursula Müller Speiser Verlag
Universitätsverlag Winter
Wilhelm Fink Verlag
World Literature Today

The editor gratefully acknowledges permission granted by the following publishers and copyright holders to reprint material in this volume:

Index
of Persons and Operas Mentioned in the Text

Abendroth, Walter 252, 269, 271
Abert, Anna Amalia 304
Acciajoli, Filippo 81
Achard, Léon 219
Achter, Morton 203
Adami, Giuseppe 35
Adamy, Bernhard 251, 269
Addison, Joseph 36, 183f., 186, 190
Algarotti, Francesco 35, 181, 183, 191f., 194, 198, 360
Almeida, Antonio de 203
Altdorfer, Albrecht 267
Ariosto, Lodovico 69
Aristotle 28f., 37, 57, 141f., 172, 177, 197
Arrivabene, Opprandino 328
Artus, Louis 108f., 111, 117, 122, 124
Auber, Daniel Francois 34, 343f., 362-364
La Muette de Portici 343f., 362-364

Auden, Wystan Hugh 4, 10, 14, 38, 43-63, 233, 270, 273-299, 348, 366f.
Auric, Georges 17
Avenarius, Cäcilie 324

Balakirev, M. A. 18
Balzac, Honoré de 69
Bambini, Eustachio 82
Barbier, Jules 203, 206-208, 210, 214-216, 220-223, 227
Bardi, Giovanni de 243
Batts, Michael S. 145
Beach, Joseph Warren 43
Beaumarchais 35-37, 41, 361
Beethoven, Ludwig van 5, 40, 62, 147, 302, 319, 330, 332-334, 364f.
Fidelio 5, 40, 62, 319, 364f.
Bellini, Vincenzo 34, 44, 60-62, 303, 305, 327
Norma 61
Benn, Gottfried 258f., 270
Bentley, Eric 150f.

Berg, Alban 4, 31, 36, 38f., 57
  Wozzeck 4, 36, 39, 57
Berlioz, Hector 11, 13f., 36-38, 302, 304, 307, 309, 321, 330-335, 341, 367
  La Damnation de Faust 14, 36, 331
  Les Troyens 331
Bertati, Giovanni 65-67, 69, 71f., 74, 82-88, 195, 369
Biancolelli, Domenico 79
Bizet, Georges 19, 202, 208, 213, 221, 304, 342
  Carmen 202, 213, 221, 342
Blair, John G. 44, 275
Blume, Friedrich 309
Bodenhausen, Eberhard von 112
Böhm, Franz Magnus 263
Borchmeyer, Dieter 231, 247, 270, 272
Bordoni 5, 190
Borodin, Alexander 18
Bouilly, Jean Nicolas 5, 364f.
Brahms, Johannes 304, 320
Brecht, Bertolt 12, 17, 20, 28-31, 36, 38, 46, 112, 348, 369
Breton, André 296, 298
Briner, Andres 260f., 268, 270

Britten, Benjamin 44, 202
  Death in Venice 202
  Peter Grimes 202
  The Turn of the Screw 202
Brockway, Wallace 304
Brooks, Cleanth. 43
Brown, Calvin S. 7
Bruckner, Anton 304
Brühl, Count Carl von 314
Büchner, Georg 4
Budden, Julian 354
Buelow, Hans von 143
Buina, Giuseppe Maria 175
Bulthaupt, Heinrich 4, 270
Bunyan, Paul 44, 49, 298
Burde, Wolfgang 275
Busoni, Ferruccio 19, 36, 41, 242, 270, 296, 360

Caccini, Giulio 37, 179
Cagliostro 66
Callan, Edward 43
Calsabigi, Raniero de 4, 186, 193
Carlyle, Thomas 228
Carré, Michel 203, 206, 208, 210, 214-216, 220-223, 227
Carroll, Lewis 297
Casanova, Giacomo 66
Cerny, Johann 146

Index of Persons and Operas

Cesti, Pietro 179
Il pomo d'oro 179
Chantavoine, Jean 315, 320
Chekhov, Anton 12, 40
Cherubini, Luigi 12, 34, 364
Les Deux Journées 364
Chézy, Helmine von 4, 34
Cicognini, Giacinto 78f., 82
Cimarosa, Domenico 34
Claudel, Paul 17, 36, 38
Cocteau, Jean 17-24, 26, 29, 36, 53, 369
Collet, Henri 17
Conrad, Peter 303
Cooke, Deryk 275
Corneille, Pierre 36f.
Crabbe, George 202
Craft, Robert 277
Csampai, Attila 349f.
Cui, César 18
Cuzzoni, Francesca 5, 190

Da Ponte, Lorenzo 4, 65-67, 69, 71f., 74, 76, 82-85, 89, 186, 188, 195, 273, 361, 369
Dahlhaus, Carl 144, 156, 163, 201, 326
Dante Alighieri 153, 233
David, Felicien 203, 249, 328
De Villiers, Pierre 79f.
Debussy, Claude 17f., 21f., 24f., 35, 201

Pelléas et Mélisande 22, 201
Dent, Edward, J. 3f., 303, 314
Dessauer, Josef 321
Diderot, Denis 36f., 111, 182
Dietsch, Pierre Louis 321, 323
Le Vaisseau fantôme 321, 323
Donizetti, Gaetano 34, 44, 60f., 281, 303, 305, 327, 353
Lucia di Lammermoor 61
Polyeucte 353
Dorimon, M. 79f.
Dryden, John 36, 41, 179
Duncan, Ronald 60
Durey, Georges 17

Einem, Gottfried von 5
Einstein, Alfred 179, 182, 185, 304f.
Eliot, T. S. 6, 40, 43, 48, 69, 233, 282
Engelbert, Barbara 275
Euripides 37, 50, 182

Faustina *see* Bordoni
Fehn, Ann Clark 258, 270
Fergusson, Francis 4, 145, 150, 155
Ferrand, Humbert 333
Foppa, Giuseppe 82

Fouqué, Friedrich de la Motte 313f.
Freytag, Gustav 8, 223, 241
Gardi, Francesco 82
Garlington, Aubrey 310
Gasparini, Michelangelo 175
Gassmann, Florian 186
Gautier, Théophile 207
Gautier, Théophile, Jr. 207
Gaveaux, Pierre 364
  Léonore ou l'amour conjugal 364
Gay, John 29, 39, 186f., 190
Gazzaniga, Giuseppe 66f., 85, 88, 186
  Don Giovanni 66f., 85, 88
Gerhard, Anselm 363
Gide, André 59
Gigli, Girolamo 185
  Dirindina 185
Gilbert, Mary E. 110, 117, 131
Glossy, Karl 365
Gluck, Christoph Willibald 7, 13, 35, 37, 60f., 182, 312
  Orfeo ed Euridice 60
Goethe, Johann Wolfgang 12, 35, 40f., 69, 201, 204f., 207, 208-210, 212, 221-225, 227, 229f., 233-236, 238, 240f., 248-250, 255, 270, 287, 302, 332, 364

Goldoni, Carlo 33, 69, 177, 180, 193
Goldschmidt, Helene 229, 232, 234, 240f., 250, 270
Golther, Wolfgang 145
Gossett, Philip 303
Gottfried von Strassburg 145
Gounod, Charles 34, 62, 208
  Faust 202
Gregor, Joseph 358
Griffiths, Paul 277
Grillparzer, Franz 36, 229, 249, 270, 319, 320
Grimm, Jacob 103
Grimm, Reinhold 229, 231, 270
Grimm, Wilhelm 103
Grout, Donald 304f.
Gründgens, Gustav 241
Grünewald, Matthias Neidhart 238, 250, 259f., 262, 268-270, 272, 370
Gustav III of Sweden 361
Gutzkow, Karl 235

Hägelin, Franz Karl 342, 344, 351-354, 356, 359f.
Halévy, Ludovic 303
Hamsun, Knut 258
Handel, George Frederic 5, 34, 39, 190, 235, 281
Hanslick, Eduard 234
Hasse, Johann Adolf 34

Hawkes, Ralph 282
Haydn, Joseph 34
Hebbel, Friedrich 229, 235, 270
Heine, Ferdinand 326
Henze, Hans Werner 50
  Die Bassariden 50
Hindemith, Paul 6, 229f., 233, 234, 237, 240f., 244, 245f., 249f., 258-261, 263f., 266f., 269-271, 370
  Mathis der Maler 6, 229-272, esp. 257ff., 370
Hitzig, Eduard Julius 313
Hoffmann, Dirk 113
Hoffmann, E. T. A. 9, 36, 73, 176, 182, 202, 224, 302, 305, 308-318, 320f., 331, 356
  Undine 36, 305, 310, 313-318
Hofmannsthal, Hugo von 4, 9f., 12, 35f., 40f., 44f., 49, 59, 105-139, 185, 274, 311, 369, 371
Hogarth, William 52, 117, 131f., 139, 274, 278-281, 284, 289f., 294, 298
Homer 233
Honegger, Arthur 17
Honolka, Kurt 344, 359
Horne, Marilyn 203

Hugo, Victor 302, 327, 331, 351
Huxley, Aldous 45, 281
Huysmans, Joris Carl 169

Isherwood, Christopher 43
Istel, Edgar 3

Jacovacci, Vincenzo 343
Janin, Jules 204
Jean Paul 316
Josipovici, Gabriel 280
Joyce, James 7

Kafka, Franz 4
Kallman, Chester 46f., 51, 273, 276, 289, 292, 294f., 298
Kant, Immanuel 37f., 167, 351
Kanzog, Klaus 343
Karl August von Weimar 234
Kaufmann, Harald 275
Kayser, Christoph Philipp 35
Kerman, Joseph 3, 5, 35, 143-145
Kessler, Harry Graf 108f., 112-116, 127f.
Khevenhüller-Metsch, Graf von 110, 119, 139
Kierkegaard, Søren 10, 36, 46, 52, 54, 56, 59, 62, 366

Kietz, Gustav 97
Kimbell, David 328
Kind, Friedrich 318
Kleist, Heinrich von 308
Koerner, Christian Gottfried 341
Kriss, Rudolf 243, 271
Kruedener, Olaf von 338
Kunze, Stefan 82, 234, 250, 271
Kupfer, Harry 324

Lagerroth, Ulla-Britta 275, 370
Lang, Paul Henry 303, 305
Leoncavallo, Ruggiero 215
  I Pagliacci 215
Leopardi, Giacomo 69
Leskov, Nicolai 347
Lessing, Gotthold Ephraim 181
Lichtenberg, Georg Christoph 110, 119
Liebeskind, J. A. 349
Liszt, Franz 148, 152-154, 159, 304, 309, 334
Lobe, Johann Christian 317
Lolli, Giuseppe 72
Lorenzi, Giambattista 82
Lortzing, Albert 304, 315f.
Louvet de Couvray 107, 117f., 121f., 131, 134
Lully, Jean-Baptiste 182

Maeterlinck, Maurice 40, 201
Mahler, Gustav 358
Malherbe, François de 218
Malipiero, Francesco 175, 260
Mandel, Oscar 77
Mann, Heinrich 174
Mann, Thomas 144, 233
Marcello, Benedetto 6, 36, 171-199
Marmontel, Jean François 33
Marschner, Heinrich 304, 316
Martello, Pier Jacopo 180
Martín y Soler, Vicente 68
  L'Arbore de Diana 68
Marzari, C. D. 328, 348, 352
Massenet, Jules 201
  Manon Lescaut 201
Melani, Alessandro 81
Mendelssohn-Bartholdy, Felix 304, 333
Menotti, Gian Carlo 3, 59
  The Consul 59
Metastasio, Pietro 4, 37, 69, 193, 195
Meyerbeer, Giacomo 34, 62, 172, 208, 303-305, 323
  Robert le Diable 323
Milhaud, Darius 17
Milton, John 233
Molière 67, 73, 79f., 83, 106, 118, 120f., 127f., 131, 139, 355
Montegut, Emile 205

Monteverdi, Claudio 35, 179, 281
Mozart, W. A. 5, 7, 10, 12, 14, 35, 37f., 41, 44, 46f., 55-57, 61f., 65-90, 103, 109, 186, 188, 213, 217, 233, 273, 281, 290, 319f., 348-350, 355, 361, 367
Così fan tutte 10, 188
Die Entführung aus dem Serail 5, 14, 41
Don Giovanni 10, 46, 55f., 62, 65-90, 186, 217, 273, 355
Le nozze di Figaro 67, 85, 109, 361
Die Zauberflöte 5, 41, 46f., 56, 213, 319, 348-350
Mühlher, Robert 120
Muratori, Ludovico 180, 190, 192, 194, 198
Musset, Alfred de 40, 126, 201
Mussorgsky, Modeste 201

Napoleon Bonaparte 338
Napoleon III. 361
Nestroy, Johann Nepomuk 172, 345
Newman, Ernest 93, 96
Nietzsche, Friedrich 19f., 36, 45, 141, 159, 170
Noufflard, Georges 36

Novalis (Friedrich von Hardenberg) 159, 205

Oehlenschläger, Adam Gottlob 231, 235, 271
Offenbach, Jacques 108, 202, 224
Orlandini, Giuseppe Maria 175

Paër, Ferdinando 365
Paisiello, Giovanni 34
Palestrina, Giovanni Pierluigi 229-272, 370
Pariati, Pietro 195
Paulding, James E. 234, 271
Pauly, Reinhard 193
Peckham, Morse 151, 158
Pepusch, John Christopher 186
The Beggar's Opera 186
Pfitzner, Hans 229-272, 370
Palestrina 229-271, 370
Piave, Francesco Maria 348
Pinagli, Palmiro 303
Pixérecourt, René 225
Plebe, Armando 245, 266, 271
Pollarolo, Antonio 175
Pollarolo, Carlo Francesco 175
Ponelle, Jean-Pierre 324
Poppenberg, Felix 107
Poulenc, Francis 17

Puccini, Giacomo 35, 38, 41, 60, 328
La Bohème
Purcell, Henry 34

Quinault, Philippe 4, 33

Ramuz, Charles Ferdinand 4, 17, 26-28, 280
Reyer, E. 228
Rich, John 186
Rie, Rherese 243
Rimsky-Korsakov, Nicolai 18, 18
Rinuccini, Ottavio 37, 179
Ritter, Karl 154
Riva, Giuseppe 5, 190
Roller, Alfred 111
Rosa, Salvator 182
Rosen, Charles 303
Rossini, Gioacchino 13, 35f., 38, 44, 58, 62, 302f., 307, 329f., 360, 363
Il Barbiere de Sevilla 329
Guillaume Tell 218, 302, 307, 329f., 360, 363f.
Rougemont, Denis de 150f.
Rousseau, Jean-Jacques 13, 36f., 348
Roussenel 207
Royer, Adolphe 344
Russell, Anna 91, 94

Sachs, Hans 237-239, 241f., 247
Saint-Evremond 35, 171, 179
Salieri, Antonio 38, 68
Tarare 68
Sappho 229, 249, 270
Satie, Eric 17f., 21-23, 39
Savonarola, Girolamo 244
Scarlatti, Alessandro 34
Scheffer, Ary 206
Schikaneder, Emanuel 5
Schiller, Friedrich 41, 205, 302, 330, 341, 343
Schlegel, August Wilhelm 204
Schlegel, Friedrich 205
Schönberg, Arnold 21, 31
Schopenhauer, Arthur 8, 36, 38, 159, 254, 308
Shostakovich, Dmitri 346f., 380
Lady Macbeth of Mtsensk 346
Schreker, Franz 259, 263
Die Gezeichneten 259
Schubert, Giselher 260, 270f.
Schuh, Willi 111, 114
Schumann, Robert 5, 154, 304, 320, 322, 333
Scribe, Eugène 4, 33, 203
Seebach, Count Nikolaus von 358

Index of Persons and Operas

Seebohm, Richard 229, 234, 250, 271
Seveling, C. F. 207
Shakespeare, William 12, 22, 40, 60, 69, 105, 225, 233, 331
Shaw, George Bernard 36, 91, 360, 369
Sitwell, Edith 17
Smetana, Bedrich 34
Smith, Patrick 304, 364
Sondheim, Steve 232
  Sunday in the Park with George 232
Sonnleitner, Josef von 365
Soubis, Albert 218
Spears, Monroe K. 44, 275
Spitzer, Leo 142, 164
Spontini, Gasparo 34
Staël, Germaine de 204, 206
Stalin 346
Stanislavsky, Konstantin 12, 40
Stendhal (Henri Beyle) 7, 13f., 36, 38f., 58, 309, 329
Stephanie, Johann, Jr. 14
Stradella, Alessandro 233
Strauss, Richard 3f., 13, 35f., 38, 41, 44, 60, 105, 111, 114f., 124, 127f., 130f., 137, 185, 274, 309, 357
  Die Ägyptische Helena 36
  Arabella 58

Ariadne auf Naxos 185
Intermezzo 36, 185, 199
Der Rosenkavalier 58f., 105-139, 218, 221, 274, 358, 369
Die schweigsame Frau 41
Salome 4, 114, 201, 358
Stravinsky, Igor 12, 17, 20, 22-28, 30f., 38, 45, 52, 61, 273-299, 369f.
  L'Histoire du Soldat 17, 61, 280f.
  The Rake's Progress 273-299
  Reynard 25
Strecker, Ludwig 260
Striggio, Alessandro 35
Strindberg, August 335

Tailleferre, Germaine 17
Tasso, Torquato 229, 232, 238
Telemann, Georg Philipp 34
Terrasse, Victor 108
  L'Ingenu libertin 108f., 111, 115, 118, 122, 124, 127, 132, 134-138
Thomas, Ambroise 6, 201-228, 370
  Mignon 6, 201-228, 370
Tieck, Ludwig 229, 231, 234, 235, 271, 316
Tirso de Molina 65, 69, 74, 76, 78, 369

Tritti, Giacomo 82
Tchaikovsky, Peter Iljitsch 233, 309
Eugene Onegin 233

Uhlig, Theodor 97

Vallas, Léon 23
Verdi, Giuseppe 4, 7, 13, 35, 38, 40, 44, 47, 56, 60, 62, 69, 110, 130, 201, 210, 233, 281, 302f., 304f., 307, 327f., 343-347, 351f., 353f., 357, 360f.
Aida 233
Un Ballo in maschera 361
La Battaglia di Legnano 344
Ernani 302, 328
Falstaff 13, 110, 130, 233, 305, 307
Giovanna d'Arco 344
I Lombardi 344
Macbeth 233, 346
Otello 40, 60, 210
Rigoletto 7, 56, 302, 347, 351, 353, 357, 360
Stiffelio 354
La Traviata 201
Il Trovatore 5
Verlaine, Paul 11

Virgil 248
Vlad, Roman 275
Voltaire 36
Voss, Egon 145

Wagner, Richard 10, 18-23, 25, 29, 36, 38-41, 44, 45, 47, 53, 61, 91-103, 109, 114, 141-170, 172, 218, 230f., 233, 236, 238f., 241f., 246f., 249, 260, 270f., 282, 304f., 308f., 311, 320-326, 330, 335, 341, 357, 360, 369
Der fliegende Holländer 320-326, 330, 335
Lohengrin 322, 323
Die Meistersinger von Nürnberg 10, 41, 109, 114, 230, 238f., 241f., 246f., 249, 271
Parsifal 25, 91, 148, 152, 305, 357
Rienzi 322f., 360
Siegfried 91-103, 154, 369
Tannhäuser 172, 246f., 322f., 341, 357
Tristan und Isolde 53, 109, 141-170, 218, 233, 242, 320, 335, 357, 369
Die Walküre 61, 357

Index of Persons and Operas

Walton, William 17
Weber, Carl Maria von 34, 36, 39, 62, 182, 302, 304, 311f., 314, 316-320, 326, 331f., 340
  Der Freischütz 36, 302, 314-320, 330, 341
Weill, Kurt 12, 28f., 31f.
  Die Dreigroschenoper 12, 17, 29-32, 36, 348
Weiner, Marc 321
Weinmann, Karl 243, 272
Weinstock, Herbert 304
Weisstein, Ulrich 230, 272
Weltrich, Richard 146, 147

Wesendonck, Mathilde 157
White, Eric Walter 275
Wiel, Taddeo 174
Wieland, Christoph Martin 36, 41, 181, 349
Wilde, Oscar 195, 201
Winckelmann, Johann Joachim 181
Wohlke, Franz 261, 263, 272
Worringer, Wilhelm 246, 272

Zanetti, Emilia 279, 285
Zanolini, Antonio 35
Zeno, Apostolo 4, 33, 69, 195
Zweig, Stefan 41

Song and Significance

Virtues and Vices of Vocal Translation

Edited by Dinda L. Gorlée

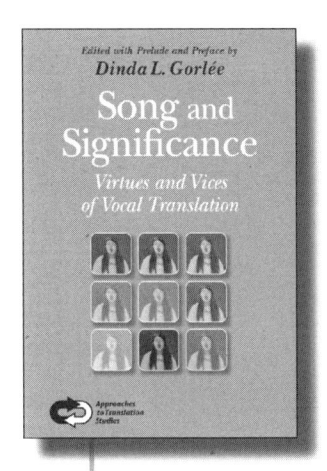

Vocal translation is an old art, but the interpretive feeling, skill and craft have expanded into a relatively new area in translation studies. Vocal translation is the translation of the poetic discourse in the hybrid art of the musicopoetic (or poeticomusical) forms, shapes and skills. This symbiotic construct harmonizes together the conflicting roles of music and language in face-to-face singing performances. The artist sings in an accurate but free flow, but sung in a language different from the original lyrics.

In opera, folksong, hymn and art song, as well as in operetta, musical song and popular song, we have musical genres allied to a libretto with lyrical text. A libretto is a linguistic text which is a pre-existing work of art, but is subordinated to the musical text. The essays in *Song and Significance: Virtues and Vices of Vocal Translation* provide interpretive models for the juxtaposition of different orders of the singing sign-events in different languages, extending the meaning and range of the musical and literary concepts, and putting the mixed signs to a true-and-false test.

Amsterdam/New York, NY,
2005 311 pp.
(Approaches to
Translation Studies 25)
Paper € 62 / US$ 74
ISBN-10: 9042016876
ISBN-13: 9789042016873

USA/Canada:
295 North Michigan Avenue - Suite 1B, Kenilworth, NJ 07033,
USA. Call Toll-free (US only): 1-800-225-3998
All other countries:
Tijnmuiden 7, 1046 AK Amsterdam, The Netherlands
Tel. +31-20-611 48 21 Fax +31-20-447 29 79
Please note that the exchange rate is subject to fluctuations

Intermediality in Theatre and Performance

Edited by Freda Chapple and
Chiel Kattenbelt

Intermediality: the incorporation of digital technology into theatre practice, and the presence of film, television and digital media in contemporary theatre is a significant feature of twentieth-century performance. Presented here for the first time is a major collection of essays, written by the *Theatre and Intermediality Research Group* of the *International Federation for Theatre Research*, which assesses *intermediality in theatre and performance*. The book draws on the history of ideas to present a concept of intermediality as an *integration of thoughts and medial processes*, and it locates intermediality at the *inter-sections situated in-between* the performers, the observers and the confluence of media, medial spaces and art forms involved in performance at a particular moment in time. Referencing examples from contemporary theatre, cinema, television, opera, dance and puppet theatre, the book puts forward a thesis that the intermedial is a space where the boundaries soften and we are *in-between and within a mixing of space, media and realities, with theatre providing the staging space for intermediality*. The book places theatre and performance at the heart of the 'new media' debate and will be of keen interest to students, with clear relevance to undergraduates and post-graduates in Theatre Studies and Film and Media Studies, as well as the theatre research community.

Amsterdam/New York, NY,
2006 266 pp.
(Themes in Theatre 2)
Paper € 54 / US$ 70
ISBN-10: 9042016299
ISBN-13: 9789042016293

USA/Canada:
295 North Michigan Avenue - Suite 1B Kenilworth, NJ 07033, USA. Call Toll-free (US only): 1-800-225-3998
All other countries:
Tijnmuiden 7, 1046 AK Amsterdam, The Netherlands
Tel. +31-20-611 48 21 Fax +31-20-447 29 79
Please note that the exchange rate is subject to fluctuations

L'Art français et Francophone depuis 1980

Contemporary French and Francophone Art

Michael Bishop/
Christopher Elson (éds)

Ce volume présente vingt-trois essais consacrés à l'art français et francophone des vingt-cinq dernières années et propose des analyses critiques d'une cinquantaine d'artistes majeurs qui travaillent sur des modes richement variés.

The volume offers 23 new critical essays on contemporary French and francophone art, dealing with some fifty major artists working in a wide range of mediums.

Amsterdam/New York, NY,
2005 238 pp.
(Faux Titre 269)
Paper € 48 / US$ 60
ISBN-10: 9042018771
ISBN-13: 9789042018778

USA/Canada:
295 North Michigan Avenue - Suite 1B, Kenilworth, NJ 07033, USA. Call Toll-free (US only): 1-800-225-3998
All other countries:
Tijnmuiden 7, 1046 AK Amsterdam, The Netherlands
Tel. +31-20-611 48 21 Fax +31-20-447 29 79
Please note that the exchange rate is subject to fluctuations

Screen Consciousness
Cinema, Mind and World

Edited by Robert Pepperell and
Michael Punt

Amsterdam/New York, NY, 2006 202 pp.
(Consciousness, Literature and the Arts 4)
Paper € 40 / US$ 54
ISBN-10: 9042020164
ISBN-13: 9789042020160

This collection of essays is driven by the question of how we know what we know, and in particular how we can be certain about something even when we know it is an illusion. The contention of the book is that this age-old question has acquired a new urgency as certain trends in science, technology and ideas have taken the discussion of consciousness out of the philosophy department and deposited it in the world at large. As a consequence, a body of literature from many fields has produced its own sets of concerns and methods under the rubric of Consciousness Studies. Each contribution in this collection deals with issues and questions that lots of people have been thinking about for many years in many different contexts, things such as the nature of film, cinema, world, mind and so on. Those of us fascinated by these diverse yet related issues may have often felt we were working in a disciplinary no-man's-land. Now suddenly, it seems with Consciousness Studies we have a coherent intellectual home – albeit one that is self-consciously eclectic.

The essays included in *Screen Consciousness: Cinema, Mind and World* are from a range of disciplines – art, philosophy, film theory, anthropology and technology studies – each represented by significant international figures, and each concerned with how their field is being transformed by the new discipline of Consciousness Studies. Together they attempt to reconcile the oncoming rush of new data from science and technology about how we know what we know, with the insights gained from the long view of history, philosophy and art. Each of the contributions seeks to interpose Consciousness Studies between film and mind, where for cultural theorists psychoanalysis had traditionally stood. This is more than simply updating Film Studies or nodding in the direction of cognitive film theory. Film, with all its sentient, sensuous and social qualities, is a common reference point between all these forces, and Consciousness Studies provides the intellectual impetus for this book to revisit familiar problems with fresh insight.

USA/Canada:
295 North Michigan Avenue - Suite 1B Kenilworth, NJ 07033,
USA. Call Toll-free (US only): 1-800-225-3998
All other countries:
Tijnmuiden 7, 1046 AK Amsterdam, The Netherlands
Tel. +31-20-611 48 21 Fax +31-20-447 29 79

Please note that the exchange rate is subject to fluctuations

The *Matrix* in Theory

Edited by Myriam Diocaretz and Stefan Herbrechter

The *Matrix* trilogy continues to split opinions widely, polarising the downright dismissive and the wildly enthusiastic. Nevertheless, it has been fully embraced as a rich source of theoretical and cultural references. The contributions in this volume probe the effects the *Matrix* trilogy continues to provoke and evaluate how or to what extent they coincide with certain developments within critical and cultural theory. Is the enthusiastic philosophising and theorising spurred by the *Matrix* a sign of the desperate state theory is in, in the sense of "see how low theory (or 'post-theory') has sunk"? Or could the *Matrix* be one of the "master texts" for something like a renewal for theory as now being mainly concerned with new and changing relations between science, technology, posthumanist culture, art, politics, ethics and the media? The present volume is unashamedly but not dogmatically theoretical even though there is not much agreement about what kind of theory is best suited to confront "post-theoretical" times. But it is probably fair to say that there is agreement about one thing, namely that if theory appears to be "like" the Matrix today it does so because the culture around it and which "made" it itself seems to be captured in some kind of Matrix. The only way out of this is through more and renewed, refreshed theorising, not less.

Amsterdam/New York, NY,
2006 314 pp.
(Critical Studies 29)
Bound € 65 / US$ 81
ISBN-10: 9042016396
ISBN-13: 9789042016392

USA/Canada:
295 North Michigan Avenue - Suite 1B Kenilworth, NJ 07033, USA. Call Toll-free (US only): 1-800-225-3998
All other countries:
Tijnmuiden 7, 1046 AK Amsterdam, The Netherlands
Tel. +31-20-611 48 21 Fax +31-20-447 29 79
Please note that the exchange rate is subject to fluctuations

Framing Borders
in Literature and Other Media

Edited by Werner Wolf and
Walter Bernhart

This book is both a contribution to an interdisciplinary study of literature and other media and a pioneering application of cognitive and frame-theoretical approaches to these fields. In the temporal media a privileged place for the coding of cognitive frames are the beginnings while in spatial media physical borders take over many framing functions. This volume investigates forms and functions of such framing spaces from a transmedial perspective by juxtaposing and comparing the framing potential of individual media and works. After an introductory theoretical essay, which aims to clarify basic concepts, the volume presents eighteen contributions by scholars from various disciplines who deal with individual media. The first section is dedicated to framing in or through the visual arts and includes discussions of the illustrations of medieval manuscripts, the practice of framing pictures from the Middle Ages to Magritte and contemporary American art as well as framings in printmaking and architecture. The second part deals with literary texts and ranges from studies centred on framings in frame stories to essays focussing on the use of paratextual, textual and non-verbal media in the framings of classical, medieval and modern German and American narrative literature; moreover, it includes studies on defamiliarized framings, e.g. by Julio Cortázar and Jasper Fforde, as well as an essay on end-framing practices. Sections on framings in film (including the trailers of Tolkien's *The Lord of the Rings*) and in music (operatic overtures and Schumann's piano pieces) provide perspectives on further media. The volume is of relevance to students and scholars from various fields: intermedia studies, cognitive approaches to the media, literary and film studies, history of art, and musicology.

Amsterdam/New York, NY,
2006 VIII-482 pp. (Studies
in Intermediality 1)
Bound € 100 / US$125
ISBN-10: 9042017899
ISBN-13: 9789042017894

USA/Canada:
295 North Michigan Avenue - Suite 1B Kenilworth, NJ 07033,
USA. Call Toll-free (US only): 1-800-225-3998
All other countries:
Tijnmuiden 7, 1046 AK Amsterdam, The Netherlands
Tel. +31-20-611 48 21 Fax +31-20-447 29 79
Please note that the exchange rate is subject to fluctuations

The Art of *Commedia*

A Study in the *Commedia dell' Arte* 1560-1620 with Special Reference to the Visual Records

M.A. Katritzky

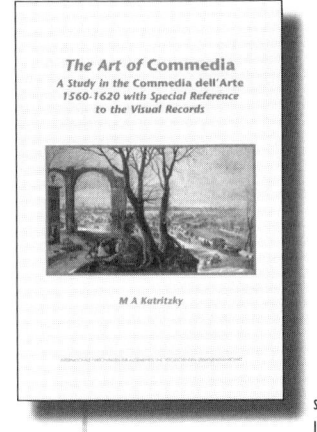

Italian comedians attracted audiences to performances at every level, from the magnificent Italian, German and French court festival appearances of Orlando di Lasso or Isabella Andreini, to the humble street trestle *lazzi* of anonymous quacks. The characters they inspired continue to exercise a profound cultural influence, and an understanding of the *commedia dell'arte* and its visual record is fundamental for scholars of post-1550 European drama, literature, art and music. The 340 plates presented here are considered in the light of the rise and spread of *commedia* stock types, and especially Harlequin, Zanni and the actresses. Intensively researched in public and private collections in Oxford, Munich, Florence, Venice, Paris and elsewhere, they complement the familiar images of Jacques Callot and the Stockholm *Recueil Fossard* within a framework of hundreds of significant pictures still virtually unknown in this context. These range from anonymous popular prints to pictures by artists such as Ambrogio Brambilla, Sebastian Vrancx, Jan Bruegel, Louis de Caulery, Marten de Vos, and members of the Valckenborch and Francken clans. This volume, essential for *commedia dell'arte* specialists, represents an invaluable reference resource for scholars, students, theatre practitioners and artists.

Amsterdam/New York, NY, 2006 625 pp, incl. 340 ill. (Internationale Forschungen zur Allgemeinen und Vergleichenden Literaturwissenschaft 100)
Bound € 180 / US$ 225
ISBN-10: 9042017988
ISBN-13: 9789042017986

USA/Canada:
295 North Michigan Avenue - Suite 1B Kenilworth, NJ 07033, USA. Call Toll-free (US only): 1-800-225-3998
All other countries:
Tijnmuiden 7, 1046 AK Amsterdam, The Netherlands
Tel. +31-20-611 48 21 Fax +31-20-447 29 79
Please note that the exchange rate is subject to fluctuations

The Abject Object
Avatars of the Phallus in Contemporary French Theory, Literature and Film

Keith Reader

This book addresses representations and constructions of masculinity in crisis in contemporary French culture by way of two important concepts – the phallus (largely but not solely in (a) Lacanian sense(s)) and abjection (Kristeva). Scrutiny of these concepts informs readings of a number of texts – literary (Bataille, Adamov, Doubrovsky, Houellebecq, Rochefort, Angot) and cinematic (Ferreri, Eustache, Godard, Noé, Bonello) – in which the abject phallus is a significant factor. The texts chosen all describe or stage crises of masculinity and mastery in ways that suggest that these supposedly beneficent qualities – and the phallus that symbolizes them – can often be perceived as burdensome or even detestable. Abjection is a widely-used concept in contemporary cultural studies, but has not hitherto been articulated with the phallus as emblem of male dominance as it is here. The volume will be of interest to those working in the areas of French, gender and film studies.

The author is Professor of Modern French Studies at the University of Glasgow and has published extensively in the areas of French culture, film and intellectual history. His most recent books are monographs on Régis Debray and Robert Bresson. He is coeditor, with Alex Hughes, of the *Encyclopedia of Contemporary French Culture*, of which a second edition is currently in preparation.

Amsterdam/New York, NY,
2006 225 pp.
(Chiasma 17)
Paper € 45 / US$ 56
ISBN-10: 9042017295
ISBN-13: 9789042017290

USA/Canada:
295 North Michigan Avenue - Suite 1B Kenilworth, NJ 07033, USA. Call Toll-free (US only): 1-800-225-3998
All other countries:
Tijnmuiden 7, 1046 AK Amsterdam, The Netherlands
Tel. +31-20-611 48 21 Fax +31-20-447 29 79
Please note that the exchange rate is subject to fluctuations